CCNP™ Support

Matthew E. Luallen

CCNP™ Support Exam Cram

Limits Of Liability And Disclaimer Of Warranty

The author and publisher of this book have used their best efforts in preparing the book and the programs contained in it. These efforts include the development, research, and testing of the theories and programs to determine their effectiveness. The author and publisher make no warranty of any kind, expressed or implied, with regard to these programs or the documentation contained in this book.

The author and publisher shall not be liable in the event of incidental or consequential damages in connection with, or arising out of, the furnishing, performance, or use of the programs, associated instructions, and/or claims of productivity gains.

Trademarks

Trademarked names appear throughout this book. Rather than list the names and entities that own the trademarks or insert a trademark symbol with each mention of the trademarked name, the publisher states that it is using the names for editorial purposes only and to the benefit of the trademark owner, with no intention of infringing upon that trademark.

The Coriolis Group, LLC
14455 N. Hayden Road
Suite 220
Scottsdale, Arizona 85260

480/483-0192
FAX 480/483-0193
http://www.coriolis.com

Library of Congress Cataloging-in-Publication Data
Luallen, Matthew.
CCNP support exam cram / by Matthew Luallen
p. cm.
ISBN 1-57610-681-0
1. Electronic data processing personnel--Certification. 2. Computer networks--Examinations--Study guides. I. Title.
QA76.3.L84 2000
004.6--dc21 00-022734
CIP

Printed in the United States of America
10 9 8 7 6 5 4 3 2 1

President, CEO
Keith Weiskamp

Publisher
Steve Sayre

Acquisitions Editor
Jeff Kellum

Marketing Specialist
Cynthia Caldwell

Project Editor
Dan Young

Technical Reviewer
Seyoum Zegiorgis

Production Coordinator
Meg E. Turecek

Cover Design
Jesse Dunn

Layout Design
April Nielsen

14455 North Hayden Road • Suite 220 • Scottsdale, Arizona 85260

Coriolis: The Smartest Way To Get Certified™

To help you reach your goals, we've listened to readers like you, and we've designed our entire product line around you and the way you like to study, learn, and master challenging subjects.

In addition to our highly popular *Exam Cram* and *Exam Prep* books, we offer several other products to help you pass certification exams. Our *Practice Tests* and *Flash Cards* are designed to make your studying fun and productive. Our *Audio Reviews* have received rave reviews from our customers—and they're the perfect way to make the most of your drive time!

The newest way to get certified is the *Exam Cram Personal Trainer*—a highly interactive, personalized self-study course based on the best-selling *Exam Cram* series. It's the first certification-specific product to completely link a customizable learning tool, exclusive *Exam Cram* content, and multiple testing techniques so you can study what, how, and when you want.

Exam Cram Insider—a biweekly newsletter containing the latest in certification news, study tips, and announcements from Certification Insider Press—gives you an ongoing look at the hottest certification programs. (To subscribe, send an email to **eci@coriolis.com** and type "subscribe insider" in the body of the email.) We also sponsor the Certified Crammer Society and the Coriolis Help Center—two other resources that will help you get certified even faster!

Help us continue to provide the very best certification study materials possible. Write us or email us at **cipq@coriolis.com** and let us know how our books have helped you study. Tell us about new features that you'd like us to add. Send us a story about how we've helped you; if we use it in one of our books, we'll send you an official Coriolis shirt!

Good luck with your certification exam and your career. Thank you for allowing us to help you achieve your goals.

Keith Weiskamp

Keith Weiskamp
President and CEO

Look For These Other Books From The Coriolis Group:

CCNP Remote Access Exam Cram
by Craig Dennis and Eric Quinn

CCNP Switching Exam Cram
by Richard A. Deal

I dedicate this book to my brother, Tim, who began laying the groundwork years ago for me through continuous support and guidance year after year. I still remember playing Empire on those "fast" 386 machines and those 10 megabyte file transfers on 9600-baud modems. I am sure glad that mom and dad had to pay for those rather than us. And without your ongoing help, from summer employment to your suffering through my inadvertently performing "format c:" instead of "format a:" on a couple of computers, I would not be where I am today. I also feel bound to mention to everyone that is near and dear to me, thanks for understanding all of the times I had to stay home to work on this book, and miss out on the family events. I would also like to say a special thank you to Jill, a very special woman in my life who has endured the long hours with me.

About The Author

Matthew E. Luallen, CCIE #5338, just recently earned the CCIE certification in November of 1999. Matthew also holds the CCNA, CCNP, and MCSE+I certifications.

In 1995, Matthew joined the internetworking rush and began his own Internet development company, The Pages Online, for which he was the controlling shareholder for two years. He graduated in 1997 from the University of Illinois at Urbana Champaign with a bachelor's degree in Industrial Engineering and a minor in Computer Science. Currently Matthew is enrolled in a Masters of Computer Science program at National Technological University. For the past two years he has served as a network engineer for Argonne National Laboratory, a U.S. Department of Energy research facility located in Chicago, Illinois, and as a consultant/owner for InternetworkingConsultant.com, LLC.

When Matthew is not internetworking, he spends time enjoying life through several electronic and athletic hobbies. Matthew currently lives in Lombard, Illinois, and continues to be a die-hard Cubs fan and a longstanding Bull's fan, even with the recent retirement of Michael Jordan. You can reach Matthew by email at **meluallen@yahoo.com**.

Acknowledgments

I would like to say thanks to all of the people at The Coriolis Group, without whom I would have never been able to complete this book. Jeff and Dan, thanks for keeping me on my toes during this revision. And to everyone at The Coriolis Group that worked on this book behind the scenes: Technical Editor, Seyoum Zegiorgis; Production Coordinator, Meg E. Turecek; Cover Design, Jesse Dunn; Marketing Specialist, Cynthia Caldwell; Acquisitions Editor, Jeff Kellum; Layout Designer, April Nielsen; and last, but certainly not least, the Project Editor, Dan Young.

Contents At A Glance

Table Of Contents

Introduction

Welcome to the *CCNP Support Exam Cram*! This book aims to help you get ready to take—and pass— the Cisco Career Certification test numbered 640-506, "Support 2.0". This Introduction explains Cisco's certification programs in general and talks about how the *Exam Cram* series prepare for Cisco's career certification exams.

Exam Cram books help you understand and appreciate the subjects and materials you need to pass Cisco Career Certification exams. *Exam Cram* books are aimed strictly at test preparation and review. They do not teach you everything you need to know about a topic. Instead, I (the author) present and dissect the questions and problems I've found that you're likely to encounter on a test. I've worked from Cisco's own training materials, preparation guides, and tests, and from a battery of third-party test preparation tools. My aim is to bring together as much information as possible about Cisco certification exams.

Nevertheless, to completely prepare yourself for any Cisco test, I recommend that you begin your studies with some instructor-led classroom training. You should also pick up and read one of the many study guides available from Cisco or third-party vendors, including The Coriolis Group's *Exam Prep* series. I also strongly recommend that you install, configure, and fool around with the Internetwork Operating System (IOS) software or environment that you'll be tested on, because nothing beats hands-on experience and familiarity when it comes to understanding the questions you're likely to encounter on a certification test. Book learning is essential, but hands-on experience is the best teacher of all!

The Cisco Career Certification Program

The Cisco Career Certification program is relatively new on the internetworking scene. The best place to keep tabs on it is the Cisco Training Web site, at **www.cisco.com/certifications**. Before Cisco developed this program, Cisco Certified Internetwork Expert (CCIE) certification was the only available Cisco certification. Although CCIE certification is still the most coveted and prestigious certification that Cisco offers (possibly the most prestigious in the

Table 1 Cisco Routing and Switching CCNA, CCNP, and CCIE Requirements

CCNA

Only 1 exam required	
Exam 640-507	CCNA

CCNP*

All 4 of these are required	
Exam 640-503	Routing
Exam 640-504	Switching
Exam 640-505	Remote Access
➤ **Exam 640-506**	**Support**

* You need to have your CCNA before you become a CCNP.

CCIE

1 written exam and 1 lab exam required	
Exam 350-001	CCIE Routing and Switching Qualification
Lab Exam	CCIE Routing and Switching Laboratory

internetworking industry), lower-level certifications are now available as stepping stones on the road to the CCIE. The Cisco Career Certification program includes several certifications in addition to the CCIE, each with its own acronym (see Table 1). If you're a fan of alphabet soup after your name, you'll like this program:

Note: Within the certification program, there are specific specializations. For the purposes of this book, I will focus only on the Routing and Switching track. Visit ***www.cisco.com/warp/public/10/wwtraining/certprog/index.html*** *for information on the other specializations.*

- **Cisco Certified Design Associate (CCDA)** The CCDA is a basic certification aimed at designers of high-level internetworks. The CCDA consists of a single exam (640-441) that covers information from the Designing Cisco Networks (DCN) course. You must obtain CCDA and CCNA certifications before you can move up to the CCDP certification.
- **Cisco Certified Network Associate (CCNA)** The CCNA is the first career certification. It consists of a single exam (640-507) that covers information from the basic-level class, primarily Interconnecting Cisco Network Devices (ICND). You must obtain CCNA certification before you can get your CCNP and CCDP certification.

- **Cisco Certified Network Professional (CCNP)** The CCNP is a more advanced certification that is not easy to obtain. To earn CCNP status, you must be a CCNA in good standing. There are two routes you can take to obtain your CCNP. For the first route, you must take four exams: Routing (640-503), Switching (640-504), Remote Access (640-505), and Support (640-506). For the second route, you must take the Foundation (640-509) and Support (640-506) exams.

Although it may seem more appealing on the surface, the second route is more difficult. The Foundation exam contains more than 130 questions and lasts almost 3 hours. In addition, it covers all the topics covered in the Routing, Switching, and Remote Access exams.

Whichever route you choose, there are four courses Cisco recommends that you take:

- **Building Scalable Cisco Networks (BSCN)** This course corresponds to the Routing exam.
- **Building Cisco Multilayer Switched Networks (BCMSN)** This course corresponds to the Switching exam.
- **Building Cisco Remote Access Networks (BCRAN)** This course corresponds to the Remote Access exam.
- **Cisco Internetworking Troubleshooting (CIT)** This course corresponds to the Support exam.

Once you have completed the CCNP certification, you can further your career (not to mention beef up your resume) by branching out and passing one of the CCNP specialization exams. These include:

- **Security** Requires you to pass the Managing Cisco Network Security exam (640-422)
- **LAN ATM** Requires you to pass the Cisco Campus ATM Solutions exam (640-446)
- **Voice Access** Requires you to pass the Cisco Voice over Frame Relay, ATM, and IP exam (640-447).
- **SNA/IP Integration** Requires you to pass the (SNA Configuration for Multiprotocol Administrators (640-445) and the SNA Foundation (640-456) exams.

- **Network Management** Requires you to either pass the Managing Cisco Routed Internetworks (MCRI [640-443]) and the Managing Cisco Switched Internetworks (MCSI [640-444]) exams.
- **Cisco Certified Design Professional (CCDP)** The CCDP is another advanced certification. It's aimed at high-level internetwork designers who must understand the intricate facets of putting together a well-laid-out network. The first step in the certification process is to obtain the CCDA and CCNA certifications (yes, both). As with the CCNP, you must pass the Foundation exam or pass the Routing, Switching, and Remote Access exams individually. Once you meet those objectives, you must pass the Cisco Internetwork Design exam (640-025) to complete the certification.
- **Cisco Certified Internetwork Expert (CCIE)** The CCIE is possibly the most influential certification in the internetworking industry today. It is famous (or infamous) for its difficulty and for how easily it holds its seekers at bay. The certification requires only one written exam (350-001); passing that exam qualifies you to schedule time at a Cisco campus to demonstrate your knowledge in a two-day practical laboratory setting. You must pass the lab with a score of at least 80 percent to become a CCIE. Recent statistics have put the passing rates at roughly 20 percent for first attempts and 35 through 50 percent overall. Once you achieve CCIE certification, you must recertify every two years by passing a written exam administered by Cisco.
- **Certified Cisco Systems Instructor (CCSI)** To obtain status as a CCSI, you must be employed (either permanently or by contract) by a Cisco Training Partner in good standing, such as GeoTrain Corporation. That training partner must sponsor you through Cisco's Instructor Certification Program, and you must pass the two-day program that Cisco administers at a Cisco campus. You can build on CCSI certification on a class-by-class basis. Instructors must demonstrate competency with each class they are to teach by completing the written exam that goes with each class. Cisco also requires that instructors maintain a high customer satisfaction rating, or they will face decertification.

Taking A Certification Exam

Alas, testing is not free. Each computer-based exam costs between $100 and $200. If you do not pass, you must pay the testing fee each time you retake the test. In the United States and Canada, tests are administered by Sylvan Prometric. Sylvan Prometric can be reached at (800) 755-3926 or (800) 204-EXAM, any time from 7:00 A.M. to 6:00 P.M., Central Time, Monday through Friday. You can also try (612) 896-7000 or (612) 820-5707.

To schedule a computer-based exam, call at least one day in advance. To cancel or reschedule an exam, you must call at least 24 hours before the scheduled test time (or you may be charged regardless). When calling Sylvan Prometric, have the following information ready for the telesales staffer who handles your call:

- Your name, organization, and mailing address.
- Your Cisco Test ID. (For most U.S. citizens, this is your Social Security number. Citizens of other nations can use their taxpayer IDs or make other arrangements with the order taker.)
- The name and number of the exam you wish to take. For this book, the exam name is "Support 2.0," and the exam number is 640-506.
- A method of payment. The most convenient approach is to supply a valid credit card number with sufficient available credit. Otherwise, Sylvan Prometric must receive check, money order, or purchase order payments before you can schedule a test. (If you're not paying by credit card, ask your order taker for more details.)

When you show up to take a test, try to arrive at least 15 minutes before the scheduled time slot. You must supply two forms of identification, one of which must be a photo ID.

All exams are completely closed book. In fact, you will not be permitted to take anything with you into the testing area. However, you are furnished with a blank sheet of paper and a pen. I suggest that you immediately write down on that sheet of paper all the information you've memorized for the test. Although the amount of time you have to actually take the exam is limited, the time period does not start until you're ready, so you can spend as much time as necessary writing notes on the provided paper. If you think you will need more paper than what is provided, ask the test center administrator before entering the exam room. You must return all pages prior to exiting the testing center.

In *Exam Cram* books, the information that I suggest you write down appears on the Cram Sheet inside the front cover of each book. You will have some time to compose yourself, to record this information, and even to take a sample orientation exam before you begin the real thing. I suggest you take the orientation test before taking your first exam, but because they're all more or less identical in layout, behavior, and controls, you probably won't need to do this more than once.

When you complete a Cisco certification exam, the software will tell you whether you've passed or failed. All tests are scored on a basis of 100 percent, and results are broken into several topic areas. Even if you fail, I suggest you ask for—and keep—the detailed report that the test administrator should print for you. You can use this report to help you prepare for another go-round, if needed. Once you see your score, you have the option of printing additional copies of the score report. It is a good idea to have it print twice.

If you need to retake an exam, you'll have to call Sylvan Prometric, schedule a new test date, and pay another testing fee. The first time you fail a test, you can retake the test the next day. However, if you fail a second time, you must wait 14 days before retaking that test. The 14-day waiting period is in effect for all tests after the first failure.

Tracking Cisco Certification Status

As soon as you pass any Cisco exam (congratulations!), you must complete a certification agreement. You can do so online at the Certification Tracking Web site (**www.galton.com/~cisco/**), or you can mail a hard copy of the agreement to Cisco's certification authority. You will not be certified until you complete a certification agreement and Cisco receives it in one of these forms.

The Certification Tracking Web site also allows you to view your certification information. Cisco will contact you via email and explain it and its use. Once you are registered into one of the career certification tracks, you will be given a login on this site, which is administered by Galton, a third-party company that has no in-depth affiliation with Cisco or its products. Galton's information comes directly from Sylvan Prometric, the exam-administration company for much of the computing industry.

Once you pass the necessary exam(s) for a particular certification and complete the certification agreement, you'll be certified. Official certification normally takes anywhere from four to six weeks, so don't expect to get your credentials overnight. When the package arrives, it will include a Welcome Kit that contains a number of elements, including:

- A Cisco certificate stating that you have completed the certification requirements, suitable for framing, along with a laminated Cisco Career Certification identification card with your certification number on it.

- Promotional items, which vary based on the certification.

Many people believe that the benefits of the Cisco career certifications go well beyond the perks that Cisco provides to newly anointed members of this elite group. We're starting to see more job listings that request or require applicants to have a CCNA, CCDA, CCNP, CCDP, and so on, and many individuals who complete the program can qualify for increases in pay or responsibility. In fact, Cisco has started to implement requirements for its Value Added Resellers: To attain and keep silver, gold, or higher status, they must maintain a certain number of CCNA, CCDA, CCNP, CCDP, and CCIE employees on staff.

There's a very high demand and low supply of Cisco talent in the industry overall. As an official recognition of hard work and broad knowledge, a Cisco Career Certification credential is a badge of honor in many IT organizations.

How To Prepare For An Exam

Preparing for any Cisco test (including Support 2.0) requires that you obtain and study materials designed to provide comprehensive information about Cisco router operation and the specific exam for which you are preparing. The following list of materials will help you study and prepare:

- **Instructor-led training** There's no substitute for expert instruction and hands-on practice under professional supervision. Cisco Training Partners, such as GeoTrain Corporation, offer instructor-led training courses for all of the Cisco Career Certification requirements. These companies aim to help prepare network administrators to run Cisco routed and switched internetworks and pass the Cisco tests. Although such training runs upwards of $350 per day in class, most of the individuals lucky enough to partake find them to be quite worthwhile.

- **Cisco Connection Online** This is the name of Cisco's Web site (**www.cisco.com**), the most current and up-to-date source of Cisco information.

- **The CCPrep Web site** This is the most well-known Cisco certification Web site in the world. You can find it at **www.ccprep.com** (formerly known as **www.CCIEprep.com**). Here, you can find exam preparation materials, practice tests, self-assessment exams, and numerous certification questions and scenarios. In addition, professional staff is available to answer questions that you can post on the answer board.

- **Cisco training kits** These are available only if you attend a Cisco class, at a certified training facility, or if a Cisco Training Partner in good standing gives you one.

- **Study guides** Several publishers—including Certification Insider Press—offer CCNP titles. The Certification Insider Press series includes:

  - **The *Exam Cram* series** These books give you information about the material you need to know to pass the tests.

  - **The *Exam Prep* series** These books provide a greater level of detail than the *Exam Cram* books and are designed to teach you everything you need to know from an exam perspective.

  Together, the two series make a perfect pair.

- **Multimedia** These Coriolis Group materials are designed to support learners of all types—whether you learn best by listening, reading, or doing:
  - **The *Practice Tests Exam Cram* series** Provides the most valuable test preparation material: practice exams. Each exam is followed by a complete set of answers, as well as explanations of why the right answers are right and the wrong answers are wrong. Each book comes with a CD-ROM that contains one or more interactive practice exams.
  - **The *Exam Cram Flash Cards* series** Offers practice questions on handy cards you can use anywhere. The question and its possible answers appear on the front of the card, and the answer, explanation, and a valuable reference appear on the back of the card. The set also includes a CD-ROM with an electronic practice exam to give you the feel of the actual test—and more practice!
  - **The *Exam Cram Audio Review* series** Offers a concise review of key topics covered on the exam, as well as practice questions.
- **Other publications** You'll find direct references to other publications and resources in this text: There's no shortage of materials available about Cisco routers and their configuration. To help you sift through some of the publications out there, I end each chapter with a "Need To Know More?" section that provides pointers to more complete and exhaustive resources covering the chapter's information. This should give you an idea of where I think you should look for further discussion.

By far, this set of required and recommended materials represents an unparalleled collection of sources and resources for Cisco routers configuration guidelines. I anticipate that you'll find that this book belongs in this company. In the next section, I explain how this book works, and I give you some good reasons why this book counts as a member of the required and recommended materials list.

About This Book

Each topical Exam Cram chapter follows a regular structure, along with graphical cues about important or useful information. Here's the structure of a typical chapter:

- **Opening hotlists** Each chapter begins with a list of the terms, tools, and techniques that you must learn and understand before you can be fully conversant with that chapter's subject matter. I follow the hotlists with one or two introductory paragraphs to set the stage for the rest of the chapter.

- **Topical coverage** After the opening hotlists, each chapter covers a series of at least four topics related to the chapter's subject. Throughout this section, I highlight topics or concepts likely to appear on a test using a special Study Alert layout, like this:

This is what a Study Alert looks like. Normally, a Study Alert stresses concepts, terms, software, or activities that are likely to relate to one or more certification test questions. For that reason, I think any information found offset in Study Alert format is worthy of unusual attentiveness on your part. Indeed, most of the information that appears on the Cram Sheet appears as Study Alerts within the text.

Pay close attention to material flagged as a Study Alert; although all the information in this book pertains to what you need to know to pass the exam, I flag certain items that are really important. You'll find what appears in the meat of each chapter to be worth knowing, too, when preparing for the test. Because this book's material is very condensed, I recommend that you use this book along with other resources to achieve the maximum benefit.

In addition to the Study Alerts, I have provided tips that will help build a better foundation for Support knowledge. Although the information may not be on the exam, it is certainly related and will help you become a better test taker.

This is how tips are formatted. Keep your eyes open for these, and you'll become an Cisco networking guru in no time!

- **Practice questions** Although I talk about test questions and topics throughout the book, a section at the end of each chapter presents a series of mock test questions and explanations of both correct and incorrect answers. I also try to point out especially tricky questions by using a special icon, like this:

Ordinarily, this icon flags the presence of a particularly devious inquiry, if not an outright trick question. Trick questions are calculated to be answered incorrectly if not read more than once, and carefully, at that. Although they're not ubiquitous, such questions make regular appearances on the Cisco exams. That's why I say exam questions are as much about reading comprehension as they are about knowing your material inside out and backwards.

- **Details and resources** Every chapter ends with a section titled "Need To Know More?" It provides direct pointers to Cisco and third-party resources offering more details on the chapter's subject. In addition, this section tries to rank or at least rate the quality and thoroughness of the topic's coverage by each resource. If you find a resource in this collection that you like, use it, but don't feel compelled to use all the resources. On the other hand, I recommend only resources I use regularly, so none of our recommendations will be a waste of your time or money (but purchasing them all at once probably represents an expense that many network administrators and would-be CCNPs might find hard to justify).

The bulk of the book follows this chapter structure slavishly, but there are a few other elements that I'd like to point out. Chapter 14 is a sample test that provides a good review of the material presented throughout the book to ensure you're ready for the exam. Chapter 15 is the answer key. In addition, you'll find a handy glossary and an index.

Finally, the tear-out Cram Sheet attached next to the inside front cover of this Exam Cram book represents a condensed and compiled collection of facts, figures, and tips that I think you should memorize before taking the test. Because you can dump this information out of your head onto a piece of paper before answering any exam questions, you can master this information by brute force—you need to remember it only long enough to write it down when you walk into the test room. You might even want to look at it in the car (not while driving) or in the lobby of the testing center just before you walk in to take the test.

How To Use This Book

If you're prepping for a first-time test, we've structured the topics in this book to build on one another. Therefore, some topics in later chapters make more sense after you've read earlier chapters. That's why I suggest you read this book from front to back for your initial test preparation. If you need to brush up on a topic or you have to bone up for a second try, use the index or table of contents to go straight to the topics and questions that you need to study. Beyond the tests, I think you'll find this book useful as a tightly focused reference to some of the most important aspects of Support 2.0.

Given all the book's elements and its specialized focus, I've tried to create a tool that will help you prepare for—and pass—Cisco Career Certification Exam 640-506, "Support 2.0" Please share your feedback on the book with us, especially if you have ideas about how I can improve it for future test-takers. We'll consider everything you say carefully, and we'll respond to all suggestions.

Please send your questions or comments to us at at **cipq @coriolis.com**. Please remember to include the title of the book in your message; otherwise, we'll be forced to guess which book you're writing about. Also, be sure to check out the Web pages at **www.certificationinsider.com**, where you'll find information updates, commentary, and clarifications on documents for each book that you can either read online or download for use later on.

Thanks, and enjoy the book!

Self-Assessment

The reason I included a Self-Assessment in this Exam Cram is to help you evaluate your readiness to tackle CCNP certification. It should also help you understand what you need to master the topic of this book—namely, Exam 640-506, "Support 2.0." But before you tackle this Self-Assessment, let's talk about concerns you may face when pursuing a CCNP, and what an ideal CCNP candidate might look like.

CCNPs In The Real World

In the next section, I describe an ideal CCNP candidate, knowing full well that only a few real candidates will meet this ideal. In fact, our description of that ideal candidate might seem downright scary. But take heart: Although the requirements to obtain a CCNP may seem pretty formidable, they are by no means impossible to meet. However, you should be keenly aware that it does take time and requires some expense and substantial effort to get through the process.

The first thing to understand is that the CCNP is an attainable goal. You can get all the real-world motivation you need from knowing that many others have gone before, so you will be able to follow in their footsteps. If you're willing to tackle the process seriously and do what it takes to obtain the necessary experience and knowledge, you can take—and pass—all the certification tests involved in obtaining an CCNP. In fact, we've designed these Exam Crams, and the companion Exam Preps, to make it as easy on you as possible to prepare for these exams. But prepare you must!

The same, of course, is true for other Cisco career certifications, including:

- **Cisco Certified Design Associate (CCDA)**—The CCDA is a basic certification aimed at designers of high-level internetworks.
- **Cisco Certified Network Associate (CCNA)**—The CCNA is the first career certification.
- **Cisco Certified Network Professional (CCNP)**—The CCNP is a more advanced certification that is not easy to obtain.

- **Cisco Certified Internetwork Expert (CCIE)**—The CCIE is possibly the most influential certification in the internetworking industry today. It is famous (or infamous) for its difficulty and for how easily it holds its seekers at bay.

The Ideal CCNP Candidate

Just to give you some idea of what an ideal CCNP candidate is like, here are some relevant statistics about the background and experience such an individual might have. Don't worry if you don't meet these qualifications, or don't come that close—this is a far from ideal world, and where you fall short is simply where you'll have more work to do.

- Academic or professional training in network theory, concepts, and operations. This includes everything from networking media and transmission techniques through network operating systems, services, and applications.
- Three-plus years of professional networking experience, including experience with Ethernet, token ring, modems, and other networking media. This must include installation, configuration, upgrade, and troubleshooting experience.
- Two-plus years in a networked environment that includes hands-on experience with Cisco routers and related equipment. A solid understanding of each system's architecture, installation, configuration, maintenance, and troubleshooting is also essential.
- A thorough understanding of key networking protocols, addressing, and name resolution, including TCP/IP, IPX/SPX, and AppleTalk.
- Familiarity with key TCP/IP-based services, including ARP, BOOTP, DNS, FTP, SNMP, SMTP, Telnet, TFTP, and other relevant services for your internetwork deployment.

Fundamentally, this boils down to a bachelor's degree in computer science, plus three years of work experience in a technical position involving network design, installation, configuration, and maintenance. I believe that well under half of all certification candidates meet these requirements, and that, in fact, most meet less than half of these requirements—at least, when they begin the certification process. But because thousands of people have survived this ordeal, you can survive it too—especially if you heed what our Self-Assessment can tell you about what you already know and what you need to learn.

Put Yourself To The Test

The following series of questions and observations is designed to help you figure out how much work you must do to pursue Cisco career certification and what kinds of resources you should consult on your quest. Be absolutely honest in your answers, or you'll end up wasting money on exams you're not yet ready to take. There are no right or wrong answers, only steps along the path to certification. Only you can decide where you really belong in the broad spectrum of aspiring candidates.

Two things should be clear from the outset, however:

- Even a modest background in computer science will be helpful.
- Extensive hands-on experience with Cisco products and technologies is an essential ingredient to certification success.

1. Have you ever taken any computer-related classes? [Yes or No]

   If Yes, proceed to question 2; if No, proceed to question 4.

2. Have you taken any classes included in Cisco's curriculum? [Yes or No]

   If Yes, you will probably be able to handle Cisco's architecture and system component discussions. If you're rusty, brush up on basic router operating system concepts, such as, RAM, NVRAM, and flash memory. You'll also want to brush up on the basics of internetworking, especially IP subnetting, access lists, and WAN technologies such as ATM, Frame Relay, and ISDN.

   If No, consider some extensive reading in this area. I strongly recommend instructor-led training offered by a Cisco Training Partner. However, a good general advanced routing technology book, such as *Cisco CCIE Fundamentals: Network Design and Cast Studies* by Andrea Cheek, H. Kim Lew, and Kathleen Wallace (Cisco Press, Indianapolis, IN, 1998 ISBN: 1-57870-066-3). If this title doesn't appeal to you, check out reviews for other, similar titles at your favorite online bookstore.

3. Have you taken any networking concepts or technologies classes? [Yes or No]

   If Yes, you will probably be able to handle Cisco's internetworking terminology, concepts, and technologies. If you're rusty, brush up on basic internetworking concepts and terminology, especially networking media, transmission types, the OSI Reference model, and networking technologies such as Ethernet, token ring, FDDI, and WAN links.

If No, you might want to read one or two books in this topic area. Check out the "Need to Know More?" section at the end of each chapter for a selection of resources that will give you additional background on the topics covered in this book.

4. Have you done any reading on routing protocols and/or routed protocols (IP, IPX, AppleTalk, and so on)? [Yes or No]

   If Yes, review the requirements stated in the first paragraphs after Questions 2 and 3. If you meet those requirements, move on to the next question.

   If No, consult the recommended reading for both topics. A strong background will help you prepare for the Cisco exams better than just about anything else.

The most important key to success on all of the Cisco tests is hands-on experience with Cisco routers and related equipment. If I leave you with only one realization after taking this Self-Assessment, it should be that there's no substitute for time spent installing, configuring, and using the various Cisco products upon which you'll be tested repeatedly and in depth. It cannot be stressed enough that quality instructor-led training will benefit you greatly and give you additional hands-on configuration experience with the technologies upon which you are to be tested.

5. Have you installed, configured, and worked with Cisco routers? [Yes or No]

   If Yes, make sure you understand basic concepts as covered in the class Introduction to Cisco Network Devices (ICND), Advanced Cisco Router Configuration (ACRC), Cisco LAN Switch Configuration (CLSC), and Configuring, Maintaining, and Troubleshooting Dial-up Services (CMTD), before progressing into the materials covered here, because this book expands on the basic topics taught there.

You can download objectives and other information about Cisco exams from the company's Training and Certification page on the Web at **www.cisco.com/training**.

   If No, you will need to find a way to get a good amount of instruction on the intricacies of configuring Cisco equipment. You need a broad background to get through any of Cisco's career certification. You will also need to have hands-on experience with the equipment and technologies on which you'll be tested.

If you have the funds, or your employer will pay your way, consider taking a class at a Cisco Training Partner (preferably one with "distinguished" status for the highest quality possible). In addition to classroom exposure to the topic of your choice, you get a good view of the technologies being widely deployed and will be able to take part in hands-on lab scenarios with those technologies.

Before you even think about taking any Cisco exam, make sure you've spent enough time with the related software to understand how it may be installed and configured, how to maintain such an installation, and how to troubleshoot that software when things go wrong. This will help you in the exam, and in real life!

Whether you attend a formal class on a specific topic to get ready for an exam or use written materials to study on your own, some preparation for the Cisco career certification exams is essential. At $100 to $200 (depending on the exam) a try, pass or fail, you want to do everything you can to pass on your first try. That's where studying comes in.

6. Have you taken a practice exam on your chosen test subject? [Yes or No]

   If Yes, and you scored 70 percent or better, you're probably ready to tackle the real thing. If your score isn't above that crucial threshold, keep at it until you break that barrier.

   If No, obtain all the free and low-budget practice tests you can find (see the list above) and get to work. Keep at it until you can break the passing threshold comfortably.

I have included a practice exam in this book, so you can test yourself on the information and techniques you've learned. If you don't hit a score of at least 70 percent after this test, you'll want to investigate the other practice test resources I mention in this section.

For any given subject, consider taking a class if you've tackled self-study materials, taken the test, and failed anyway. The opportunity to interact with an instructor and fellow students can make all the difference in the world, if you can afford that privilege. For information about Cisco classes, visit the Training and Certification page at **www.cisco.com/training** or **www.geotrain.com** (use the "Locate a Course" link).

If you can't afford to take a class, visit the Training and Certification page anyway, because it also includes pointers to additional resources and self-study tools. And even if you can't afford to spend much at all, you should still invest in some low-cost practice exams from commercial vendors, because they can help you assess your readiness to pass a test better than any other tool. The following Web sites offer some practice exams online:

- CCPrep.com at **www.ccprep.com** (requires membership)
- Network Study Guides at **www.networkstudyguides.com** (pay as you go)

When it comes to assessing your test readiness, there is no better way than to take a good-quality practice exam and pass with a score of 70 percent or better. When we're preparing ourselves, I shoot for 80-plus percent, just to leave room for the "weirdness factor" that sometimes shows up on Cisco exams.

Assessing Readiness For Exam 640-506

In addition to the general exam-readiness information in the previous section, there are several things you can do to prepare for the Support exam. You will find a great source of questions and related information at the CCprep Web site at **www.ccprep.com**. This is a good place to ask questions and get good answers, or simply to watch the questions that others ask (along with the answers, of course).

You should also cruise the Web looking for "braindumps" (recollections of test topics and experiences recorded by others) to help you anticipate topics you're likely to encounter on the test.

When using any braindump, it's OK to pay attention to information about questions. But you can't always be sure that a braindump's author will also be able to provide correct answers. Thus, use the questions to guide your studies, but don't rely on the answers in a braindump to lead you to the truth. Double-check everything you find in any braindump.

For Support 2.0 preparation in particular, I'd also like to recommend that you check out one or more of these resources as you prepare to take Exam 640-506:

- Cisco Connection Online (CCO) Documentation (**www.cisco.com/univercd/home/home.htm**). From the CCO Documentation home page you can select a variety of topics, including but not limited to Troubleshooting Internetworking Systems and Internetwork Troubleshooting guides, as well as Internetwork Technologies Overviews and Design Guides.

- Cisco Routers in a Nutshell (**www.clark.net/pub/rbenn/cisco.html**). An excellent resource for all levels of Cisco expertise. This Web site provides direct links to several white papers within Cisco's Web site, such as protocol explanations and sample network configurations.
- Douglas Comer. *Internetworking with TCP/IP, Volume 1: Principles, Protocols, and Architecture*, Prentice Hall, Englewood Cliffs, NJ, 1995. ISBN: 0-13-216987-8.
- Laura A. Chappell. *Novell's Guide to LAN/WAN Analysis: IPX/SPX*. IDG Books Worldwide, Foster City, CA, 1998. ISBN: 0764545086.
- Perlman, Radia: *Interconnections: Bridges and Routers*, Addison-Wesley, Reading, PA, 1992. ISBN: 0-201-56332-0.

Stop by your favorite bookstore or online bookseller to check out one or more of these resources. I believe the first two are the best general all-around references on TCP/IP and advanced routing available, and the second two complement the contents of this Exam Cram for test preparation very nicely.

One last note: Hopefully, it makes sense to stress the importance of hands-on experience in the context of the Support 2.0 exam. As you review the material for that exam, you'll realize that hands-on experience with the Cisco IOS with various technologies and configurations is invaluable.

Onward, Through The Fog!

Once you've assessed your readiness, undertaken the right background studies, obtained the hands-on experience that will help you understand the products and technologies at work, and reviewed the many sources of information to help you prepare for a test, you'll be ready to take a round of practice tests. When your scores come back positive enough to get you through the exam, you're ready to go after the real thing. If you follow our assessment regime, you'll not only know what you need to study, but when you're ready to make a test date at Sylvan Prometric. Good luck!

Cisco Certification Exams

Terms you'll need to understand:

- √ Radio button
- √ Checkbox
- √ Exhibit
- √ Multiple-choice question formats
- √ Careful reading
- √ Process of elimination

Techniques you'll need to master:

- √ Assessing your exam-readiness
- √ Preparing to take a certification exam
- √ Practicing (to make perfect)
- √ Making the best use of the testing software
- √ Budgeting your time
- √ Saving the hardest questions until last
- √ Guessing (as a last resort)
- √ Breathing deeply to calm frustration

Exam taking is not something that most people anticipate eagerly, no matter how well prepared they may be. In most cases, familiarity helps ameliorate test anxiety. In plain English, this means you probably will not be as nervous when you take your fourth or fifth Cisco certification exam, as you will be when you take your first one.

Whether it is your first exam or your tenth, understanding the details of exam taking (how much time to spend on questions, the environment you'll be in, and so on) and the exam software will help you concentrate on the material rather than on the setting. Likewise, mastering a few basic exam-taking skills should help you recognize—and perhaps even outfox—some of the tricks and gotchas you're bound to find in some of the exam questions.

This chapter, besides explaining the exam environment and software, describes some proven exam-taking strategies that you should be able to use to your advantage.

Assessing Exam-Readiness

Before you take any Cisco exam, I strongly recommend that you read through and take the Self-Assessment included with this book (it appears just before this chapter, in fact). This will help you compare your knowledge base to the requirements for obtaining a CCNP, and it will also help you identify parts of your background or experience that may be in need of improvement, enhancement, or further learning. If you get the right set of basics under your belt, obtaining Cisco certification will be that much easier.

Once you've gone through the Self-Assessment, you can remedy those topical areas where your background or experience may not measure up to an ideal certification candidate. But you can also tackle subject matter for individual tests at the same time, so you can continue making progress while you're catching up in some areas.

Once you've worked through an *Exam Cram*, have read the supplementary materials, and have taken the practice test at the end of the book, you'll have a pretty clear idea of when you should be ready to take the real exam. Although I strongly recommend that you keep practicing until your scores top the 70 percent mark, 75 percent would be a good goal to give yourself some margin for error in a real exam situation (where stress will play more of a role than when you practice). Once you hit that point, you should be ready to go. But if you get through the practice exam in this book without attaining that score, you should keep taking practice tests and studying the materials until you get there. You'll find more information about other practice test vendors in the Self-Assessment, along with even more pointers on how to study and prepare. But now, on to the exam itself!

The Exam Situation

When you arrive at the testing center where you scheduled your exam, you will need to sign in with an exam coordinator. He or she will ask you to show two forms of identification, one of which must be a photo ID. After you have signed in and your time slot arrives, you will be asked to deposit any books, bags, or other items you brought with you. Then, you will be escorted into a closed room. Typically, the room will be furnished with anywhere from one to half a dozen computers, and each workstation will be separated from the others by dividers designed to keep you from seeing what is happening on someone else's computer.

You will be furnished with a pen or pencil and a blank sheet of paper, or, in some cases, an erasable plastic sheet and an erasable felt-tip pen. You are allowed to write down any information you want on both sides of this sheet. Before the exam, you should memorize as much of the material that appears on The Cram Sheet (inside the front cover of this book) as you can so you can write that information on the blank sheet as soon as you are seated in front of the computer. You can refer to your rendition of The Cram Sheet anytime you like during the test, but you will have to surrender the sheet when you leave the room.

Most test rooms feature a wall with a large picture window. This permits the exam coordinator standing behind it to monitor the room, to prevent exam takers from talking to one another, and to observe anything out of the ordinary that might go on. The exam coordinator will have preloaded the appropriate Cisco certification exam—for this book, that's Exam 640-506—and you will be permitted to start as soon as you are seated in front of the computer.

All Cisco certification exams allow a certain maximum amount of time in which to complete your work (this time is indicated on the exam by an onscreen counter/clock, so you can check the time remaining whenever you like). Exam 640-506 consists of 61 randomly selected questions. You may take up to 75 minutes to complete the exam and need a score of 696 out of 1,000 to pass.

All Cisco certification exams are computer generated and use a multiple-choice format. From time to time you may be prompted to enter actual configuration commands as if you were at the command-line interface. It is important not to abbreviate the commands in any way when this type of question is posed. Although this may sound quite simple, the questions are constructed not only to check your mastery of basic facts and figures about Cisco router configuration, but they also require you to evaluate one or more sets of circumstances or requirements. Often, you will be asked to give more than one answer to a question. Likewise, you might be asked to select the best or most effective solution to a problem from a range of choices, all of which technically are correct. Taking the exam is quite an adventure, and it involves real thinking. This book shows you what to expect and how to deal with the potential problems, puzzles, and predicaments.

Exam Layout And Design

Some exam questions require you to select a single answer, whereas others ask you to select multiple correct answers or fill in the blank with a code command. The following multiple-choice question requires you to select a single correct answer. Following the question is a brief summary of each potential answer and why it is either right or wrong.

Question 1

What is the key piece of information on which routing decisions are based?

❍ a. Source network-layer address

❍ b. Destination network-layer address

❍ c. Source MAC address

❍ d. Destination MAC address

Answer b is correct. The destination network-layer (or Layer 3) address is the protocol-specific address to which this piece of data is to be delivered. The source network-layer address is the originating host and plays no role in getting the information to the destination. Therefore, answer a is incorrect. The source and destination MAC addresses are necessary for getting the data to the router, or the next hop address. However, they are not used in pathing decisions. Therefore, answers c and d are incorrect.

This sample question format corresponds closely to the Cisco certification exam format—the only difference on the exam is that questions are not followed by answer keys. To select an answer, position the cursor over the radio button next to the answer. Then, click the mouse button to select the answer.

Let's examine a question that requires choosing one or more answers. This type of question provides checkboxes rather than radio buttons for marking all appropriate selections.

Question 2

Which of the following are possible encapsulations for an ISDN capable interface? [Choose the four best answers]

- ❑ a. Frame Relay
- ❑ b. LAPB
- ❑ c. PPP
- ❑ d. HDLC
- ❑ e. ATM

Answers a, b, c, and d are correct. ISDN is also capable of supporting X.25 encapsulation. Answer e is incorrect because Basic Rate Interfaces are not capable of providing Asynchronous Transfer Mode (ATM) services. Specialized ATM interfaces are required for utilization of that technology.

For this type of question, more than one answer is required. Cisco does not give partial credit for partially correct answers when the test is scored. For Question 2, you have to check the boxes next to items a, b, c, and d to obtain credit for a correct answer. Notice that picking the right answers also means knowing why the other answers are wrong!

Question 3

Enter the command to display information regarding IP-enabled interfaces. [Fill in the blank]

____

"**show ip interfaces**" is the correct answer. You will have to know the exact command. Unfortunately for most of us, you cannot abbreviate the commands in the blank as if you were actually at the command-line interface. You must know the exact syntax and command variables of the question to get credit.

Although these three basic types of questions can appear in many forms, they constitute the foundation on which all the Cisco certification exam questions rest. More complex questions include so-called exhibits, which are usually network scenarios, screenshots of output from the router, or even pictures from the course materials. For some of these questions, you will be asked to make a selection by clicking on a checkbox or radio button on the screenshot itself. For others, you will be expected to use the information displayed therein to guide your answer to the question. Familiarity with the underlying utility is your key to choosing the correct answer(s).

Other questions involving exhibits use charts or network diagrams to help document a workplace scenario that you will be asked to troubleshoot or configure. Careful attention to such exhibits is the key to success. Be prepared to toggle frequently between the exhibit and the question as you work.

Using Cisco's Exam Software Effectively

Unlike the former Cisco examinations that allowed you to checkmark each question and return to it at any time during the testing period, now Cisco only gives you one chance to answer each question correctly. All Cisco tests will not allow users to mark, skip, or return to questions. In other words, fixed-length Cisco exams will act like adaptive tests in that a user must answer a question and move on to the next question. Also, remember to limit the amount of time that you work on a question or you will risk running out of time. If a question stumps you, eliminate all answers that you know are incorrect and guess from the remaining choices. Not answering a question guarantees you won't receive credit for it, but a guess has at least a chance of being correct.

You are better off guessing than leaving questions unanswered.

Exam-Taking Basics

The most important advice about taking any exam is this: Read each question carefully. Some questions are deliberately ambiguous, some use double negatives, and others use terminology in incredibly precise ways. I have taken numerous exams—both practice and live—and in nearly every one have missed at least one question because they did not read it closely or carefully enough.

Here are some suggestions on how to deal with the tendency to jump to an answer too quickly:

- Make sure you read every word in the question. If you find yourself jumping ahead impatiently, go back and start over.

- As you read, try to restate the question in your own terms. If you can do this, you should be able to pick the correct answer(s) much more easily.
- Try to articulate to yourself what you do not understand about the question, why the answers do not appear to make sense, or what appears to be missing. If you "chew" on the subject for a while, your subconscious might provide the details that are lacking or you might notice a "trick" that will point to the right answer.

Above all, try to deal with each question by thinking through what you know about Cisco routers and their configuration—the characteristics, behaviors, facts, and figures involved. By reviewing what you know (and what you have written down on your information sheet), you will often recall or understand things sufficiently to determine the answer to the question.

Question-Handling Strategies

Based on exams I have taken, some interesting trends have become apparent. For those questions that take only a single answer, usually two or three of the answers will be obviously incorrect, and two of the answers will be plausible—of course, only one can be correct. Unless the answer leaps out at you (if it does, reread the question to look for a trick; sometimes those are the ones you are most likely to get wrong), begin the process of answering by eliminating those answers that are most obviously wrong.

Things to look for in obviously wrong answers include spurious menu choices or utility names, nonexistent software options, and terminology you have never seen. If you have done your homework for an exam, no valid information should be completely new to you. In that case, unfamiliar or bizarre terminology probably indicates a totally bogus answer.

Numerous questions assume that the default behavior of a particular utility is in effect. If you know the defaults and understand what they mean, this knowledge will help you cut through many Gordian knots.

As you work your way through the exam, another counter that Cisco thankfully provides will come in handy—the number of questions completed and questions outstanding. Budget your time by making sure that you have completed one-quarter of the questions one-quarter of the way through the exam period (or the first 15 questions in the first 18 minutes) and three-quarters of them three-quarters of the way through (45 questions in the first 56 minutes).

If you are not finished when 70 minutes have elapsed, use the last 5 minutes to guess your way through the remaining questions. Remember, guessing is potentially more valuable than not answering, because blank answers are always wrong, but a guess may turn out to be right. If you do not have a clue about any of the remaining questions, pick answers at random, or choose all a's, b's, and so on. The important thing is to submit an exam for scoring that has an answer for every question.

Mastering The Inner Game

In the final analysis, knowledge breeds confidence, and confidence breeds success. If you study the materials in this book carefully and review all the practice questions at the end of each chapter, you should become aware of those areas where additional learning and study are required.

Next, follow up by reading some or all of the materials recommended in the "Need To Know More?" section at the end of each chapter. The idea is to become familiar enough with the concepts and situations you find in the sample questions that you can reason your way through similar situations on a real exam. If you know the material, you have every right to be confident that you can pass the exam.

After you have worked your way through the book, take the practice exam in Chapter 14. This will provide a reality check and help you identify areas you need to study further. Make sure you follow up and review materials related to the questions you miss on the practice exam before scheduling a real exam. Only when you have covered all the ground and feel comfortable with the whole scope of the practice exam should you take a real one.

If you take the practice exam and do not score at least 75 percent correct, you will want to practice further.

Armed with the information in this book and with the determination to augment your knowledge, you should be able to pass the certification exam. However, you need to work at it; otherwise, you'll spend the exam fee more than once before you finally pass. If you prepare seriously, you should do well. Good luck!

Additional Resources

A good source of information about Cisco certification exams comes from Cisco itself. Because its products and technologies—and the exams that go with them—change frequently, the best place to go for exam-related information is online.

If you haven't already visited the Cisco Certified Professional site, do so right now. The Cisco Career Certifications home page (shown in Figure 1.1) resides at **www.cisco.com/warp/public/10/wwtraining/certprog/index.html**.

> *Note: This page might not be there by the time you read this, or it might have been replaced by something new and different, because things change regularly on the Cisco site. Should this happen, please read the sidebar titled "Coping with Change on the Web."*

The menu options in the left column of the home page point to the most important sources of information in the Career Certifications pages. Here's what to check out:

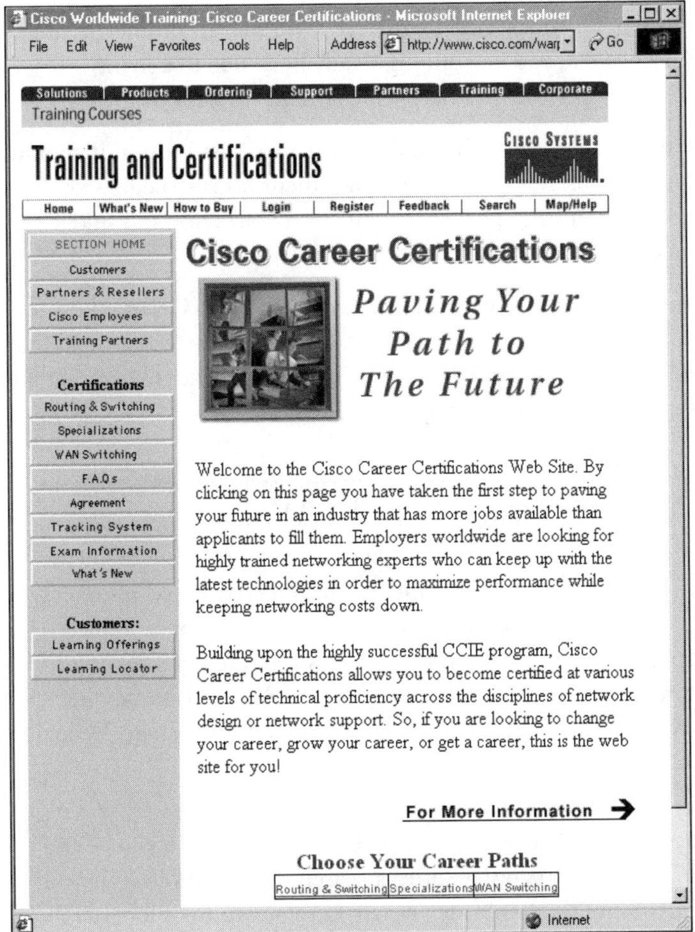

Figure 1.1 The Cisco Career Certifications home page.

- **Routing and Switching** Use this entry to explore the CCIE certification track for routing and switching.
- **Specializations** Use this entry to explore different CCNP specialization options.
- **WAN Switching** Use this entry to explore the CCIE certification track for WAN Switching.
- **FAQs** Use this entry to access the most commonly asked questions regarding any Cisco Career Certification.
- **Agreement** Prior to certification, all candidates must complete the certification agreement or Cisco will not recognize them as certified professionals.
- **Tracking System** Once you have registered with Sylvan Prometric, and taken any Cisco exam, you will automatically be added to a living certification tracking system so that you can keep up with your progress.
- **Exam Information** This entry actually points to a class locator. It should be noted that no book is an adequate replacement for instructor-led, Cisco-authorized training. This entry will assist your efforts to find a class that meets your scheduling needs.

These are just the high points of what's available in the Cisco Certified Professional pages. As you browse through them—and we strongly recommend that you do—you will probably find other informational tidbits mentioned that are every bit as interesting and compelling.

Coping With Change On The Web

Sooner or later, all the information we have shared with you about the Cisco Certified Professional pages and the other Web-based resources mentioned throughout the rest of this book will go stale or be replaced by newer information. In some cases, the URLs you find here might lead you to their replacements; in other cases, the URLs will go nowhere, leaving you with the dreaded "404 File not found" error message. When that happens, do not give up.

There's always a way to find what you want on the Web if you are willing to invest some time and energy. Most large or complex Web sites—and Cisco's qualifies on both counts—offer a search engine. As long as you can get to Cisco's site (it should stay at **www.cisco.com** for a long while yet), you can use this tool to help you find what you need.

The more focused you can make a search request, the more likely the results will include information you can use. For example, you can search for the string "training and certification" to produce a lot of data about the subject in general, but if you are looking for the preparation guide for Exam 640-506, "Support 2.0," you will be more likely to get there quickly if you use a search string similar to the following:

```
"Exam 640-506" AND "preparation guide"
```

Finally, feel free to use general search tools—such as **www.search.com**, **www.altavista.com**, and **www.excite.com**—to search for related information. The bottom line is this: If you can't find something where the book says it lives, start looking around. If worst comes to worst, you can always email us. We just might have a clue.

Support Resources

Terms you'll need to understand:

- ✓ Cisco Connection Online (CCO)
- ✓ Network management systems (NMSs)
- ✓ CiscoWorks 2000
- ✓ Remote Monitoring (RMON)
- ✓ Simple Network Management Protocol (SNMP)
- ✓ Network monitors
- ✓ Protocol analyzers

Techniques you'll need to master:

- ✓ Navigating with CCO
- ✓ Debugging with the CCO Stack Decoder
- ✓ Understanding the capabilities of network management software
- ✓ Using media testing equipment

Several troubleshooting tools are available to aid you in diagnosing network failures. Network monitors can provide baseline information, protocol analyzers can probe local area network (LAN) traffic, and complete network management systems (NMSs) can monitor, analyze, and manage your entire internetwork. Network management equipment cannot satisfy all the requirements of administering a network—the ease of access to documentation and support resources is also essential.

Cisco Connection Online (CCO)

Cisco Connection Online (CCO), located at **www.cisco.com**, provides online support and services and gives immediate access to information about developing and administering an internetwork (see Figure 2.1). CCO can be accessed

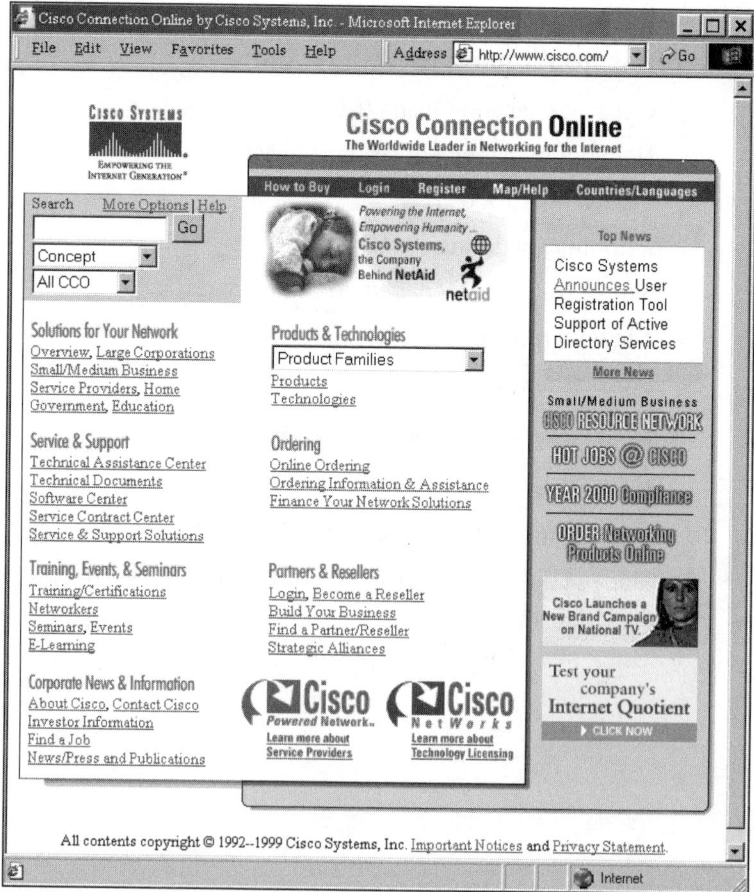

Figure 2.1 The Cisco Connection Online (CCO) Web page, located at **www.cisco.com**.

in two flavors—guest users have general access to company and product information, and registered users have access to in-depth information and more online services. Registration with CCO requires a corporate contract number; this number can be attained by signing a Cisco service contract. Once registered, you will have access to several additional resources, such as the CCO Marketplace, Software Center, and online Technical Assistance Center (TAC).

Cisco Marketplace

The Cisco Marketplace, available by selecting the Online Ordering link on the CCO home page, enables you to configure and purchase Cisco networking software and products over the Internet. The Cisco Marketplace also provides management of product orders, shipment tracking, maintenance contracts, and warranty information. The availability of these business processes on the Web allows for 24-hour purchasing support, which, in turn, leads to increased consumer efficiency.

Software Center

The Software Center, which can be accessed by clicking on the Software Center link on the CCO home page, provides online major upgrades and maintenance releases of Cisco software products. Current releases of Cisco's Internetwork Operating System (IOS) can be selected by answering a series of questions, such as the type of Network layer protocols that must be supported (such as IP, IPX, or AppleTalk) and the IOS revision level (such as 11.1, 11.2, or 12.0). Also, using the Product Upgrade tool, you can gather current product literature, release information, and documentation.

Cisco IOS software, available within the Software Center, is named according to a scheme that identifies what features are included in the image and what platform it runs on. The names have three sections, separated by dashes, in the form xxxx-yyyy-ww, where xxxx is the platform, yyyy specifies the features, and ww indicates where it executes from and whether it's compressed.

Documentation

Cisco Documentation, located at **www.cisco.com/univercd/home/home.htm**, provides complete Cisco product catalogs and configuration manuals for all types of internetworks. The material contained in this area of the Web site provides general internetworking information and detailed sample Cisco router and switch configurations. This is a very valuable resource; familiarity with the navigation of and the content contained in this section of the Web site is helpful, especially if you're on track to attain the Cisco Certified Internetworking Expert (CCIE) certification.

Technical Assistance Center

The Technical Assistance Center (TAC), available by selecting the Technical Assistance Center on the CCO home page, provides Cisco customers and third-party support providers around-the-clock technical support for all Cisco products. All TAC support cases are processed by the Global Call Center, where the case is assigned a unique case number and a Cisco Customer Support Engineer (CSE) is assigned to the case as the *call owner*. Cisco CSEs are guaranteed to have a bachelor's degree in electrical engineering (or equivalent). What's more, a third of the CSEs have passed at least one of the examinations needed to become Cisco Certified Internetworking Experts (CCIEs). Support cases are originally submitted to the TAC either by phone or email.

Case Submission

Prior to submitting a case to the TAC, you should gather all your facts and thoroughly define your problem, including your maintenance number and product serial number. After enough information is compiled for the Cisco engineer, a case can be opened using the online TAC submission form. Make sure you provide any relevant **show tech-support** data for the routers involved and any other information that the Cisco engineer feels is feasible for submission (see Table 2.1 for a list of common requests). The **show tech-support** command provides core data that's essential to all the router's currently running processes. This command will be covered in more detail in Chapter 4. Each case is constantly monitored for further details, but if network degradation continues you may be required to promote the case to a higher priority level.

Case Escalation

Cases that eventually result in critical events, such as the network being down, may require case escalation. This requires you to contact the TAC Duty Manager and request the case be escalated to a priority level that meets your expectations of service. Available priority levels are shown in Table 2.2. This can also be handled online via the Case Management Toolkit.

Do not rely on email or the Web to submit Priority 1 or Priority 2 problems to Cisco. High priority situations should be reported to Cisco via a phone call directly to the Cisco TAC.

Table 2.1 Common commands requested by Customer Service Engineers (CSEs).

Problem Area	Commands Requested
ISDN	**show isdn status, debug isdn events, debug isdn q921, debug isdn q931, show dialer, debug dialerPPP, debug ppp negotiation, debug ppp authentication**
Frame Relay	**show frame map, show frame pvc, show interface**
IP Routing	**show ip protocol, show ip route, show ip route summary**
OSPF Routing	**show ip ospf database, show ip ospf interface, show ip ospf neighbor, show ip route ospf**
EIGRP Routing	**show ip eigrp topology, show ip eigrp neighbors, show ip route eigrp**
IP Client	**show ip arp, show ip interface, show ip traffic**
IPX Client	**show ipx servers, show ipx interface, show ipx traffic**
Apple Client	**show apple zone, show apple interface, show apple neighbor, show apple traffic**

Table 2.2 TAC problem priority levels.

Priority Level	Description
1	Production network down
2	Production network severely degraded
3	Network performance degraded
4	Information needed on Cisco product capabilities, installation, and configuration

Case Management Toolkit

The Case Management Toolkit, embedded in the TAC, provides online processing and management of cases submitted to the TAC. Usage of this toolkit requires submission of the TAC case number that was originally assigned to the problem by the CSE. The Case Management Toolkit enables you to open new cases, check the status of existing cases, and update information for existing cases, as described in Table 2.3.

Troubleshooting

Every valuable network engineer has a standard troubleshooting technique to use in the event of network difficulties. CCO provides several online troubleshooting tools to assist you in solving problems, from simple networking issues to highly visible network down events.

Table 2.3 The Case Management Toolkit's primary tools.

Tools	Function
Open a TAC case	Allows you to fill out a technical assistance request to open a new TAC case
Update a TAC case	Allows you to check on the current status of any currently open TAC cases
Query a TAC case	Allows you to send updates to the TAC concerning the status of a currently open case

Stack Decoder

The Stack Decoder, found at **www.cisco.com/stack/stackdecoder.shtml**, provides diagnostic capabilities of the low-level processes running within the Cisco router. The Stack Decoder can be used when the router encounters a set of conditions it has not been programmed to handle. To use this tool during the time of the router failure, paste the information returned from a **show stack** command into the Stack Decoder. If key information is available as to the nature of the current failure, such as an IPX/SPX issue, insert these comments into the comment line and then submit the report. Results will be posted to the Web site almost immediately. Sample output from the **show stack** command is shown in Listing 2.1.

Listing 2.1 Output of the **show stack** command.

```
Router>show stack
Minimum process stacks:
 Free/Size Name
 5364/6000 BOOTP Server
 10032/12000 Init
 5640/6000 CDP Protocol
 4808/6000 Router Init
 4736/6000 MSDP Open
 4328/6000 BGP Open
 2000/3000 BGP Accepter
 9972/12000 Exec
 9116/12000 Virtual Exec

Interrupt level stacks:
Level Called Unused/Size Name
 1 735327018 7848/9000 Network Interrupt
 2 28598 7964/9000 Network Status Interrupt
 3 0 8692/9000 OIR Interrupt
 4 0 9000/9000 PCMCIA Interrupt
 5 617288 8620/9000 Console Uart
 6 0 9000/9000 Error Interrupt
 7 89549543 8608/9000 NMI Interrupt Handler
```

Bug Navigator II

The Bug Navigator II (shown in Figure 2.2), which is available at **www.cisco.com/support/bugtools/bugtool.shtml**, allows you to perform keyword searches to find available resources for handling symptom diagnostics and upgrade planning. For example, a keyword search of currently known bugs for IOS version 12.0 on the Cisco 2600 series router with regard to Ethernet would not return any responses with the keyword "Ethernet" included in the search, but would return the result set of all identified problems in using IOS 12.0 on a Cisco 2600 series router. Selecting the option to Watch This Bug will include these criteria within the bug watcher profile associated with the CCO account.

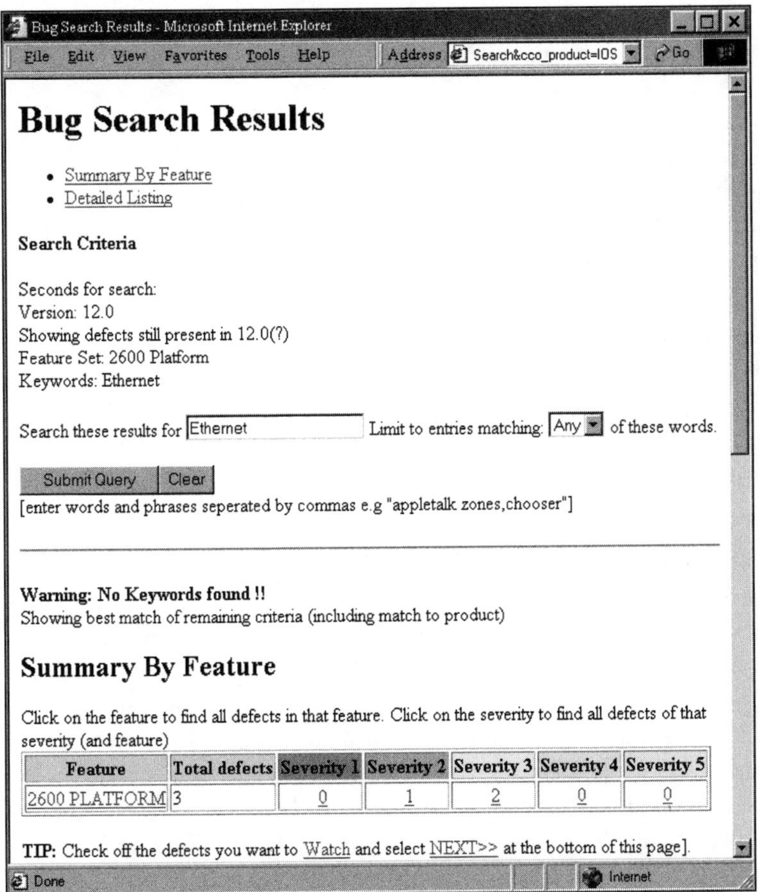

Figure 2.2 The Bug Navigator II program located on Cisco's Web site.

Troubleshooting Assistant

The Troubleshooting Assistant, also available by clicking on the Technical Assistance Center within the CCO home page, can be used for common troubleshooting scenarios involving hardware, software, and performance issues. While performing a query, it interactively steps you through a series of questions within the technology suspected of causing a problem, such as IP routing not working correctly or AppleTalk zones not being displayed in the Macintosh Chooser window. Each answer subsequently narrows the scope of the issue, until either a solution is suggested or the problem is defined as "uncommon." In the latter case, additional information may be returned directing you to further probes into Cisco documentation or the TAC.

> *Note: To effectively use the Troubleshooting Assistant, it is recommended that you have a current network topology map and a printout of the router's running configuration.*

Open Forum

The Open Forum is an online question-and-answer whiteboard that allows Cisco customers to pose questions to Cisco employees and Cisco Certified Internetworking Experts (CCIEs). When your search of the forum is complete, you'll be presented with a list of similar problems and solutions. If no valid question-and-answer pairs are returned, you can post your questions to the open forum.

> *Note: Submission to the forum is similar to a public chat room; it's globally accessible and should be treated as such.*

Network Management

Network management systems (NMSs) are required as an internetwork becomes more complex and network failure becomes more difficult to diagnose. The International Standards Organization (ISO) has defined five functional areas of network management: fault management, accounting management, configuration and name management, performance management, and security management. Network faults and performance degradation can be monitored by protocols ratified by the Internet Engineering Task Force (IETF), such as the Simple Network Management Protocol (SNMP) and Remote Monitoring (RMON). Several tools exist that can be used to monitor the network, such as protocol analyzers and network monitors. Also, Cisco has produced several software applications that can be used to analyze networks implementing Cisco devices.

Cisco Software

Cisco Systems is a premiere provider of network-management software for configuring, analyzing, and troubleshooting network problems within a Cisco environment. Its software is available for several variations of Unix as well as Microsoft Windows NT 4. Cisco software products are available to provide configuration management and performance baselining. These applications are covered in more detail in the following sections.

CiscoWorks 2000

CiscoWorks 2000 is Cisco's premiere network management package. It provides realtime device-level monitoring and fault- and configuration-change management. CiscoWorks 2000 also provides tools for change management within IOS configurations—including notifications of changes identified in running router configurations—and can also serve as a Trivial File Transfer Protocol (TFTP) server for configuration uploading and downloading. CiscoWorks 2000 is entirely Web-based and can easily be integrated with third-party network management systems, such as Hewlett-Packard's OpenView Network Node Manager. The package contains Cisco Resource Manager Essentials, Internetwork Performance Monitor, Cisco Access Control List Manager, and CiscoWorks for Switched Internetworks Campus:

- **Resource Manager Essentials** Cisco Resource Manager (CRM) Essentials, included with CiscoWorks 2000, simplifies network support tasks through Web-based resource management for routers, switches, and hubs. CRM provides inventory management, change audit reports, a software image manager, and a system-logging analyzer.

- **Internetwork Performance Monitor** Internetwork Performance Monitor (IPM) is a network response time and availability troubleshooting application. IPM provides a proactive approach for network engineers to troubleshoot their networks using real-time and historical report functions.

- **Cisco Access Control List Manager** The Cisco Access Control List (ACL) Manager provides a Web-based interface to manage the access lists located within Cisco network devices. ACL Manager dramatically reduces the time needed to develop new ACLs as well as time required to maintain them.

- **User Registration Tool** The User Registration tool provides a graphical interface to reconfigure switch ports. This may be helpful when managerial changes are made to corporate policies or institute divisional reorganizations requiring user mobility and dynamic application services.

- **CiscoWorks For Switched Internetworks Campus** CiscoWorks for Switched Internetworks (CWSI) Campus is Cisco's graphical user interface (GUI) solution for managing switch-based networks, including the 1900, 2800, 2900, and 5000 series Catalyst switches. Using CWSI Campus, via SNMP, you can set everything that's available via the command-line interface (CLI), such as port speeds, descriptions, Cisco Group Management Protocol (CGMP) attributes, and virtual LAN (VLAN) configurations. CWSI contains TrafficDirector and VlanDirector:
- **TrafficDirector** Cisco TrafficDirector software provides advanced traffic-analysis tools and the monitoring capabilities of embedded RMON agents within the catalyst switches and standalone Cisco SwitchProbe products. Traffic data acquired via the RMON agents can be used to outline network performance at the Data Link, Network, Transport, and Application layers.
- **VlanDirector** VlanDirector is a GUI-based management interface for Cisco switches. Individual or multiple ports can be configured via SNMP with descriptions, speed selection, VLAN membership, CGMP membership, and bridge priorities. All of these changes can be made through simple mouse selections or by using drag-and-drop utilities. These integrated features reduce the management costs of new installations and configuration changes.

You can be sure that a Cisco product will be the correct answer for questions on the exam regarding network management software and solutions. If questions have answers that are not Cisco-centric, you can rule those answers out immediately.

Netsys Baseliner

Netsys Baseliner is a simulation and modeling tool that can aid you in initial network design and performance testing of a current production network. Netsys uses object-oriented code to simulate the performance of an internetwork's configuration. By importing the existing infrastructure's code into Netsys and making changes to the code prior to live implementation, you can see and test network performance before committing the design changes.

Network Monitors

Network monitors are software that monitor the network for performance evaluation and degradation—for example, packet loss, high CPU utilization, and host reachability. Monitors can provide baselining information to aid you in pinpointing faulty conditions through variations from the normal performance measures. Common areas to baseline are CPU utilization, bandwidth utilization, the number of collisions, cyclical redundancy checksum (CRC) errors, and carrier transitions.

Protocol Analyzers

Protocol analyzers provide realtime traffic analysis and dissemination, as well as packet generation. These tools are used most often to interactively monitor the network by capturing network data on a per-packet basis. The captured information can then be used to analyze data at each layer of the OSI model. Physical, Data Link, Network, and Transport layer functionality, as well as the purpose of each byte of the packet, normally categorize the information recorded by the analyzer.

The differences between protocol analyzers and network monitors may be confusing at first. To separate the two, remember that network monitors work at higher layers, monitoring the performance of the network through SNMP and keepalives, whereas protocol analyzers break down and display individual data packets flowing on the network.

Media Testing Equipment

A majority of network faults, such as improperly terminated cabling, broken segments, and faulty wiring, can be traced back to the physical infrastructure. Several solutions exist to reduce the stress involved in troubleshooting—each with its own market niche.

Breakout Boxes

Breakout boxes, pictured in Figure 2.3, are used to verify pinouts on serially connected devices. Although the information can be found on Cisco's Web site, locating the proper cabling to connect to the console port on random routers and switches can be very time consuming. With the use of a breakout box, you can verify the correct data exchange sequence and create your connection to the console.

Cable Testers

Cable testers, pictured in Figure 2.4, check the physical continuity and termination of the networking infrastructure. Terminated cables can be easily verified against the corporate standard as to whether the wires are straight through or crossed, as well as whether they're properly inserted into the terminal jack or patch panel.

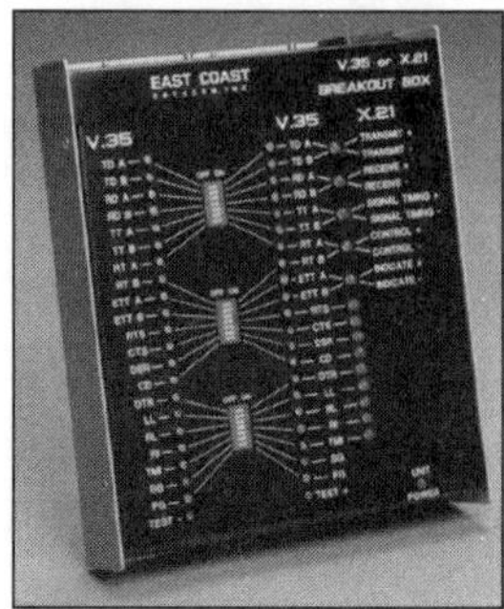

Figure 2.3 A breakout box can be used to verify cable integrity.

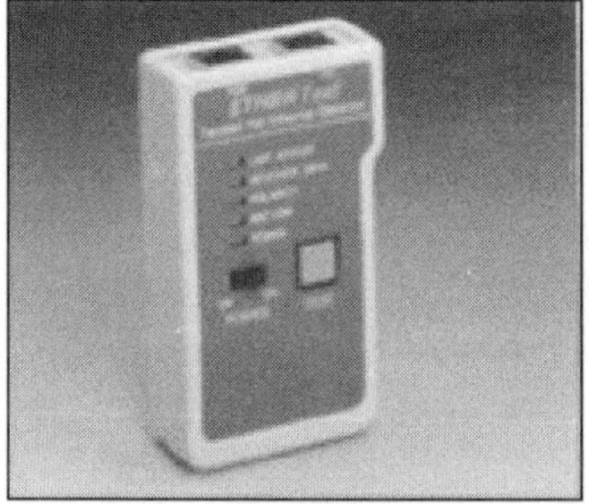

Figure 2.4 Cable testers come in various forms.

Digital Multimeters

Digital multimeters (DMMs), pictured in Figure 2.5, are used to take measurements of voltage, current, and resistance. Both alternating current (AC) and direct current (DC) signals can be measured using a DMM. Thinnet and thicknet cable installations use terminators that should have an impedance of

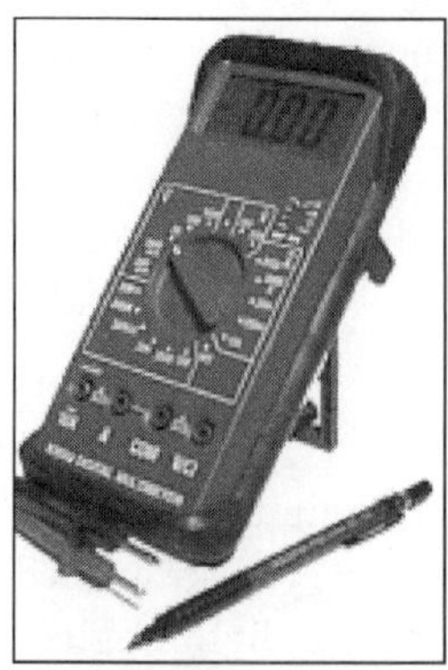

Figure 2.5 Digital multimeters can be used to verify correct cable termination.

50 ohms to within plus or minus 4 percent (if you're in doubt, this can be verified using a multimeter).

Time Domain Reflectors

Time domain reflectors (TDRs), pictured in Figure 2.6, have been around for many years and provide a very accurate way to pinpoint cabling problems. TDRs send pulses along a cable to identify shorts, breaks, and imperfections that may be affecting network throughput. A good TDR can locate a break within a few feet of the actual location. Optical time domain reflectors (OTDRs) analyze fiber media using optical pulses rather than electronic signals.

Oscilloscopes

Oscilloscopes, pictured in Figure 2.7, measure the amount of signal using the number of volts per a unit of time (for example, 1.5 volts/second). Normally, an

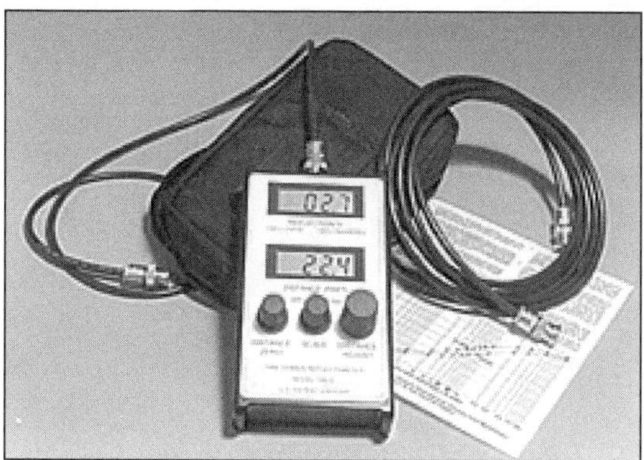

Figure 2.6 Time domain reflectors are very accurate in pinpointing cable problems.

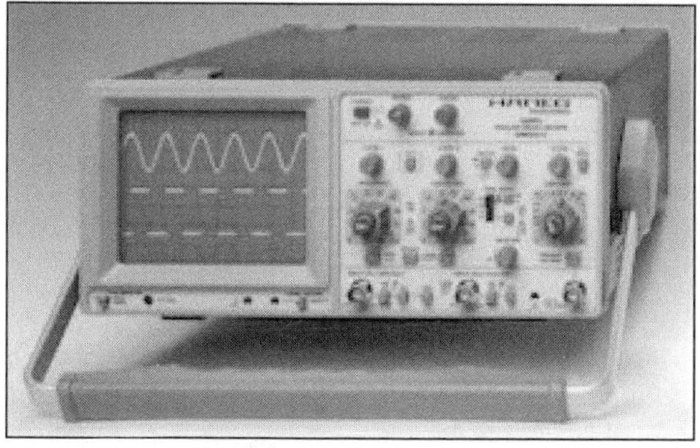

Figure 2.7 Oscilloscopes can be used in conjunction with a TDR.

oscilloscope would be used in conjunction with a TDR to verify cable shorts, sharp bends, and attenuation (loss of signal power).

Know how and when each type of media-testing equipment is used. If a cable break is thought to be the problem, you'll use a TDR. If you feel that a port has gone bad on a router, switch, or patch panel, you'll use a cable tester. Knowing the answers to these type of scenarios will not only help you during the examination, they'll also help you during real-world experiences.

Practice Questions

Question 1

Which type of troubleshooting tool is commonly used to display packet data?

❍ a. Network monitor

● b. Protocol analyzer

❍ c. Breakout box

❍ d. Oscilloscope

The correct answer is b. A protocol analyzer displays individual packets corresponding to the layers of the OSI model. A network monitor displays performance measurements and the overall status of the internetwork. Therefore, answer a is incorrect. A breakout box is used to distinguish the functionality of serial pinouts. Therefore, answer c is incorrect. An oscilloscope is used to test for cable continuity and attenuation. Therefore, answer d is also incorrect.

Question 2

On the Cisco Connection Online (CCO) Web site, what is the Stack Decoder?

❍ a. It executes simple router and switch configuration commands.

❍ b. It provides information on how to set up the Catalyst stackable modules.

● c. A tool that decodes the information given by the router's **show stack** command.

❍ d. A password cracker that decodes Cisco type 7 passwords.

The correct answer is c. The Stack Decoder is used to process the information generated by the **show stack** command executed on a Cisco router. This online tool can locate valuable information and solutions for common network failures. Cisco IOS commands can either be entered via the command-line interface (CLI) or by Cisco management tools, such as CiscoWorks 2000. Therefore, answer a is incorrect. Although information about the Catalyst stackable modules can be found on the CCO Web site, the Stack Decoder is not part of this system. Therefore, answer b is incorrect. Several tools are available freely over the Internet to crack Cisco type 7 passwords, but the Stack Decoder is not one of them. Therefore, answer d is incorrect.

Question 3

Which tool is most useful for analysis of redesign, reconfiguration, and stress testing within a Cisco network?

❍ a. A cable tester

❍ b. Cisco Netsys Baseliner

❍ c. An oscilloscope

❍ d. Network management systems

The correct answer is b. Cisco Netsys Baseliner can compile current infrastructure configurations and then analyze their design for performance. The configurations can then be altered prior to implementation on a production network. Remember that when answering questions, you should look for the most specific answer as well as an answer based around Cisco technology. Cable testers and oscilloscopes are used to verify infrastructure integrity. Therefore, answers a and c are incorrect. Network management systems (NMSs) can be used to analyze a Cisco network, but not to the extent that Cisco Netsys Baseliner can by using proprietary extensions. Therefore, answer d is incorrect.

Question 4

What is the name of the area within the CCO Web site that provides online purchasing?

____

The correct answer is the Cisco Marketplace. The Marketplace provides 24-hour access to product order status, delivery tracking, warranty information, and maintenance contracts.

Question 5

Which Cisco troubleshooting software provides remote traffic-analysis statistics through the Remote Monitoring (RMON) protocol?

❍ a. CiscoWorks 2000

❍ b. TrafficDirector

❍ c. Netsys Baseliner

❍ d. VlanDirector

The correct answer is b. TrafficDirector, which is included with the CiscoWorks for Switched Internetworks Campus product, provides traffic statistics using the RMON protocol. CiscoWorks 2000 provides configuration and change management primarily via SNMP, but it does not provide traffic analysis. Therefore, answer a is incorrect. Netsys Baseliner analyzes the network for performance and redesign criteria. Therefore, answer c is incorrect. VlanDirector, also included with CWSI, provides virtual LAN (VLAN) management and configuration tools. Therefore, answer d is incorrect.

Question 6

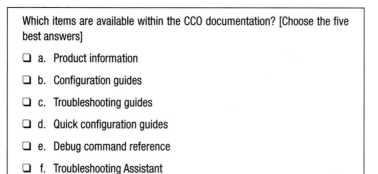

Which items are available within the CCO documentation? [Choose the five best answers]

- ❑ a. Product information
- ❑ b. Configuration guides
- ❑ c. Troubleshooting guides
- ❑ d. Quick configuration guides
- ❑ e. Debug command reference
- ❑ f. Troubleshooting Assistant

The correct answers are a, b, c, d, and e. Complete product guides are available online to aid in installation and maintenance. Guides detailing how to configure popular protocols and common scenarios are also available through the online documentation. Troubleshooting guides, along with the troubleshooting engine, are available online for step-by-step support on common issues, and template configurations are available online to reduce the complexity of original equipment installations. Finally, although debug commands need to be performed with extreme caution, a complete listing of debug capabilities is available online as well. Answer f is incorrect because the Troubleshooting Assistant is available within Online Technical Support.

Question 7

Current network management systems (NMSs) provide which of the following features? [Choose the three best answers]

- ❑ a. Performance monitoring
- ❑ b. Complete package integration with other systems
- ❑ c. Configuration and change management
- ❑ d. Security management

The correct answers are a, c, and d. NMS stations monitor network performance, which can provide a baseline for the network. Management stations also can interoperate with intrusion detection devices that send SNMP traps and CiscoWorks 2000 can be used to track router and switch configuration changes, providing a change management solution. Current network management systems cannot be integrated together. Therefore, answer b is incorrect. However, the IETF is currently working on network management standards that will allow all vendor management systems to interoperate with one another.

Question 8

Which tool is best suited for testing signals and pinouts across an RS-232 interface?

- ❍ a. Breakout box
- ❍ b. Physical inspection
- ❍ c. Cable tester

The correct answer is a. Breakout boxes provide signal testing for RS-232 serial devices. The physical inspection of wiring does not provide adequate knowledge of the cable itself. Therefore, answer b is incorrect. Cable testers are used for wiring and termination certification. Therefore, answer c is incorrect.

Question 9

Which tool can manage Internet Operating System (IOS) configurations through the Internet?

❍ a. TrafficDirector

❍ b. CiscoWorks 2000

❍ c. Network monitor

❍ d. Protocol analyzer

The correct answer is b. CiscoWorks 2000 provides a complete management package that can administer all of your Cisco products, including both routers and switches. TrafficDirector is a traffic-analysis tool—it does not manage networking equipment. Therefore, answer a is incorrect. Network monitors only provide current statistics about an internetwork. Therefore, answer c is incorrect. Protocol analyzers are used to view the contents of each packet captured by the analyzer. Therefore answer d is also incorrect.

Question 10

You are having difficulties establishing a connection between a local and a remote router via an ISDN connection. What commands might a CSE ask you to enter into the router while diagnosing the problem? [Choose the two best answers]

❑ a. **show ip route**

❑ b. **show isdn status**

❑ c. **show ip arp**

❑ d. **debug ppp authentication**

The correct answers are b and d. A Cisco Support Engineer (CSE) would most likely ask you to enter the **show isdn status** command to verify at what layers the connection is establishing correctly. If it is found that there is a problem at Layer 2 of the OSI model, then the CSE would also want the information generated from the **debug ppp authentication** command. Answers a and c are incorrect because the commands would only give information about Layer 3 and Layer 3 to Layer 2 address mappings, whereas in this case the ISDN connection is never to be established so that problem resides either in Layer 1 or 2.

Need To Know More?

Kauffels, Franz-Joachim. *Network Management: Problems, Standards, and Strategies*. Addison Wesley Publishing Company. Reading, MA, 1992. ISBN: 020156534X. Although a bit outdated, this book still does a good job describing the management processes used by popular network management systems, such as Hewlett-Packard's HP Openview and IBM's Netview for several individual network protocols.

McCabe, James D. *Practical Computer Network Analysis and Design*. Morgan Kaufmann Publishers, Inc. San Francisco, CA, 1998. ISBN: 1558604987. This book covers several key perfomance and design analysis characteristics that can help to isolate network faults prior to complete network degradation.

Rose, Marshall T. *The Simple Book: An Introduction to Networking Management, Second Edition*. Prentice Hall, Inc. Upper Saddle River, NJ, 1996. ISBN: 0134516591. An excellent resource to learn the inner workings of the Simple Network Management Protocol (SNMP).

For information about network management, navigate to the Cisco Connection Online (CCO) Documentation page at **www.cisco.com/univercd/home/home.htm**. From there, select Internetworking Technology Overview, and then the Network Management Basics link. These Web pages describe the distinct management processes performed on a network.

For information about SNMP, navigate to the CCO Documentation page at **www.cisco.com/univercd/home/home.htm**. From there, select Internetworking Technology Overview, and then the Simple Network Management Protocol link. There you'll find information on the actual packet details of SNMP messages.

CCO Documentation also contains good troubleshooting information. Go to **www.cisco.com/univercd/home/home.htm** and select Internetworking Troubleshooting Guide, then choose Troubleshooting Tools. This page provides a general introduction to network management and the tools available.

Troubleshooting Methodology

Terms you'll need to understand:

- √ Network baseline
- √ Frame error statistics and variation
- √ Bandwidth utilization

Techniques you'll need to master:

- √ Generating network baseline reports
- √ Implementing a general troubleshooting method

When a user complains that the "network is down," what does this really mean? Is he or she unable to browse a Web site, log in, or use a certain application? It's possible that the problem resides only with this single workstation, or several users may also be experiencing the problem.

Network Baselines

A *network baseline* defines the typical protocol activity of all devices within your network infrastructure. It involves recording performance measurements during the normal operation of the network to serve as a basis for comparison. The information collected provides network administrators with patterns and trends, which allows identification of potentially problematic issues.

By understanding the relationship between network growth and performance, you can better plan the expansion of your network. Understanding the normal operating conditions of the network can serve as a valuable asset in a troubleshooting situation. Additionally, the network's ability to support future applications can be foreseen rather than using the assumption that the network can support growth.

What Statistics Should Be Gathered?

Always gather statistics over the same time period each day so that your baseline reflects activity accurately. Your statistics would not be accurate if, for example, you gathered network statistics during business hours some days and nonbusiness hours other days and then averaged that data. In general, the following variables should be monitored to provide adequate information about the operational state of your network:

- **Error statistics** For collisions, runts, jabbers, and CRC errors
- **Bandwidth utilization** During peak and normal operation
- **Frame variation** Peak and average number per second/size
- **CPU utilization** For infrastructure equipment (routers and servers)
- **Protocol distribution** For infrastructure equipment (routers and servers)
- **Top *n* talkers** Identifying the top (*n*) points of high network utilization

This information could then be stored in a centralized database that will manipulate the information into detailed analysis reports that can serve as a valuable reference for the network.

How Should The Collected Data Be Analyzed?

The gathered statistics should allow for a thorough evaluation of the operational state of the network. You can analyze the characteristics of the network through the following reports:

- Infrastructure utilization of each network segment displayed with the minimal, average, and peak data points. This can be useful in identifying saturated networks and dramatic increases in network load.
- Infrastructure error statistical charts to indicate the overall health of the network. This can be used to indicate failing cabling or network interfaces.
- Short- and long-term traffic statistics to provide a history of network growth, track changes in network performance, and plan for future expansion.
- Evaluate the effect of changes to the network, such as bandwidth upgrades, device relocation, or application installation.

Troubleshooting Model

Experts solve real problems in several steps. You must interpret the problem in light of your own knowledge and experience. This enables you to decide what information is important, what information can be ignored, and what additional information may be needed, even though it was not explicitly provided. The seven-step strategy shown in Figure 3.1 represents an effective way to organize your thinking to produce a solution based on your best understanding of internetworking. The quality of the solution depends on the information you use when determining the solution. Using this strategy also makes it easier to look back through your solution to check for incorrect information and assumptions. The following sections discuss the steps in more detail.

If you learn to use the strategy effectively, you'll find it a valuable tool to use for solving new and complex problems.

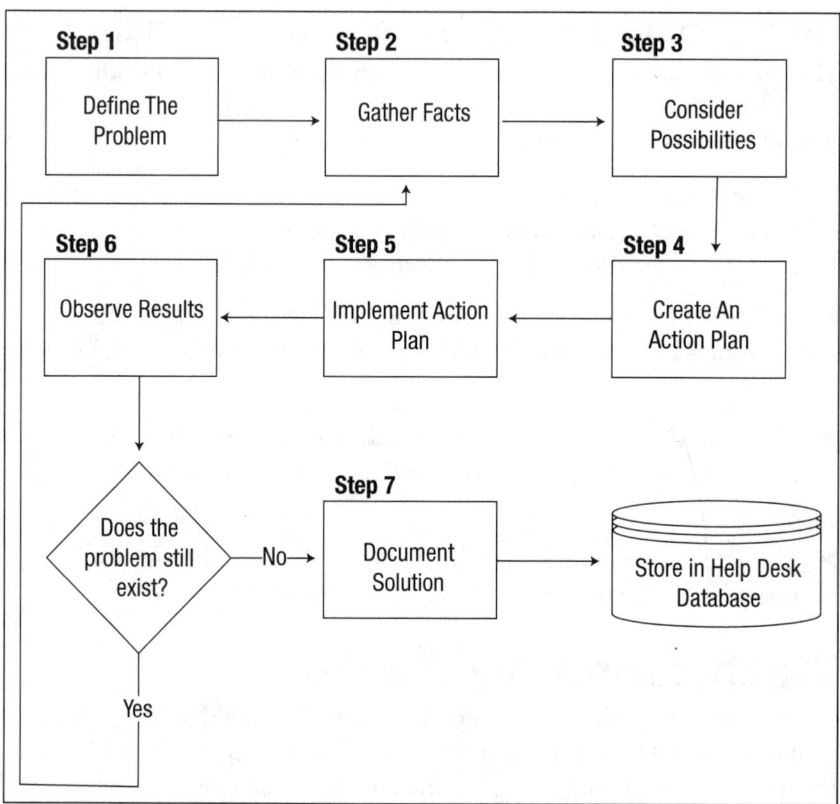

Figure 3.1 A sample troubleshooting flow chart.

Define The Problem

The first step to take is to develop a clear statement of what the problem is and its complexity. This should be done carefully to ensure that there's no vagueness or misconception as to just what is to be corrected. Generate a list of symptoms and their associated potential causes to define the problem space. In short, identify the problem correctly so that you won't be solving the wrong problem.

Gather Facts

The next step is to gather all available statistical and historical information about the problem. You'll need to ask the users, system administrators, and other involved individuals to adequately identify the nature of the problem. Collect as much information as possible, such as network baseline statistics, whether this is a recurring problem, and which portions of the network are currently affected.

Consider Possibilities

Based on your analysis of the problem and your criteria gathered from all involved individuals and documentation, brainstorm possible courses of action. Generate as many relevant courses of action as you can without carefully evaluating each of them. Don't rule out any solution just because at first glance it seems infeasible or unconventional. After you've generated a good list of possibilities, narrow the list down to a manageable number of possibilities that you can evaluate more carefully.

Create An Action Plan

An action plan describes the steps to be taken to achieve the goals and objectives. The steps are specific events that must occur to accomplish all or part of an objective. The action plan should identify what must be done, who is responsible, what resources will be required to take the steps, and any other conditions or items that must exist to accomplish the steps. An action plan will often suggest priorities and potential back-off plans that apply when it's not possible to implement all the proposed actions within a specified time.

Implement Action Plan

Next, carefully execute the action plan step by step, judiciously modifying a single parameter and then observing the results. Verifying each action and the associated repercussions is the most important step while troubleshooting.

Observe Results

Observe the results and check that the action plan has generated a reasonable and error-free solution, and that your answer satisfies the criteria and the goal. If the problem has been solved, you should look at the process used to solve the problem and explore what was learned. If the problem continues, you'll need to gather more facts about the problem and start the process again, until an acceptable solution is reached.

Document Solution

Documentation is very difficult to produce, but it's required of all IT professionals. Without the proper documents describing the reasoning behind a change, the steps taken, and the results observed, a network is potentially a disaster waiting to happen. You should identify "experience factors" that were encountered and that may be useful in the future. Above all, you should identify other problems that would be solved using the same subject fundamentals.

Scenario 1: Troubleshooting

Networking problems have been occurring all Monday morning on the link between the remote office and corporate headquarters. Currently, the connection is up between the two locations, but users located at the remote office are unable to access records located on corporate headquarters' file server. The following steps detail the entire troubleshooting process:

1. **Define The Problem** The link between the remote office and corporate headquarters is unstable and some applications are currently not available. This may be caused by poor service provider connections, failing router hardware, or invalid router configurations.

2. **Gather Facts** By asking peer network engineers, you find out that the corporate router was upgraded to a new version of Cisco IOS over the weekend. You also were able to get a copy of last week's router configuration from the corporate Trivial File Transfer Protocol (TFTP) server.

3. **Consider Possibilities** Cisco router IOS upgrades could cause access lists to become malformed. Or, if Internetwork Packet Exchange (IPX) is enabled on the WAN link, Get Nearest Server requests may not be functioning correctly. Also, mistyped configuration statements could have been introduced to the router during the upgrade.

4. **Create An Action Plan** First, identify the old and new versions of Cisco IOS loaded on the corporate router. Next compare the pre-upgrade and post-upgrade running configuration for differences. If differences exist between the two configurations, load the old configuration into the corporate router and check for improvements; otherwise, load the previous version of Cisco IOS and check if the problem is now solved. If the problem continues beyond this point, restore the original Monday configuration, notify the Cisco Technical Assistance Center, and regroup to discuss further options.

5. **Implement Action Plan** Evaluate each line item within the action plan, taking care that if a step fails you return the configuration to its previous state. Performing a comparison of the previous and currently running configuration you notice that the **permit any** statement is missing on the WAN interface's access list. You then load the previous configuration into memory and check for improvements.

6. **Observe Results** Checking with the remote office users acknowledges that the missing access list configuration statement solved the problem and they are now able to access remote file services.

7. **Document Solution** The link between the remote office and corporate headquarters was unstable and some applications were not available. The problem was isolated to a missing **permit any** access list configuration statement on corporate headquarters' router WAN interface. The reason the statement was located with the previous week's configuration and not Monday's is unknown, but the process to upgrade Cisco router IOS may need to be redeveloped to reduce the chance of typographical errors. Resources such as CiscoWorks 2000 Essentials that perform automated IOS rollout may need to be evaluated and potentially incorporated into the internetwork.

Practice Questions

Question 1

Which step of the troubleshooting process recommends that you contact users and inspect the available network management tools?

- ❍ a. Consider Possibilities
- ◉ b. Gather Facts
- ❍ c. Implement Action Plan
- ❍ d. Create An Action Plan

The correct answer is b. You should gather as much information as possible about the network (baseline and current operating state) and any changes that may have been made recently by system administrators and users. Answer a is incorrect because you shouldn't consider the possibilities until after gathering enough information about the problem. Creating and implementing an action plan follows considering the possibilities and cannot be done until problem research has been completed. Therefore, answers c and d are also incorrect.

Question 2

Which step of the troubleshooting process isolates the problem to a set of explicit characteristics and associated causes?

- ❍ a. Observe results
- ❍ b. Document facts
- ◉ c. Define the problem
- ❍ d. Generate errors

The correct answer is c. Defining the problem requires a simple yet detailed analysis of what is currently malfunctioning in the internetwork. Answer a is incorrect because observing the results is the step taken after implementing the action plan. The last procedure within the seven-step troubleshooting model is to document all relevant information that was learned during the process. Therefore, answer b is also incorrect. Answer d is incorrect because it isn't a step within the model.

Question 3

During the action plan implementation phase, you make changes to the network that render it inoperable. Which step should be done next after a change does not solve the original problem?

- ❍ a. Continue making network changes, per the action plan, until the problem goes away.
- ❍ b. Discard the current action plan and begin debugging the problem immediately.
- ● c. Remove all changes, returning the network to its original state.

The correct answer is c. Whenever a change is made that generates problems or does not solve the currently defined problem, you should remove the change immediately before proceeding. This helps you avoid haphazardness. Answer a is incorrect because the action plan was put into place with the assumption that all changes will work; however, continuing on may render the entire network unusable. Answer b is also incorrect because you should never completely discard an action plan and begin making random changes to the network, especially when new problems were introduced to the network after a change was previously made.

Question 4

What are the reasons to retrieve network statistics and perform a general baseline? [Choose the three best answers]

- ☑ a. It defines the typical activity within the network infrastructure, which can then be used while troubleshooting.
- ❑ b. It provides network administrators with pattern and trend analysis data.
- ❑ c. It provides a metric to evaluate the effect of changes to the network.
- ❑ d. It can be used directly to pinpoint Cisco IOS misconfigurations.

The correct answers are a, b, and c. Network baselines are very useful and can be leveraged throughout an internetwork's life span, from potential problem identification to future planning. Although the baseline may help while troubleshooting the network, it still can't take all of the guesswork out of why the results are occurring; a detailed understanding of the Cisco IOS is required. Therefore, answer d is incorrect.

Question 5

Long-term traffic statistics can be used to help do what while managing a network? [Choose the two best answers]

- ❑ a. Provide a history of network growth.
- ❑ b. Generate a report of infrastructure equipment CPU utilization.
- ❑ c. Expose areas of potential network problems.
- ❑ d. Plan for future expansion.

The correct answers are a and d. Long-term statistics provide a historical report of network growth and show areas of high growth where equipment may need to be replaced. General traffic statistics do not include CPU utilization information. Therefore, answer b is incorrect. Short-term traffic statistics, not long term, can be used to evaluate immediate network changes and potential network problems. Therefore, answer c is also incorrect.

Need To Know More?

McCabe, James D. *Practical Computer Network Analysis and Design*. Morgan Kaufmann Publishers, Inc. San Francisco, CA, 1998. ISBN 1-55860-498-7. This book is a fantastic resource that provides a general overview of networks and the potential areas of focus for baselining and improving a network's overall performance and reliability.

From the CCO Documentation home page at **www.cisco.com/univercd/home/home.htm**, select Internetworking Troubleshooting Guide|Troubleshooting Overview. This section contains a more-detailed description of the general troubleshooting model recommended by Cisco.

4

Troubleshooting Tools

Terms you'll need to understand:

- √ Cisco Internetwork Operating System (IOS)
- √ Privileged and EXEC modes
- √ **ping**
- √ **traceroute**
- √ Cisco Discovery Protocol (CDP)
- √ System logging
- √ Protocol analyzer

Techniques you'll need to master:

- √ Using **show** commands
- √ Using **debug** commands
- √ Using **clear** commands
- √ Understanding **ping** and **traceroute** output
- √ Operating a protocol analyzer
- √ Workstation troubleshooting tools

A network engineer is only as good at troubleshooting a network as the tools that are at his or her disposal. Common troubleshooting tools may be embedded in the host workstation, routers, or self-contained protocol analyzers. In this chapter, we'll discuss the basic tools available within intermediate hosts, such as Cisco routers, and end hosts, such as Windows, Macintosh, and Unix workstations.

Cisco Tools

Cisco has embedded several extremely useful troubleshooting tools into its routing software. These tools can provide enough granularity to allow the experienced network engineer to solve common networking problems strictly through Cisco's Internetwork Operating System (IOS) command-line interface.

The **show** Commands

The **show** commands list the output of the currently running configuration and the state of the router. They can provide you with valuable information while troubleshooting network performance and failure issues. A very valuable but often overlooked item that the Cisco IOS provides with all available software commands is a limited description of each of the commands. Listing 4.1 does not include the complete list of **show** commands, but it does include several of the commands that will be covered in more detail in later chapters.

Listing 4.1 A list of several commonly used **show** commands.

```
Router>show ?
  access-lists        List access lists
  appletalk           AppleTalk information
  arp                 ARP table
  atm                 ATM information
  bridge              Bridge Forwarding/Filtering Database[verbose]
  buffers             Buffer pool statistics
  cdp                 CDP information
  configuration       Contents of Non-Volatile memory
  controllers         Interface controller status
  debugging           State of each debugging option
  diagbus             Show diagnostic bus information
  frame-relay         Frame-Relay information
  hosts               IP domain-name, name servers, and host table
  interfaces          Interface status and configuration
  ip                  IP information
  ipx                 Novell IPX information
  line                TTY line information
  logging             Show the contents of logging buffers
```

```
memory            Memory statistics
ppp               PPP parameters and statistics
processes         Active process statistics
protocols         Active network routing protocols
queue             Show queue contents
rif               RIF cache entries
running-config    Current operating configuration
sessions          Information about Telnet connections
snapshot          Snapshot parameters and statistics
snmp              snmp statistics
source-bridge     Source-bridge parameters and statistics
spanning-tree     Spanning tree topology
stacks            Process stack utilization
standby           Hot standby protocol information
startup-config    Contents of startup configuration
stun              STUN status and configuration
subsys            Show subsystem information
tcp               Status of TCP connections
tech-support      Show system information for Tech-Support
users             Display information about terminal lines
version           System hardware and software status
vlans             Virtual LANs Information
x25               X.25 information
```

Three of the **show** commands can be used in identifying the current Cisco infrastructure. They are listed in Table 4.1 and will be further described in the next sections.

show cdp neighbors

The **show cdp neighbors** command is a very valuable tool that can be used to identify an internetwork using a Layer 2 protocol. If used with the **details** switch, Cisco IOS and Network layer information can also be retrieved. Listing 4.2 displays the output from the standard command.

Table 4.1 The show commands that can be used to identify a Cisco network.

Command	Function
show cdp neighbors	Displays information about the directly connected Cisco devices
show tech-support	Displays a detailed list of the results from several **show** commands
show version	Displays Cisco IOS and hardware information

Listing 4.2 You can view all directly connected Cisco devices with the **show cdp neighbors** command.

```
Router>show cdp neighbors
Capability Codes: R - Router, T - Trans Bridge,
                  B - Source Route Bridge, S - Switch, H - Host,
                  I - IGMP, r - Repeater

Device ID  Local Intrfce  Holdtme   Capability  Platform  Port ID
cat_5500   Eth 0          163       T B S       WS-C5500  7/1
cat_5000   Fas 1/1        179       T S         WS-C5000  1/1
```

show tech-support

To assist TAC engineers in locating and finding a solution to a specific problem, Cisco has embedded a single command, **show tech-support**, into its IOS. This command performs several common **show** commands at the same time. A list of **show** commands performed by **show tech-support** is provided in Table 4.2.

Each of the **show** commands in Table 4.2 retrieves valuable information that can be analyzed to isolate network problems. They will all be covered in more detail in the following chapters.

show version

The **show version** command displays Cisco IOS version details, software location, router hardware, router uptime, and configuration register information. This information can be very useful when you're trying to troubleshoot a network for the first time and network documentation is at a minimum. Also, if password recovery is required, the configuration register will show the current setting and the setting that will be used during the subsequent booting of the router. Listing 4.3 displays the output of a **show version** command on a router.

Table 4.2 The show tech-support command performs several commands at one time.

show appletalk traffic	show bootflash:	show bootvar
show buffers	show context	show controllers
show controllers cbus	show diagbus	show interfaces
show ip traffic	show novell traffic	show process cpu
show process memory	show running-config	show stacks
show version		

Listing 4.3 The output of the **show version** command.

```
Router>show version
Cisco Internetwork Operating System Software
IOS (tm) RSP Software (RSP-JSV-M), Version 11.2(13)P,
    RELEASE SOFTWARE (fc1)
Copyright (c) 1986-1998 by cisco Systems, Inc.
Compiled Tue 07-Apr-98 20:29 by dschwart
Image text-base: 0x60010900, data-base: 0x60B78000

ROM: System Bootstrap, Version 11.1(2), RELEASE SOFTWARE (fc1)
BOOTFLASH: RSP Software (RSP-BOOT-M), Version 11.2(13)P,
    RELEASE SOFTWARE (fc1)

Router uptime is 5 weeks, 3 days, 20 minutes
System restarted by reload at 16:58:01 CST Tue May 4 1999
System image file is "slot0:rsp-jsv-mz.112-13.P.bin",
    booted via slot0

cisco RSP2 (R4700) processor with 131072K/2072K bytes of memory.
R4700 processor, Implementation 33, Revision 1.0
Last reset from power-on
G.703/E1 software, Version 1.0.
SuperLAT software copyright 1990 by Meridian Technology Corp).
Bridging software.
X.25 software, Version 2.0, NET2, BFE and GOSIP compliant.
TN3270 Emulation software.
Chassis Interface.
1 EIP controller (6 Ethernet).
1 FIP controller (1 FDDI).
1 VIP2 controller (1 ATM).
1 FEIP controller (2 FastEthernet).
6 Ethernet/IEEE 802.3 interface(s)
2 FastEthernet/IEEE 802.3 interface(s)
1 FDDI network interface(s)
1 ATM network interface(s)
123K bytes of non-volatile configuration memory.

20480K bytes of Flash PCMCIA card at slot 0 (Sector size 128K).
8192K bytes of Flash internal SIMM (Sector size 256K).
Configuration register is 0x2102
```

The first three highlighted sections describe the version of Cisco IOS running on the system, the version of Cisco IOS burned into the bootrom, the running Cisco IOS file source, and the time and date of the last reload. This information can be very valuable when first identifying a network topology. The next section describes the interfaces installed into the chassis. In this case, Ethernet,

FDDI, ATM, and Fast Ethernet line modules have been installed. This is another key area that you should check while learning about a network's topology. The final highlighted section describes the current value of the configuration register. Changing this value can set boot parameters, such as where to load the Cisco IOS from or if the system startup configuration should be bypassed. The configuration register will be gone over in more detail in Chapter 5, when we discuss router password recovery.

The **debug** Commands

If properly utilized, the debugging tools embedded within the Cisco IOS can contribute answers to several difficult problems. The information you can obtain through debugging may lead to finding invalid host address assignments on subnetworks or the notification of incorrect propagation of routing information from upstream routers. You may want to consider debugging events, rather than debugging packets, because of the finer granularity that can be achieved. If you must debug packets, consider using an access list to limit the scope of the output.

You can issue the **terminal monitor** command to view debugging information from a virtual terminal session.

A limited listing of available **debug** commands can be found in Listing 4.4. You should note that **debug** commands are only available in privileged mode (which is indicated by Router#). Always verify the impact of **debug** commands prior to using them on a production network. Commands such as **debug all** can bring down a fully functional network in seconds. The **debug all** command can greatly decrease the performance of a router and can even cause the router to crash. If you've typed this command from a terminal session, the priority of screen updates to terminals is very low, and it will seem like the session has hung. You can always use the **undebug all** command to delete all debug processes.

To reduce the negative impact of using **debug** commands enter the command **no logging console** on your router within the global configuration mode. This command will disable all logging to the console terminal. Then use the **terminal monitor** command to copy **debug** command output and system error messages to your current telnet session.

Listing 4.4 A partial listing of the more commonly used **debug** commands.

```
Router#debug ?
  all                   Enable all debugging
  apple                 Appletalk information
  arap                  Appletalk Remote Access
  arp                   IP ARP and HP Probe transactions
  atm                   ATM interface packets
  cBus                  ciscoBus events
  cdp                   CDP information
  dialer                Dial on Demand
  eigrp                 EIGRP Protocol information
  ethernet-interface    Ethernet network interface events
  fastethernet          Fast Ethernet interface information
  fddi                  FDDI information
  frame-relay           Frame Relay
  ip                    IP information
  ipc                   Interprocess communications debugging
  ipx                   Novell/IPX information
  llc2                  LLC2 type II Information
  packet                Log unknown packets
  ppp                   PPP (Point to Point Protocol) information
  serial                Serial interface information
  snapshot              Snapshot activity
  snmp                  SNMP information
  spanning              Spanning-tree information
  standby               Hot standby protocol
  token                 Token Ring information
  tunnel                Generic Tunnel Interface
  vlan                  vLAN information
  x25                   X.25 information
```

The **clear** Commands

clear commands can be used to reset statistical counters, delete entries from internal router tables, or even reset hardware logic. The most common commands that you will encounter throughout this book will refer to resetting counters to zero and deleting routing table or arp-cache entries. Almost all **clear** commands are only available in privileged mode, as shown in Listing 4.5.

Listing 4.5 A list of **clear** commands.

```
Router#clear ?
  access-list          Clear access list statistical information
  access-template      Access-template
  appletalk            Reset AppleTalk information
  arp-cache            Clear the entire ARP cache
  atm                  ATM information
```

```
bridge              Reset bridge forwarding cache
cdp                 Reset cdp information
clns                CLNS
controller          Clear controller
counters            Clear counters on one or all interfaces
decnet              Reset DECnet information
dialer              Clear dialer statistics
dlsw                Data Link Switching (DLSw)
frame-relay-inarp   Clear inverse ARP entries from the map table
host                Delete host table entries
interface           Clear the hardware logic on an interface
ip                  IP
ipx                 Reset Novell/IPX information
isis                Clear IS-IS data structures
kerberos            Clear Kerberos Values
lane                lane
line                Reset a terminal line
logging             Clear logging buffer
ncia                Native Client Interface Architecture (NCIA)
netbios-cache       Clear the entire NetBIOS name cache
rif-cache           Clear the entire RIF cache
smrp                Simple Multicast Routing Protocol statistics
snapshot            Clear Snapshot timers
source-bridge       Clear counters displayed in show source-bridge
tarp                Reset tarp information
tcp                 Clear a TCP connection or statistics
vines               VINES neighbor and routing table entries
vlan                Clear vLAN statistical information
vpdn                Clear a VPDN entity
x25-vc              Clear X.25 virtual circuits on an interface
xns                 Reset XNS information
```

The **ping** Command

The **ping** command tests Network layer end-to-end connectivity between the source host and destination address. If **ping** responds that the connection is valid between the two hosts, you at least know that the Data Link layer is up. What's more, if a router is between the two hosts, the Network layer has also been verified, and routing is taking place correctly. **ping** can also be used to test protocols other than IP, such as IPX and AppleTalk, as shown in Listing 4.6.

Listing 4.6 The **ping** command can be used to verify Network layer connectivity for several different protocols.

```
Router>ping ?
  WORD       Ping destination address or hostname
  apollo     Apollo echo
```

```
appletalk  Appletalk echo
clns       CLNS echo
decnet     DECnet echo
ip         IP echo
ipx        Novell/IPX echo
vines      Vines echo
xns        XNS echo
```

ping is very useful in splitting up the troubleshooting concentration area because it can be used to isolate between a routing, data link, or physical infrastructure issue and an application/transport problem. **ping** will respond with a series of characters that describes the answer to the command; the available response codes are listed in Table 4.3.

Within the Cisco IOS, **ping** comes in two formats: user mode and privileged mode.

User Mode

The version of **ping** provided in user mode displays information regarding the overall success rate of the command as well as minimum, average, and maximum roundtrip statistics. Listing 4.7 displays the results from the **ping** command initiated with The Coriolis Group's Web site address.

Listing 4.7 The user mode **ping** command can verify end-to-end Network layer connectivity.

```
Router>ping www.coriolis.com
Type escape sequence to abort.
```

Table 4.3 The standard response codes returned by the IP version of the ping command.

Character	Description
!	Each exclamation point indicates the receipt of a reply.
.	Each period indicates a router timeout while waiting for the reply.
?	Unknown packet type.
A	The path taken was administratively prohibited.
M	The data packet sent could not be fragmented along the path.
N	Indicates that the network is unreachable.
P	Indicates that the protocol is unreachable.
Q	A source quench message was received.
U	Indicates that the destination is unreachable.

```
Sending 5, 100-byte ICMP Echos to 209.140.152.4,
     timeout is 2 seconds:
!!!!!
Success rate is 100 percent (5/5),
     round-trip min/avg/max = 80/89/100 ms
```

To abort a **ping** session, use the escape sequence. The default is to simultaneously press Ctrl+Shift+6, let go, and then press the X key.

Privileged Mode

The privileged mode **ping** command provides the complete **ping** facility available within user mode plus several advanced features. The extended features allow hundreds of Internet Control Message Protocol (ICMP) packets to be sent with sweeping datagram sizes, carrying user-defined data. Listing 4.8 shows the **ping** tool using the extended commands that become available when you answer "yes" to the **Extended commands [n]** question shown in the highlighted section. The privileged mode **ping** command can test Maximum Transmission Unit (MTU) variances via the Don't Fragment (DF) bit, source routing, and even other protocols.

Listing 4.8 The privileged mode **ping** command.

```
Router#ping
Protocol [ip]:
Target IP address: www.coriolis.com
Repeat count [5]: 20
Datagram size [100]:
Timeout in seconds [2]:
Extended commands [n]: y
Source address or interface: 10.1.1.2
Type of service [0]:
Set DF bit in IP header? [no]: yes
Data pattern [0xABCD]: 0x1234
Loose, Strict, Record, Timestamp, Verbose[none]:
Sweep range of sizes [n]: y
Sweep min size [36]:
Sweep max size [18024]:
Sweep interval [1]:
Type escape sequence to abort.
Sending 20, [36..18024]-byte ICMP Echos to 209.140.152.4,
     timeout is 2 seconds:
```

```
Packet has data pattern 0x1234
!!!!!!!!!!!!!!!!!!!!
Success rate is 100 percent (20/20),
    round-trip min/avg/max = 56/76/92 ms
```

ping has many options available when used in the extended mode—almost to the point that it becomes confusing. In Table 4.4, each variable within **ping** is listed along with a general description.

If you're trying to verify connectivity of several hosts on a LAN, log into the locally attached router in privileged mode and **ping** the broadcast address of the LAN. All hosts on this network will respond to the **ping** request. This is only available if IP-directed broadcasts are enabled. (It should be noted that this may violate your local security policy.)

Table 4.4 The definitions of commonly used parameters available within the privileged mode ping command.

Variable	Description
Protocol	Default protocol is IP. IPX, AppleTalk, DECnet, Vines, and others are available.
Target IP Address	The destination node that will be pinged.
Repeat Count	Default is 5. Number of **ping** packets to be sent to the destination.
Datagram Size	Default is 100. Size of the **ping** packet, in bytes.
Timeout	Default is 2. Timeout interval, in seconds.
Source Address	Default is Best Source. IP address that appears in the packet's source address field; other choices can be any configured IP address within the router.
Type of Service	Default is 0. The quality of service to be issued to this packet.
DF Bit	Default is No. States whether the router can fragment this packet.
Data Pattern	Default is 0xABCD. Sets a 16-bit hexadecimal pattern to generate in the data field.
Routing Options	Default is None. Set in the IP header; other options are Loose, Strict, Record, Timestamp, and Verbose.
Sweep Sizes	Default is No. Allows variance in the size of echo packets being sent.

The **traceroute** Command

traceroute tracks the path a packet takes throughout an internetwork. The path taken from source to destination and from destination to source may vary with each packet. This should be taken into consideration while troubleshooting a network. **traceroute** works by using the error messages generated by routers when a datagram exceeds its Time To Live (TTL) value. The first three probes generated by **traceroute** are sent with a TTL equal to 1, which causes the first router to discard the probe and reply with a "TTL exceeded" error message. The **traceroute** command will record the roundtrip time for each of the probes and will then increase the TTL value by one and send another three probes. This continues until the trace is complete. The available protocols that **traceroute** functions with are shown in Listing 4.9.

Listing 4.9 The **traceroute** command can be used to track the paths of packets for a variety of protocols.

```
Router>traceroute ?
  WORD        Trace route to destination address or hostname
  appletalk   AppleTalk Trace
  clns        ISO CLNS Trace
  ip          IP Trace
  oldvines    Vines Trace (Cisco)
  vines       Vines Trace (Banyan)
```

As with **ping**, **traceroute** has two available styles: user mode and privileged mode.

User Mode

The version of **traceroute** provided in user mode supplies simple functionality, with only the path results and minimum, average, and maximum roundtrip times returned (see Listing 4.10). This mode does not allow any variables to be set for the **traceroute** facility.

Listing 4.10 The user mode version of **traceroute** provides hop-by-hop statistics.

```
Router>traceroute www.coriolis.com
Translating "www.coriolis.com"...domain server (10.1.1.8) [OK]

Type escape sequence to abort.
Tracing the route to www.coriolis.com (209.140.152.4)

  1 Router.company.com (10.1.1.2) 0 msec 0 msec 4 msec
  2 gateway.company.com (198.32.130.49) 4 msec 0 msec 4 msec
  3 phxchi-gw.phoenix.good.net (209.54.110.121)
    68 msec 76 msec 80 msec
```

```
 4 coriolis.phoenix.good.net (207.98.136.203)
   108 msec 132 msec 104 msec
 5 www.coriolis.com (209.140.152.4) 124 msec 192 msec 120 msec
```

Privileged Mode

Using **traceroute** while in privileged mode adds several variables, such as protocol type, display characteristics, and Time To Live (TTL) information, that can be set to influence the results returned (see Listing 4.11). **traceroute** can then provide a more granular approach to tracing packets.

Listing 4.11 The privileged version of **traceroute** has several variables that can influence output.

```
Router#traceroute
Protocol [ip]:
Target IP address: www.coriolis.com
Source address: 10.1.2.1
Numeric display [n]: y
Timeout in seconds [3]:
Probe count [3]:
Minimum Time to Live [1]:
Maximum Time to Live [30]:
Port Number [33434]:
Loose, Strict, Record, Timestamp, Verbose[none]:
Type escape sequence to abort.
Tracing the route to 209.140.152.4

  1 10.1.1.2 12 msec 0 msec 0 msec
  2 198.32.130.49 0 msec 0 msec 4 msec
  3 209.54.110.121 48 msec 72 msec 60 msec
  4 207.98.136.203 132 msec 160 msec 160 msec
  5 209.140.152.4 204 msec 252 msec 80 msec
```

You can use the extended **traceroute** command to determine the unique transmit and receive data paths from source to destination. Table 4.5 describes the variables within the extended **traceroute** command.

System Logging

By default, system error messages are sent to the console port of the router. Connecting a computer to the console port and using a terminal emulation program to log into the router can capture this information. Another option that you can define within the configuration is to have logging point to an IP address where system-logging messages can be understood. Information sent into the system can vary according to any of the seven system categories that can be defined within the IOS.

Table 4.5 The fields that are unique to the extended traceroute command.

Variable	Description
Protocol	Default protocol is IP. IPX, AppleTalk, DECnet, Vines, and others are available.
Target IP Address	The destination node to perform a trace to.
Source Address	Default is Best Source. The IP address that appears in the packet's source address field. Other choices can be any configured IP address within the router.
Numeric Display	Default is both displays. Sets whether addresses should use DNS resolution.
Timeout	Default is 3. The time, in seconds, to wait for a probe response.
Minimum TTL	Default is 1. The minimum TTL for trace probes.
Maximum TTL	Default is 30. The maximum TTL for trace probes. **traceroute** terminates when this value is reached.
Port Number	Default is 33434. The destination port to be used by the UDP probes.
Routing Options	Default is None. Set in the IP header; other options are Loose, Strict, Record, Timestamp, and Verbose.

Logging Options

System logs can be logged to four different locations: the console, the virtual terminal, the syslog server, and an internal buffer. The location of the logs can be changed using the Cisco commands shown in Table 4.6.

The logging destination will affect the overhead of the system. A list of the available methods, from highest to lowest in terms of the overhead produced are: console logging, virtual terminal logging, syslog server logging, and internal buffer logging.

System Categories

Currently, the Cisco IOS software generates seven major categories of system logging messages, four of which are the most important: Error, Notification, Informational, and Debugging. Error messages about software or hardware malfunctions are displayed at the Errors level. Interface up/down transitions and system restart information is displayed at the Notification level. Reload requests and process-level stack messages are displayed at the Informational level. Output generated by any **debug** commands is displayed at the Debugging level. Table 4.7 relates the IOS configuration-required level number with the appropriate description.

Table 4.6 The Cisco commands for setting the logging location.

Command	Description
logging [IP address]	Sends logging messages to the syslog server specified by the IP address
logging buffered	Sends logging messages to an internal buffer
logging console [level]	Limits the logging to the console to messages up to the level specified
logging monitor [level]	Limits the logging to virtual terminal sessions based on the level specified
logging trap [level]	Limits the logging messages sent to the syslog server to the level specified
no logging on	Enables logging to the console only

Table 4.7 The settings for the detail of information sent to the system logs.

Level	Description
0	Emergencies
1	Alerts
2	Critical
3	Error
4	Warning
5	Notifications
6	Informational
7	Debugging

It's very useful for all the system logging information to have valid timestamps. This can be accomplished by doing two things:

- Including the command **service timestamps log datetime localtime** in the configuration
- Having all routers within an administrative domain use the same NTP server so that timestamps are equivalent

Protocol Analyzer Operation

A *protocol analyzer* is a software-based fault and performance management tool that captures data, monitors network traffic, and collects key network statistics. These tools enable network managers to extract and review vital and detailed information needed to effectively troubleshoot, manage, and migrate to today's complex network environments. Protocol analyzers can decode traffic based on the OSI model and individual protocol stacks. Upscale analyzers may include features such as traffic generation, fault analysis and isolation tools, and remote management interfaces.

Several vendors have written protocol analyzer software, including Microsoft's Network Monitor application (which is included with Microsoft Windows NT/2000). Due to the large deployment base of this operating system and the ease of accessibility to the product, this is the protocol analyzer that will be discussed briefly in this section (see Figure 4.1).

Data Capturing

Capturing data on most protocol analyzers is very simple and normally requires only a single mouse click. More advanced criteria can be included during data captures, such as host address and protocol filtering, traffic generation,

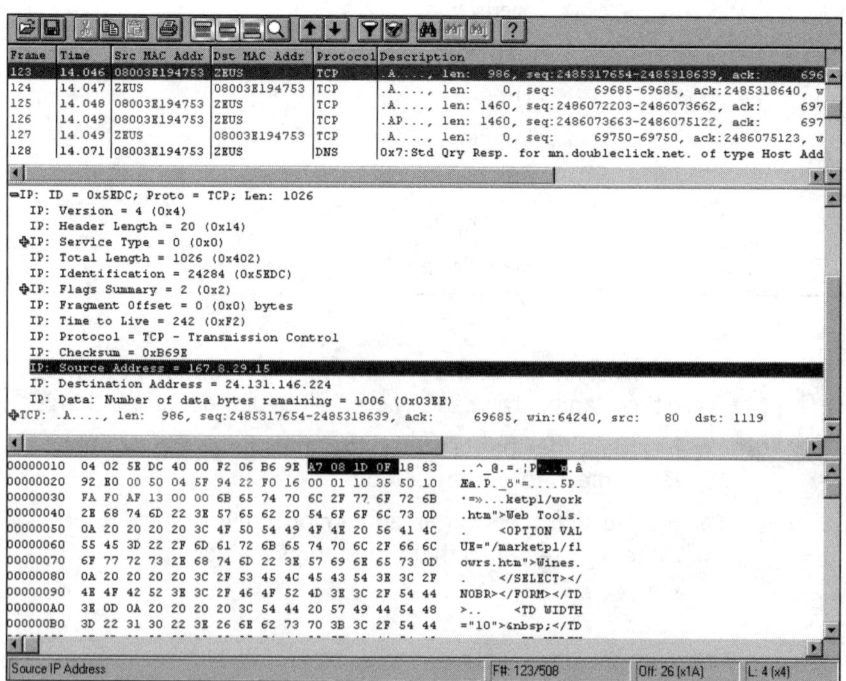

Figure 4.1 The network monitor application embedded within Microsoft Windows NT/2000.

record and playback, alarm triggers, and performance statistics. During the data-capturing process, network statistics are available so that you can verify the total number of packets on the network and the total number of captured packets that meet all filtering criteria (see Figure 4.2).

Protocol Decoding

For analyzers to provide useful data analysis, they must support a variety of LAN, WAN, and networking protocols, such as Ethernet, Fast Ethernet, ATM, IP, IPX, and AppleTalk. Normally, the protocol packages that are purchased provide hardware and software to monitor a variety of network topologies. Figure 4.3 shows Protocol Data Unit (PDU) headers decoded at the Ethernet, IP, and TCP layers.

Make certain that you fully understand each layer of the OSI model and how to break down the information presented by the protocol analyzer. Use examples, such as the one depicted in Figure 4.3, to learn more about standard protocols like FTP, Telnet, POP3, SMTP, and SHTTP.

Some analyzers allow protocol decoding while capturing data, whereas other analyzers must stop capturing to be able to decode the data. Also, several protocol analyzers provide post-capture analysis and automatic identification of commonly occurring network problems (this normally depends on the buffer size within the analyzer—the larger the buffer, the more data that can be acquired).

Traffic Filters

Quite often, the amount of network data captured can be abundant and not within the scope of troubleshooting a current network problem. For instance, suppose TCP connectivity between host A and host B is sporadic and the analyzer has captured data from all hosts on the subnetwork rather than the

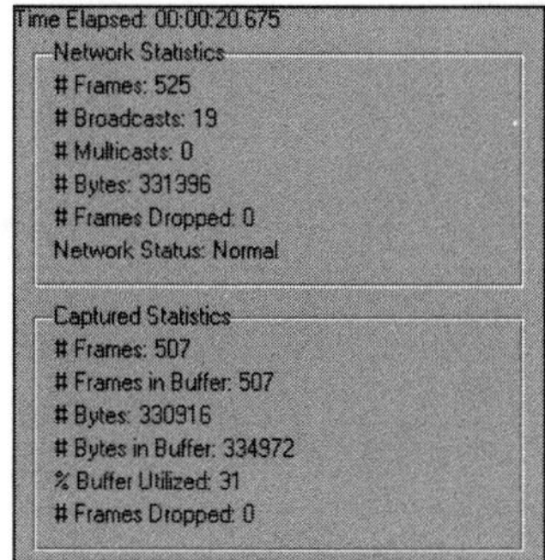

Figure 4.2 Network statistics are available during the data-capturing process.

specifics needed. To reduce the amount of data captured so that it fits the troubleshooting criteria, you can create traffic filters to restrict the data captured to traffic between host A and host B using TCP/IP as the transport mechanism (see Figure 4.4).

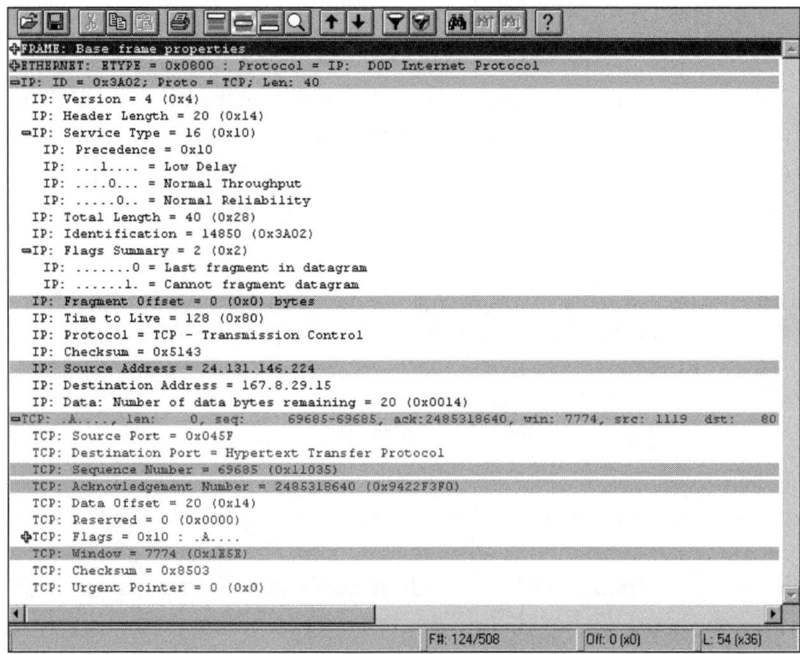

Figure 4.3 The protocol analyzer can view each individual frame, packet, and transport header field's content.

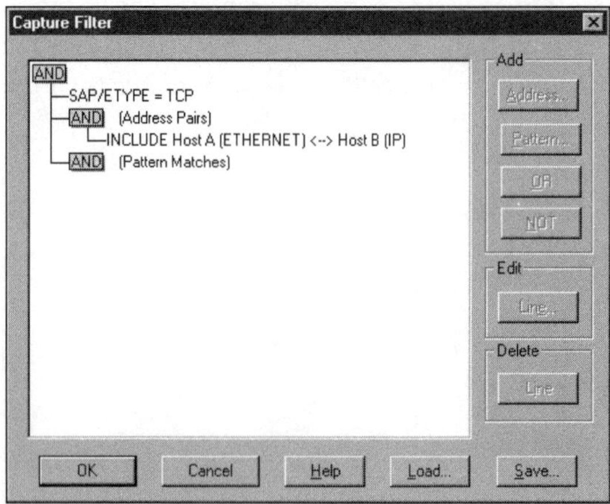

Figure 4.4 Traffic filters can narrow the scope of a capture operation, thus reducing the amount of data captured to only what may be relevant.

Workstation-Specific Tools

Networks are installed to allow host workstations to connect to resources available over an internetwork. These hosts require tools to assist in verifying connectivity and correct configuration. A small section of this chapter will also cover troubleshooting tools available on client workstations so that the end-to-end troubleshooting tools available can be conceptualized.

Note that almost all TCP/IP stack implementations contain versions of **ping** and **traceroute**.

Microsoft Windows

Several tools are available on the Windows NT Workstation and Windows 95/98 platforms to assist in finding networking faults for TCP/IP and IPX/SPX.

winipcfg And ipconfig

When troubleshooting a computer experiencing TCP/IP connectivity problems, begin by checking the TCP/IP configuration using either **winipcfg** or **ipconfig /all** (for Windows NT/2000). The output of these commands can be reviewed for proper IP address, subnet mask, default gateway, and WINS/DNS server settings.

netstat

netstat displays protocol statistics and a list of current TCP/IP connections. Several valuable switches exist for **netstat**, as shown in Table 4.8.

Table 4.8 A few of the switches available for the netstat command.

Switch	Description
Netstat -a	Displays all connections and listening port numbers
Netstat -n	Displays addresses and port numbers in a numerical format
Netstat -p proto	Displays statistics for the protocol specified; this can be IP, TCP, or UDP
Netstat -r	Displays the routing table plus active connections
Netstat -s	Displays per-protocol statistics

route

Even client workstations have to make routing decisions—for example, a workstation might need to determine whether a destination address is located on the local network or a remote network so that it can identify the hardware address to use. Windows NT/2000 automatically builds a simple routing table that can be viewed by using the **route** command.

IPXroute

The **IPXroute** tool provides information on the current IPX settings, such as frame type, IPX network number, and internal network number. It also can provide IPX routes if the workstation is configured as an IPX router. Several extensions exist for **IPXroute**, as shown in Table 4.9.

Unix

The Unix operating system is available through several vendors, each with their own graphical interfaces, but all with generally the same command-line references. A couple of commonly used commands are **ifconfig** and **netstat**.

ifconfig

The **ifconfig** utility is used to verify and configure network interface parameters, such as IP address, subnet mask, and the default gateway. This command displays data very similar to the **ipconfig** command for Microsoft Windows.

netstat

netstat displays the status of network connections on either TCP, UDP, RAW, or Unix sockets on the system. It has several switches that can alter the output of the information presented, such as per-protocol statistics. The Unix version of the **netstat** command is very similar to the same command found in Microsoft Windows.

Table 4.9 The IPXroute command can show configuration, routing, and server information.

Switch	Description
IPXroute config	Displays the current IPX settings for frame types and network numbers
IPXroute servers	Displays the SAP table
IPXroute show	Displays current IPX internal routing statistics
IPXroute table	Displays the IPX routing table (if IPX routing is enabled)

Novell NetWare

Novell provides three separate NetWare Loadable Modules (NLMs) for troubleshooting and monitoring TCP/IP, IPX/SPX, and AppleTalk networks. They are TCPcon, IPXcon, and ATcon, respectively.

- **TCPcon** This utility can monitor routing tables and provide information for ICMP, IP, OSPF, TCP, and UDP.
- **IPXcon** A utility that provides access to statistics and information about the status of various components of the IPX protocol. It uses SNMP to access this information from any local or remote system on the network. IPXcon operates over IPX and TCP/IP networks and uses UDP to run over the networks.
- **ATcon** This utility provides information on routing tables and can monitor the status of AURP connections.

Apple

Apple operating systems do not, by default, include IP connectivity utilities such as **ping**. To resolve this, many **ping** utilities, such as MacTCP Watcher, are available for free download on the Internet. Another option for verifying general network connectivity (AppleTalk or IP) is to check the availability of network resources through the Macintosh Chooser window.

The Chooser, which can be selected from the Macintosh menu, can give you valuable information about the network (see Figure 4.5). Here are several items to check:

- Is the AppleTalk Active radio button selected?
- Do you see the AppleShare icon in the upper-left box?

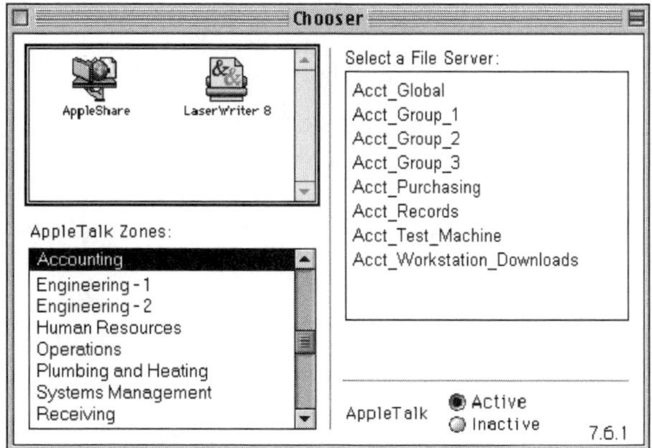

Figure 4.5 The Apple Chooser can verify network connectivity.

- Do you see any names in the Select A File Server box?
- Do you see the name of the file server or shared disk you want in the Select A File Server box?
- Do you see any zone names in the AppleTalk Zones box?
- Do you see the name of your zone?

Practice Questions

Question 1

Where are the system error messages sent by default?

❍ a. An internal buffer.

❍ b. The console.

❍ c. System logs are turned off by default.

❍ d. Virtual terminal sessions.

The correct answer is b. By default, system logs are sent to the console. This can be changed by entering logging commands to direct the output to an internal buffer (**logging buffered**), the virtual terminals (**logging monitor**), or a syslog server (**logging [*IP address*]**), but these are not the default. Therefore, answers a and d are incorrect. System logs can never be completely turned off; the command **no logging on** still logs to the console. Therefore, answer c is incorrect.

Question 2

Which router command will list the current version of IOS running on a router?

❍ a. **show running-config**

❍ b. **show IOS**

❍ c. **show version**

❍ d. **view current-config**

The correct answer is c. The **show version** command will list the current IOS version along with several other pieces of information, such as the router hardware, the configuration register, and the time of the last reboot. **Show running-config** lists the currently running configuration on the router. Therefore, answer a is incorrect. The other answers are not IOS commands. Therefore, answers b and d are incorrect.

Question 3

After you've captured several packets on an Ethernet IPX network with your protocol analyzer, the counter reads 3,813 frames received, 513 frames captured. What do these two statistics mean?

- ❍ a. 3,300 frames contained invalid checksums and were dropped.
- ❍ b. Excessive collisions are being seen on the network.
- ❍ c. The protocol analyzer is set for the wrong Ethernet frame type.
- ❍ d. 3,813 frames were seen by the network interface, but 513 frames met the criteria specified in a traffic filter.

The correct answer is d. Traffic filters can be set on protocol analyzers so that only relevant traffic can be captured. A protocol analyzer only counts valid packets in the received frames field; errors may be shown in invalid, collision, or other fields. Therefore, answer a is incorrect. All captured data does not include collisions; this is a separate statistic. Therefore, answer b is incorrect. If the wrong frame type was selected on the network, no traffic would be seen. Therefore, answer c is incorrect.

Question 4

Which command maps the path of a data packet through a network by incrementing the TTL value in the IP header?

- ❍ a. **ping**
- ❍ b. **ICMP**
- ❍ c. **traceroute**
- ❍ d. **netstat**

The correct answer is c. **traceroute** increments the TTL value by one after sending three probes to the first hop, and with each subsequent hop between the source and destination address. The **traceroute** command uses **ping** and **ICMP** as transport mechanisms, but they do not automatically increment the TTL value. Therefore, answers a and b are incorrect. The **netstat** command only shows statistics for host computers. Therefore, answer d is also incorrect.

Question 5

What is the default console escape sequence to abort a **ping** command or suspend a session?

- ❍ a. Press the Esc key.
- ❍ b. Simultaneously press Ctrl+Shift+X.
- ❍ c. Simultaneously press Ctrl+Shift+6, let go, and then press the X key.
- ❍ d. Simultaneously press Ctrl+Alt+Delete.

The correct answer is c. However, other escape sequences can be configured in the router, and general escape sequences can vary by terminal emulator packages. Although this is not the case here, you should keep this in mind while performing password recovery. Because answer c is correct, answers a, b, and d are incorrect.

Question 6

Which fields within the extended **ping** command set can be used to detect performance problems associated with a node configured with a large MTU size? [Choose the two best answers]

- ❑ a. The type of service.
- ❑ b. Setting the data pattern to 0x0000.
- ❑ c. The DF bit in the IP header set to Yes.
- ❑ d. Sweeping the range of echo packet sizes.

The correct answers are c and d. The Don't Fragment (DF) bit states whether the packet can be fragmented by interim routers. By sweeping the range of echo packet sizes and turning the DF bit on, detection of internetwork MTU sizes can be found. If a low MTU size is in the middle of the network, a high amount of fragmentation may take place, thus causing the receiver to reassemble several packets. This may lead to higher CPU utilization of the receiver, and the transmitter may be required to resend several packets, if the network is unreliable. The type of service would only affect the quality given to the packet by the network and would not detect MTU sizes. Therefore, answer a is incorrect. Setting the data pattern can help sometimes to troubleshoot problems on frame relay networks, but it will not help in detecting large MTU size. Therefore, answer b is also incorrect.

Question 7

Performing the **ping** command returns the following results. What's the most likely cause of this?

```
Router>ping www.company.com
Type escape sequence to abort.
Sending 5, 100-byte ICMP Echos to 10.10.3.4, timeout
     is 2 seconds:
.!!!!
Success rate is 80 percent (4/5),
     round-trip min/avg/max = 26/53/72 ms
```

- ❍ a. Network performance was very low and the first packet was dropped.
- ❍ b. The destination network was unreachable at first, then routing flipped and the network was available.
- ❍ c. An interim router administratively prohibited the first packet.
- ❍ d. The first packet timed out because the system sending the **ping** had to send an ARP request for the default gateway's hardware address and the probe timed out before a response was returned.

The correct answer is d. Host machines on a network must send an ARP request for a machine's hardware address prior to sending any data on a local network, or they must send an ARP request for the default gateway's hardware address for external devices. In this case, it's not mentioned whether this is a locally connected host, but you can derive that the MAC address was not stored in the host machine's ARP cache because the host did have to send an ARP request. If the packet was dropped due to network performance, subsequent packets would have most likely also been lost. Therefore, answer a is incorrect. If the destination network was unreachable or administratively prohibited, the letter U or A would have been displayed rather than a period. Therefore, answers b and c are also incorrect.

Question 8

After you entered several **debug** commands, the performance of the router degraded dramatically, and no debugging statements reached the terminal. Which of the following reasons are most likely to have caused the problem? [Choose the two best answers]

- ❑ a. The router has lost its configuration stored in NVRAM.
- ❑ b. The **terminal monitor** command has never been issued.
- ❑ c. A **debug** command was entered that was not understood by the version of IOS on the router.
- ❑ d. The **debug all** command was entered, which overloaded the router and caused severe performance degradation.

The correct answers are b and d. Always make sure that you use the command **terminal monitor** prior to sending **debug** commands from a virtual terminal session. This allows system-logging events to be sent to terminal sessions. If a router had lost its configuration in NVRAM, (this is where the **startup-config** is stored), the router would not have problems until the next system reload occurred. Therefore, answer a is incorrect. The user will be notified of any IOS commands not understood by the router. These will not be entered into the configuration. Therefore, answer c is incorrect.

Question 9

Which command should be performed on the router so that its data can be submitted to the Technical Assistance Center (TAC) during a case submission?

- ❍ a. **show protocols**
- ❍ b. **show tech-support**
- ❍ c. **type running-config**
- ❍ d. **show support**

The correct answer is b. **show tech-support** issues a variety of **show** commands, as listed previously in this chapter. The **show protocols** command displays the current protocols enabled on each router interface and the addresses assigned to those protocols. This does not provide enough information for the TAC to resolve a problem. Therefore, answer a is incorrect. **type running-config** and **show support** do not exist within Cisco IOS, and they would generate an Invalid Input error. Therefore, answers c and d are incorrect.

Question 10

Which two commands limit system logs to only warning messages (and lower) being sent to a syslog server at address 10.1.1.10?

- ❍ a. **logging 10.1.1.10** and **logging trap 4**
- ❍ b. **logging monitor 10.1.1.10** and **logging trap 5**
- ❍ c. **syslog server 10.1.1.10** and **logging trap 5**
- ❍ d. **syslog level 4** and **logging 10.1.1.10**

The correct answer is a. As described earlier in the chapter, system error messages can be sent to four different locations—the console, virtual terminals, an internal buffer, and a syslog server. Also, seven different information levels exist to provide event information. The other answers do not adhere to the correct command structure. Therefore, answers b, c, and d are incorrect.

Need To Know More?

Haugdahl, J. Scott. *Network Analysis and Troubleshooting*. Addison-Wesley. Berkley, CA, 1999. ISBN: 0-20143-319-2. This book features proven network analysis techniques and experience-based strategies for isolating and solving network problems.

Miller, Mark. A. *LAN Troubleshooting Handbook*. M&T Books. San Mateo, CA, 1990. ISBN: 1-55851-054-0. This book contains general LAN troubleshooting techniques and scenarios that can be used to help diagnose network failures.

From the CCO Documentation home page (**www.cisco.com/univercd/home/home.htm**), select Internetworking Troubleshooting Guide and then Troubleshooting Tools. Visit this section for more information about the **show**, **debug**, **ping**, and **trace** Cisco IOS commands.

From the CCO Documentation home page (**www.cisco.com/univercd/home/home.htm**), select Troubleshooting Internetworking Systems and then Troubleshooting Overview. These Web pages provide further details on how and when to use the Cisco IOS troubleshooting tools.

Cisco Router Processes

Terms you'll need to understand:

- √ Route processor
- √ Switch processor
- √ Silicon switch processor
- √ Process, fast, autonomous, and silicon switching
- √ Flash memory
- √ Access, Distribution, and Core network layers

Techniques you'll need to master:

- √ Generating core dumps
- √ Performing router password recovery
- √ Identifying Cisco network devices

Cisco routers come in a variety of families, from the Access layer 2500/2600 series, all the way up to core-level 7500 series routers, to the recently introduced Gigabit Switch Routers (GSR 12000). Each family can play specific roles within an internetwork, but all have a large amount of overlap in general functionality. This chapter briefly discusses the general architecture of the routers and then introduces some of the Cisco IOS commands available to check the current state of the router.

Architecture

General Cisco router architecture includes a system bus and a CxBus or CyBus used to transport packets from individual interfaces to a route or switching processor. Data is copied from buffer to buffer, with the path each packet takes dependent on the switching method chosen. Other types of architectures exist, such as route switch processors (RSPs), versatile interface processors (VIPs), and switch route processors (SRPs), but these areas are outside the scope of this book.

Route Processors

Route processors (RPs) contain the CPU and system software image that manage the entire device. The route processor also controls and manages all tables and caches (ARP, route, and switching flows), a range of MAC addresses for interfaces, routing protocol updates, and interfaces and internal environmental status. Network management capabilities such as SNMP and remote administration are also handled by the RP.

Switching Modes

Different IP switching modes exist, and each provides its own subset of performance and reliability measures. The following sections describe the available switching types as well as the process each type performs in moving packets between router interfaces.

Process Switching

Process switching requires the route processor to perform a routing table lookup for every packet on an individual basis, thus greatly increasing the latency of packet traversal throughout the router. Accurately processing **debug** commands requires the use of process switching so that each packet is checked for the events the **debug** command is searching for.

All other switching methods rely on process switching to transmit the first packet within a packet flow. After the first packet, the switching process is defined by what processes have been enabled on an interface or the type of available hardware.

Fast Switching

The RP contains the fast switch cache used to enable fast switching of packets. Fast switching relies on previously defined header information that's copied out of the cache directly, without the route processor performing a routing table lookup.

Optimum Switching

The 7500 series does not have silicon or autonomous switching capabilities; new caching methods were developed to enhance internal packet flows known as *optimum switching*. Optimum switching is only available for the Cisco 7500 series routers. It's enabled by default for IP on Ethernet, FDDI, and serial interfaces, as well as on all ATM port adapter interfaces.

Autonomous Switching

The switch processor (SP) uses an entry within the autonomous switching cache and encapsulates each packet with this previously determined information. The packet is then placed in the output queue of the interface processor and transmitted.

Silicon Switching

The silicon switch processor (SSP), used by the 7000 series routers, compares entries within the silicon switch cache. Matching entries are encapsulated with the appropriate addressing information, copied to the output queue of the interface processor, and transmitted.

NetFlow Switching

In addition to moving packets throughout the router, NetFlow switching (by far the most popular of the switching techniques) keeps a detailed table of traffic statistics and flows that can be exported to a database and charted. A *network flow* is identified as a stream of packets between a given source and destination IP and TCP/UDP identification. Specifically, each individual traffic flow is identified as the combination of the following fields:

- Source IP address
- Destination IP address

- Source TCP/UDP port number
- Destination TCP/UDP port number
- Protocol type
- Type of service
- Input interface

NetFlow also provides a highly efficient processing of security access lists in comparison to other switching methods.

Series Routers

Even within a series, Cisco's routers vary greatly—for instance, the 2505 with 8 Ethernet and 3 serial ports versus a 2507 router with 16 Ethernet and 3 serial ports. This allows you to purchase a router that fits your specific needs. The high-end routers, such as a 7513, are modular in design and therefore can be custom-tailored throughout the life of the device. Each individual series also performs a bit differently than the others and may be used at different layers of the networking infrastructure model (Access, Distribution, and Core):

- **2500/2600, 3600, and 4000 series (Access/Distribution)** These have shared memory space for all packet buffers and cache.
- **7000 series (Core)** This series utilizes a silicon switch processor (SSP) to store the silicon switch cache and autonomous switch cache. Silicon switching can only occur if the SSP is installed.
- **7500 series (Core)** This series uses an integrated route switch processor (RSP) to increase frame transmission rates, but it cannot provide silicon or autonomous switching. Instead, it provides optimum switching, which is similar to fast switching but with reduced latency.

2500/2600, 3600, And 4000 Series

The Cisco 2500/2600 series represents Cisco System's low-cost entry into the router marketplace. The Cisco 2500 series of Ethernet and token ring routers provides a wide range of branch office solutions including integrated router/ hub and router/access server models. The Cisco 2600 series shares modular interfaces with the Cisco 1600, 1700, and 3600 series with added support for Voice over Frame relay (VoFR), Voice of IP (VoIP), and enhanced queuing functionality. The Cisco 4500-M is a midrange router with a 100-MHz reduced instruction set (RISC) CPU for supporting medium-sized LAN and WAN connectivity. The higher-end Cisco 4700-M router has a 133-MHz RISC CPU and produces approximately 40 percent more processing performance than the Cisco 4500-M. All of the latest Cisco equipment is highly modular in style so that you can choose what interfaces are required for your infrastructure, such as Ethernet, Fast Ethernet, ISDN, token ring, or ATM.

7000 Series

The 7000 series routers utilize the Cisco Extended Bus (CxBus), operating at 533 Mbps, for transmitting data to and from processor modules. The standard system requires one route processor and one switch processor (or silicon switch processor). An upgraded RSP7000 system requires one 7000 series route switch processor (RSP7000) and one 7000 series Chassis Interface (RSP7000CI). The RSP7000 contains the system processor and performs packet switching functions, while the RSP7000CI board contains all of the environmental monitoring functions. The 7000 series supports Online Insertion and Removal (OIR), which allows you to add, replace, or remove interface processors without interrupting the system power or entering any console commands.

Take the time to study the internal architecture of the 7000 and 7500 series routers, this information may be very useful while attempting to troubleshoot a problem.

7500 Series

The Cisco Extended Bus (CyBus), operating at 1.067 Mbps, is the data bus used for processor modules in the Cisco 7505 and 7513 routers. There are two CyBuses on the routers for an aggregated bandwidth of 2134 Gbps. An arbiter controls traffic across the CyBus by prioritizing access requests from the interface processors to ensure that each request is processed and to prevent any interface processor from jeopardizing the CyBus and interfering with the ability of the other interface processors to access the RSP. The 7500 series also supports OIR.

Interface processors designed for the 7000 series' CxBus work with the CyBus architecture in the 7500 series; however, they will not be able to utilize the increased bandwidth capability provided by the CyBus.

Cisco IOS Commands

The Cisco IOS contains several commands for listing information about a router's performance, current operational state, and internal devices, as well as ways to generate crash reports and even "hack" into a router if the passwords have been lost. This section describes in detail the available Cisco IOS commands and how they can be used to maintain a Cisco router.

The show Commands

Several **show** commands can be used to identify the active state of a router; the most commonly used commands are described in Table 5.1. The next few sections go into more detail on each of these commands and describe how they may be useful in identifying information in a Cisco internetwork.

show buffers

The **show buffers** command, shown in Listing 5.1, lists buffer pool statistics for several frame size categorizations, such as small, middle, and big buffers. Buffers are allocated on a frame-by-frame basis according to the frame's overall size. Therefore, a 700-byte frame would be allocated space within the "big" buffers.

Listing 5.1 The output generated by the **show buffers** command.

```
Router>show buffers
Buffer elements:
     499 in free list (500 max allowed)
     630098897 hits, 0 misses, 0 created

Public buffer pools:
Small buffers, 104 bytes (total 120, permanent 120):
     111 in free list (20 min, 250 max allowed)
     264091817 hits, 1439 misses, 558 trims, 558 created
```

Table 5.1 Frequently used show commands for troubleshooting Cisco routers.

Command	Description
show buffers	Displays router buffer pool statistics
show diagbus	Displays port adapter, controller, and interface processor diagnostic information
show environment all	Displays temperature and voltage information on 7000, 7200, and 7500 series routers
show flash	Displays the file contents of FLASH
show interfaces stats	Displays the number of packets that are distributed switched, process switched, and fast switched
show memory	Displays free and allocated memory statistics
show processes	Displays information about active processes
show running-config	Lists the current running configuration
show startup-config	Lists the startup configuration stored either in FLASH or Non-Volatile Random Access Memory (NVRAM)

```
     1119 failures (0 no memory)
Middle buffers, 600 bytes (total 90, permanent 90):
     88 in free list (10 min, 200 max allowed)
     309914979 hits, 2703 misses, 29 trims, 29 created
     1089 failures (0 no memory)
Big buffers, 1524 bytes (total 90, permanent 90):
     89 in free list (5 min, 300 max allowed)
     120456213 hits, 504 misses, 165 trims, 165 created
     418 failures (0 no memory)
VeryBig buffers, 4520 bytes (total 10, permanent 10):
     9 in free list (0 min, 300 max allowed)
     391274 hits, 318 misses, 11 trims, 11 created
     318 failures (0 no memory)
Large buffers, 5024 bytes (total 10, permanent 10):
     10 in free list (0 min, 30 max allowed)
     105 hits, 221 misses, 3 trims, 3 created
     221 failures (0 no memory)
Huge buffers, 18024 bytes (total 9, permanent 0):
     9 in free list (0 min, 13 max allowed)
     2182729 hits, 186 misses, 0 trims, 9 created
     183 failures (0 no memory)
```

The highlighted area describes small buffer allocations, which include all frames under 104 bytes in size (**small buffers, 104 bytes**). The buffer has a total of 120 allocated buffer regions, of which 120 are permanent (**total 120, permanent 120**). At the time the command was issued, 111 buffers were empty and available for use (**111 in free list**) and there was a minimum of 20 and a maximum of 250 small buffers allowed at any given time (**20 min, 250 max allowed**). A small buffer has been used to transport a frame 264,091,817 times, and 1,439 times space has not been available to allocate, so the buffer pool was enlarged (**264091817 hits, 1439 misses**). Hits are good; misses are what you need to concern yourself with. Look at the buffer misses as a percentage of all traffic passing through the buffers. The number of allocated buffers have been reduced and created 558 times (**558 trims, 558 created**). The number of frames that have been discarded due to unavailable memory is 1119 (**1119 failures**).

Buffer pools can be manipulated, but buffer tuning must be evaluated on a case-by-case basis. Don't try it yourself if you don't know precisely what you're doing. The best thing to do is to open a case with TAC and have an engineer evaluate your network before any adjustments are made.

show diagbus

Cisco routers may contain several additional modules, such as versatile interface processors (VIPs), Fast Ethernet interface processors (FEIPs), and ATM interface processors (AIPs). The **show diagbus** command, shown in Listing 5.2, displays general and diagnostic information for each installed line module.

Listing 5.2 The **show diagbus** command lists the status of internal Cisco buses.

```
Router>show diagbus
Slot 0:
        Physical slot 0, ~physical slot 0xF, logical slot 0, CBus 0
        Microcode Status 0x4
        Master Enable, LED, WCS Loaded
        Board is analyzed
        Pending I/O Status: Debug I/O
        EEPROM format version 1
        FEIP controller, HW rev 2.01, board revision C0
        Serial number: 03510246  Part number: 73-1374-04
        Test history: 0x00        RMA number: 00-00-00
        Flags: cisco 7000 board; 7500 compatible

        EEPROM contents (hex):
          0x20: 01 13 02 01 00 35 8F E6 49 05 5E 04 00 00 00 00
          0x30: 60 00 00 00 00 00 00 00 00 00 00 00 00 00 00 00

        Slot database information:
        Flags: 0x4      Insertion time: 0x1488 (13w0d ago)

        PA 0 Information:
                Fast-Ethernet PA, 1 port, 100BaseTX-nISL
                EEPROM format version 1
                HW rev 1.00, Board revision A0
                Serial number: 03543009  Part number: 73-1376-03

        PA 1 Information:
                Fast-Ethernet PA, 1 port, 100BaseTX-nISL
                EEPROM format version 1
                HW rev 1.00, Board revision A0
                Serial number: 03542974  Part number: 73-1376-03
[output omitted from listing]
```

This command shows an FEIP line module containing two Fast Ethernet port adapters (PA 0 and 1). The output contains the serial and part numbers for all devices, as well as the hardware revision. This information can be very useful while troubleshooting, especially if a problem eventually is isolated to a bug due to hardware or software incompatibilities.

You can use the **show diagbus** command to retrieve the serial numbers for each module installed in the router.

show environment all

Environmental sensors monitor the chassis and record statistics once every minute. If a threshold is reached, a warning message is displayed on the console (or sent to system logs if configured to do so). Warning messages are sent out, at most, once per hour. The **show environment all** command, shown in Listing 5.3, can be used to display system status information such as power supplies, fan activity, and temperature points, although the output from this command varies by chassis type.

Listing 5.3 Use the **show environment all** command to view a detailed device status report.

```
Router>show environment all
Arbiter type 1, backplane type 7513 (id 2)
Power supply #1 is 1200W AC (id 1),
     power supply #2 is removed (id 7)
Active fault conditions: none
Fan transfer point: 1%
Active trip points: none
15 of 15 soft shutdowns remaining before hard shutdown

                        1
             0123456789012
Dbus slots: XX XX X X

 card      inlet        hotpoint      exhaust
RSP(6)   24C/75F       34C/93F       28C/82F

Shutdown temperature source is 'hotpoint' on RSP(6),
    requested RSP(6)

+12V measured at 12.12
 +5V measured at 5.19
-12V measured at -11.98
+24V measured at 23.68
+2.5 reference is 2.49

PS1 +5V Current    measured at 39.22 A (capacity 200 A)
PS1 +12V Current   measured at 0.00 A (capacity 35 A)
PS1 -12V Current   measured at 0.00 A (capacity 3 A)
PS1 output is 203 W
```

Environmental conditions can have a drastic effect on overall longevity and performance on any electrical equipment and should be considered while troubleshooting any network problem.

A simpler way to monitor environmental statistics and check for errors is to set up SNMP trap generation when values exceed the configured threshold values. This can be used to notify a central network management station of the problem and reduce the overhead of constantly monitoring each individual device manually.

show flash

FLASH memory can contain Cisco IOS software images, router configuration files, or even general network management files. These files can be listed using the **show flash** command, as shown in Listing 5.4.

Listing 5.4 The **show flash** command displays the contents of the internal FLASH memory.

```
Router>show flash
-#- ED -type- -crc-    -seek-  nlen -length- -date-     name
1   .. unknown  8C95B40E  75861C   23   7570844  May 10 1999 12.0-1

12986244 bytes available (7592060 bytes used)

Router>show flash devices
slot0, slot1, bootflash
```

FLASH devices can be the bootflash, PCMCIA cards (slot0 and slot1), or other devices. This command, in conjunction with the boot variable, can pinpoint the location of the startup router configurations on the 7000, 7200, 7500, and 12000 series routers.

show interfaces stats

The **show interfaces stats** command generates a detailed table indicating the number of packets and characters that have been process-, fast-, and distributed-switched. Listing 5.5 displays the output from this command.

Listing 5.5 Switching statistics can be seen using the **show interfaces stats** command.

```
Router>show interfaces stats
FastEthernet1/0
          Switching path    Pkts In    Chars In    Pkts Out   Chars Out
               Processor   10960590  1200994658    22954680  3617533219
             Route cache 1288210380  2825155602  2005418319  2138562880
       Distributed cache          0           0           0           0
                   Total 1299170971  4026150364  2028373000  1461130343
```

Packet-switching techniques can have a dramatic impact on the network, degrading or increasing overall network performance. Sometimes situations may require process switching (**debug** commands), whereas others require distributed switching (multicast). This is an excellent measure for verifying exactly how your traffic is being switched.

show memory

You should always make certain to check the overall memory usage of a router before and after making any changes by using the **show memory** command (see Listing 5.6). Some routers, such as a 3640, may even require you to specify the amount of memory used for input/output transactions and the amount used for the processor.

Listing 5.6 The **show memory** command lists the actively running processes and their associated memory addresses.

```
Router>show memory
                Head Total(b) Used(b) Free(b)  Lowest(b) Largest(b)
Processor  60F6A7E0 59026448 4823486 54202962 2312636   53822784
     Fast  60F4A7E0 131072   58744   72328    72328     72284

          Processor memory

 Address Bytes Prev.    Next     Ref N P Alloc PC  What
60F6A7E0  1064 0        60F6AC34   1     6018077C  List Elements
60F6AC34  2664 60F6A7E0 60F6B6C8   1     6018077C  List Headers
60F6B6C8  9000 60F6AC34 60F6DA1C   1     60199610  Interrupt Stack
60F6DA1C    44 60F6B6C8 60F6DA74   1     60876420  *Init*
60F6DA74  9000 60F6DA1C 60F6FDC8   1     60199610  Interrupt Stack
60F6FDC8    44 60F6DA74 60F6FE20   1     60876420  *Init*
60F6FE20   164 60F6FDC8 60F6FEF0   1     6019FD0C  *Init*
60F6FEF0  2656 60F6FE20 60F7097C   1     601393D4  TTY data
[output omitted from listing]
```

The output displays the amount of allocated memory for process- and fast-switched frames, as well as the memory address space and total bytes consumed by each router process currently running on the router. Installing updated software versions or additional equipment on a router normally increases the processor load, thus increasing the overall memory requirements. Shortages of unused memory can cause unexpected results that could lead to hours of unwarranted troubleshooting.

show processes

The **show processes** command, shown in Listing 5.7, generates a report of active internal router processes and their associated runtime and invocation numbers. Also shown is the five-second, one-minute, and five-minute average CPU utilization statistics. These statistics can help to identify problems if, for instance, the average CPU utilization exceeds a baseline value for an extended period of time.

Listing 5.7 Use the **show processes** command to view the current CPU utilization and each process's individual load.

```
Router>show processes
CPU utilization for five seconds: 6%/4%;
     one minute: 6%; five minutes: 7%
 PID QTy        PC Run(ms) Invoked uSecs     Stacks TTY Process
   1 Csp 601A0410     1256 1573717     0 2640/3000    0 Load Meter
   2 Hwe 6002AEE4    62528 1203710    51 4952/6000    0 SSCOP Input
   3 Lst 6018837C 4279944  140794 30398 5756/6000    0 Check heaps
   4 Cwe 6018D7A0      112     219   511 5652/6000    0 Pool Manager
   5 Mst 60131148        0       2     0 5612/6000    0 Timers
   6 Mwe 601E6CCC        0       1     0 2644/3000    0 OIR Handler
   7 ME  6023B3D8        0       1     0 5840/6000    0 IPC Zone
   8 Lwe 60240FA8 2165792 5951693   363 4840/6000    0 ARP Input
   9 Mwe 6005EE2C        0       1     0 5648/6000    0 SERIAL A'dct
  10 Hwe 602F4464      220     232   948 4640/6000    0 ATM ILMI Inp
  11 ME  602ED208      188     356   528 5272/6000    0 ILMI Process
  12 Mwe 60230B50        0       1     0 5636/6000    0 IP Crashinfo
  13 Lsi 60235B28     4116  131101    31 2752/3000    0 Slave Time
  14 M*         0      252     275   916 9828/12000   2 Virtual Exec
  [output omitted from listing]
```

This command can be used to view the overall impact of an individual routing process, such as ARP requests. The listing shows that 5,951,693 times (running for a total 2,165,792 ms), the ARP input process has been invoked and given a low priority (L). The ARP input scheduling service is currently waiting for an event to process (**we**). For more detailed information about this command, check the Cisco Web site.

show running-config/show startup-config

Two of the best troubleshooting tools show the currently running router's configuration and the startup configuration, respectively. The **show running-config** command displays the currently running Cisco IOS configuration set, whereas the **show startup-config** command displays the configuration that would be processed if the router were reloaded. Values and commands that appear to be out of the ordinary may be the cause of network problems or performance issues. Always take the time to view a router's current configuration; this may be the only way to alleviate hours or even days of troubleshooting.

Viewing the startup and running configurations and comparing any discrepancies can save a lot of valuable time while troubleshooting. You will find that a majority of configuration mistakes can be easily noticed while you are scrolling through router configurations.

Generating Core Dumps

Full memory images can be obtained using the **write core** command, as shown in Listing 5.8. These are generally useful during times of hard router crashes. The image that's written to the TFTP server can then be analyzed by Cisco personnel and may help identify the router's problem.

Listing 5.8 The **write core** command generates an internal core dump.

```
Router#write core
Remote host? 10.3.1.1
Name of core file to write [router-core]?
Write file router-core on host 10.3.1.1? [confirm]
Writing router-core !!!!!!!!!!!!!!!!!!!!!!!!!!!!!!!!!!!!!!!!!!!!!!
!!!!!!!!!!!!!!!!!!!!!!!!!!!!!!!!!!!!!!!!!!!!!!!!!!!!!!!!!!!!!!!!!!
!!!!!!!!!!!!!!!!!!!!!!!!!!!!!!!!!!!!!!!!!!!!!!!!!!!!!!!!!!!!!!!!!!
!!!!!!!!!!!!!!!!!!!!!!!!!!!!!!!!!!!!!!!!!!!!!!!!!!!!!! [OK]
```

You can also use the IOS command **exception dump** *ip address*, where *ip address* is the address of your TFTP server. This will automatically generate a core dump when the router crashes. It should be noted that internal router core dumps should only be performed with the guidance of a Cisco TAC engineer.

Password Recovery

To perform password recovery on a Cisco router you must have console access. Password recovery for routers is in essence a relatively simple task, but it can become quite cumbersome if not performed correctly. Also, keep in mind that certain series of routers may require a slightly different recovery method than others. The most common way to recover a lost password can be done by performing these 12 steps:

1. Attach an ASCII terminal to the console port.
2. Configure the terminal to operate at 9600 baud, 8 data bits, no parity, 1 stop bits.
3. Power cycle the router.

4. Within 60 seconds of turning on the router, press the **Break** key. This action causes the terminal to display the bootstrap program prompt (rommon 1 >).

5. From the ROM monitor prompt, set the configuration register value to "0×2142". This causes the router to bypass the configuration contents stored in NVRAM upon next bootup. To do this, type **o/r 2142**:

```
rommon 1 > o/r 0x2142
```

6. Once the configuration register has been changed, initialize the router by typing **i**:

```
rommon 1 > i
```

7. After the router boots up, you'll be prompted to indicate whether you want to enter the initial configuration dialog box. Type **n** for no.

8. Enter privileged EXEC mode by typing **enable**. No password will be required.

9. Load the original configuration back into the router by entering the command **copy startup-config running-config**. You must be very careful not to enter this in the reverse order; otherwise, the old configuration will be lost forever.

10. Set the new enable password using the password commands for the console, virtual terminals, auxiliary port user mode, and general privileged mode (either the standard **enable** or the **enable secret password**):

```
Router(config)#line console 0
Router(config-line)#password 0 <new password>
Router(config)#line vty 0 4
Router(config-line)#password 0 <new password>
Router(config)#line aux 0
Router(config-line)#password 0 <new password>
Router(config)#enable password 0 <new password>
Router(config)#enable secret 0 <new password>
```

11. Restore the configuration register and exit configuration mode. The configuration register must be reset so the router will properly boot using the configuration now stored in NVRAM. Do this by typing **config-register 0×2102** in configuration mode.

12. Save changes using the **copy running-config startup-config** command.

Practice Questions

Question 1

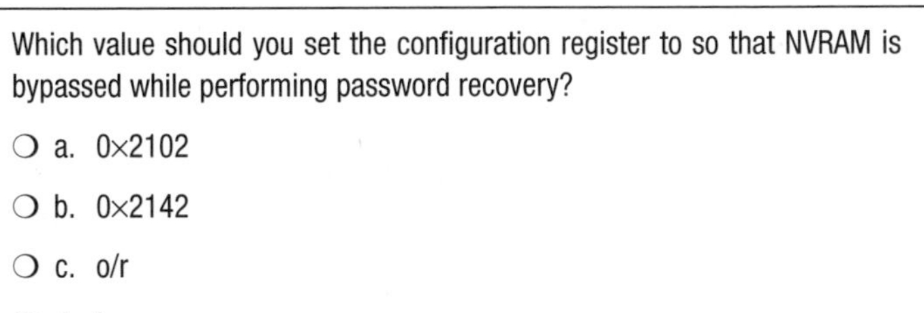

Which value should you set the configuration register to so that NVRAM is bypassed while performing password recovery?

❍ a. 0×2102

❍ b. 0×2142

❍ c. o/r

❍ d. i

The correct answer is b. The configuration register value can be used to identify the location of the startup configuration, and 0×2142 bypasses NVRAM. Answer a is incorrect because it indicates that the startup configuration is to be loaded from NVRAM. Answers c and d are invalid configuration register values—they're used to set and initialize the router while in ROM monitor mode—and are therefore incorrect.

Question 2

You need to find the serial numbers of all line modules located within a Cisco 7513 router. Which command can be used to display these values?

❍ a. **show running-config**

❍ b. **show diagbus**

❍ c. **show processes**

❍ d. **show system**

The correct answer is b. The **show diagbus** command can be used to display the individual line module type and serial number. The **show running-config** command displays the active Cisco IOS configuration. Therefore, answer a is incorrect. The **show processes** command generates a table of active router processes and CPU utilization. Therefore, answer c is also incorrect. Answer d is incorrect because it is not a valid Cisco IOS command.

Question 3

What Cisco IOS command displays the current running configuration contents?

____

The correct answer is **show running-config**. This command displays the entire contents of the current Cisco IOS running configuration. The **show startup-config** command, on the other hand, displays the configuration that would be processed during a reload.

Question 4

Repeatedly, a 4500 series Cisco router is crashing unexpectedly and then reloading immediately. After speaking with the Technical Assistance Center, you enter a command in the router so that core dumps will be sent to a TFTP server at the IP address 10.1.1.1 if a crash occurs. Which command did you enter?

❍ a. **tftp crashinfo 10.1.1.1**

❍ b. **copy crash tftp 10.1.1.1**

❍ c. **write core**

❍ d. **exception dump 10.1.1.1**

The correct answer is d. Crash information files are sent to a TFTP server using the format **exception dump** ***ip address of TFTP server***. Answers a and b are incorrect because they are not valid Cisco IOS commands. Answer c is incorrect because the **write core** command generates a core dump to a remote host immediately and does not initiate an automated process during a failure.

Question 5

Which switching process is required so that all packets are processed by the **debug** commands?

❍ a. fast switching

❍ b. autonomous switching

❍ c. process switching

❍ d. silicon switching

The correct answer is c. Process switching sends every packet to the route processor. Therefore, they can be seen by the debugging processes. Answers a, b, and d are incorrect because they all provide a cache-based switching feature that only sends a few packets to the route processor for table lookups. Therefore, the packets will not be seen by the debugging processes.

Question 6

Performing the **show buffers** command reveals that there have been 1,217 big buffer misses. What does this mean?

- ❍ a. Space was not available within the buffer pool, so 600 bytes of buffer memory was allocated.
- ❍ b. 1,524 bytes of buffer memory has been allocated 1,217 times.
- ❍ c. Packets have been discarded 1,217 times due to buffer allocation failures.

The correct answer is b. Big buffers consist of 1,524-byte buffers, and each time a miss occurs, a new memory range is allocated to that buffer (in this case, 1,217 times). 600-byte buffers are allocated to middle buffers. Therefore, answer a is incorrect. Packets are dropped only when buffer failures, not misses, occur. Therefore, answer c is incorrect.

Question 7

You've recently converted from completely process-switching packets to fast-switching them, and now you would like to see how many packets are using each method. Which command will provide these statistics for you?

- ❍ a. **show switching**
- ❍ b. **show processes**
- ❍ c. **show interfaces stats**
- ❍ d. **show environment**

The correct answer is c. The **show interfaces stats** command displays switching information for processor, fast, and distributed switching. **show switching** is not a valid Cisco IOS command. Therefore, answer a is incorrect. The **show processes** command generates a table of active router processes and CPU utilization. Therefore, answer b is incorrect. The **show environment** command displays the active internal state of the router (such as temperature, voltages, and fan activity). Therefore, answer d is incorrect.

Need To Know More?

From the CCO Documentation home page at **www.cisco.com/univercd/home/home.htm**, select Internetworking Troubleshooting Guide|Troubleshooting Hardware and Booting Problems. Check out this section for more general information about hardware and boot processes, categorized by router type.

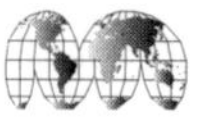

From the CCO Documentation home page at **www.cisco.com/univercd/home/home.htm**, select Troubleshooting Internetworking Systems|Troubleshooting Router Startup Problems. Here, you can find step-by-step instructions for identifying and correcting several common router symptoms.

Protocol Review

Terms you'll need to understand:

- √ Open Systems Interconnection (OSI) reference model
- √ Fiber optic, twisted pair, and coax transmission media
- √ Asynchronous Transfer Mode (ATM)
- √ Ethernet
- √ Token ring
- √ Fiber Distributed Data Interface (FDDI)
- √ Serial Link Internet Protocol (SLIP)
- √ Point-to-Point Protocol (PPP)
- √ High-Level Data Link Control (HDLC)
- √ Synchronous Data Link Control (SDLC)
- √ Internet Protocol (IP)
- √ Internetwork Packet Exchange (IPX)/Sequenced Packet Exchange (SPX)
- √ AppleTalk protocols
- √ Distance-vector routing protocols
- √ Link-state routing protocols
- √ IP multicast

Techniques you'll need to master:

- √ Identifying Ethernet frame types
- √ Recognizing IP protocols
- √ Understanding IP addressing and subnet masking
- √ Recognizing IPX protocols
- √ Understanding IPX addressing and SAP announcements
- √ Recognizing AppleTalk protocols
- √ Understanding AppleTalk addressing and zoning
- √ Using IP multicast methods

Protocols are defined to furnish a guide for data transmission and communication on an internetwork, just as protocols are defined to promote legislature into law in the federal government. Without guidelines, proprietary extensions would govern the network and the Internet would have never come to fruition. This chapter describes the layers within the OSI reference model and their functions, as well as the types of protocols that reside at each one of these layers. We'll cover, in detail, the IP, IPX, and AppleTalk protocols and their relationship to three of the four lower layers of the model—the Data Link, Network, and Transport layers.

OSI Reference Model

The OSI reference model is based on a proposal developed by the International Standards Organization (ISO). The model is called the ISO Open Systems Interconnection (OSI) reference model because it deals with connecting open systems—that is, systems that are open for communication with other systems. Figure 6.1 displays the OSI model and the path taken by data transmitted between two hosts on disparate networks, and Table 6.1 compares the functionality at each level.

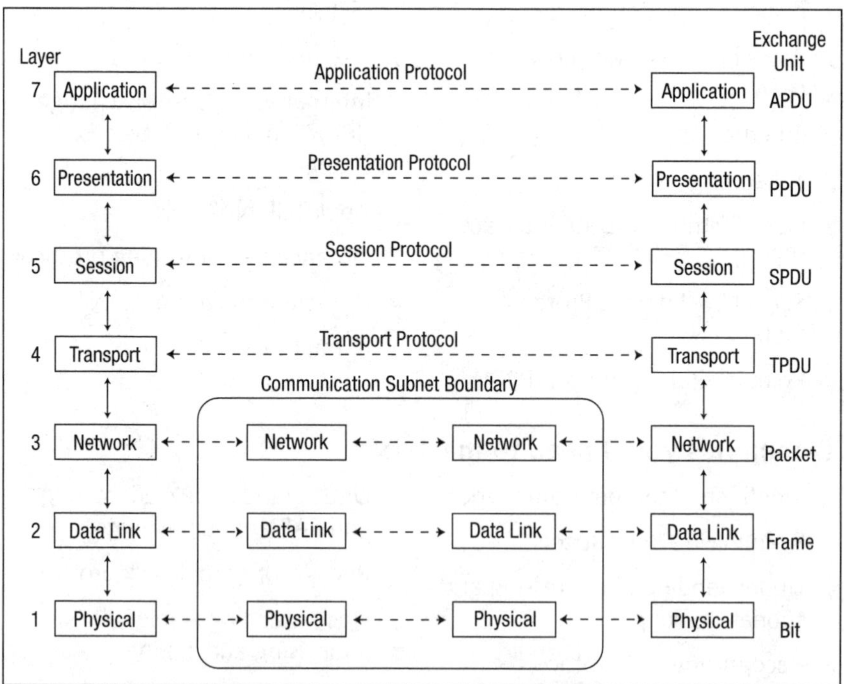

Figure 6.1 A snapshot of the OSI reference model.

Table 6.1 The hardware or software functionality at each layer of the OSI reference model.

Layer	Function
Physical	This level contains network interfaces, RS-232 ports, wires, cards, voltage requirements, and repeaters.
Data Link	This level provides hardware addresses, bridges, and switches.
Network	This level provides software addresses and routers.
Transport	This level provides reliability and error checking.
Session	This level manages logical communication sessions.
Presentation	This level provides translation and encryption.
Application	This is the application's interface.

Physical Layer

As the lowest layer of the reference model, the Physical layer defines the physical and electrical characteristics of the interface to the network and provides a transparent transmission path for the information across the chosen physical medium. Data transmission takes place using binary zeros and ones over a circuit according to rules such as electrical voltages, timing, full duplex/half duplex, and connector cable standards.

Data Link Layer

The second layer, the Data Link layer, is responsible for providing error-free transfer of frames from one computer to another through the Physical layer. In essence, it manages the data being transferred and corrects the transmission errors of bits, not the actual data. It's divided into two sublayers: the Media Access Control (MAC) and the Logical Link Control (LLC). The MAC performs most of the Data Link layer functions, whereas the LLC is an interface between the MAC layer and the Network layer.

Network Layer

The Network layer controls the operation of each network. A key design issue is determining how packets are routed from source to destination. Routes can be based on static tables that rarely change, they can be determined at the start of each conversation (for example, a terminal session), or they can be highly dynamic, being redetermined for each packet to reflect the current network load.

Transport Layer

The fourth layer provides data transport from machine to machine, independent of the physical network. The Transport layer establishes, maintains, and terminates logical connections between hosts. It also provides segmentation of large data transmissions into smaller packets, if required. In general, this layer deals with end-to-end issues of data entering and departing the network.

Connection-oriented Transport layer protocols guarantee delivery of data to higher layers, whereas connectionless protocols check for valid transmissions but don't retransmit data; therefore, no guaranteed delivery of data can be assumed.

Session Layer

The Session layer is responsible for initiating, maintaining, and terminating each logical session between end users. This layer performs name recognition and the functions, such as security, needed to allow two applications to communicate over the network. Session layer applications frequently map directly to Transport layer services.

Presentation Layer

This layer provides such features as peripheral device coding, formatting, encryption, and compaction. In essence, it handles data presentation conversions between internal formats and the network format for data to solve the problems of different data representation models between nodes. An example of a protocol residing at this layer is External Data Representation (XDR), which is used by remote procedure call (RPC) applications to provide interoperability between heterogeneous computer systems.

Application Layer

This layer's name is misleading, because the ultimate application processes do not reside in this layer. The Application layer provides services to applications and a window for applications to gain access to the OSI environment. Different file systems have different file naming conventions, different ways of representing text lines, and so on. Transferring a file between two different systems requires handling these and other incompatibilities. This work belongs to the Application layer, as does electronic mail, file transfer, remote job entry, directory lookup, and various other general-purpose and special-purpose facilities.

A simple pneumonic for remembering the layers of the OSI model in order is "Please Do Not Throw Sausage Pizza Away."

Physical Layer Specifications

Physical layer protocols are concerned with the transmission of data bits and are specific to the media, such as optical, coax, twisted pair, and the like. They specify the data signal encoding and the type of physical connector, including pinouts. The next few sections do not go into too much detail, but instead briefly cover three of the most popular types of transmission media.

Coax

Coaxial cable consists of a solid copper core surrounded by insulation, a braided metal shielding, and an outer cover. The cable core carries the electronic data signals throughout the network. Each end of a coaxial cable must be terminated to prevent signal repetition. There are two type of coaxial cable:

- **Thinnet** Thinnet, or 10Base2, coaxial cable can carry a signal for about 185 meters. British Naval Connectors (BNCs) provide host connections into the network.
- **Thicknet** Thicknet, or 10Base5, coaxial cable can carry a signal for about 500 meters. BNCs can be used, but generally Attachment Unit Interface (AUI) cables connected into vampire taps provide host connections into the network.

Fiber Optic

Fiber-optic cables consist of glass fibers, one receive and one transmit, that carry digital data signals in the form of pulses of light. Fiber-optic cabling is an excellent selection if you have any plans for a high-speed, high-capacity network in the future. There are two modes in which traffic can be sent across a fiber link:

- **Singlemode** Singlemode fibers are designed to carry a single wave of light for distances of up to 10 kilometers.
- **Multimode** Multimode fibers are designed to carry multiple waves of light at the same time, but are not designed for long distances. The maximum distance for a multimode fiber is 2 kilometers. Multimode fiber has a larger core than Singlemode.

Twisted Pair

Twisted-pair cabling consists of strands of copper wire twisted around each other to reduce interference. Host connections generally consist of RJ-45 connectors that are slightly larger than RJ-11 phone connectors. There are two major categories of twisted-pair cable:

- **Unshielded Twisted Pair (UTP)** UTP consists of two to eight wires and is most commonly used for telephone systems; the maximum cable length is 100 meters. It uses the 10BaseT specification. Five categories exist for UTP, with Category 5 cabling being the most common in data networks because it provides 100Mbps connectivity.

- **Shielded Twisted Pair (STP)** STP uses a woven copper jacket, which provides much more protective shielding than UTP. Thus, STP is more tolerant of electrical interference and supports longer distances and higher rates of transmission than does UTP.

Data Link Layer Protocols

Data Link layer protocols ensure reliable and error-free data transfer across links between adjacent network nodes. Every Data Link layer frame is composed of Network layer information and control information. The following sections describe some of the most common Data Link layer protocols, including ATM, Ethernet, token ring, Fiber Distributed Data Interface (FDDI), Serial Link Internet Protocol (SLIP), Point-to-Point Protocol (PPP), High-Level Data Link Control (HDLC), and Synchronous Data Link Control (SDLC).

ATM

ATM is a cell-based, connection-oriented, switching, and multiplexing technology designed to be a fast, general purpose transfer mode for multiple services. ATM is a technology defined by protocol standards created by the ITU-T, ANSI, and the ATM Forum. It is asynchronous because cells are not transferred periodically; cells are actually given time slots on demand. The ATM cell, shown in Figure 6.2, is the fixed length data unit used to transmit data. The data is encapsulated into a 48-byte payload and is preceded by a 5-byte header. Because ATM is connection-oriented it requires end-to-end virtual connections to be established before data transfer. To accomplish this, ATM uses two types of Virtual Circuits, which are PVCs and SVCs. The ATM PVCs are similar to frame relay DLCIs.

In an ATM network, all data is switched and multiplexed in these cells. A switch is responsible for data forwarding. ATM uses address switching to connect communicating ends. At each switch, the cell header may be assigned a

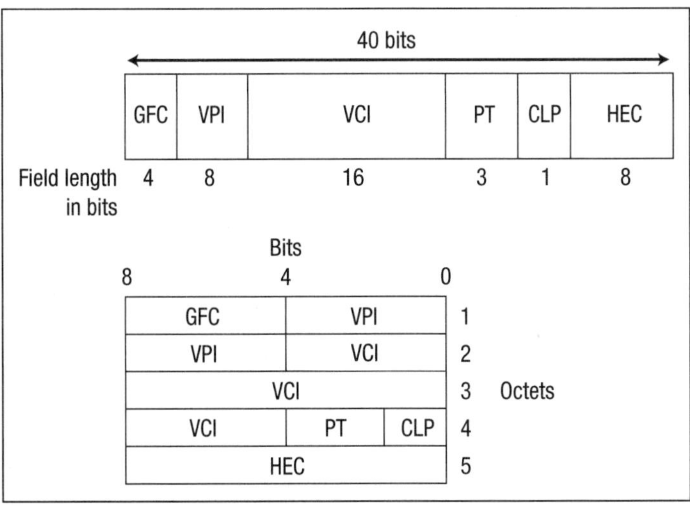

Figure 6.2 An ATM cell.

different VPI and VCI based on the routing table information. The circuit established between the two ends for one transmission may not be the same the next time the two ends communicate. The connection path is identified in the cell header by the VPI and VCI. The VPI and VCI can be reassigned at each switch. Each switch contains a routing table, which stores routing information. The switch guides the cells along the network using information in the routing table.

Ethernet

A variety of Ethernet frame types can be found in Novell NetWare LAN environments, including Ethernet 802.3 (RAW), Ethernet 802.2, Ethernet II, and Ethernet SNAP, as shown in Figure 6.3. The frame types being used depend on the version of NetWare deployed and the individuals administering the network. For example, NetWare 2.x supports only 802.3 (RAW) and Ethernet II, whereas NetWare 3.x supports all four Ethernet frame types. All variations of Ethernet are Carrier Sense Multiple Access with Collision Detect (CSMA/CD) LANs. Hosts on a CSMA/CD LAN can access the network at any time, but before sending data, CSMA/CD stations listen to the network to see if it's already in use. If it is in use, the station wanting to transmit will wait; on the other hand, if the network isn't in use, the station will begin transmitting data. A *collision* occurs when two stations listen for network traffic, hear none, and transmit simultaneously. In this case, both transmissions are damaged, and the stations must retransmit at some later time. *Backoff algorithms* based upon the Ethernet MAC address determine when the colliding stations retransmit.

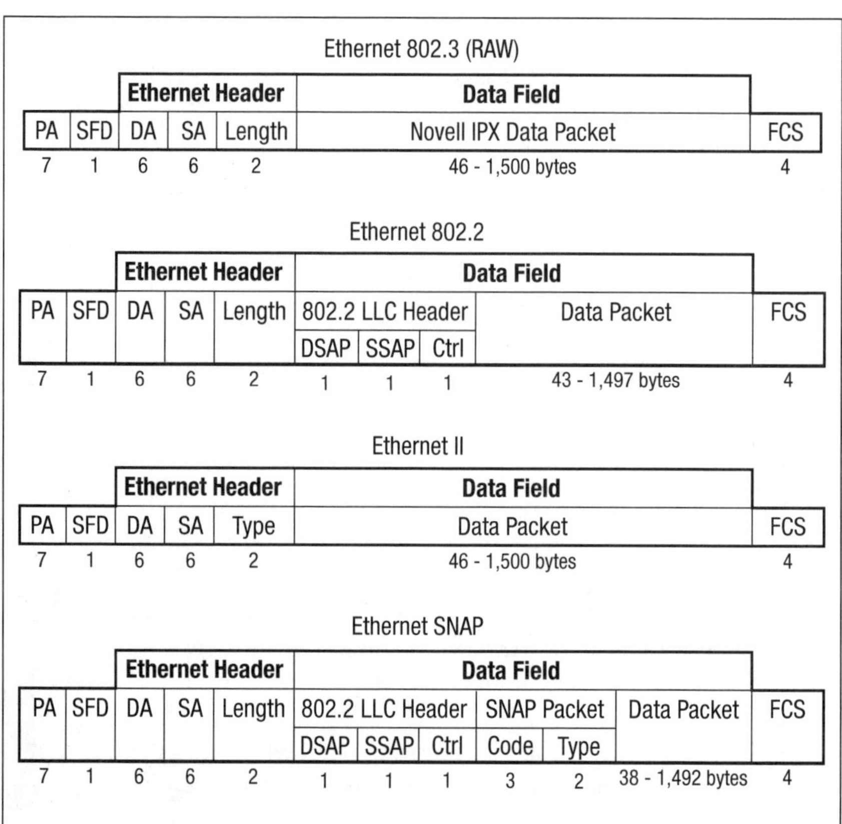

Figure 6.3 The four variations of an Ethernet frame.

Ethernet 802.3 (RAW)

The 802.3 (RAW) frame format, depicted in Figure 6.3, is the original and the default frame type used by NetWare 3.11 or earlier, and can only support IPX/SPX traffic. Novell's proprietary frame format was developed based on a preliminary release of the 802.3 specification. After Novell released their proprietary format, the LLC header was added, making Novell's format incompatible with the formal specification.

Ethernet 802.2

The Ethernet 802.2 frame type, illustrated in Figure 6.3, contains both the 802.2 LLC and 802.3 fields and can support the IPX/SPX protocols. The frame parameters are identical to those in the 802.3 (RAW) format, except the first three bytes within the data field are used for the 802.2 header LLC information. All NetWare IPX/SPX packets assign a hexadecimal value of E0 to the destination service access point (DSAP) and source service access point

(SSAP) fields and a hexadecimal value of 03 to the control field. Ethernet 802.2 is the default encapsulation type for NetWare 3.12 and later.

Ethernet II

This frame type is also similar to the 802.3 specification, except the 2-byte length field has been replaced with a 2-byte Ethernet type field (see Figure 6.3). The Ethernet II frame format can support IP, IPX, and AppleTalk protocols.

The Ethernet type field provides Network layer information at the Data Link layer. Table 6.2 describes some of the field assignments.

Ethernet SNAP

The Ethernet Subnetwork Access Protocol (SNAP) is similar to the 802.2 frame format, but with expanded LLC capabilities. Ethernet SNAP, the bottom frame in Figure 6.3, can support IPX/SPX, IP, and AppleTalk Phase II protocols.

After analyzing an Ethernet frame, the easiest way to distinguish among the four different frame types is to perform the following three steps in order:

1. If the Ethernet type/length field value is greater than 0x05DC, the frame is Ethernet II.
2. If the IPX header (0xFFFF) follows the length field, the frame is interpreted as an 802.3 (RAW) frame with IPX/SPX traffic.
3. Finally, examine the byte following the length field (DSAP). If the value is 0xAA, the frame type is SNAP; otherwise, it's an 802.2 frame.

Table 6.2 Some of the standard hexadecimal variable assignments for the Ethernet type field.

Hexadecimal Value	Description
0000-05DC	IEEE 802.3 length field
0800	Internet Protocol
0806	ARP (for IP and CHAOS)
809B	AppleTalk
80F3	AppleTalk ARP
8137-8138	Novell

Token Ring

Token ring networks operate by passing a single token from computer to computer around a physical ring network. To send data, a computer must wait for this token to reach it; the data is then attached to the token and sent back onto the network. When the token reaches the intended destination, the receiving computer copies the data from the token and then resends the token and data back to the source. The original sender finally strips the token and data from the network, and a new token is released onto the network. The token ring frame is shown in Figure 6.4.

Fiber Distributed Data Interface

The Fiber Distributed Data Interface (FDDI) specification outlines a 100Mbps, dual-ring, token-passing LAN over fiber-optic media, very similar to that of token ring. One of the most important advantages of FDDI is its use of optical fiber (singlemode or multimode) as a transmission medium. The FDDI frame format is shown in Figure 6.5.

Due to the nature of token-passing networks, collisions will never occur on a token ring or Fiber Distributed Data Interface (FDDI) network at any time, even if the network supports early token release. Early token release allows a new token to be released as soon as frame transmission is completed.

Serial Link Internet Protocol

Serial Link Internet Protocol (SLIP) was the first protocol used for remotely connecting to an IP network over a modem connection. SLIP defines a Layer 2

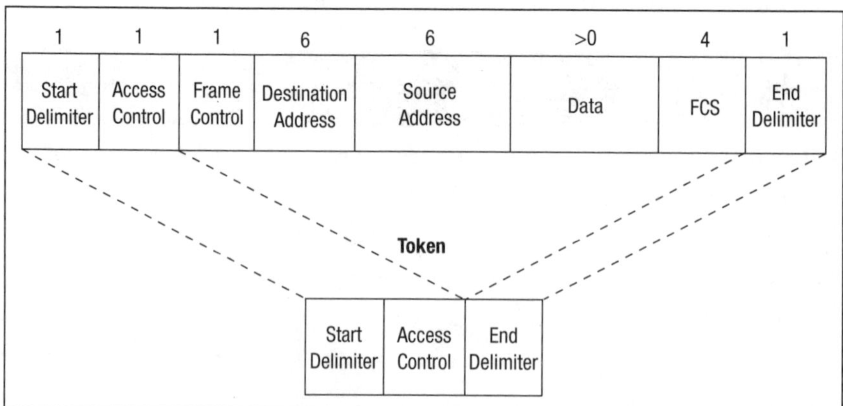

Figure 6.4 A token ring frame.

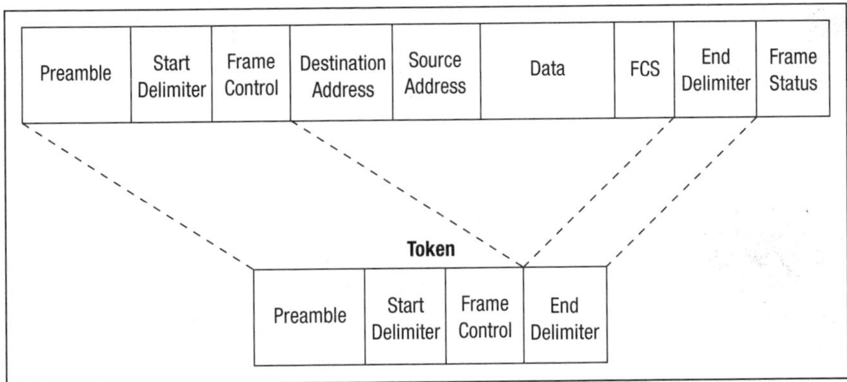

Figure 6.5 An FDDI frame.

encapsulation protocol, but there's no support for dynamic IP address assignment, link testing, or different Network layer protocol multiplexing over a single connection. SLIP is now superceded by PPP.

Point-To-Point Protocol

Point-to-Point Protocol (PPP) utilizes a layering mechanism for data transmission. The connection begins with the Line Control Process (LCP) establishing the initial link through configuration and testing. Once the LCP has completed initialization, one or more Network Control Protocols (NCPs) can be used to provide Network layer support for a protocol suite. NCPs are available for IP, IPX, and AppleTalk.

High-Level Data Link Control

There are two distinct High-Level Data Link Control (HDLC) implementations: HDLC Normal Response Mode (NRM) and HDLC Link Access Procedure Balanced (LAPB). Usually when referring to HDLC, people mean LAPB or some variation. HDLC LAPB is a very efficient protocol; a minimum of overhead is required to ensure flow control, error detection, and recovery. If data is flowing in both directions (full duplex), the data frames themselves carry all the information required to ensure data integrity. HDLC LAPB is usually used by X.25, the CCITT standard for packet-switched networks.

Synchronous Data Link Control

The Synchronous Data Link Control (SDLC) is a serial transmission control developed by IBM to support its Systems Network Architecture (SNA). A variation of the ISO HDLC protocol called HDLC NRM is essentially the same as SDLC. SDLC is not a peer-to-peer protocol like HDLC, frame relay, or X.25. An SDLC network is made up of a primary station that controls all communications and one or more secondary stations. Multiple secondary stations connected to a single primary are known as a *multidrop network.*

Internet Protocols

In 1969, the U.S. Department of Defense's Advanced Research and Projects Authority (DARPA) funded the development of the Internet Protocol (IP) as a research project. The current Internet succeeded the original network that they developed, known as ARPANET, in 1984. At that time, hundreds of organizations, several of them commercial, were actively participating in the worldwide network.

IP networks are covered in great detail on the exam. Make sure you know everything, inside and out, within the scope of IP networking. You can find more information about IP in Chapter 10.

IP's key functionality is connecting software-addressed hosts and the routing of packets throughout an internetwork. The current version of IP widely deployed on the Internet is defined in Request for Comments (RFC) 791, and the updated version, IPv6, is defined in RFC 1883. The next few sections cover the protocols and specifications that are encompassed within the IP protocol stack, shown in Figure 6.6.

Address Resolution Protocol

The Address Resolution Protocol (ARP) is a method for determining a host's Ethernet address based on its IP address. The sender broadcasts an ARP packet containing the IP address of another host and waits for it (or some other host) to send back its Ethernet address. Each host maintains an ARP cache of address translations to reduce delay and loading. ARP allows the Internet address to be independent of the Ethernet address, but it only works if all hosts support it. ARP is defined in RFC 826.

Reverse ARP

Reverse ARP, or RARP, is a protocol used by routers to determine the IP address of a host for which the router knows only the MAC address. Routers using RARP broadcast a packet containing the known MAC address; the host with that address returns its IP address.

Proxy ARP

Proxy ARP enables machines to reach devices connected to remote networks without specifying a default gateway. This can make the management of hosts

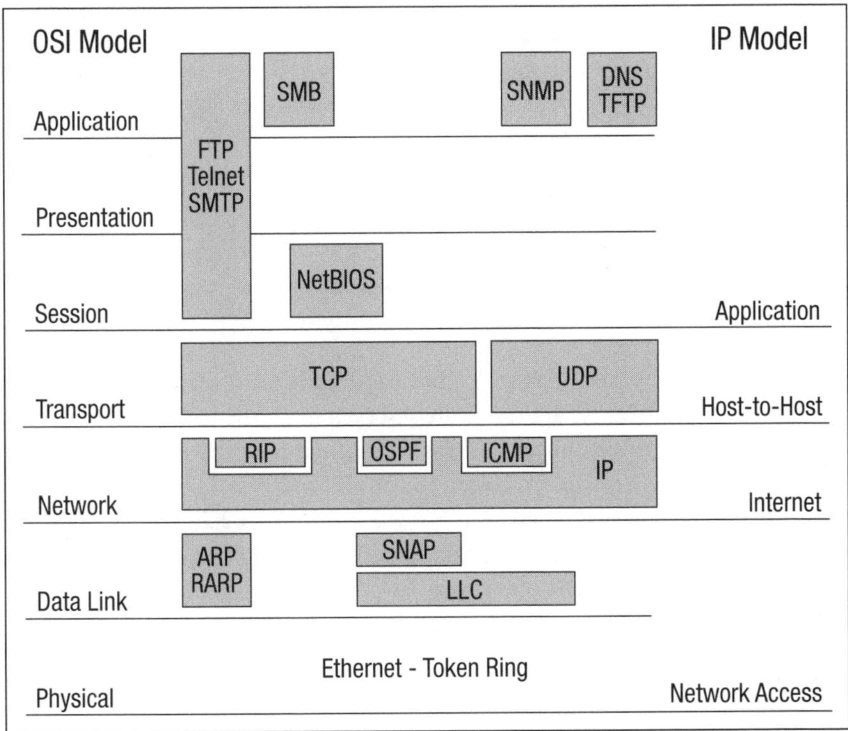

Figure 6.6 IP maps to a four-layer model rather than the seven-layer OSI model.

much simpler throughout an internetwork, but it will increase overall network traffic through the increased number of ARP requests on a subnet. Also, an examination of the host's ARP cache will reveal that all entries located off of the local subnet will be created, each mapped to the local default gateway's MAC address.

IP Host Addressing

Host addresses in a TCP/IP network are 32 bits in length and have both a network number and a host number. Valid addresses, therefore, range from 0.0.0.0 to 255.255.255.255—a total of about 4.3 billion addresses.

Classful Addresses

Classful addressing splits IP addresses into five separate ranges, Classes A, B, C, D, and E. The first few bits of the address indicate the class that the address belongs to, as listed in Table 6.3.

The bits are labeled in network order, so that the first bit is bit 0 and the last is bit 31, reading from left to right. Class A, B, and C addresses are used to define

Table 6.3 A listing of the classful address space.

Class	Prefix	Network Number	Host Number
A	0	1.0.0.0 – 127.0.0.0	Bits 8-31
B	10	128.0.0.0 – 191.255.0.0	Bits 16-31
C	110	192.0.0.0 – 223.255.255.0	Bits 25-31
D	1110	224.0.0.0 – 247.255.255.255	N/A
E	1111	248.0.0.0 – 255.255.255.255	N/A

individual hosts on the Internet. Class D addresses are reserved for multicast applications, and Class E addresses are reserved as experimental. Any address starting with 127 is a loopback address and should never be used for addressing outside of the host. A host number of all binary 1s indicates a directed broadcast over the specific network. For example, 10.10.2.255 would indicate a broadcast over the 10.10.2 network. In order to designate this network the node number is set to 0, thus the Class A address of 10.10.2.255 would have a network address of 10.0.0.0.

Class A, B, and C addresses are most commonly known for their availability for commercial use. Within these three classes, we can make a further distinction between public address space and private address space, which is unroutable by the Internet. Within class A, B, and C the following ranges, listed in Table 6.4, have been defined by RFC 1597 as private address space.

Classless Addresses

To make more efficient use of addresses in the Internet community, the original classes of IP addresses had to be segmented further than what was originally defined. Therefore, the Class A and B address spaces can be subnetted with several Class C masks to allow more IP network administrative domains. Classful addresses are still very common, especially in government institutions, but the introduction of Classless Interdomain Routing (CIDR) and variable-length subnet masks (VLSMs) has allowed for the more efficient division of address space to create arbitrarily sized networks.

Table 6.4 A listing of the private address space.

Network Number
10.0.0.0 – 10.255.255.255
172.16.0.0 – 172.31.255.255
192.168.0.0 – 192.168.255.255

Subnet Masks

When setting up each node with its IP address, you must also specify the subnet mask. This mask is used to specify which part of the address is the network number and which is the host number. This is accomplished by a logical bitwise AND between the subnet mask and the IP address. The result specifies the network number. For Class C, the subnet mask will always be 255.255.255.0; for Class B, the subnet mask will always be 255.255.0.0; and so on. The subnet mask becomes very important, and more complicated, when classless addressing is used. Variable length subnet masks allow classless subnet mask ranges for partitioning of IP networks. For instance, you could partition the IP address space of 200.100.50.0 between two remote offices. This could be accomplished by using a 255.255.255.252 subnet mask for a point-to-point link between the sites; while using a 255.255.255.192 subnet mask for a 50-user network at each endpoint on the connection.

IP Header Information

For a datagram to be forwarded by gateways or other intermediate systems, it must add its own header. The IP header, shown in Figure 6.7, is composed of several fields that provide an end-to-end transportation mechanism for any encapsulated data. The main fields in this header are the source and destination Internet addresses, the protocol number (listed in Table 6.5), and another checksum. The source Internet address is simply the address of your machine. The destination Internet address is the address of the remote machine. The protocol number tells IP at the other end to send the datagram using a specific protocol, such as Transmission Control Protocol (TCP), User Datagram Protocol (UDP), and so on. Although most IP traffic uses TCP, other protocols can use IP, so you have to tell IP which protocol to send the datagram to. Finally, the checksum allows IP at the other end to verify that the header wasn't damaged in transit.

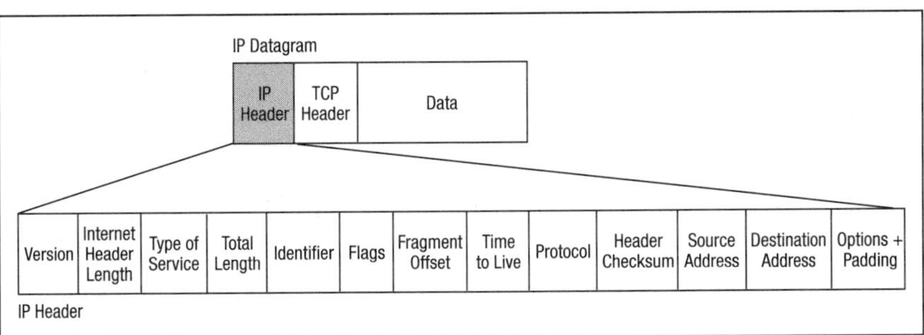

Figure 6.7 The IP header contains source and destination IP addresses and other valuable information.

Table 6.5 The values of the protocol field, as defined by RFC 1700.

Value	Name	Protocol
1	ICMP	Internet Control Messages Protocol
2	IGMP	Internet Group Management Protocol
4	IP	IP in IP
6	TCP	Transmission Control Protocol (TCP)
17	UDP	User Datagram Protocol (UDP)
45	IDRP	Interdomain Routing Protocol (IDRP)
88	IGRP	Internet Group Routing (Cisco Routing) Protocol

***Note:** TCP and IP have separate checksums. IP needs to be able to verify that the header didn't get damaged in transit, or it could send a message to the wrong place.*

Internet Control Message Protocol

The Internet Control Message Protocol (ICMP) provides error reporting, reachability testing, and flow control at the IP layer. The general troubleshooting tool that ICMP is most popular for is ping. ICMP echoes and replies can then be used to verify connectivity at the Network layer, thus segmenting the scope of network troubleshooting.

To avoid the infinite number of informational messages and the eventual collapse of the network, no ICMP messages are sent about ICMP messages.

Often overlooked, the ICMP Router Discovery Protocol (IRDP) can be a useful tool for system administrators because it eliminates the need to configure a default route on each host. IRDP is defined as a proposed standard in RFC 1256. Its sole function is to advertise IP addresses for routers on a LAN. Properly configured hosts can then use these addresses as default routes in their routing tables. If the default router ever changes, the hosts automatically adjust their default routes.

User Datagram Protocol

User Datagram Protocol (UDP) is a simple, datagram-oriented, connectionless Transport layer protocol. Each operation by a process produces exactly one UDP datagram. UDP sends these datagrams with no guarantee that they'll reach the destination correctly. The receiver verifies the checksum, and if the sending and receiving checksums do not match, the datagram is silently discarded and no error messages are generated. The checksum detects any modification of the UDP header (shown in Figure 6.8) or data anywhere between the sender and receiver. Therefore, the protocol is very simple.

Transmission Control Protocol

IP is not a very reliable protocol, so it needs to have a protocol over and above it in order to add some dependability to the transactions. The Transmission Control Protocol (TCP), outlined in RFC 761, is the protocol of choice when it comes to file transfers, which need to be reliable. Therefore, Hypertext Transfer Protocol (HTTP), Simple Mail Transport Protocol (SMTP), Post Office Protocol 3 (POP3), File Transfer Protocol (FTP), and so on all rely on TCP/IP for data transfer. TCP also provides reliability with checksums and sequencing, as well as flow control through request/reply mechanisms and sliding windows. These fields and others are shown within the TCP header in Figure 6.9.

Request/reply flow control is needed to pace the data transfer if one host begins transmitting to another at speeds higher than it can accept. For example, consider a host connected via 10Mbps Ethernet and another host connected at 28.8Kbps—the modem connection would quickly become overwhelmed without the capabilities of flow control.

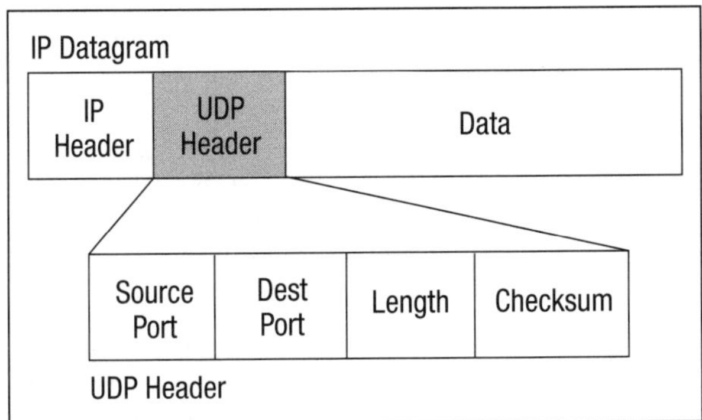

Figure 6.8 UDP header layout.

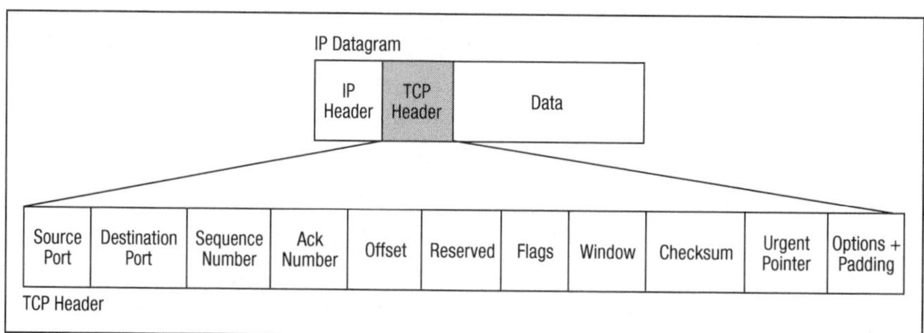

Figure 6.9 A snapshot of the fields inside of the TCP header.

The sliding window algorithms within TCP provide a method of flow control. The algorithm places a buffer between the application program and the network data flow. Data received from the network is placed in the buffer so that the application can then read at its own pace. As the application moves the data from the buffer, the space is freed and the buffer can then accept more data from the network. The window is the amount of data that can be read ahead—that is, the size of the buffer minus the amount of valid data currently stored in it. Window announcements are then used to inform the remote host of the current window size. If the window size falls to zero, a window announcement will be sent to the remote host, and it will stop sending data until a new announcement is received with a higher window size.

TCP/UDP Port Assignments

The source port and destination port fields within the TCP and UDP headers identify the points at which the upper-layer source and destination processes receive services. Table 6.6 lists the common TCP and UDP universally reserved port assignments. Check RFC 1700 for a complete list of port numbers.

NetBIOS

NetBIOS is an application environment that can use TCP/IP services for data transmission over a LAN. NetBIOS provides an interface specification for access to network services, such as name-to-address resolution and sending and receiving data. For communication between stations of a network, each station is given one or more names. These names are alphanumeric, 15 characters in length, and should be in ASCII format. When NetBIOS was originally designed and implemented, it was envisioned that it would only be required to run on individual LANs. Over time, computer networks have exploded in size and have overgrown the capabilities of NetBIOS. NetBIOS is quickly being replaced, and applications are now using the services of TCP/IP directly.

Table 6.6 Common TCP and UDP port assignments.

Decimal	Type	Description
7	UDP	Echo
20	TCP	FTP Data
21	TCP	FTP Control
23	TCP	Telnet
25	TCP	Simple Mail Transfer Protocol (SMTP)
53	UDP	Domain Name Server (DNS)
69	UDP	Trivial File Transfer Protocol (TFTP)
80	TCP	Hypertext Transfer Protocol (HTTP)
110	TCP	Post Office Protocol 3 (POP3)
119	TCP	Network News Transfer Protocol (NNTP)
137	UDP	NetBIOS Name Service
138	UDP	NetBIOS Datagram Service
139	UDP	NetBIOS Session Service
161	UDP	Simple Network Management Protocol (SNMP)
162	UDP	SNMP Traps

General IP Networking

In Figure 6.10, there are two separate Ethernet segments—each network has its own address space. If A wants to send a packet to E, it must first send the packet to router C, which can then forward the packet to E. This is accomplished by having A use ARP to determine router C's MAC address. Then the packets are sent to the local default gateway at Layer 2, but the data packet is still addressed to E's Network layer IP address. Router C will receive the packet destined to E and will perform a routing table lookup to locate the interface to send the data packet out of. In this case, the network is directly connected, and the packet will be forwarded out of router C's interface onto the 10.1.1.0 network. Host E will receive the packet and pass it up to the appropriate application.

NetWare Protocols

The following sections contain descriptions of the most prominent Novell NetWare protocols, starting at the Network layer. Physical and Data Link layer protocols are not discussed because these are usually hardware-specific, with the exception of the Logical Link Control (LLC) sublayer of the Data Link layer.

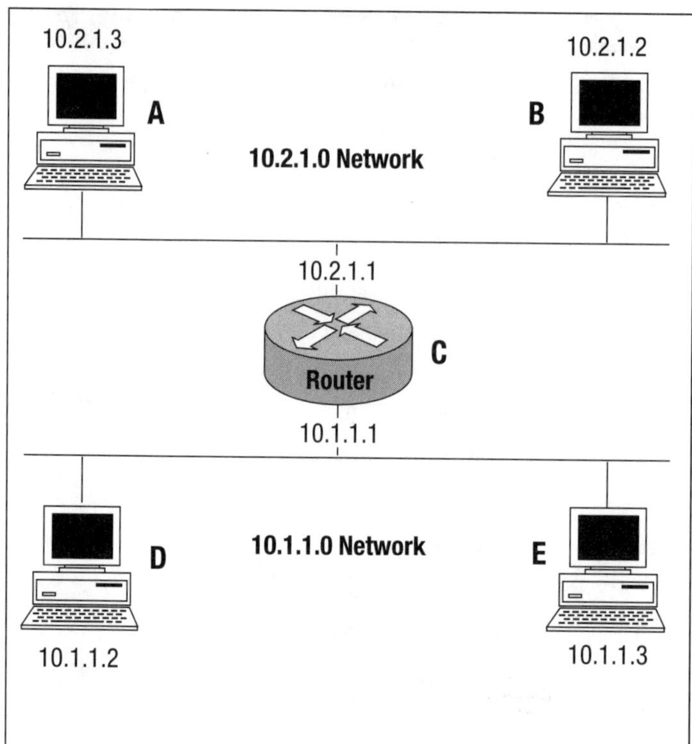

Figure 6.10 A depiction of several computers attached to two separate network segments connected via a router.

The LLC sublayer defines the guidelines for providing an error-free transmission path to the Network layer and service access points. The IEEE 802.2 standard is classified within the LLC sublayer. In contrast to the OSI model, the NetWare model consists of only five layers, as shown in Figure 6.11.

IPX Node Addressing

An IPX address consists of a 4-byte network number, a 6-byte node number, and a 2-byte socket number. The node number is usually the hardware address of the interface card and must be unique inside the particular IPX network. The network number must be the same for all nodes on a particular physical network segment. Socket numbers correspond to the particular service being accessed. Table 6.7 describes the contents of an IPX network address.

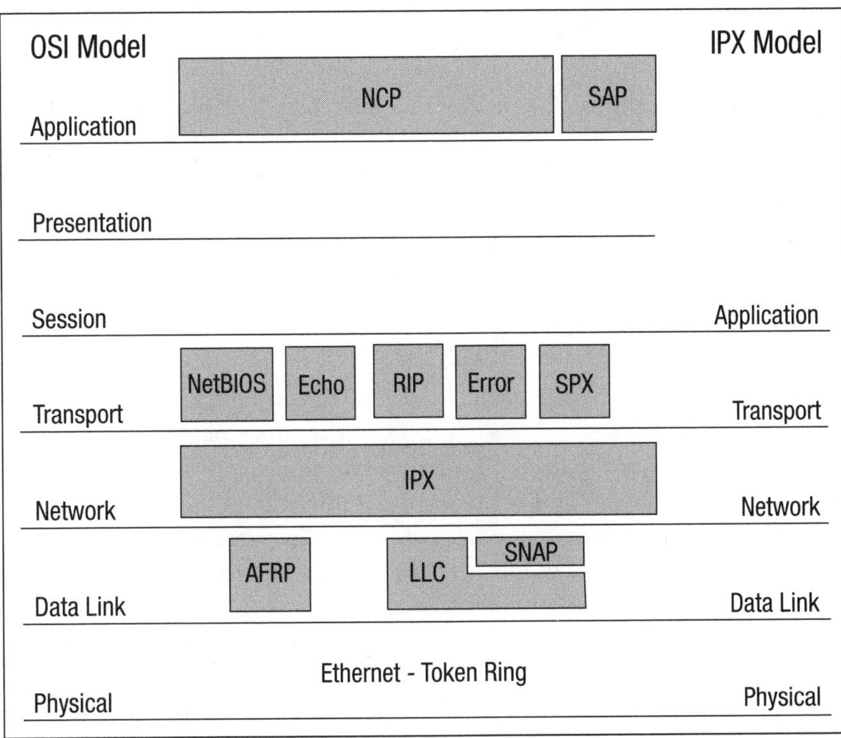

Figure 6.11 Novell's networking protocols follow a five-layer model rather than the seven-layer OSI model.

Table 6.7 IPX delivers packets using a 12-byte network address, which consists of three address components.

Component	Size	Description
Network address	4 bytes	Identifies a specific logical network or LAN on an IPX internetwork.
Node address	6 bytes	Identifies the individual nodes on the network. Server machines can have a logical node address.
Socket address	2 bytes	Identifies processes or functions within a node.

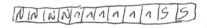

Internetwork Packet Exchange

Novell's IPX is a connectionless protocol derived from Xerox Network Systems (XNS). Therefore, IPX provides no guarantee that source host packets will be delivered to the target host. In addition, IPX packets, pictured in Figure 6.12, may arrive in any sequence. IPX depends on upper-layer protocols to ensure packet retransmission and sequencing. It also provides addressing and traffic-control functions for communications between end stations and NetWare servers.

Sequenced Packet Exchange

Sequenced Packet Exchange (SPX) provides end-to-end, guaranteed virtual connections similar to IP's Transmission Control Protocol (TCP). SPX verifies and acknowledges successful packet delivery to any network destination by requesting verification that the data was received. Within this verification must be a value that matches the value calculated from the data before transmission. Therefore, SPX ensures not only that the data packet arrived, but that it arrived intact. The SPX header is illustrated in Figure 6.13.

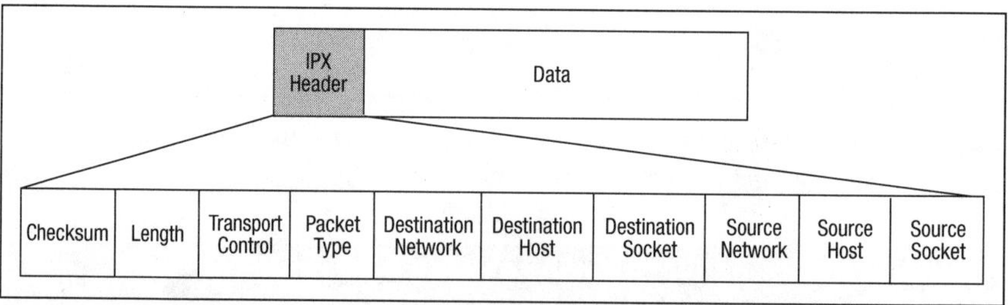

Figure 6.12 A detailed view of the fields within an IPX header.

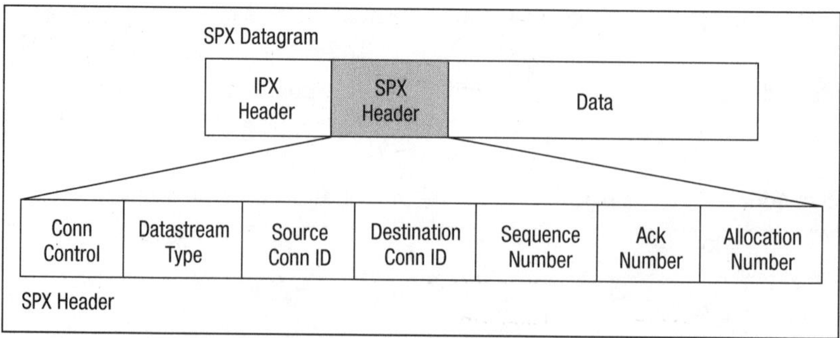

Figure 6.13 A look at the SPX header and the available fields.

Service Advertisement Protocol

The Service Advertisement Protocol (SAP) advertises available network services every 60 seconds through the direct use of IPX. Applications written by third parties may use SAP announcements to advertise the presence of their custom network services. Several common SAP types are listed in Table 6.8.

Clients using SAP announcements produce Get Nearest Server (GNS) broadcasts. The nearest NetWare file server responds with another SAP announcement. From this point on, the client can make a connection to the server and request resources. If a NetWare server is located on the local segment, it will respond to all GNS requests; otherwise, the local router will respond to all requests.

NetWare Core Protocol

The NetWare Core Protocol (NCP) uses SAP announcements to find file servers and print servers on the network. NetWare file and print services are implemented through NCP. Despite the name, the NetWare Core Protocol is a high-level protocol that's similar to Microsoft's Server Message Block (SMB) LAN Manager Protocol, which is used to share files and printers in a pure-Microsoft environment.

General IPX Networking

In Figure 6.14, nodes A and D are Novell NetWare workstations, nodes B and E are Novell NetWare servers, and node C is a router located between the two networks. The NetWare servers broadcast routing information and service advertisements to all nodes on the network segment using RIP and SAP announcements or NLSP. Router C forwards this information to its connected

Table 6.8 A list of common SAP types.

Decimal	Hex	Object Description
4	0004	File server
7	0007	Print server
32	0020	NetBIOS
567	0237	NMS IPX discovery
632	0278	Directory server (NetWare 4.x)
1659	067b	Microsoft Windows 95/98 file and print sharing
1660	067c	Microsoft Windows 95/98 file and print sharing
34238	85be	Cisco EIGRP

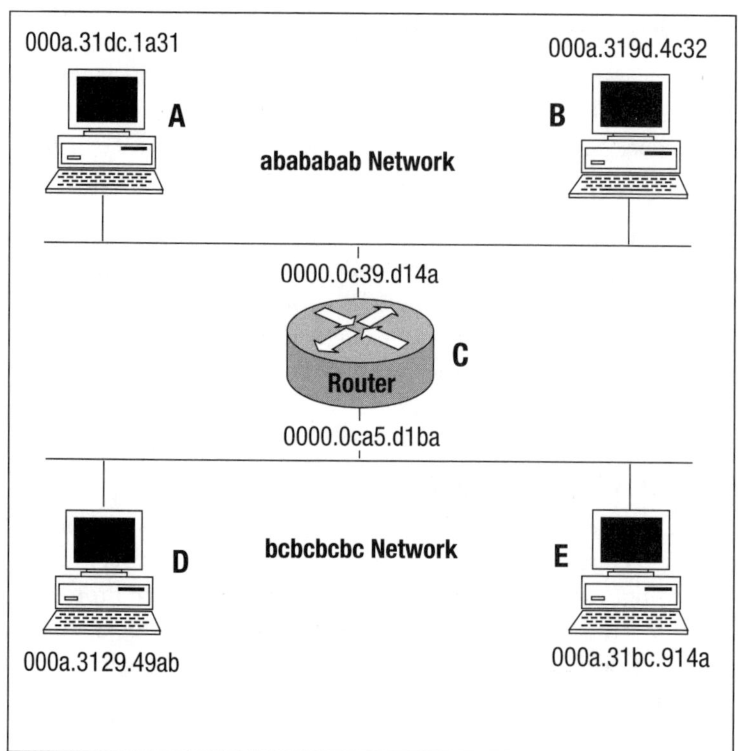

Figure 6.14 Two Novell IPX networks segmented by a router.

networks so that workstations are made aware of the addresses of all file and print servers available and servers are made aware of the routes to these other servers. To address a service running on a server, each server has its own internal network number, which is placed in the network number field of the IPX header.

For example, suppose A wants to access the file server E, whose internal network number is 5E1C0155. A would have been made aware of E's address through service advertisements broadcast by router C. To learn how to reach E, A broadcasts a routing request. Router C receives this request and returns its own hardware node number. A, therefore, addresses an IPX packet to E using E's internal network number, 5E1C0155, and node number, 000a.31bc.914a. The Ethernet header's destination address is Router C's node address: 0000.0c39.d14a. Router C then receives this IPX packet and observes that the IPX packet header's destination address is not its own, so it transmits the packet on network bcbcbcbc, knowing that E is on that network, using an Ethernet header destination address of 000a.31bc.914a.

AppleTalk Protocols

Networking for Apple computers is implemented through AppleTalk. Applications and processes can communicate across a single AppleTalk network or an AppleTalk internetwork, which is a number of interconnected AppleTalk networks. Using AppleTalk, applications and processes can transfer and exchange data and share resources. The AppleTalk networking system includes a number of protocols arranged in layers, which are collectively referred to as the *AppleTalk protocol stack*. Each of these protocols provides a set of functions and services that a protocol above it can use and build upon. As shown in Figure 6.15, the AppleTalk protocols adhere to the seven-layer OSI model.

Phase I Vs. Phase II Networks

AppleTalk Phase I networks do not support multiple zones and are only equipped to support the LocalTalk network protocol. Phase I networks were enhanced in 1989 to provide support for large Apple internetworks—Apple introduced AppleTalk Phase II networks, which support thousands of nodes, multiple AppleTalk zones on a network, and token ring networks. AppleTalk Phase II also implements more efficient routing techniques, such as the Routing Table Maintenance Protocol (RTMP), that improve performance in multiprotocol environments.

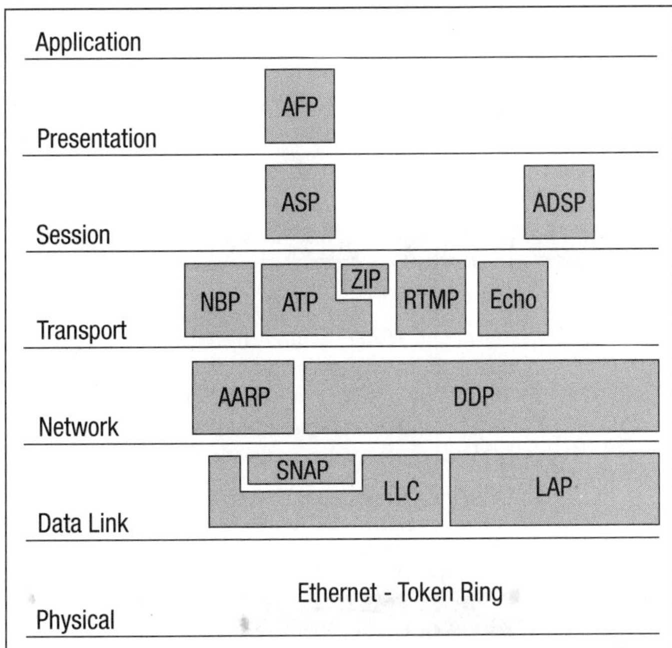

Figure 6.15 The AppleTalk protocols adhere to the seven-layer OSI model.

AppleTalk Node Addressing

Valid AppleTalk addresses contain a 16-bit network number and an 8-bit node number. Node addresses are reserved using a technique called *dynamic node assignment*, a mechanism that automatically assigns node numbers to hosts using an 8-bit node identification number (node ID). When an Apple client boots, it guesses its own node ID, either by a number stored in NVRAM or through AppleTalk Address Resolution Protocol (AARP) assigning a tentative AppleTalk address. AARP verifies whether the address is currently in use by broadcasting 10 AARP probe messages. If a node is already using the address, it will notify the station indicating the problem, and the Apple client will generate another random number and try again. This process is repeated until the initializing node is assigned a unique address, such as 4.101. Table 6.9 lists the different sections of an AppleTalk address.

Link Access Protocol

The Link Access Protocol (LAP), a Data Link layer protocol, receives packets of information and converts them into the proper signals for your network card. Several variations, based upon the network media, of the LAP exist:

- **LocalTalk LAP (LLAP)** Allows the LocalTalk hardware built into Macintosh computers to communicate on LocalTalk networks.
- **Ethernet LAP (ELAP)** Allows a Macintosh computer with an installed Ethernet network card to communicate with devices on AppleTalk networks.
- **Token ring LAP (TLAP)** Allows devices using token ring technology to communicate with devices on AppleTalk networks.

Table 6.9 AppleTalk addressing numbers and names.

Addressing Information	Description
Network number	A unique 16-bit number that identifies the network to which a node is connected. A single AppleTalk network can be either extended or nonextended. A range of network numbers defines an extended network.
Node ID	A unique 8-bit number that identifies a node on an AppleTalk network.
Socket number	A unique 8-bit number that identifies a socket. A maximum of 254 different socket numbers can be assigned in a node.

Datagram Delivery Protocol

The protocol implementations at the Physical and Data Link layers of the AppleTalk protocol stack provide node-to-node delivery of data on the Internet. Datagram Delivery Protocol (DDP) uses the node-to-node delivery services provided by the data link to send and receive data. DDP is central to the process of sending and receiving data across an AppleTalk internetwork. Regardless of which data link is being used and which higher-level protocols are processing data, all AppleTalk data is carried in the form of DDP packets, known as *datagrams*. DDP lets you send and receive data a packet at a time. If you use DDP, you must address each data packet to the socket for which it is intended. Fields included within the DDP header are shown in Figure 6.16.

Zone Information Protocol

The Zone Information Protocol (ZIP) provides applications and processes with access to zone names. A *zone* is a logical grouping of nodes in an AppleTalk internetwork, and each zone is identified by a name. A zone name is typically used to identify an affiliation between a group of nodes, such as a group of nodes belonging to a particular department within an organization. ZIP maintains the mapping of networks and the zones they include for all networks belonging to an AppleTalk internetwork. The ZIP header is shown in Figure 6.17.

Name Binding Protocol

The Name Binding Protocol (NBP) allows you to bind a name to the internal storage address for your host and then register this mapping so that other hosts can look it up. Applications can display NBP names to users and use addresses internally to locate entities. When you register your entity's name and address pair, NBP validates its uniqueness. The mapping of names to addresses that NBP maintains is important for AppleTalk because the addressing numbers

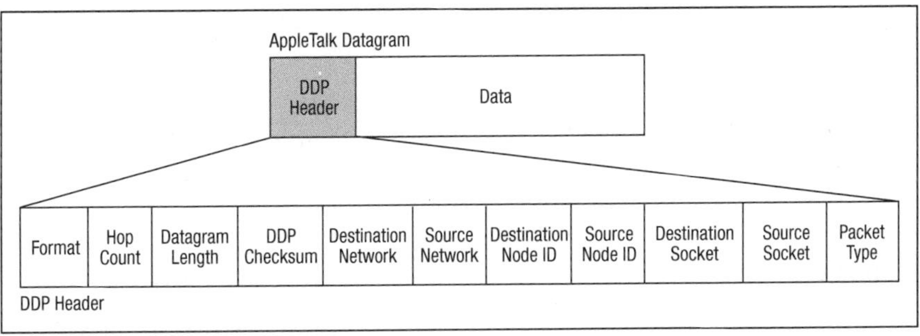

Figure 6.16 The DDP header.

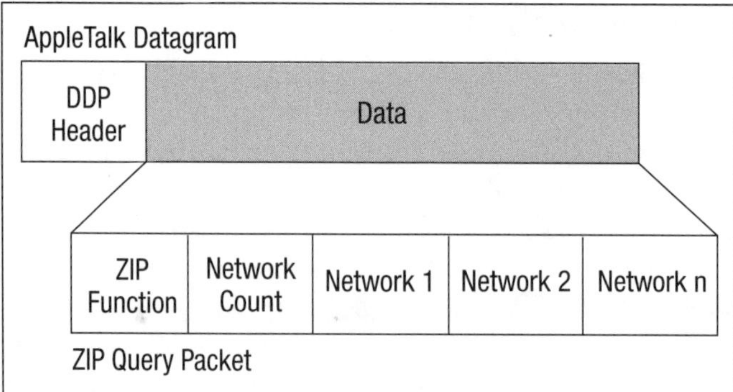

Figure 6.17 The ZIP header contains zone information.

that AppleTalk uses are not fixed. As described earlier, AppleTalk assigns an address dynamically to a node when the node first joins the network and whenever the node is rebooted. The mappings of addresses are sent within the NBP header, as shown in Figure 6.18.

AppleTalk Address Resolution Protocol

Network layer addresses are mapped to their corresponding MAC sublayer addresses via AppleTalk Address Resolution Protocol (AARP). AppleTalk nodes maintain this information in their address mapping table (AMT). The table is scanned each time a node sends a packet to an AppleTalk address. If a MAC sublayer address cannot be found, the sending node broadcasts an AARP request packet. When a node or router with the appropriate address responds, the address is entered into the requesting end station's AMT.

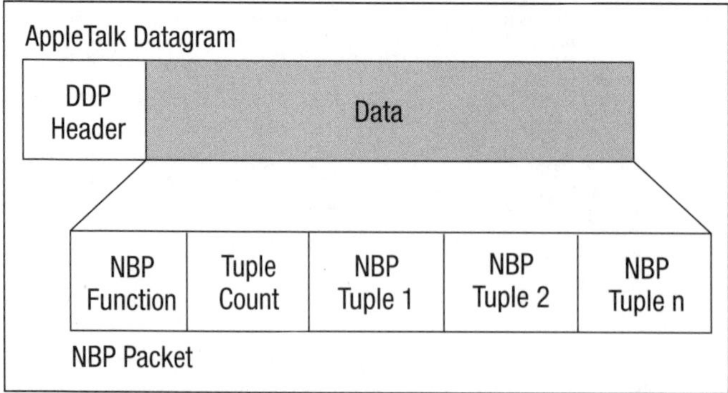

Figure 6.18 The NBP header contains name-to-address mappings.

AppleTalk Echo Protocol

The AppleTalk Echo Protocol (AEP) is an extremely simple protocol that generates packets that can be used to test the reachability of various network nodes. Implemented on socket number 4, the echoer listens for packets to be received. If a packet of the correct DDP type is received, the packet is determined to be an AEP packet, and a copy is returned to the sender.

AppleTalk Transaction Protocol

The AppleTalk Transaction Protocol (ATP) offers a simple, efficient means of transferring small amounts of data across a network. ATP ensures that data is delivered without error or packet loss through the use of transaction identifiers (TIDs), sequences, and control checksums. ATP provides the request/response transaction mechanisms on which the session-oriented services of the AppleTalk Session Protocol (ASP) are based. The ATP header is illustrated in Figure 6.19.

AppleTalk Session Protocol

The AppleTalk Session Protocol (ASP) allows one or more ASP workstation applications or processes to establish a session with the same server at the same time. To track communication from various sessions, ASP assigns a unique session identifier, referred to as a *session reference number*, to each session. The ASP workstation application always initiates the process of setting up a session and the communication across a session, and the ASP server replies to the commands it receives.

AppleTalk Data Stream Protocol

The AppleTalk Data Stream Protocol (ADSP) includes both session and transport services, and it's the most commonly used of the AppleTalk transport protocols. ADSP allows you to establish and maintain a connection between

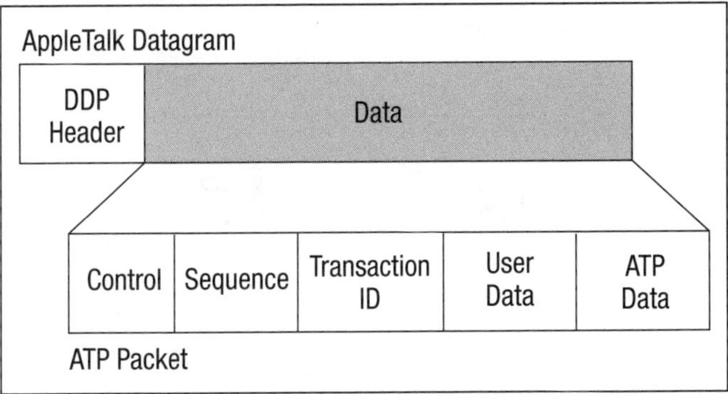

Figure 6.19 A look at the ATP header inside of an AppleTalk datagram.

two AppleTalk hosts and transfer data across this connection as a continuous stream. Because ADSP is a client of DDP, data that you transmit using ADSP is actually sent and received over the AppleTalk internetwork in packets. However, ADSP builds a session connection on top of the packet transfer services that DDP provides so that applications using ADSP can exchange data as a continuous stream.

AppleTalk Filing Protocol

The AppleTalk Filing Protocol (AFP) provides communication and data transmission between file servers and clients in an AppleShare network. AFP allows Macintosh users to share files by interacting directly with the NetWare file system on the same level as the NetWare Core Protocol (NCP).

General AppleTalk Networking

Device nodes are assembled into logical groups called *zones*, and each device can be in only one zone, whereas zones can span multiple AppleTalk network cable ranges, as shown in Figure 6.20. When a Macintosh user requests a service through the chooser, the client sends a ZIP request to the local router for

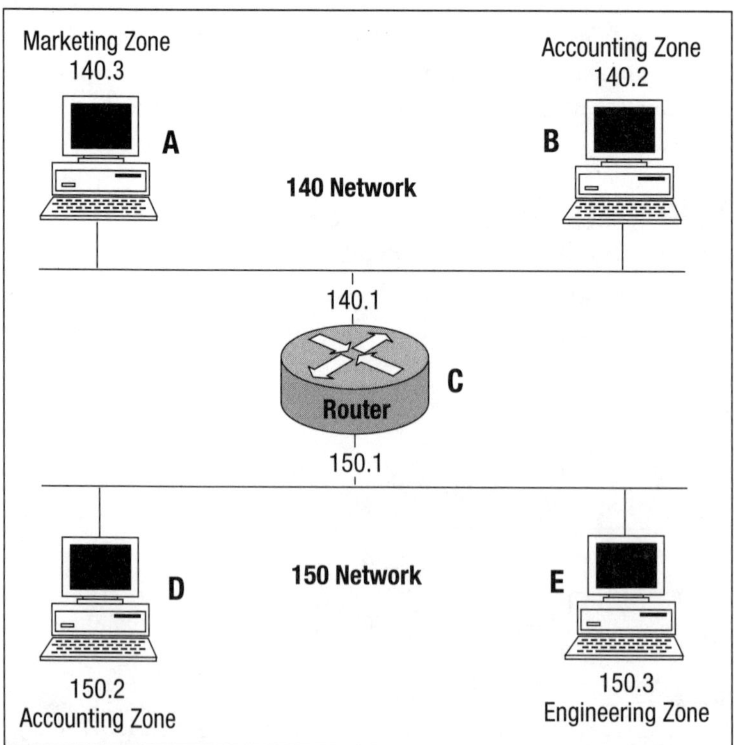

Figure 6.20 An AppleTalk network segmented by a router.

a list of available zones. The chooser window is then propagated with the list of zones received by the ZIP reply. The client may now select a zone from within the chooser, and an NBP request to locate AppleTalk servers will be sent to all routers within the cable groups of the selected zone. The routers send a multicast to all devices that match the type selected, and the devices individually reply to the originating client. The user can now select the preferred service through the chooser window.

Routing Protocols

Network routes are required to transport data across subnetworks. The routes can be statically entered by engineers or dynamically created by routing protocols. Small networks may be able to withstand statically entered routing information, but any network that might increase in size in the foreseeable future should use dynamically updating routing protocols.

In determining the best route to a destination, different routing protocols use a number of different measurements. These measurements are called *metrics*. Each routing protocol uses one or more metrics to calculate the best route to a particular destination. The most common metrics include path length (hop count), reliability, delay, bandwidth, load, and the cost of a link. One or more metrics are used by a routing protocol in order to calculate the quality of a route.

Another major difference between routing protocols is how they handle updating each other with current information. There are many methods of accomplishing this. Given these major differences, there are two primary categories for dynamic routing protocols: distance-vector and link-state.

Distance-Vector Routing Protocols

Distance-vector routing protocols require each router to send a copy of its entire routing table to each of its neighbors. For each route received by a router, the lowest cost path is selected and placed into the router's local routing table and then readvertised to its directly connected neighbors. Common additions to this protocol to prevent routing loops include split horizon, poison reverse, triggered updates, and hold-down timers.

Split Horizon

Routing loops can potentially destroy an internetwork and propagate for a very long time. The split horizon rule originates from the fact that sending routes out of an interface from which they are received is not useful. Therefore, if a router receives an update that network X is available on interface Y, the router will not propagate the route to X through router's Y interface. Distance-vector protocols send routing updates according to this rule.

Split Horizon With Poison Reverse

Although split horizon should prevent routing loops between routers that have formed adjacencies, larger routing loops may still occur. Poison reverse allows networks to be advertised with a hop count set to infinity (16 hops for RIP), thus causing the route to be immediately flushed from all routing tables. This will quickly stop two-node routing loops and substantially reduce the possibility of large network routing loops.

Hold-Down Timers

Hold-downs can be used to prevent regular routing updates from being sent that may inaccurately reinstate a route that's invalid. Hold-downs indicate to routers to stop any changes that could affect recently modified routes for a period of time. This hold-down time is usually just greater than the amount of time that's required for updating the entire network of a routing change.

Triggered Updates

Triggered updates allow routers to inform their neighbors immediately of routing changes, without waiting for the regular update periods. This will cause a wave of routing updates to be propagated throughout a network. These updates will not arrive at every device simultaneously; therefore, a device that has not yet received the update could release a regular update message indicating that an invalid route is good. Hold-down timers are used to prevent this from happening.

Link-State Routing Protocols

Link-state routing protocols issue flood notifications to all routers during link-up or link-down state changes—this is called a *link-state advertisement (LSA)*. All the routers will then note the change and recompute their routing tables accordingly. This method is more reliable and less bandwidth-intensive than distance-vector routing protocols, due to the low probability of routing loops occurring. Also, complete routing tables are not transferred every 60 seconds, only individual route updates. The downfall is that this is more complex and more CPU-intensive than distance-vector routing protocols.

Routing Information Protocol

The Routing Information Protocol (RIP) provides dynamic routing by replicating routing tables between all routers within a RIP domain. Configuring a RIP system requires little effort beyond setting path costs. Another advantage is that RIP uses an algorithm that does not impose serious computation or storage requirements on hosts or routers. RIP is available for both IP and IPX.

IP Version

RIP is a distance-vector protocol that implements split horizon, poison reverse, hold-down timers, and triggered updates to prevent routing loops. RIP eliminates the need to manually create routing tables by enabling the embedded system to dynamically gather and supply gateway IP addresses that are needed for routing. With RIP, neighboring routers periodically exchange their entire routing tables and use timers, described in Table 6.10, to remove these routes from their tables. RIP uses a hop count as the metric of a path's cost; a path is limited to 15 hops. RIP version 1 is a classful protocol, whereas version 2, described in RFC 2453, allows classless addressing.

IPX Version

Novell's implementation of RIP uses the lowest network delay metric, called *tick-based routing*, and then the hop count to determine the best path over a network; a tick is measured in 1/18 of a second increments. When multiple tick-based, equal least-cost routes exist, the best path is selected as the one with the lowest hop count. If both routes are still equal, RIP will randomly select the best path.

Internet Gateway Routing Protocol

Cisco's proprietary routing protocol, the Internet Gateway Routing Protocol (IGRP), was released as an upgrade from the only other existing routing protocol at the time—RIP. IGRP alleviates RIP's small hop count limit of 15—it provides up to 255 hops. IGRP also includes a more diverse routing metric than hop count. It uses a combination of internetwork delay, bandwidth, link reliability, and load to choose the best available path. This enhancement would mandate the selection of a T1 link over a 128Kbps ISDN connection, whereas RIP cannot differentiate between the two and would load balance across the

Table 6.10 RIP sends updates at predefined intervals to peer routers.

Variable	Default Time	Description
Update timer	30 seconds	Frequency of routing updates
Invalid timer	90 seconds	Time to wait for updates before declaring a route invalid
Hold-down timer	100 seconds	Time to wait before announcing route updates
Flush timer	270 seconds	Time before route is flushed from routing table

two links. IGRP also uses split horizon, poison reverse, hold-downs, and triggered updates, as described earlier in the "Distance-Vector Routing Protocols" section. Poison reverse updates implemented in IGRP are set if a routing metric has increased by a factor of 1.1 or greater, due to the concept that increases in routing metrics generally indicate routing loops. IGRP implements a number of timers, similar to RIP, as shown in Table 6.11.

Border Gateway Protocol

The Border Gateway Protocol version 4 (BGP-4) is used to provide routing information between Internet routing domains. BGP-4 is a distance-vector protocol, like RIP, but unlike almost all other distance-vector protocols, BGP-4 tables store the actual route to the destination network. BGP-4 also supports policy-based routing, which allows a network's administrator to create routing policies based on political, security, or economic issues rather than technical ones. The transition to BGP-4 was largely sparked due to its support of CIDR and the rapidly decreasing number of available IP addresses. BGP-4 is described in RFC 1771.

Enhanced IGRP

Cisco introduced an enhanced version of IGRP, called EIGRP, that combines the advantages of link-state protocols with the advantages of distance-vector protocols. EIGRP incorporates the diffusing update algorithm (DUAL), which is the algorithm used to obtain loop freedom at every instant throughout a route computation. This allows all routers involved in a topology change to synchronize at the same time. Routers that are not affected by topology changes are not involved in the recomputation. The convergence time with DUAL rivals that of any other existing routing protocol.

EIGRP does not make periodic updates; instead, it sends partial updates only when the metric for a route changes, similar to OSPF. Propagation of partial

Table 6.11 IGRP maintains a number of timers.

Variable	Default Time	Description
Update timer	90 seconds	Frequency of routing updates
Invalid timer	270 seconds	Time to wait for updates before declaring a route invalid
Hold-down timer	280 seconds	Time to wait before announcing route updates
Flush timer	630 seconds	Time before route is flushed from routing table

updates is restricted so that only those routers that need the information are updated. As a result of these two capabilities, EIGRP consumes less bandwidth than IGRP. EIGRP also includes multiple-protocol support, including AppleTalk, IP, and Novell IPX/SPX. Each implementation also redistributes route entries between EIGRP and the major routing protocols of each of the Network layer protocols.

Routing Table Maintenance Protocol

The Routing Table Maintenance Protocol (RTMP) is a distance-vector protocol that's very similar to RIP. RTMP is the process by which AppleTalk routers propagate the local network information from one router to the rest of the routers on a network. RTMP packets are broadcast packets containing the entire routing table that every router on a network segment sends out every ten seconds. Also like RIP, RTMP uses hop count as the metric for route preference, and it only allows for up to 15 hops—any more than 15 hops and AppleTalk routing will fail.

Open Shortest Path First

The Open Shortest Path First (OSPF) protocol, as defined in RFC 1131, is a link-state routing algorithm that's more robust than RIP, converges faster, requires less network bandwidth, and is better able to scale to larger networks. OSPF is based on the Dijkstra algorithm to perform the Shortest Path First (SPF) calculations, which helps OSPF address some of RIP's shortcomings, and is therefore better suited for modern, large, dynamic networks. For example, in contrast to RIP sending the entire routing table from router to router every 30 seconds, OSPF sends its link-state information every 30 minutes. OSPF can get away with this, because OSPF routers also send each other small update messages, known as link-state advertisements (LSAs), whenever they detect a change in the network. OSPF version 2, described in RFC 1583, is rapidly replacing RIP on the Internet. When OSPF routers exchange updates that reflect changes in the network, they quickly converge on a new representation of the topology.

NetWare Link-State Protocol

The NetWare Link-State Protocol (NLSP) is a link-state routing protocol that has several distinct advantages over its distance-vector counterpart, RIP. NLSP does not send SAP updates every 60 seconds; instead, SAP updates are sent the same way as routing updates—only when changes occur. This feature alone can reduce IPX/SPX traffic overhead by as much as 20 percent or more.

AppleTalk Update-Based Routing Protocol

AppleTalk Update-Based Routing Protocol (AURP) operates like RTMP, but it's a link-state protocol, so it only sends updates when changes occur within the network. AURP also provides AppleTalk protocol tunneling within TCP/IP and update-based routing within these tunnels.

IP Multicast Routing

Most high-level network protocols, such as TCP and UDP, only provide a unicast transmission service. That is, nodes of the network only have the ability to send to one other node at a time. IP multicasts provide a single stream of data to a multicast router, and then the stream is split accordingly to groups that have subscribed to the multicast session. IP multicasting provides organizations with significant cost and bandwidth savings over traditional systems for voice, video, and data. A comparison between multicast and unicast streams is shown in Figure 6.21.

Distance-Vector Multicast Routing Protocol

Distance-Vector Multicast Routing Protocol (DVMRP) maintains topological knowledge of available multicast routes via a distance-vector routing protocol, upon which it implements a multicast forwarding algorithm called *truncated reverse path broadcasting*. DVMRP suffers from the well-known scaling problems of any distance-vector routing protocol. Table 6.11 lists the multicast addresses used for DVMRP routers as well as several other addresses used by routing protocols.

Protocol Independent Multicast

Protocol Independent Multicast (PIM) is an efficient and robust multicast routing protocol that's capable of supporting thousands of groups and different

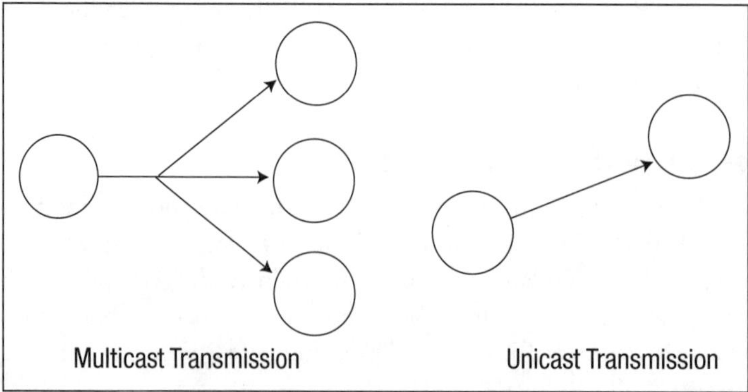

Figure 6.21 A comparison between unicast and multicast.

types of multicast applications. The protocol independence of PIM allows it to support all major underlying Layer 2 subnetwork technologies. The objective is to develop a standard multicast routing protocol that can provide scalable interdomain multicast routing across the Internet. The PIM routing protocol explicitly defines two different multicast distribution scenarios—dense mode and sparse mode:

- **Dense mode** In dense mode, multicast group members are densely located—that is, many or most of the routers in the area need to be involved in routing multicast datagrams. Dense mode PIM uses reverse path forwarding and looks a lot like DVMRP.
- **Sparse mode** In sparse mode, the number of routers with attached group members is small with respect to the total number of routers; group members are widely dispersed, and a defined rendezvous point is used for the multicast senders to send data to and for the receivers to receive data from. Sparse mode PIM assumes that no hosts want the multicast traffic unless they specifically ask for it.

Internet Group Management Protocol

The Internet Group Management Protocol (IGMP) was primarily designed for hosts on multiaccess networks to inform locally attached routers of their group membership information. Multicast routers listen for these messages and then can exchange group membership information with other multicast routers. This allows distribution trees to be formed to deliver multicast datagrams; in the case of PIM, sparse mode traffic will be delivered to the host.

Practice Questions

Question 1

Which Internet protocol can hosts use to discover all locally attached router addresses?

- ❍ a. IGMP
- ❍ b. UDP
- ❍ c. IRDP
- ❍ d. ICMP

The correct answer is c. ICMP Router Discovery Protocol (IRDP) provides router information to locally attached hosts. The Internet Gateway Management Protocol (IGMP) subscribes hosts to local multicast sessions. Therefore, answer a is incorrect. UDP, or User Datagram Protocol, is the Transport layer connectionless protocol for IP. Therefore, answer b is also incorrect. The Internet Control Message Protocol, or ICMP, provides end-to-end control messages at the Network layer. Therefore, answer d is incorrect.

Question 2

ICMP provides which basic IP management functions? [Choose the two best answers]

- ❑ a. Reachability testing to verify host connectivity, using Echo and Echo Reply
- ❑ b. Reliable transport methods, using sequencing and sliding window techniques
- ❑ c. MAC address resolution and caching
- ❑ d. Flow control, using Source Quench messages

The correct answers are a and d. ICMP is the Network layer management protocol for IP and, within that realm, does provide reachability information and flow control. The Transmission Control Protocol (TCP) provides a reliable transport protocol for IP. Therefore, answer b is incorrect. MAC address resolution and caching is provided by the Address Resolution Protocol (ARP). Therefore, answer c is also incorrect.

Question 3

Which of the following methods might eventually cause a routing loop? [Choose the two best answers]

❑ a. Split horizon has been disabled on an interface.

❑ b. IP multicast routing is not enabled.

❑ c. Hold-down timers are not consistent across the network.

❑ d. Invalid IP addresses are assigned on the network.

The correct answers are a and c. Split horizon prevents networks from being advertised out of the same interface in which they were received. The only time it may be a viable option to disable split horizon is when a map statement is used—for example, in a frame relay network with multiple logical connections on a single interface but only one physical connection. If hold-down timers are not consistent across a network, this will cause route flapping, which might lead to routers in a RIP environment to not converge quickly enough, thus leading to routing loops. IP multicasting has no effect on general routing principals. Therefore, answer b is incorrect. Invalid IP address assignments on a network might lead to address conflicts and hosts becoming unreachable, but routing loops will not propagate due to this. Therefore, answer d is incorrect.

Question 4

What's the protocol number for ICMP within the IP header?

❍ a. 88

❍ b. 17

❍ c. 1

❍ d. 45

The correct answer is c. ICMP messages are sent with the protocol set to 1. The other protocol assignments are as follows: 88 is IGRP, 17 is UDP, and 45 is IDRP. Therefore, answers a, b, and d are incorrect.

Question 5

Which of the following protocols provides routing for AppleTalk?

❍ a. ATP

❍ b. ZIP

❍ c. AARP

❍ d. RTMP

The correct answer is d. Routing Table Maintenance Protocol (RTMP) provides distance-vector routing for the AppleTalk Phase II protocol. ATP, or AppleTalk Transaction Protocol, provides a reliable transport mechanism for AppleTalk applications. Therefore, answer a is incorrect. The Zone Information Protocol (ZIP) relays AppleTalk zone information between the routers and hosts. Therefore, answer b is incorrect. The AppleTalk Address Resolution Protocol (AARP) provides functionality that's similar to what ARP does for IP (software-address-to-hardware-address resolution). Therefore, answer c is incorrect.

Question 6

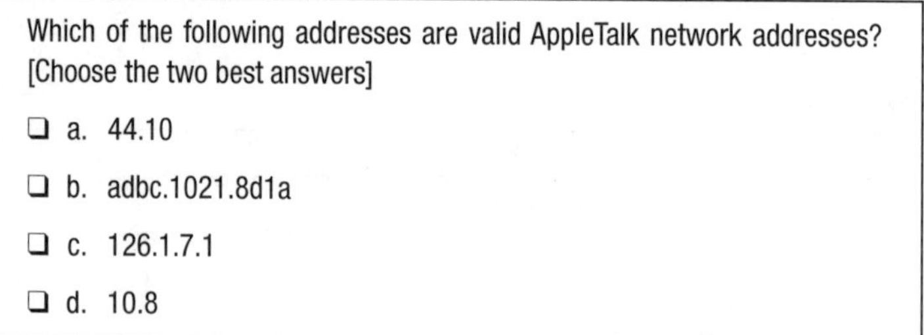

Which of the following addresses are valid AppleTalk network addresses? [Choose the two best answers]

❏ a. 44.10

❏ b. adbc.1021.8d1a

❏ c. 126.1.7.1

❏ d. 10.8

The correct answers are a and d. AppleTalk addresses are composed of a 16-bit network address and an 8-bit node address, which makes all values between 1 and 255 available for the network address and all values between 1 and 253 available for the node address (the node address values 254 and 255 are reserved). adbc.1021.8d1a is the MAC address of a host and does not fall within the viable range of addressing as defined by AppleTalk. Therefore, answer b is incorrect. 126.1.7.1 is a 32-bit IP address. Therefore, answer c is incorrect.

Question 7

Which of the following addresses are valid IPX network addresses? [Choose the two best answers]

- ❑ a. 8.34
- ❑ b. DEADBEEF.0000.0d31.3a1e
- ❑ c. 001c.3a1d.43d1
- ❑ d. E.001c.3a1d.43d1

The correct answers are b and d. Valid IPX network addresses contain up to eight hexadecimal values for the network address with the host's MAC address appended to it. 8.34 is an acceptable AppleTalk address, and 001c.3a1d.43d1 is an acceptable MAC address without the network address. Therefore, answers a and c are incorrect.

Question 8

Which of the following addresses is a valid IP network address?

- ❍ a. 127.0.0.1
- ❍ b. 224.0.0.4
- ❍ c. 192.168.12.255
- ❍ d. 138.3.25.37

The correct answer is d. A valid node address cannot be the network number, a broadcast address, a loopback address, or a multicast address. Therefore, answers a, b, and c are incorrect.

Question 9

Which type of protocol requires the application to request retransmission of lost or corrupt packets?

- ❍ a. Connection oriented
- ❍ b. Connectionless
- ❍ c. TCP
- ❍ d. SPX

The correct answer is b. Connectionless protocols do not provide any guarantee of delivery to higher layers, such as applications; therefore, any error-recovery mechanisms must reside within the application. Connection-oriented protocols, such as TCP and SPX, have their own methods for guaranteeing packet delivery to upper applications. Therefore, answers a, c, and d are incorrect.

Question 10

Disjointed, classful subnet masks can be utilized by which of the following routing protocols? [Choose the two best answers]

❑ a. IGRP

❑ b. EIGRP

❑ c. OSPF

❑ d. RIP

The correct answers are b and c. EIGRP and OSPF support variable-length subnet masks (VLSMs) and classless address space. Neither IGRP nor RIP support VLSMs or classless addressing. Therefore, answers a and d are incorrect.

Question 11

What's the standard SAP type for Novell Print Servers?

❍ a. 1

❍ b. 4

❍ c. 7

❍ d. 24

The correct answer is c. The other SAP types characterize the following:

- SAP type 1 defines the user.
- SAP type 4 defines a file server.
- SAP type 24 defines a remote bridge server.

Therefore, answers a, b, and d are incorrect.

Question 12

Which of the following addresses is an IP multicast address?

- ❍ a. 10.0.0.255
- ❍ b. 172.168.0.1
- ❍ c. 224.0.0.5
- ❍ d. 255.255.255.255

The correct answer is c. The multicast address space spans the IP address range from 224.0.0.0 to 239.255.255.255. Any address ending with 255 is a broadcast to all hosts on the local network segment, and an address consisting of all 255 values is an all-networks, all-hosts broadcast. Therefore, answers a and d are incorrect. 172.168.0.1 is a standard host address. Therefore, answer b is also incorrect.

Question 13

If a protocol analyzer records a high number of collisions on a FDDI network, which of the following scenarios is most likely the cause?

- ❍ a. A network card has failed and is now generating invalid signaling.
- ❍ b. The current utilization of the network is greater than 30 percent.
- ❍ c. Collisions cannot occur on a token-based network; therefore, the protocol analyzer is reporting incorrect data.

The correct answer is c. Collisions can never occur on a token-based network. If a network card were to fail in a FDDI network, a wrapping of the network would take place, thus alleviating the problem. Token-passing networks allow only one workstation to transmit at any given time. Therefore, answer a is incorrect. The usual 30 percent maximum thresholds seen by 10Mbps Ethernet networks is not valid. Therefore, answer b is also incorrect.

Question 14

Which of the following routing protocols are categorized as link-state protocols? [Choose the two best answers]

- ❑ a. RIP
- ❑ b. OSPF
- ❑ c. NLSP
- ❑ d. EIGRP

The correct answers are b and c. RIP and EIGRP are considered distance-vector routing protocols, whereas OSPF and NLSP are link-state protocols. Therefore, answers a and d are incorrect. The functionality of EIGRP is very similar to that of link-state protocols such as OSPF, but the same distance-vector technology found in IGRP is used in EIGRP, and the underlying distance information remains unchanged.

Question 15

After analyzing a packet with a protocol analyzer, you notice that the Ethernet type/length field within the frame is set to 0×809b. Which Ethernet frame type is this?

- ❍ a. Ethernet SNAP
- ❍ b. 802.3 (Raw)
- ❍ c. 802.2
- ❍ d. Ethernet II

The correct answer is d. As listed in the section on Ethernet, if the ethertype/length field is greater than the hexadecimal value of 0×05DC, the frame is interpreted as Ethernet II. Therefore, answers a, b, and c are incorrect.

Question 16

Which TCP/IP reference model layer performs functions similar to the OSI model's Network layer?

❍ a. Transport layer

❍ b. Protocol layer

❍ c. Internet layer

❍ d. Presentation layer

The correct answer is c. The Internet layer provides the services of IP, which correspond directly to the Network layer in the OSI reference model. The Transport layer maps to the Host-to-Host layer in TCP/IP. Therefore, answer a is incorrect. The Protocol and Presentation layers do not exist within the TCP/IP model. Therefore, answers b and d are also incorrect.

Need To Know More?

Burk, Robin, Martin Bligh, Thomas Lee, et al. *TCP/IP Blueprints*. Sams Publishing. Indianapolis, IN, 1997. ISBN 0-672-31055-4. An excellent resource for learning about the protocols within IPv4 and the new version of IP (IPv6).

Malamud, Carl. *Analyzing Novell Networks*. Van Nostrand Reinhold. New York, NY, 1992. ISBN 0-442-00364-1. Malamud details how to analyze NetWare environments from the perspective of using a protocol analyzer. This book can really help in troubleshooting IPX networks.

Sidhu, Gursharan S., Richard F. Andrews, and Alan B. Oppenheimer. *Inside AppleTalk, 2nd Edition*. Addison-Wesley. Reading, MA, 1990. ISBN 0-201-55021-0. For a comprehensive look inside the AppleTalk protocol, there's no better reference than this one.

Check out the information within the Internetworking Technologies Overview section at Cisco Connection Online (CCO) (**www.cisco.com/univercd/home/home.htm**). Click on the Internetworking Technologies Overview link to find detailed areas for virtually everything described in this chapter. Browse through this information if you faltered in any area covered in this chapter.

Physical And Data Link Diagnostics

Terms you'll need to understand:

- √ Cisco Discovery Protocol (CDP)
- √ Cisco controller bus (cBus)
- √ Ethernet
- √ Serial
- √ Token ring
- √ Fiber Distributed Data Interface (FDDI)
- √ Asynchronous Transfer Mode (ATM)
- √ Frame relay

Techniques you'll need to master:

- √ Understanding information displayed by **show** commands
- √ Using **debug** commands to verify physical and data link operation
- √ Troubleshooting Ethernet networks
- √ Verifying and identifying interface status messages

Approximately 80 percent of all network failures are the result of Physical layer errors. You might think that statement is quite bold, but a network going down after being properly configured is a rarity unless it's due to a hardware failure. This chapter describes an assortment of Cisco IOS commands that can be used to identify whether a problem resides at the Physical layer, Data Link layer, or one of the higher layers of the OSI reference model. A few of the common Physical and Data Link layer scenarios incurred while troubleshooting internetworks follow these descriptions.

Cisco IOS Commands

Troubleshooting Physical and Data Link layer issues can be very troublesome, because sporadic, inconsistent failures occur while hardware is malfunctioning, and Layer 2 addresses are very difficult to use in pinpointing a culprit. Within the Cisco IOS are several commands that can help you identify hardware failures, physical connections, and Data Link layer protocol functionality.

The **show** Commands

Narrowing the scope of a problem is one of the first steps in troubleshooting. Starting at the bottom of the OSI model first and checking for a loss of physical connectivity or hardware failures can greatly reduce the time spent diagnosing a problem. Checking the appropriate hardware and interfaces that are in the path of the failing network components can accomplish this verification process. Within the Cisco IOS are several **show** commands that can display the integrity of the various types of hardware as well as the appropriate data link connectivity statistics to confirm correct operation. Table 7.1 lists and describes all the most commonly used **show** commands.

show cdp neighbors

The Cisco Discovery Protocol (CDP) is a proprietary protocol that allows configuration and Network layer information to be propagated within a Layer 2 protocol among Cisco devices. Listing 7.1 displays the output of the **show cdp neighbors** command performed on a Cisco device that's directly connected to three other Cisco devices.

Listing 7.1 Neighboring Cisco devices can be seen with the **show cdp neighbors** command.

```
Router>show cdp neighbors
Capability Codes: R - Router, T - Trans Bridge,
                  B - Source Route Bridge, S - Switch, H - Host,
                  I - IGMP, r - Repeater
```

```
Device ID      Local Intrfce   Holdtme  Capability  Platform   Port ID
014595(congo)    Fas 1/1         125       T B S    WS-C5500   3/2
017843(falcon)  ATM3/0/0.3       125       T B S    WS-C5000   3/1
Panther         ATM3/0/0.6       146         R      RSP2       Eth 5
```

The **Device ID** field contains the serial number, MAC address, or hostname of the attached Cisco device. The **Local Intrfce** describes the locally connected interface name and number. The **Holdtme** field shows the amount of time before the entry expires from the CDP table. The **Capability** field lists all the potential functions of the remotely attached device, as listed in the **Capability Codes** section. The **Platform** and **Port ID** fields detail the Cisco device type and the remotely connected interface, respectively. This information can be incredibly useful for troubleshooting links and verifying the configurations of higher-layer protocols through Data Link layer transmissions.

Table 7.1 Several show commands can be used to pinpoint physical and data link problems.

Command	Description
show cdp neighbors	Displays proprietary Cisco, Data Link, and Network layer information on all directly connected Cisco devices
show controllers	Displays memory handling and device error values
show controllers cbus	Displays information about the internal Cisco controller Bus interface card
show controllers fddi	Displays low-level information about the FDDIs processor
show controllers serial	Displays low-level information about the serial interfaces
show controllers token	Displays low-level information about the token ring interface processor
show interfaces	Displays the current status of and general statistics for all configured interfaces
show interfaces atm	Displays information about ATM interfaces
show interfaces ethernet	Displays information about Ethernet interfaces
show interfaces fddi	Displays information about FDDIs
show interfaces serial	Displays information about serial interfaces
show interfaces tokenring	Displays information about token ring interfaces

show controllers

You can display low-level information about memory management and error counters for every interface processor installed by issuing the **show controllers** command. The output from this command will vary depending on the card and microcode loaded, which is generally proprietary and only useful to technical support personnel. This command actually displays a compilation of the results of the commands listed in the next few sections.

The information displayed by the **show controllers** commands is generally useful for diagnostic tasks performed by technical support personnel only, but can also be used to verify correct configuration settings within the IOS itself. Note that the information retrieved by the following commands has a dependence on the version of the microcode loaded, so the command results may vary.

show controllers cbus

You can display descriptions of the current Cisco controller bus (cBus) card and the interfaces installed in the controller bus slots by issuing the **show controllers cbus** command. This information can be used to retrieve the name and controller type of every card, as well as the slot number each card is inserted into and the microcode version installed. The command also shows the capabilities of the card and reports controller-related failures. The output from the **show controllers cbus** command is displayed in Listing 7.2.

Listing 7.2 The **show controllers cbus** command can be used to verify installed line cards.

```
Router>show controllers cbus
MEMD at 40000000, 2097152 bytes (unused 960, recarves 1, lost 0)
  [Output omitted from listing]
  slot0: FIP, hw 2.9, sw 20.02, ccb 5800FF20, cmdq 48000080,
    vps 4096, software loaded from system
    Fddi0/0, addr 00e0.12ab.4900 (bia 00e0.12ab.4900)
      gfreeq 48000160, lfreeq 48000178 (4512 bytes)
      rxlo 4, rxhi 78, rxcurr 4, maxrxcurr 30
      txq 48000180, txacc 48000082 (value 78), txlimit 78
  slot1: FEIP, hw 2.1, sw 20.06, ccb 5800FF30, cmdq 48000088,
    vps 8192, software loaded from system
  FLASH ROM version 160.5, VPLD version 2.2
    FastEthernet1/0, addr 00e0.12ab.4920 (bia 00e0.12ab.4920)
      gfreeq 48000140, lfreeq 48000188 (1536 bytes)
```

```
    rxlo 4, rxhi 129, rxcurr 4, maxrxcurr 27
    txq 48000190, txacc 4800008A (value 79), txlimit 79
  FastEthernet1/1, addr 00e0.12ab.4921 (bia 00e0.12ab.4921)
    gfreeq 48000140, lfreeq 48000198 (1536 bytes)
    rxlo 4, rxhi 129, rxcurr 2, maxrxcurr 7
    txq 480001A0, txacc 48000092 (value 79), txlimit 79
```

This command can be useful when you need to verify that line modules are correctly seen by the cBus interface card and to check for the correct microcode version for certain configuration considerations. If the microcode component is not installed correctly, or if any of the pins are bent during installation, the ciscoBus card will not recognize that a card exists in that cBus slot and it will not be displayed by this command.

show controllers fddi

The **show controllers fddi** command details the internal state of the microchips, and information the system uses for bridging and routing that's specific to the FDDIs line card. The first line of the display shows the FDDIs hardware and microcode version, as displayed in Listing 7.3. The last line of output indicates how many times the specific physical interface, **Phy-A** or **Phy-B**, encountered a physical error on the fiber-optic cable.

Listing 7.3 The **show controllers fddi** command displays process information about the FDDI module.

```
Router>show controllers fddi
Fddi0/0 - hardware version 2.9, microcode version 20.2
  Phy-A registers:
    cr0 4, cr1 0, cr2 0, status 6, cr3 0
  Phy-B registers:
    cr0 4, cr1 4, cr2 0, status 3, cr3 0
  FORMAC registers:
    irdtlb  7275, irdtneg F85E, irdthtt EF14, irdmir  FFFF0BDC
    irdtrth F867, irdtmax FBC5, irdtvxt 8585, irdstmc 0810
    irdmode 6A21, irdimsk E000, irdstat 8060, irdtpri 0000
FIP registers
 ccbptr:         7F90  event_ptr:    0088  cmdreg:          0006
 [Output omitted from listing]
 unused:         0000  bogus_claim:  0000  robin:           0007
 Total LEM: phy-a 200, phy-b 56
```

This information can be used to verify that the line card is installed properly as well as whether the hardware and microcode versions support certain IOS configurations. An increase in Total Link Error Monitor (Total LEM) events may foreshadow a failing fiber-optic cable or interface.

show controllers serial

The **show controllers serial** command displays information about serial line cards and can be used to verify correct installation and configured parameters. The **show controllers serial** command displays the type of cable installed, any line errors that have occurred, and the values of several internal hardware logic variables. The output from the **show controllers serial** command is shown in Listing 7.4.

Listing 7.4 Use the **show controllers serial** command to identify the data terminal equipment (DTE) or data communications equipment (DCE).

```
Router>show controllers serial
MK5 unit 0, NIM slot 0, NIM type code 7, NIM version 1
idb = 0x4A58, driver structure at 0x4796E0, regaddr = 0x8000300
IB at 0x6006E60: mode=0x0108, local_addr=0, remote_addr=0
N1=1524, N2=1, scaler=100, T1=1000, T3=2000, TP=1
buffer size 1524
DTE V.35 serial cable attached
RX ring with 2 entries at 0x06EC0 : RLEN=5, Rxhead 20
00 pak=0x47DBD4  ds=0x60187E4 status=80 max_size=1524 pak_size=64
01 pak=0x47A0DC  ds=0x6008EB8 status=80 max_size=1524 pak_size=78
[Output omitted from listing]
bad_frames=0, frmrs=0, T1_timeouts=0, rej_rxs=0, runts=0
0 missed datagrams, 0 overruns, 0 bad datagram encapsulations
0 user primitive errors, 0 provider primitives lost
0 unexpected provider primitives, 0 spurious primitive interrupts
0 memory errors, 0 transmitter underruns
mk5025 registers: csr0 = 0x0E00, csr1 = 0x0302, csr2 = 0x0700
                  csr3 = 0x6E60, csr4 = 0x0214, csr5 = 0x0008
```

This command can be used to troubleshoot serial cable connections. In this case, the serial interface is configured as the data terminal equipment (DTE). However, if the cable is reversed, the serial interface will be configured as the data communications equipment (DCE), which would be incorrect and will cause errors. Rising hardware and data link line errors can pinpoint a misconfigured or problematic interface prior to complete failure.

show controllers token

You can display a description of the current token ring interfaces by issuing the **show controllers token** command. The card type, microcode version, ring statistics, internal controller statistics, and the nearest available upstream neighbor (NAUN) information is also available, as shown in Listing 7.5.

Listing 7.5 The **show controllers token** command displays ring state information as well as hardware and microcode version information.

```
Router>show controllers token 4/1
Interface TokenRing4/1 state: up
  Data from IDB:
    Current MAC address: 0008.2a36.1a84,
    Burned in MAC address: 0008.2a36.1a84
    Group address: 80000000
    Functional address: 08000000, enables: CDP
    Ring mode: 0000, enables:

  Last Ring Status: none
    Stats: soft: 0/0, hard: 0/0, sig loss: 0/0, throttle: 0/0
           tx beacon: 0/0, wire fault 0/0, recovery: 0/0
           only station: 0/0, remote removal: 0/0
  Interface failures: 0

  Current operating mode:
    DTR concentrator
      MAC state: port open, station connected
      Mode: port
      Duplex: full
      Access protocol: TXI
      Ring speed: 16 Mbps
      Ring monitor role: Standby monitor

  Internal controller data:
    [Output omitted from listing]
    Internal controller soft error counts:
      Line errors: 0/0, Internal errors: 0/0
      Burst errors: 0/0, ARI/FCI errors: 0/0
      Abort errors: 0/0, Lost frame errors: 0/0
      Copy errors: 0/0, Receiver congestion: 0/0
      Token errors: 0/0, Frequency errors: 0/0
    Internal controller SMT state:
      Adapter MAC:     0008.2a36.1a84, Physical drop:     00000000
      NAUN address:    0008.2a36.1a44, NAUN drop:         00000000
      [Output omitted from listing]
```

The output first shows the number of soft and hard errors on the token ring itself—the first number being the number of soft errors since the command was last performed and the latter being the number since the last reboot. Also displayed in this section is the number of times this station was the only one on the ring and the number of times it has transmitted a beaconing frame. *Beaconing* is used to detect and attempt repair on network faults, such as signal loss on the wire. The configured duplex state and ring speed for the controller card are shown in the **Current operating mode** section. Within the **Internal controller data** section is more information about internal software errors, such as burst errors, which describe the number of times a signaling problem (such as noise or crosstalk) has occurred. The **Receiver congestion** statistic counts the number of times the station has not been able to keep up with the traffic bound for it. Also, within the **Internal controller SMT state** section, **NAUN address** describes the MAC address of the nearest upstream network station. This can help you learn about the ring's topology, which can then be used to isolate failures. All this information can be helpful when you're troubleshooting token ring failures, especially in combination with a protocol analyzer.

show interfaces

Information and statistics are available for each interface or all installed interfaces when you issue the **show interfaces** command. Individual interfaces could have information pertaining to only that type of interface, such as ring status for FDDI or virtual circuit status for Asynchronous Transfer Mode (ATM). Although the individual results may vary somewhat, each interface shares a few common informational descriptions. Listing 7.6 generalizes some of the commands' output and also displays the most commonly used statistical counters.

Listing 7.6 All **show interfaces** commands contain some similar characteristics.

```
<interface-name> is <physical-status>,
   line protocol is <datalink-status>
 Hardware is <hardware-type>, address is <mac-address>
   (bia <factory-mac-address>)
 MTU 1500 bytes, BW 10000 Kbit, DLY 1000 usec,
    rely 255/255, load 1/255
 Encapsulation <encapsulation-type>, loopback not set,
    keepalive set (10 sec)
 ARP type: ARPA, ARP Timeout 04:00:00
 Last input 2w0d, output 00:00:01, output hang never
 Last clearing of "show interface" counters never
 Queueing strategy: fifo
 Output queue 0/40, 0 drops; input queue 0/75, 146 drops
 30 second input rate 9000 bits/sec, 7 packets/sec
 30 second output rate 24000 bits/sec, 16 packets/sec
 1490379533 packets input, 75096157 bytes, 0 no buffer
 Received 0 broadcasts, 0 runts, 0 giants
 3 input errors, 0 CRC, 0 frame, 2 overrun, 0 ignored
 1251738156 packets output, 3838228792 bytes, 0 underruns
 62 output errors, 56250903 collisions, 3 interface resets
```

Variables such as the *<interface-name>*, *<physical-status>*, and *<datalink-status>*, as well as several other statistical counters, are described in detail in Table 7.2.

Table 7.2 Several of the variables shown here are displayed by most show interfaces commands.

Variable	Description
<interface-name>	This can be the media type and physical card/port of the interface, such as Ethernet1/1, or it can be in the form of **VLAN number**.
<physical-status>	Indicates whether the interface hardware is currently active and whether an administrator has taken it down. Disabled indicates that the router has received more than 5,000 errors in a keepalive interval (which is 10 seconds by default).
<datalink-status>	Indicates whether the software processes that handle the line protocol believe the interface is usable (that is, whether keepalives are successful) or whether it has been taken down by an administrator.
<hardware-type>	Displays the hardware type (for example, MCI Ethernet, SCI, cBus Ethernet) and address.
<mac-address>	Displays the MAC address configured on the interface.
<factory-mac-address>	Displays the burned-in address (BIA), which is the MAC address assigned to the interface at the factory.
MTU	Displays the maximum transmission unit (MTU) of the interface.
BW	Displays the bandwidth of the interface in kilobits per second.
Dly	Displays the delay of the interface in microseconds.
Rely	Displays the reliability of the interface as a fraction of 255 (255/255 is 100 percent reliability), calculated as an exponential average over 5 minutes.
Load	Displays the load on the interface as a fraction of 255 (255/255 is completely saturated), calculated as an exponential average over 5 minutes.
<encapsulation-type>	Displays the encapsulation method assigned to the interface.
ARP Type	Displays the frame's encapsulation type. Valid states are ARPA, SNAP, Novell-ether, and SAP.

(continued)

Table 7.2 Several of the variables shown here are displayed by most show interfaces commands (continued).

Variable	Description
ARP Timeout	Displays the amount of time entries stay within the ARP table.
Loopback	Indicates whether loopback is set.
Keepalives	Indicates whether keepalives are set.
Last Input/Output	Displays the amount of time since the last packet was successfully received by an interface.
Last Clearing	Displays the time at which the counters that measure cumulative statistics shown by this command were last reset to zero.
Input/Output Queues	Displays the number of packets in the output and input queues (each number is followed by a slash). These values are the maximum size of the queue and the number of packets dropped due to a full queue.
Input/Output Rates	Displays the average number of bits and packets transmitted per second in the last five minutes.
Packets Input	Displays the total number of error-free packets received by the interface.
No Buffer	Displays the number of received packets discarded because there was no buffer space in the main system.
Broadcasts	Displays the total number of broadcast or multicast packets received by the interface.
Runts	Displays the number of packets that were discarded because they were smaller than the medium's minimum packet size.
Giants	Displays the number of packets that were discarded because they exceeded the medium's maximum packet size.
Input Errors	Displays the total number of errors (including runts, giants, no buffer, CRC, frame, overrun, and ignored counts).
CRC	Displays the number of CRC errors on an interface.
Frame	Displays the number of packets received with CRC errors.
Overrun	Displays the number of times the receiver was unable to move data to a buffer because the input rate exceeded the receiver's ability.

(continued)

Table 7.2 Several of the variables shown here are displayed by most show interfaces commands (continued).

Variable	Description
Ignored	Displays the number of received packets ignored by the interface because the interface hardware was running low on internal buffers.
Packets Output	Displays the total number of messages transmitted by the interface.
Underruns	Displays the number of times the transmitter has run faster than the router could handle.
Output Errors	Displays the sum of all errors that prevented the final transmission of datagrams out of the interface being examined.
Collisions	Displays the number of messages retransmitted due to an Ethernet collision.
Interface Resets	Displays the number of times an interface has been completely reset. This can happen if packets queued for transmission were not sent within several seconds.

The information and counters displayed by the **show interfaces** commands are very useful for baselining the network and providing details about general network traffic. You'll find that these commands are used quite often in all aspects of networking, including troubleshooting.

Increasing error counters displayed by the **show interfaces** commands point to a failing device and prove helpful in troubleshooting a network. Here are a few of the more common error counters to watch for and what their diagnoses could be:

- **No Buffer Errors** Broadcast storms on Ethernet networks and bursts of noise on serial lines are often responsible for these events.
- **CRC Errors** These usually indicate noise or transmission problems on the LAN interface or the LAN bus itself. A high number of CRCs is usually the result of collisions or a station transmitting bad data.
- **Frame Errors** An increasing value is normally the result of collisions or a malfunctioning Ethernet device located on the LAN.

- **Ignored Errors** Broadcast storms and bursts of noise can cause this value to increase.
- **Collisions** This is usually the result of an overextended LAN due to the Ethernet or transceiver cable being too long, more than two repeaters appearing between stations, or too many cascaded multiport transceivers.
- **Interface Resets** On a serial line, this can be caused by a malfunctioning modem that's not supplying the transmit clock signal or by a cable problem. If the system notices that the carrier detect line of a serial interface is up but the line protocol is down, it periodically resets the interface in an effort to restart it. Interface resets can also occur when an interface is looped back or shut down.

show interfaces atm

Virtual circuit statistics, supported encapsulations, and the Network Service Access Point (NSAP) address can be displayed using the **show interfaces atm** command, as shown in Listing 7.7.

Listing 7.7 The **show interfaces atm** command displays the NSAP address and other useful information.

```
Router>show interfaces atm3/0/0
ATM3/0/0 is up, line protocol is up
  Hardware is cyBus ATM
  Description: External OC-3 Connection
  Internet address is 10.0.1.1/24
  MTU 9180 bytes, sub MTU 9180, BW 156250 Kbit, DLY 80 usec,
     rely 255/255, load 2/255
  NSAP address: 47.00058000570000000010FA00.235234319341.00
  Encapsulation ATM, loopback not set, keepalive not supported
  Encapsulation(s): AAL5, PVC mode
  512 TX buffers, 512 RX buffers,
  2048 maximum active VCs, 1024 VCs per VP, 567 current VCCs
  VC idle disconnect time: 300 seconds
  Signalling vc = 105, vpi = 0, vci = 5
  UNI Version = 3.1, Link Side = user
  Last input 00:00:00, output 00:00:00, output hang never
  Last clearing of "show interface" counters never
  Queueing strategy: fifo
  Output queue 0/40, 0 drops; input queue 1/75, 3754 drops
  30 second input rate 938000 bits/sec, 335 packets/sec
  30 second output rate 1342000 bits/sec, 314 packets/sec
  1490379533 packets input, 75096157 bytes, 0 no buffer
```

```
Received 0 broadcasts, 0 runts, 0 giants, 66 throttles
3 input errors, 0 CRC, 0 frame, 2 overrun, 0 ignored, 3 abort
1251738156 packets output, 3838228792 bytes, 0 underruns
```

Several of the informational and statistical variables are similar to other commands, but a few aren't shown in Listing 7.7 because they are only seen within ATM interfaces. These are referenced in Table 7.3.

Troubleshooting ATM can be very difficult, and protocol analyzers equipped to decode ATM protocols are very expensive. Using this **show** command can provide some insight into potential errors, such as faulty cabling or hardware failures, improperly configured signaling VCs, and incorrect NSAP address structures. ATM is a technology that once it has become operational, doesn't really fail. Therefore, if a failure does occur, a protocol analyzer is the only way to provide enough detail to diagnose the problem.

show interfaces ethernet

Information about Ethernet interfaces installed in the router can be displayed using the **show interfaces ethernet** command. This command, like other **show interfaces** commands, can be used to view interface statistics, but it also can be used to verify the Ethernet encapsulation type used on the interface. This can be very useful when you're troubleshooting incorrectly defined IPX encapsulations, which will be discussed further in Chapter 11. Listing 7.8 displays the output from the **show interfaces ethernet** command.

Table 7.3 Definitions of the ATM interface statistics.

Variable	Description
NSAP Address	The ATM switch prefix followed by the end station identifier (ESI).
Encapsulation(s)	The ATM encapsulation type. Valid states are AAL5, PVC, and SVC.
TX/RX buffers	The number of configured transmit/receive buffers.
Maximum VCs	The maximum number of virtual circuits supported.
Current VCs	The current number of virtual circuits.
VC Idle Disconnect	The time before a Virtual Circuit (VC) is labeled inactive and torn down.
Signalling	The VC and the Virtual Path Identifier/Virtual Circuit Identifier (VPI/VCI) pair associated with the signaling PVC.

Listing 7.8 The **show interfaces ethernet** command displays several statistics and encapsulation types for Ethernet interfaces.

```
Router>show interfaces ethernet4/3
Ethernet4/3 is up, line protocol is up
  Hardware is cxBus Ethernet, address is aa00.0400.2bbf
    (bia 00e0.3400.4883)
  Description: Marketing Department
  Internet address is 10.1.1.1/24
  MTU 1500 bytes, BW 10000 Kbit, DLY 1000 usec, rely 255/255,
    load 1/255
  Encapsulation ARPA, loopback not set, keepalive set (10 sec)
  ARP type: ARPA, ARP Timeout 04:00:00
  Last input 00:00:02, output 00:00:00, output hang never
  Last clearing of "show interface" counters never
  Queueing strategy: fifo
  Output queue 0/40, 0 drops; input queue 0/75, 29 drops
  30 second input rate 8000 bits/sec, 9 packets/sec
  30 second output rate 42000 bits/sec, 20 packets/sec
    144949313 packets input, 1420823097 bytes, 1 no buffer
    Received 172733 broadcasts, 43184 runts, 0 giants, 1 throttles
    384482 input errors, 34817 CRC, 304094 frame, 2387 overrun,
    0 ignored, 0 abort
    244901601 packets output, 517810397 bytes, 0 underruns
    42 output errors, 31946862 collisions, 3 interface resets
    0 babbles, 0 late collision, 0 deferred
    0 lost carrier, 0 no carrier
    0 output buffer failures, 0 output buffers swapped out
```

show interfaces fddi

To obtain more information about the interfaces, such as the state of the lines and protocol types, you can use the **show interfaces fddi** command to display statistics about each of the FDDI interfaces in the chassis. The highlighted lines in Listing 7.9 report the state of the two physical FDDI rings and the directly connected upstream and downstream neighbors.

Listing 7.9 The **show interfaces fddi** command describes the current state of the ring, the MAC addresses of the directly connected neighbors, and the token rotation time.

```
Router>show interfaces fddi0/0
Fddi0/0 is up, line protocol is up
  Hardware is cxBus FDDI, address is 00e0.3400.4800
    (bia 00e0.3400.4800)
  Description: FDDI Ring Two
  Internet address is 10.10.100.1/24
```

```
MTU 4470 bytes, BW 100000 Kbit, DLY 100 usec, rely 255/255,
  load 1/255
Encapsulation SNAP, loopback not set, keepalive not set
ARP type: SNAP, ARP Timeout 04:00:00
FDX supported, FDX enabled, FDX state is operation
Phy-A state is  active, neighbor is   B,
   cmt signal bits 008/20C, status ILS
Phy-B state is  active, neighbor is   A,
   cmt signal bits 20C/028, status ILS
ECM is in, CFM is thru, RMT is ring_op
Requested token rotation 5000 usec, negotiated 5000 usec
Upstream neighbor 1000.e150.bf7f,
   downstream neighbor 0800.2bb6.b8ce
Last input 00:00:12, output 00:00:13, output hang never
Last clearing of "show interface" counters never
Queueing strategy: fifo
Output queue 0/40, 0 drops; input queue 0/75, 0 drops
5 minute input rate 0 bits/sec, 0 packets/sec
5 minute output rate 0 bits/sec, 0 packets/sec
   62 packets input, 6024 bytes, 0 no buffer
   Received 18 broadcasts, 0 runts, 0 giants
   0 input errors, 0 CRC, 0 frame, 0 overrun, 0 ignored, 0 abort
   71 packets output, 4961 bytes, 0 underruns
   0 output errors, 0 collisions, 0 interface resets
   0 output buffer failures, 0 output buffers swapped out
   3 transitions, 0 traces,  100 claims, 0 beacon
```

This information can be useful to troubleshoot FDDI ring failures and/or frequent ring transitions. The MAC addresses of the upstream and downstream neighbors can be used to identify the next computer in the FDDI ring and potentially pinpoint ring failures. Table 7.4 provides descriptions and possible states of the information provided by initiating the command.

Table 7.4 Definitions of FDDI interface statistics.

Variable	Description
FDX	Displays whether full duplex operation is supported. Valid states are supported and unsupported.
FDX State	Defines whether the negotiations have completed successfully. Valid states are idle (interface working but not full duplex), request (interface working but not full duplex), confirm (temporary state), and operation (FDX successful).
Phy-A/Phy-B state	Describes the state of the physical A port connection. Valid states are off, active, trace, connect, next, signal, join, verify, and break.

(continued)

Table 7.4 Definitions of FDDI interface statistics (continued).

Variable	Description
Neighbor	Displays the state of the directly connected neighbor. Valid states are A (CMT connection established with a dual attachment station [DAS]), S (CMT connection established with a single attachment station [SAS]), B (CMT connection established with a DAS or concentrator with secondary ring IN and primary OUT), M (CMT connection established with a concentrator), and unk (CMT connection not established).
Status	Displays the status of the fiber connection. Valid states are LSU (line state unknown), NLS (noise line state), MLS (master line state), ILS (idle line state), HLS (halt line state), QLS (quiet line state), ALS (active line state), and OVUF (buffer overflow).
ECM	Monitors the host configurations within station management transactions (SMT). Valid states are out (isolated from network), in (normal state), trace (attempting to localize a stuck beacon), leave (waiting for current connections to break before leaving network), path_test (testing internal paths), insert (optical bypass insertion), check (verifying optical bypass activity), and deinsert (optical bypass deinsertion).
CFM	Displays information about the current state of MAC connections. Valid states are isolated (MAC not attached), wrap_a (MAC attached to Phy-A only), wrap_b (MAC attached to Phy-B only), wrap_s (MAC attached to Phy-S [normal for SAS]), and thru (MAC attached to Phy-A and Phy-B [normal for DAS]).
RMT	Monitors ring management within SMT. Valid states are isolated (MAC is not participating in ring), non_op (MAC taking part in ring recovery), ring_op (MAC is taking part in operational ring), detect (ring is nonoperational), non_op_dup (MAC address is a duplicate and ring is not operational), ring_op_dup (MAC address is a duplicate and ring is operational), directed (MAC is sending beaconing frames), and trace (a trace has been initiated).
Requested Token rotation	Displays the token rotation time used by all stations on the ring.
Upstream/ Downstream neighbor	Displays the MAC address of the directly connected upstream and downstream neighbors. If the address is unknown, the MAC address 0000.f800.0000 will be displayed.

show interfaces serial

Serial interfaces encompass a wide range of utilities, but their most common use is for wide area networking. The **show interfaces serial** command displays different statistics based on the Data Link layer encapsulation method. If the High-Level Data Link Control (HDLC) protocol is chosen for the frame encapsulation type, the first **show** command within Listing 7.10 will be returned; if frame-relay is selected, the information displayed by the latter command will be returned.

Listing 7.10 The **show interfaces serial** command lists the encapsulation method, carrier transitions, and data terminal settings.

```
Router>show interfaces serial2/1
Serial2/1 is up, line protocol is up
  Hardware is cxBus Serial
  Description: External T-1 Connection
  Internet address is 10.5.5.1/30
  MTU 1500 bytes, BW 1544 Kbit, DLY 20000 usec, rely 255/255,
     load 1/255
  Encapsulation HDLC, loopback not set, keepalive set (10 sec)
  [Output omitted from listing]
     9 carrier transitions
     RTS up, CTS up, DTR up, DCD up, DSR up


Router>show interfaces serial0
Serial0 is up, line protocol is up
  Hardware is MK5025
  Internet address is 10.6.5.1/24
  MTU 1500 bytes, BW 256 Kbit, DLY 20000 usec,
     rely 255/255, load 1/255
  Encapsulation FRAME-RELAY, loopback not set,
      keepalive set (10 sec)
  LMI enq sent  355149, LMI stat recvd 355150,
     LMI upd recvd 26, DTE LMI up
  LMI enq recvd 0, LMI stat sent  0, LMI upd sent  0
  LMI DLCI 1023  LMI type is CISCO  frame relay DTE
  [Output omitted from listing]
```

The information displayed can be used to troubleshoot common serial line problems, such as verification of line transitions, correct autoconfiguration of the Local Management Interface (LMI) data link connection identifier (DLCI), and accurate receipt of LMI announcements. Table 7.5 describes the variables listed in the **show interfaces serial** command.

Table 7.5 Several statistics are displayed by the show interfaces serial command.

Variable	Description
Carrier transitions	The number of times the line status has gone up or down. Problems that can cause carrier transitions to increment include bad modems, poor serial cables, noisy lines, and unreliable LAN media.
RTS	Request To Send (RTS) signaling is up or down.
CTS	Clear To Send (CTS) signaling is up or down.
DTR	Data Terminal Ready (DTR) signaling is up or down.
DCD	Data Carrier Detect (DCD) signaling is up or down.
DSR	Data Set Ready (DSR) signaling is up or down.
LMI	Local Management Interface (LMI) information.
LMI DLCI	The LMI data link connection identifier (DLCI).
LMI Type	The LMI type used to send management information and updates.
Frame Relay DTE	Identifies the type of device connected. This can be data terminal equipment (DTE) or data communications equipment (DCE).

show interfaces tokenring

To verify that token ring interfaces are correctly configured and are in the appropriate line state, you can use the **show interfaces tokenring** command. The output of this command is shown in Listing 7.11.

Listing 7.11 The **show interfaces tokenring** command lists information about the configured ring speed and bridging capabilities.

```
Router> show interfaces tokenring1
TokenRing 1 is up, line protocol is up
  Hardware is 16/4 Token Ring,
     address is 0000.0c00.dc77 (bia 0000.0c00.dc77)
  Internet address is 10.1.20.20/24
  MTU 8136 bytes, BW 16000 Kbit,
     DLY 630 usec, rely 255/255, load 1/255
  Encapsulation SNAP, loopback not set, keepalive ste (10 sec)
  ARP type: SNAP, ARP Timeout 4:00:00
  Ring speed: 16 Mbps
  Single ring node, Source Route Bridging capable
  Group address: 0x00000000, Functional Address: 0x60840000
```

```
Last Input 0:00:01, output 0:00:01, output hang never
Output queue 0/40, 0 drops; input queue 0/75, 0 drops
Five minute input rate 0 bits/sec, 0 packets/sec
Five minute output rate 0 bits/sec, 0 no buffer
   1204582 packets input, 356785003 bytes, 0 no buffer
   Received 0 broadcasts, 0 runts, 0 giants
   0 input errors, 0 CRC, 0 frame, 0 overrun, 0 ignored, 0 abort
   992349 packets output, 351631825 bytes, 0 underruns
   0 output errors, 0 collisions, 0 interface resets, 0 restarts
   5 transitions
```

This command can be used to check for correctly configured ring speeds within the Cisco IOS and whether the node is capable of using source routing information fields (RIFs). The **Group Address** and **Functional Address** fields describe the ring's general multicast address and the current restricted multicast address, respectively.

The **debug** Commands

Interface debugging at the Physical and Data Link layers provides information that can be used to troubleshoot hardware failures and misconfigured frame encapsulations. Three primary **debug** commands can be used to troubleshoot ATM, FDDI, and serial interfaces, as listed in Table 7.6 and described in more detail in the following sections.

Ethernet and Fast Ethernet **debug** commands do exist, but they do not provide useful troubleshooting information that isn't already available through easier means, such as **show interfaces** commands.

Table 7.6 Some of the available Data Link layer debug commands.

Command	Description
debug atm sig-all	Displays information about ATM signaling events
debug fddi smt-packets	Displays information on station management (SMT) packets
debug serial interface	Displays information on serial line timing

debug atm sig-all

Use the **debug atm sig-all** command to monitor all switched virtual circuit (SVC) signaling events. The output from this command is shown in Listing 7.12.

Listing 7.12 Use the **debug atm sig-all** command to view ATM circuit initiation and teardown.

```
Router#debug atm sig-all
ATM Signalling All debugging is on

ATMSIG(I): 09 03 80 b3 c8 4d 80 00 06 08 80 00 02 81 a9
ATMSIG: index = 200, callref = 460, lic = TRUE
ATMSIG: i Rcvd Release msg in active State, length 6, call ref 460
ATMSIG: cause = temporary failure, vcnum = 939, call ref = 460
ATMAPI: notifying Release event to client
ATMSIG: state changed from Active to Release Indication
ATMAPI: RELEASE_COMP from ATMSIG Input (PC 0x607026F4)
ATMSIG: o Rel Complete msg, Release Indication state,
        length 20, call ref 460, pad 1
ATMSIG(O): 09 03 00 b3 c8 5a 80 00 06 08 80 00 02 80 9f 01
ATMSIG: state changed from Release Indication to Null
ATMSIG: removeHashEntry: svc remvd from hash table
```

This utility can be used to verify correct called and calling party addresses for each circuit initiation and teardown. If an invalid address is displayed, the end station will need to be checked for valid NSAP addresses. If any **cause** statements exist within the output, this indicates that the problem is downstream from this individual ATM client, and Private Network-Network Interface (PNNI) debugging may need to be enabled to continue troubleshooting (this topic is outside the scope of this book).

debug fddi smt-packets

You can issue the **debug fddi smt-packets** command to show information about FDDI station management (SMT) frames received by the router. The output from this command is shown in Listing 7.13.

Listing 7.13 The **debug fddi smt-packets** command can be used to display information about station management frames.

```
Router#debug fddi smt-packets
SMT packets debugging is on

SMT I: Fddi0/0, FC=NSA, DA=ffff.ffff.ffff, SA=0800.0945.3df1,
       class=NIF, type=Request, vers=1,
       station_id=1000.90a2.bc8f, len=40
```

```
- code 1, len 8 -- 0000100090A2BCE4
- code 2, len 4 -- 00010100
- code 3, len 4 -- 00002000
- code 200B, len 8 -- 0000000100000000
```

The information contained in an SMT packet can be used to troubleshoot neighbor identification, fault detection and reconfiguration, insertion and removal from the ring, and traffic statistics monitoring information.

debug serial interface

The **debug serial interface** command can be used to isolate timing problems or line problems at either end of the serial connection. The output can vary depending on the encapsulation type configured on the interface. Listing 7.14 displays the output from the command on an interface configured with HDLC.

Listing 7.14 Use the **debug serial interface** command to display information about connection failures.

```
Router#debug serial interface
Serial network interface debugging is on

Serial0: HDLC myseq 223858, mineseen 223858,
         yourseen 545874, line up
Serial0: HDLC myseq 223859, mineseen 223859,
         yourseen 545875, line up
Serial0: HDLC myseq 223860, mineseen 223859,
         yourseen 545876, line up
Serial0: HDLC myseq 223861, mineseen 223859,
         yourseen 545877, line up
Serial0: HDLC myseq 223862, mineseen 223859,
         yourseen 545878, line down
Serial0: HDLC myseq 223863, mineseen 223863,
         yourseen 545875, line up
```

The third through fifth **Serial0** statements show that the remote router is not seeing all the keepalive messages that the local router is sending. After the third attempt shown in the highlighted sequence, the line is brought down and reset. This can be very valuable in troubleshooting link integrity—in this case, it may pinpoint a malfunction with the service provider's network or increased line latency.

The clear counters Command

Interface counters may need to be cleared to verify link integrity or network failures or to retrieve a current reading of network traffic on an interface. The **clear counters** command can be used by itself to clear the statistics on all interfaces or on individual interfaces, as shown in Listing 7.15.

Listing 7.15 The **clear counters** command can be performed on all interfaces or individual interfaces.

```
Router#clear counters ?
  ATM           ATM interface
  Ethernet      IEEE 802.3
  FastEthernet  FastEthernet IEEE 802.3
  Fddi          ANSI X3T9.5
  Loopback      Loopback interface
  Null          Null interface
  Serial        Serial
  <cr>
```

Always remember to clear any counters used prior to troubleshooting any network connections. This will set a frame of reference for the statistics collected on the interface.

Common Physical And Data Link Issues

Because most network failures do occur at the lower two layers of the OSI model, your ability to troubleshoot common problems needs to be top notch. The following sections describe several scenarios related to Physical and Data Link layer issues and discuss how to potentially resolve these problems.

Scenario 1: Host Connectivity

Hosts are unable to access file services located on a remote server. After researching the situation, the network topology is found to be two routers, A and B, connected via their serial interfaces, whereas their Ethernet interfaces are connected to the workstations (as depicted in Figure 7.1). Therefore, clients connected behind Router A cannot access services behind Router B, and vice versa. Several attempts have been made to ping the remote workstations, but this also fails. The next step should be to verify the status of the Ethernet and serial interfaces and also to check for any misconfigurations.

Interface Status

After using the **ping** command to verify that Network layer connectivity is not functioning properly, you should check the physical router interfaces on the interim routers—in this case, Routers A and B. Four variations of the status

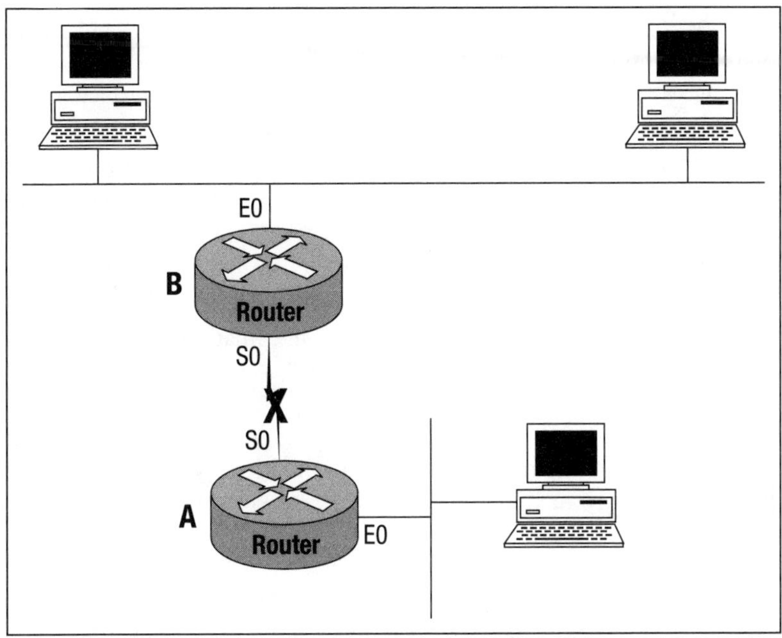

Figure 7.1 Hosts cannot access services across the serial link between Routers A and B.

information that can be listed by the **show interfaces** command exist; they're shown in Listing 7.16.

Listing 7.16 Four variations of the status information displayed by the **show interfaces** command can occur.

```
1.    Router>show interfaces Ethernet1/0
      Ethernet1/0 is administratively down, line protocol is down

2.    Router>show interfaces Ethernet1/0
      Ethernet1/0 is up, line protocol is up

3.    Router>show interfaces Ethernet1/0
      Ethernet1/0 is up, line protocol is down

4.    Router>show interfaces Ethernet1/0
      Ethernet1/0 is down, line protocol is down
```

An interface that's shown as being administratively down (the first variation listed) has been disabled using the **shutdown** configuration command. To remedy this problem, log into the router and enter the command **no shutdown** in the interface configuration mode. The second variation describes a healthy interface at the Physical and Data Link layers. This shows that problems associated with the interface are related to the Network layer and higher or, potentially, access list denials at any layer. The third type of interface status shows that the signal is being received on the wire, but the Data Link layer information is not being received correctly. This could be due to framing errors or an incorrect encapsulation type configured on a connected interface, as will be described in more detail later. The **show interfaces** command also can be used to verify the correct encapsulation type on each end of the link. The final variation describes a link that has lost physical connectivity or indicates that no signaling is being received on the wire. Incorrect termination, spliced wiring, or failing hardware could cause this type of failure.

You must be able to distinguish the scope of a network fault by examining an interface's status and identifying potential errors, such as the interface status, line errors, and FDDI ring faults.

Encapsulation Mismatch

Physical layer connectivity has been verified using the **show interfaces** command and using a line tester, but the Data Link layer is still shown to be in the *down* state. Most likely this is a problem due to disparate frame encapsulations being used on locally connected links. In this scenario, the encapsulation type across the serial interface may be different on each side of the link—HDLC could be used on one side, whereas the other is using Synchronous Data Link Control (SDLC). Several possibilities exist, including frame-relay and general WAN misconfigurations, which will be covered in Chapters 8 and 9.

Scenario 2: Transmission Media Failure

Users report that remote file and print services are currently unavailable and even network traffic to and from the default gateway is timing out. This could be due to one of several things. Researching the network topology, you find out that the users are connected to a Catalyst 5500 switch that then uplinks to a Cisco 7500 series router via an ATM interface card. After logging into the local router and performing the **show interfaces** command, you notice that the physical and data link status indicators both report *up*. The counters displayed by the command show several errors on the network, so you perform the **clear counters** command so that a pertinent frame of reference for the statistics is known. After performing several **show interfaces** commands in a row, you notice that the packets' input value is increasing and the packets' output is staying at zero; this is most likely a physical problem with the fiber. Placing an optical Time Domain Reflector (OTDR) on the fiber cable shows that a break has occurred 100 feet away. A new fiber is then patched to the existing 7500 router, and the users report that network connectivity has been restored.

When you're using fiber optics as a transmission medium, individual fibers are used to receive and transmit data. If the receive fiber becomes inactive, the line and protocol status will indicate a down state. However, if the transmit fiber becomes inactive, this notification will not take place locally. In a situation where fiber ends are not under the same administrative unit, you should make certain that your team will be notified in the event that the receiver becomes inactive.

Scenario 3: Network Latency

Network response times on the research LAN have increased dramatically over the past week, and the users are beginning to complain. The users are connected into a 10MB hub, which then connects into a Cisco 7500 router on interface Ethernet 4/1. Performing the **ping** command from the client workstation to a remote server results in only 60 percent of the packets responding. Checking the locally attached router interface using the **show interfaces ethernet 4/1** command reveals that the interface and protocols are up, but a high number of frame errors and collisions have occurred. Because the statistics have never been cleared, you issue the **clear counters ethernet 4/1** command. You then issue the **show interfaces** command again, and 2,300 collisions are shown to have occurred in the past 7 seconds.

After speaking with the other members in your team, you find out that a new network interface card was installed over the weekend in a server located on the research LAN. Disconnecting the server from the network decreases the response times for the users dramatically. What's more, after clearing the counters once again and performing the **show interfaces ethernet 4/1** command, you see that the collisions have stopped. The team then replaces the failed network card in the server and reconnects it to the rest of the network. All the users still report excellent response times. In this scenario, a new card was placed into a computer, but the card sent out corrupted packets and malformed broadcasts onto the LAN, thus causing network disruptions.

If a switch had been in place instead of the hub, the other hosts would have never seen the collisions. Hubs work at the Physical layer, essentially as repeaters, and switches work at Layer 2, only transmitting broadcasts to all ports.

Scenario 4: Device Discovery

As a consultant, you've been brought into a company to document its current network configurations and propose a three-year infrastructure upgrade plan. Documentation is unavailable, so you'll have to find out the network topology using any method possible. The networking manager does remember that the networking equipment is entirely Cisco and that CDP has been enabled on every device.

In order to discover the installed infrastructure equipment, you Telnet into the default gateway configured for your workstation and perform the **show cdp neighbors detail** command. This lists all the locally connected Cisco devices, the IOS versions, and all Network layer protocols running on each device. Spanning out from here, device to device, you can now map out the current infrastructure.

Once the topology map has been created, you need to acquire a baseline to evaluate the current load on the network. The **show interfaces** command can be performed hourly on each router and the statistics placed in a spreadsheet. This will give you a performance measure to identify the fundamental areas for future expansion.

Practice Questions

Question 1

Performing the **show interfaces Ethernet 0** command displays a high number of collisions. Which series of events should happen next?

❍ a. Remove all stations from the network and see whether the collisions stop.

❍ b. Reload the router and then shut down the interface and bring it back up.

❍ c. Clear all the Ethernet 0 counters using the **clear counters Ethernet 0** command and then perform the **show interfaces** command several times in succession.

❍ d. Perform the **show controllers ethernet** command to verify correct installation of the interface.

The correct answer is c. All statistics on the interface may have been accumulating for an extended period of time prior to any networking problems; therefore, the first thing to do is always to clear all the counters so that a frame of reference is developed. If you remove all stations from the network, regardless of the transmission medium, all collisions will eventually stop. Therefore, answer a is incorrect. Reloading the router may correct problems with configuration changes, but this is not the next step while troubleshooting increasing collisions. Therefore, answer b is incorrect. The interface is correctly installed because it's seeing network traffic. Therefore, answer d is incorrect

Question 2

Several new line cards have been installed into a Cisco 7500 series router. Which command can be used to verify that all modules have been properly inserted and are seen by the router?

❍ a. **show controllers cbus**

❍ b. **show controllers**

❍ c. **show interfaces**

❍ d. **show all**

The correct answer is a. The **show controllers cbus** command verifies all interface slots and identifies the type and microcode version of the installed module. **show controllers** will only show the details for individually installed controllers, without including the cBus. Therefore, answer b is incorrect. The **show interfaces** command can be used to verify that all interface types are available, but it will not display information as to whether the route processor card is correctly installed. Therefore, answer c is incorrect. **show all** is not available within the Cisco IOS. Therefore, answer d is incorrect

Question 3

Performing the **show interfaces ethernet 1/1** command returns the following results:

```
Router>show interfaces ethernet 1/1
Ethernet1/1 is up, line protocol is up
  Hardware is cxBus Ethernet, address is
     aa00.0400.2bbf
    (bia 00e0.3400.4883)
```

Which MAC address will the Ethernet 1/1 interface respond to?

- ❍ a. fbb2.0040.00aa
- ❍ b. 00e0.3400.4883
- ❍ c. 3884.0043.0e00
- ❍ d. aa00.0400.2bbf

The correct answer is d. The two MAC addresses displayed represent the MAC address that the interface will respond to and the MAC address that was physically imprinted by the manufacturer, in that order. fbb2.0040.00aa and 3884.0043.0e00 are the two MAC addresses listed in reverse. Therefore, answers a and c are incorrect. 00e0.3400.4883 is the burned-in address (BIA), not the software configured address. Therefore, answer b is also incorrect.

Question 4

The CFM state on the FDDI 0/0 interface is listed as **wrap_a** by the **show interfaces fddi 0/0** command. What does this state signify?

❍ a. The station is no longer connected to either of the FDDI rings.

❍ b. The station is now using the optical bypass switch.

❍ c. The station is currently only attached to the PHY-A ring.

❍ d. The station is attempting to diagnosis and resolve a failure using beaconing.

The correct answer is c. **wrap_a** identifies that the PHY-A ring has looped back upon itself because an error has occurred on the PHY-B port disabling it. The CFM state is labeled as isolated if both the PHY-A and PHY-B ports become disabled. Therefore, answer a is incorrect. The ECM field, not the CFM, describes the current state of the optical bypass. Therefore, answer b is incorrect. Answer d is incorrect because the RMT field describes this type of activity.

Question 5

A customer would like to implement a new feature within a new version of Cisco IOS. After upgrading its router to the latest version, the FDDIs no longer works correctly. Which commands can be used to display the microcode revision on the FDDI line module? [Choose the two best answers]

❑ a. **show microcode fddi**

❑ b. **show controllers cbus**

❑ c. **show controllers fddi**

❑ d. **show interfaces fddi**

The correct answers are b and c. These two commands list the hardware and microcode version numbers as well as other information pertaining to the FDDI interface. **show microcode fddi** is not a valid Cisco IOS command. Therefore, answer a is incorrect. The **show interfaces fddi** command lists Data Link and Network layer-specific information rather than the physical hardware information required. Therefore, answer d is also incorrect.

Question 6

The electrical system within your building is currently being tested for instabilities, at the same time clients are complaining that the network is down. Inspection of the network reveals that all users are directly connected into a hub that then connects to a Cisco router. Performing the **show interfaces** command on the locally connected router interface displays the following results:

```
Router>show interfaces Ethernet 0
Ethernet0 is down, line protocol is down
```

Which of the following answers best describes the problem?

❍ a. There's a protocol mismatch on the network.

❍ b. The network cable between the router and the hub has been spliced.

❍ c. The Ethernet 0 interface has been disabled administratively.

❍ d. The hub ports that clients are connected to have malfunctioned.

The correct answer is b. Physical cable splices or even the simple aggravation of loose cable connections frequently occur during routine maintenance. The network has been operational for some period. If the incorrect protocol encapsulation were to be configured on a router, the network would have never become operational. Therefore, answer a is incorrect. If the interface had been disabled administratively, the **show interfaces** command would have listed the interface as being *administratively down* rather than *down*. Therefore, answer c is incorrect. The hub ports malfunctioning would have caused the clients to complain that the network was down; however, if only the client ports were failing and the router's port was not, the interface would not be down. Therefore, answer d is also incorrect.

Question 7

Users in a remote office are complaining that they are intermittently not able to access the corporate database. Issuing the **show interfaces serial** command on the router reveals that the serial connection between corporate headquarters and the remote office is experiencing numerous carrier transitions. Which command could also be issued on the router to help in diagnosing the problem?

❍ a. **show controllers cbus**

❍ b. **debug atm-sig all**

❍ c. **debug serial interface**

❍ d. **debug all**

The correct answer is c. Debugging the serial interface will provide information on line timing, which is generally the reason carrier transitions occur. This information can then be used to distinguish whether the problem is on the local interface, within the carrier's network, or the remote interface. The **show controllers cbus** command would show the version of microcode that's installed, but this would not help in resolving an intermittent issue. Therefore, answer a is incorrect. The **debug atm-sig all** command would only debug ATM signaling events, not serial events. Therefore, answer b is incorrect. The **debug all** command would overload the router with all types of debugging material and would not prove useful. Therefore, answer d is also incorrect.

Question 8

Which command will display all directly connected Cisco devices and information about the device's software, data link, and network configuration?

____

The **show cdp neighbors detail** command lists the Network layer addresses and other information using Cisco's proprietary Cisco Discovery Protocol (CDP). This command will only work if each end of the connection is configured within each router's configuration with the **cdp enable** command.

Question 9

Which **debug** command displays information about FDDI ring transitions?

❍ a. **debug fddi transitions**

❍ b. **debug fddi-all**

❍ c. **debug fddi smt-packets**

❍ d. **debug fddi packets**

The correct answer is c. SMT packets contain information about neighbor identification, fault detection and reconfiguration, and insertion and removal from the ring. Answers a, b, and d are incorrect because they're not valid commands within the Cisco IOS.

Question 10

Which of the following specifications outlined in FDDI handles data link addressing?

❍ a. SMT

❍ b. PMD

❍ c. PHY

❍ d. MAC

The correct answer is d. The MAC layer is used in several specifications, such as Ethernet, to handle data link addressing. Station management (SMT) defines the FDDI host configuration, ring control features, host insertion and removal, and fault isolation and recovery. Therefore, answer a is incorrect. The Physical layer medium (PMD) defines the characteristics of the transmission medium. Therefore, answer b is incorrect. The Physical layer protocol (PHY) defines the data encoding/decoding procedures and framing. Therefore, answer c is incorrect.

Need To Know More?

Check out the Internetwork Troubleshooting Guide in the Cisco Connection Online (CCO) documentation at **www.cisco.com/univercd/home/home.htm** and select the Internetwork Troubleshooting Guide link. Within this section are links for troubleshooting LAN media problems, serial line problems, and ATM switching environments. This information provides several common scenarios as well as the commands to enter to identify and solve these problems.

Also check out the Troubleshooting Internetworking Systems section of the Cisco Connection Online (CCO) documentation. Go to **www.cisco.com/univercd/home/home.htm** and select the Troubleshooting Internetworking Systems link. Within this section are links for troubleshooting serial line problems and internetwork performance. These sections detail several common configuration problems that occur when the technology internetworks with other systems.

Frame Relay Issues

Terms you'll need to understand:

- √ Wide area networks (WANs)
- √ Permanent virtual circuits (PVCs)
- √ Data link connection identifiers (DLCIs)
- √ Data terminal equipment (DTE)
- √ Data communications equipment (DCE)
- √ Channel service unit/data service unit (CSU/DSU)
- √ Split horizon

Techniques you'll need to master:

- √ Knowing the variables presented by each Cisco IOS command
- √ Identifying frame relay problems using Cisco IOS commands
- √ Troubleshooting frame relay installations
- √ Looping data signals for fault isolation

Frame relay networks are by far the most popular infrastructure used to support WAN applications, such as connections between corporate headquarters and several remote offices. The underlying network relies on point-to-point PVCs between each site that needs direct communication. This chapter focuses on the pertinent Cisco IOS commands that can be used when troubleshooting a new or existing frame relay network installation.

Frame Relay

Frame relay is a connection-oriented data service that provides LAN connectivity over a wide area network (WAN). Frames are relayed through network nodes instead of packets being switched. This section briefly discusses the components used to construct a frame relay network. Several of the key frame relay terms that will be used throughout the chapter are outlined in Table 8.1.

General Functionality

Frame relay relies on the customer's equipment to perform end-to-end error correction. Each switch inside a frame relay network just relays the frames to the next switch. The networks of today are sufficiently error free to move the burden of error correction to the end points. Connection to the service provider's frame relay network is typically via a frame relay–capable access device, which attaches to a standard channel service unit/data service unit (CSU/DSU). There is **no flow control** on frame relay; the network simply discards frames it cannot deliver.

The only way to guarantee that a frame will not be dropped within the frame relay network is to never transmit the frame at all.

Layer 3: Addressing

A method must exist to hand data between Layer 3 and Layer 2. Specifically, the DLCI Layer 2 address is mapped to an IP address at Layer 3. The most basic method for DLCI to higher-level address resolution is *Inverse ARP*. Router 1 receives a Full Status Response from the frame relay network informing it that the PVCs with DLCIs 100 and 400 are active. Router 1 sends out Inverse ARP requests on both PVCs. Routers 2 and 3 receive their Inverse ARP message and respond with their respective IP address. Router 1 then maps IP address 192.168.1.20 to DLCI 100 and 192.168.1.30 to DLCI 400.

Table 8.1 Several key frame relay terms and their definitions.

Term	Definition
Backward explicit congestion notification (BECN)	A bit set in a frame by the frame relay network to tell the data terminal equipment (DTE) receiving the frame that congestion was experienced in the path opposite that of the source to the destination.
Committed information rate (CIR)	The minimum rate at which the network guarantees transfer of information under all conditions.
Data link connection identifier (DLCI)	A locally significant value, symbolizing the logical connection that's multiplexed into the physical channel.
Discard eligibility (DE)	A bit set in a frame by the frame relay network to signal to the switches that if congestion occurs on the network, this frame can be dropped.
Forward explicit congestion	A bit set in a frame by the frame relay notification (FECN) network to tell the data terminal equipment (DTE) receiving the frame that congestion was experienced in the path from the source to the destination.
Frame relay access device (FRAD)	An access device that encapsulates outgoing frames with a frame relay header and trailer and de-encapsulates incoming frame relay packets.
Local Management Interface (LMI)	LMI exchange messages create, destroy, and manage PVCs.
Network-to-network interface (NNI)	The interface between different carriers' frame relay networks.
Permanent virtual circuits (PVCs)	The electronic equivalent of a private line between two sites.
User-to-network interface (UNI)	The standard interface used to connect end users to the frame relay network.

Service Provider Networks

Your local service provider will specify the line speed (for example, 56Kbps or T1) of your connection, which is called a *subscription*. Also, you'll be asked to specify a committed information rate (CIR) for each data link connection identifier (DLCI). This value specifies the maximum average data rate that the network will use under normal conditions. If you send information faster than the CIR on a given DLCI, the network will flag some frames with the discard eligibility (DE) bit. DE-flagged packets will be discarded first if congestion is encountered within the network. Frame relay provides indications that the network is becoming congested by means of the forward explicit congestion notification (FECN) and backward explicit congestion notification (BECN) bits in data frames. These are used to tell the application to reduce the amount of traffic being sent.

Mesh networks allow many remote sites to use just a single connection to a service provider by assigning multiple DLCIs to a single physical interface. The carrier routes the data to the destination address according to available bandwidth. Each DLCI has a permanently configured switching path to each destination.

Local Management Interface

The Local Management Interface (LMI) was created by an industry group comprising Stratacom, Digital Equipment Corporation, and Northern Telecom (and assisted by Cisco). The LMI specification, operating on DLCI 1023, makes supporting large and complex internetworking easier through active PVC, multicast, and flow-control management. Some of the features include:

- **Virtual circuit status messages** Provide communication and synchronization between the network and the user device, periodically reporting the existence of new PVCs and the deletion of already existing PVCs.
- **Multicasting** Allows a sender to transmit a single frame but have it delivered by the network to multiple recipients.
- **Simple flow control** Provides devices whose higher layers cannot use the FECN and BECN congestion notification bits with a generic flow mechanism.

LMI types must be the same across directly connected interfaces. When connecting other vendors' routers to Cisco routers, use the IETF standard encapsulation.

Split Horizon

IP split horizon checking is disabled by default for frame relay interfaces; therefore routing updates will be propagated in and out of the same interface. The routers learn the DLCIs via LMI from the Frame Relay switches. Then, using Inverse ARP, the router learns of the remote Layer 3 network address and creates a mapping of local DLCIs and their associated remote network addresses. Additionally, certain protocols such as AppleTalk and IPX cannot be supported on partially meshed networks because they require split horizon to be enabled. Configuring frame relay subinterfaces ensures that a single physical interface is treated as multiple virtual interfaces. This capability allows Frame Relay interfaces to overcome split horizon rules because packets received on one virtual subinterface can now be forwarded out another virtual subinterface.

Cisco IOS Commands

The Cisco IOS provides several frame relay troubleshooting tools that can be used to isolate network problems from the local router to the remote router, as well as through both the local and remote CSUs/DSUs. The following sections describe the available **show**, **clear**, and **debug** commands.

Several statistics are displayed within the Cisco IOS commands. You must be able to understand the variables returned and how they can be applied while troubleshooting an internetwork.

The show Commands

Several interesting **show** commands can be used to observe and dissect the condition of a frame relay network. The commands are described in Table 8.2 and covered in further detail in the next few sections.

show frame-relay lmi

Local Management Interface (LMI) statistics can be displayed using the **show frame-relay lmi** command. LMI provides communication and synchronization between the network and the user device, periodically reporting the

Table 8.2 Frequently used show commands for troubleshooting a frame relay internetwork.

Command	Description
show frame-relay lmi	Displays LMI statistics
show frame-relay map	Displays the mappings between Network layer protocols and DLCIs
show frame-relay pvc	Displays detailed information on each configured DLCI
show interfaces serial	Displays the interface configuration and statistics

existence of new PVCs and the deletion of already existing PVCs, and generally providing information about PVC integrity. Virtual circuit status messages prevent the sending of data over PVCs that no longer exist. Listing 8.1 displays the output from the **show frame-relay lmi** command.

Listing 8.1 The **show frame-relay lmi** command displays LMI statistics.

```
Router>show frame-relay lmi

LMI Statistics for interface Serial0
    (Frame Relay DTE) LMI TYPE = CISCO
  Invalid Unnumbered info 0             Invalid Prot Disc 0
  Invalid dummy Call Ref 0              Invalid Msg Type 0
  Invalid Status Message 0              Invalid Lock Shift 0
  Invalid Information ID 0              Invalid Report IE Len 0
  Invalid Report Request 0              Invalid Keep IE Len 0
  Num Status Enq. Sent 20853            Num Status msgs Rcvd 20853
  Num Update Status Rcvd 12             Num Status Timeouts 0
```

These statistics can indicate potential problems within the frame relay network. The first line displayed describes the role and LMI type configured on the interface—in this example, the Serial0 interface is acting as a DTE using Cisco's LMI type. You need to make sure this information is consistent across all directly connected interfaces. Also, rising values in the number of status timeouts (the number of times the status message wasn't received within the keepalive time value) can potentially indicate faulty network equipment. All other items can be decoded using a protocol analyzer; however, descriptions of these items are outside the scope of this topic.

show frame-relay map

Direct mappings between the Network layer protocols and frame relay DLCI identifiers are displayed with the **show frame-relay map** command. The output, shown in Listing 8.2, describes the interface, protocol address, DLCI being used to reach the destination address, and compression and encapsulation characteristics. Status information is also displayed if provided by the configured LMI type.

Listing 8.2 Use the **show frame-relay map** command to view DLCI-to-network layer mappings.

```
Router>show frame-relay map

Serial0 (up): ip 10.4.9.155 dlci 155(0x9B,0x24B0), static,
              broadcast, CISCO, status defined, active
              TCP/IP Header Compression (enabled)
```

```
Serial0 (up): ipx ab.0000.0c13.d45a dlci 155(0x9B,0x24B0), static,
              broadcast, CISCO, status defined, active
Serial1 (up): ip 10.4.9.220 dlci 220(0xDC,0x34C0), static,
              broadcast, CISCO, status defined, inactive
Serial1 (up): ip 10.4.9.160 dlci 160(0xA0,0x2800), static,
              broadcast, CISCO, status deleted
```

Looking at the first example, all data packets destined for the IP address 10.4.9.155 must be transported out of Serial 0 through DLCI 155 using Cisco's encapsulation with TCP/IP header compression. This statement and the others are configured using mapping statements that define the protocol for DLCI address pairs. These address pairs can be very tedious to define, which can make the router's configuration prone to errors.

Quickly checking the information provided by the **show frame-relay map** command and then comparing it against all other locally attached interfaces for consistency will simplify the frame relay connectivity troubleshooting process.

show frame-relay pvc

The **show frame-relay pvc** command describes statistics about the PVCs configured on an interface. This information can be used to check for dropped packets, backward and forward explicit congestion notifications (BECNs and FECNs), and discard eligibility (DE) bits. The output from this command is shown in Listing 8.3.

Listing 8.3 The **show frame-relay pvc** command displays PVC statistics for each DLCI.

```
Router>show frame-relay pvc

PVC Statistics for interface Serial0 (Frame Relay DTE)
DLCI = 100, DLCI USAGE = LOCAL, PVC STATUS = ACTIVE,
    INTERFACE = Serial0
  input pkts 1822583      output pkts 1958562     in bytes 595710613
  out bytes 170501598     dropped pkts 1          in FECN pkts 217
  in BECN pkts 0          out FECN pkts 0         out BECN pkts 0
  in DE pkts 0            out DE pkts 0
  pvc create time 35w4d  last time pvc status changed 1d11
```

The interface can be configured as a DCE or a DTE, depending on the cable connected to the interface. The value displayed in the PVC STATUS field describes the status of the outgoing interface and PVC. The status of the PVC is carried by the LMI message exchange throughout the internetwork. This information can be useful for troubleshooting FECNs, BECNs, and dropped packets, which signify increased network congestion and potentially a service provider malfunction.

A high number of dropped packets in conjunction with rapidly increasing FECN and BECN values could be a warning sign that the network is saturating the connection and that additional bandwidth may be required.

show interfaces serial

Serial interfaces configured with frame relay encapsulation display information about the multicast DLCI, the DLCI of the interface, and the LMI DLCI as well as the type used for the LMI. The output from the **show interfaces serial** command is shown in Listing 8.4.

Listing 8.4 Use the **show interfaces serial** command to view the data link and LMI encapsulation type.

```
Router>show interfaces serial 0

Serial0 is up, line protocol is up
  Hardware is MK5025
  Internet address is 10.4.9.1 255.255.255.0
  MTU 1500 bytes, BW 256 Kbit, DLY 20000 usec,
     rely 255/255, load 1/255
  Encapsulation FRAME-RELAY, loopback not set,
     keepalive set (10 sec)
  LMI enq sent  208529, LMI stat recvd 208530,
      LMI upd recvd 12, DTE LMI up
  LMI enq recvd 0, LMI stat sent  0, LMI upd sent  0
  LMI DLCI 1023  LMI type is CISCO  frame relay DTE
```

The serial interface should report an up/up condition within line one. If the serial interface reports that it's physically down, check the local cabling and the CSU/DSU for failures. You may also want to check with the local service provider for potential frame relay network problems. If the serial interface reports that it is active but the line protocol is down, the problem could be with unseen remote keepalive messages, local or remote router misconfigurations, service provider misconfigurations, or failed hardware.

Refer to the section on the **show interfaces serial** command in Chapter 7. This section provides a list of what to look for based on the statistics acquired from this command.

The **debug** Commands

The various **debug** commands can be used to troubleshoot and monitor activity on a configured frame relay interface. Debug information can then be used to reduce network downtime and diagnose problems that may have taken hours to pinpoint without it. Table 8.3 lists several **debug** commands that can be used to isolate problems within a frame relay network.

debug frame-relay events

This command can be used to analyze packets and events on a frame relay network. Frame relay ARP input and replies are also displayed using the **debug frame-relay events** command. Listing 8.5 displays the output of this command.

Listing 8.5 The **debug frame-relay events** command displays detailed network and DLCI information.

```
Router#debug frame-relay events
Frame Relay events debugging is on

Serial0(i): reply rcvd 10.1.17.3 117
Serial0: FR ARP input, datagramstart = 0x600D8CC,
         datagramsize = 46, FR encap = 0x24B10300
         80 00 00 00 08 06 00 0F 81 37 02 0A 00 08 00 00 00
         31 00 00 00 00 0C 05 60 67 13 09 20 21 00 00 00 00
         00 00 00 00 00 00 00 00
```

Table 8.3 Frequently used debug commands for troubleshooting a frame relay internetwork.

Command	Description
debug frame-relay events	Enables logging of transmission or reception events
debug frame-relay lmi	Enables logging of LMI packets sent between the local and remote frame relay devices
debug frame-relay packet	Enables logging of all packets sent to this device within the frame relay network
debug serial interface	Displays information about events occurring on a serial interface

The first line indicates that the Serial0 interface received an ARP reply from the host with IP address 10.1.17.3 on DLCI 117. The second line displays the actual ARP packet returned by the remote host. The highlighted line contains the Ethernet type code 0×0806, which indicates that this is an IP ARP packet (all other Ethernet type codes are applicable to this type of packet as well). This information can be used to help troubleshoot the cause of connectivity problems during the installation of a new frame relay network.

debug frame-relay lmi

Information regarding the LMI packets exchanged between the local router and the service provider's frame relay network are conveyed using the **debug frame-relay lmi** command. The first three lines of information displayed in Listing 8.6 describe an LMI exchange between the local router, and the last two lines provide information about the remote frame relay switch.

Listing 8.6 LMI datagrams can be viewed using the **debug frame-relay lmi** command.

```
Router#debug frame-relay lmi
Frame Relay LMI debugging is on

Serial0(out): StEnq, myseq 209, yourseen 162, DTE up,
              datagramstart = 0x60747B8, datagramsize = 13,
              FR encap = 0xFCF10309, 00 75 01 01 01 03 02 D1 A2

Serial0(in): Status, myseq 209, RT IE 1, length 1, type 1,
             KA IE 3, length 2, yourseq 163, myseq 209
```

This command can be used to verify that the local router is communicating correctly with the service provider's frame relay network. Although this isn't shown in Listing 8.6, the command can also be used to view exchange PVC information (such as the service provider announcing that a specific DLCI has been added or has become inactive) and information pertaining to the committed information rate (CIR) that the service provider is guaranteeing.

debug frame-relay packet

This command can also be used to analyze all packets transmitted across an individual frame relay interface using the keyword *interface*. The **debug** command consists of groups of output lines describing the various packets transiting the network. The number of lines pertaining to a single packet can vary in accordance to the number of DLCIs the packet will be sent across. Listing 8.7 displays the output from the **debug frame-relay packet** command.

Listing 8.7 Every packet that transits the frame relay network can be shown using the **debug frame-relay packet** command.

```
Router#debug frame-relay packet
Frame Relay packet debugging is on

Serial0(i): dlci 155(0x24B1), pkt type 0x800, datagramsize 204
Serial0(o): dlci 110 type 800 size 24
Serial0: broadcast = 1, link 809B, addr 65535.255
Serial0(i): dlci 155(0x24B1), pkt type 0x800, datagramsize 92
Serial0(i): dlci 205(0x30D1),
          pkt encaps 0x0300 0x8000 0x00 00 0x806 (ARP),
          datagramsize 46
Serial0: frame relay INARP received
```

The highlighted code represents an Apple EtherTalk frame addressed to the "all networks, all hosts" broadcast address, 65535.255. In general, the information provided can be used to debug packets and evaluate the frame type, the network protocol, and the source and destination DLCIs for application correctness.

Be aware that this command generates a lot of information. On a large internetwork, it may crash the router. Use this command sparingly, in situations where all else has failed.

debug serial interface

Debugging a serial interface using frame relay encapsulation is very similar to the command described in Chapter 7. The information displayed in Listing 8.8 checks for the line and DTE status as well as for sequencing information. This information can be used to verify that the line is behaving correctly.

Listing 8.8 Interface and line protocol status messages can be viewed by the **debug serial interface** command.

```
Router#debug serial interface
Serial network interface debugging is on

MK5(0): New serial state = 0xE104
MK5(0): DCD is up.
Serial0(out): StEnq, myseq 229, yourseen 182, DTE up
Serial0(in): Status, myseq 229
```

Troubleshooting a frame relay link using the **debug serial interface** command will not display keepalive information if the LMI is down. To get around this issue, enable HDLC encapsulation to view the keepalive traffic that's seen on the network.

The **clear** Commands

The **clear** commands listed in Table 8.4 can be used to reset statistics and internal caches while troubleshooting a frame relay network.

clear counters serial

The counters listed by the **show interfaces serial** command can be reset using this command. You should reset the counters prior to troubleshooting any type of connection so that a frame of reference is established.

clear frame-relay-inarp

Dynamically created frame relay maps, which are created by using the Inverse Address Resolution Protocol (ARP), can be cleared using the **clear frame-relay-inarp** command. This can be used to flush incorrect addresses from the ARP table. For example, suppose that Inverse ARP has resolved a Network layer address to a local DLCI, but the Network layer address was misconfigured and is in a different subnetwork. The first step would be to log into the remote router and reconfigure the serial interface to the correct network mask. This will generate another Inverse ARP, and another mapping will be entered using the same local DLCI. The **clear frame-relay-inarp** command can then be used to flush this table and force another Inverse ARP.

Common Frame Relay Issues

Frame relay connections can be very difficult to troubleshoot, especially due to the reliance on outside service providers to set up and maintain the network effectively and efficiently. The largest problem with frame relay is the original

Table 8.4 Frequently used clear commands for troubleshooting a frame relay internetwork.

Command	Description
clear counters serial	Clears all counters shown by the **show interfaces serial** command
clear frame-relay-inarp	Clears dynamically created frame relay maps

setup of the connection. However, once the network is up, it's usually stable for quite some time. This section provides sample troubleshooting scenarios and then reviews the steps to take to solve the router connectivity problems using several of the Cisco IOS commands previously discussed in this chapter.

You will not be able to ping your own IP address on a multipoint frame relay interface because frame relay multipoint subinterfaces are non-broadcast. Furthermore, you will not be able to ping from one spoke to another spoke in a hub and spoke configuration because there is no mapping for your own IP address within the remote spoke and vice versa.

Scenario 1: Router Connectivity

A company wants to install a new frame relay network to attach their corporate headquarters to two remote offices. Corporate has purchased 2500 series routers for each location, and the service provider has been contacted for installation of the network at each office. The network configuration that will be installed is depicted in Figure 8.1.

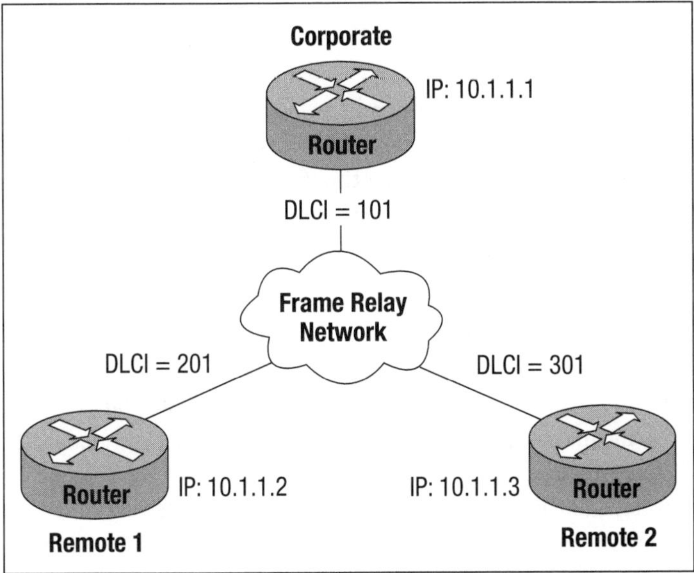

Figure 8.1 The frame relay network between corporate headquarters and two satellite offices.

Your team has completed the configuration of each router, and the service provider has contacted you verifying that the network should be up at each location. Corporate's router, the centrally located router, is configured with two subinterfaces, and each remote router is configured only with the default interface. Pings to the IP address of the first remote office (Remote 1) from headquarters are successful, but pings to the second remote office (Remote 2) located at IP address 10.1.1.3 fail. The following steps should be performed to troubleshoot the failure:

1. Issue the **show interfaces serial** command on each router that's not able to connect. Verify that the connected serial interface on all routers is active and that it's sending and receiving LMI data. If it isn't, check for the correct LMI type (Cisco, IETF, or ANSI). The LMI type must be the same on each end of the link. If it is, proceed to Step 2; otherwise, verify physical and data link connectivity and/or check with your local service provider for correct settings.

2. Verify that the CSU/DSU is configured properly for the correct clocking, framing, and line encoding, as specified by the local service provider. LMI information should now be exchanging, which can be viewed by issuing the **show frame-relay lmi** command, and the interface should be active. If not, contact your local service provider. If pings are still not available, continue to Step 3.

3. Use the **show frame-relay pvc** command to view the status of each DLCI and check for the correct assignment to each subinterface. If the DLCIs appear to be correct, shut down the interface and then bring it back up using the **shutdown** and **no shutdown** command, respectively. Attempt to ping the remote router again. If this is unsuccessful, proceed to Step 4.

4. Check the DLCI to protocol mappings using the **show frame-relay map** command. Verify that each serial interface is displayed with the active message. If the interface is not active, review the central site router configuration (in this case, Corporate's) to verify that it's connected and configured correctly. If an address mapping is not available, issue the **clear frame-relay-inarp** command and then view the active map statement again using the **show frame-relay map** command. Also, check with the local service provider to validate that the frame relay network is operating correctly. Proceed to Step 5.

5. Attempt to ping Corporate's IP address. If more than 60 percent of the packets are successful, the connection is successful.

Always verify that the map statements are correct. Mapping the incorrect IP address to a DLCI will cause the connection to fail, as will subnet variances between interface IP addresses.

Scenario 2: Loopback Testing

Users are complaining that they're not able to access services at a remote location. The **show interfaces serial** command performed on Router A says that the data link connection is down. In order for you to isolate the problem's location, the CSUs/DSUs attached to Router A and Router B need to be placed into loopback mode (see Figure 8.2). Cisco's IOS defines four different **loopback** commands that can place a local or remote CSU/DSU into loopback mode.

Perform the following steps to isolate the serial line trouble using the loopback modes:

1. Loop the connection from Router A to the local CSU/DSU (Loop 1) using the serial interface command **internal loopback**. The status of the interface should be displayed as *looped*, and the keepalive counter should be incrementing. You can verify that the connection is looped by issuing the **show interfaces serial** command. Next, use the extended **ping** command, varying the data pattern and size of the packet, to the local serial interface's IP address. This tests the connectivity up to the modem. If the success rate is not greater than 80 percent, a problem exists with the physical connection between Router A and the local CSU/DSU. Otherwise, continue to Step 2.
2. Loop the connection from Router A through the local CSU/DSU (Loop 3) using the serial interface command **local loopback**. Verify the

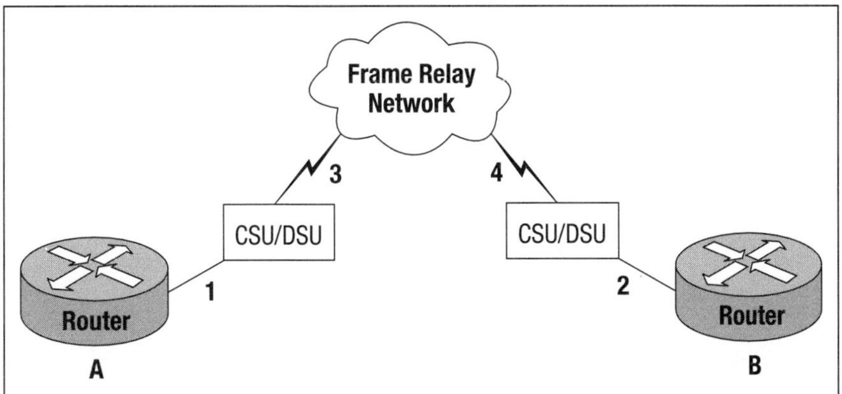

Figure 8.2 Granular loopback tests can check four different locations to isolate frame relay network faults.

interface status and keepalive counter with the **show interfaces serial** command. Perform the **ping** command as outlined in Step 1. This tests the connectivity through the local CSU/DSU. If the success rate is not greater than 80 percent, the local CSU/DSU is not configured properly or is failing. Otherwise, continue to Step 3.

3. Loop the connection from Router A to the remote CSU/DSU (Loop 4) using the serial interface command **remote line loopback**. Verify the interface status and keepalive counter with the **show interfaces serial** command. Again, perform the **ping** command outlined in Step 1. This tests connectivity through the service provider to the remote side. If the success rate is less than 60 percent, a problem exists with the service provider's network. Otherwise, continue to Step 4.

4. Loop the connection from Router A through the remote CSU/DSU (Loop 2) using the serial interface command **external loopback**. Verify the interface status and keepalive counter with the **show interfaces serial** command. Perform the **ping** command as outlined in Step 1. This will test the connectivity through the remote CSU/DSU. If the success rate is below 60 percent, a problem exists with the remote CSU/DSU. If the problem still exists, verify that the interface is still down using the **show interfaces serial** command.

Practice Questions

Question 1

After issuing the **show frame-relay pvc** command, you notice that the number of "in BECN pkts" is increasing. What does this mean?

❍ a. There's congestion on the network in the direction opposite of which the frames were traveling.

❍ b. There's congestion on the network in the direction the frames were traveling.

❍ c. It indicates the number of ring beaconings received on the network.

The correct answer is a. Backward explicit congestion notifications (BECNs) are bits set by the frame relay network that indicate traffic congestion was encountered in the reverse direction of the frames that are received by the device. Forward explicit congestion notifications (FECNs) indicate network congestion in the direction of the frames. Therefore, answer b is incorrect. Ring beacons occur on FDDI and token ring networks, not on serial devices. Therefore, answer c is incorrect.

Question 2

Your team is having difficulties configuring a new frame relay network, and it seems that one engineer configured a subinterface with the incorrect network address. Which command needs to be issued after the network address is correctly reconfigured?

❍ a. **clear counters serial**

❍ b. **clear ip arp**

❍ c. **delete frame arp**

❍ d. **clear frame-relay-inarp**

The correct answer is d. This command will force new DLCI-to-network address mappings by deleting all the entries in the frame relay Inverse ARP table. **clear counters serial** will only clear the statistical counters available for the various frame relay **show** commands. Therefore, answer a is incorrect. Clearing the IP ARP table will delete all IP-to-MAC address correlations, which is not what is required. Therefore, answer b is incorrect. **delete frame arp** is not a valid Cisco IOS command. Therefore answer c is also incorrect.

Question 3

The local service provider has established a transfer rate guarantee of service. What is this guarantee called?

❍ a. DLCI

❍ b. CIR

❍ c. LMI

❍ d. FRAD

The correct answer is b. The committed information rate (CIR) establishes a minimum line rate that the service provider's network will always have available for your connections. If the transmission speeds fall below this level, the contract is breached. The data link connection identifier (DLCI) is the locally significant number assigned to a logical connection transferred on a single physical channel. Therefore, answer a is incorrect. Connection management data is exchanged via the Local Management Interface (LMI) protocol. Therefore, answer c is incorrect. Frame relay access devices (FRADs) are systems that connect to frame relay networks. Therefore, answer d is incorrect.

Question 4

The local office installs a Cisco 2500 series router, and the remote office installs a Nortel (formerly Bay Networks) router. Which frame relay encapsulation type should be run between the two routers?

❍ a. IETF

❍ b. CISCO

❍ c. Frame

❍ d. Serial

The correct answer is a. The IETF standardized frame relay encapsulation allows routers from disparate vendors to communicate. The CISCO encapsulation method is proprietary—only Cisco devices can communicate via this protocol. Therefore answer b is incorrect. Answers c and d are incorrect because they are not Data Link layer encapsulations.

Question 5

Which Cisco IOS command will display information about all frame relay packets transiting the network?

____

The correct answer is **debug frame-relay packet**. The frame type, size, destination address, and the actual hex-encoded data can be viewed for all frame relay packets.

Question 6

Which Cisco IOS interface command will verify the serial and line connection from the local router, through the service provider's network, to the remote CSU/DSU?

❍ a. **external loopback**

❍ b. **remote line loopback**

❍ c. **internal loopback**

❍ d. **local loopback**

The correct answer is b. The **remote line loopback** interface command loops the signal prior to transiting through the remote CSU/DSU. **external loopback** will transit through the remote CSU/DSU. Therefore, answer a is incorrect. **internal loopback** will only loop to the first CSU/DSU, without transiting it. Therefore, answer c is incorrect. Finally, the **local loopback** command will transit the local CSU/DSU and then loop back without crossing the service provider's network. Therefore, answer d is incorrect.

Question 7

Which bit is set to indicate to the frame relay network that this frame can be dropped if a congested link is encountered?

❍ a. FECN

❍ b. DE

❍ c. BECN

❍ d. CIR

The correct answer is b. The discard eligibility (DE) bit can be set to indicate to the frame relay network that the packet can be dropped if congestion is encountered. The forward explicit congestion notification (FECN) bit notifies the connected device that congestion was experienced in the direction of the traveling frame. Therefore, answer a is incorrect. BECNs provides the opposite information of FECNs, notifying the next hop device that congestion was encountered in the direction opposite of the traveling frame. Therefore, answer c is incorrect. The committed information rate (CIR) is established by the service provider and guarantees levels of service within the frame relay network. Therefore, answer d is incorrect.

Question 8

Which roles should a frame relay router play in the network when connected directly to a CSU/DSU and then the service provider's network? [Choose the two best answers]

- ❑ a. User-to-Network Interface (UNI)
- ❑ b. Data communications equipment (DCE)
- ❑ c. Data terminating equipment (DTE)
- ❑ d. Network-to-Network Interface (NNI)

The correct answers are a and c. The router will play the role of the UNI and the DTE. The frame relay network switches play the roles of the DCE and the NNI. Therefore, answers b and d are incorrect.

Question 9

The local serial interface's physical state is up, but the line protocol is down. Which command can be used to trace management traffic to and from the interface?

- ❍ a. **debug lmi**
- ❍ b. **debug frame-relay events**
- ❍ c. **debug frame-relay lmi**
- ❍ d. **show frame-relay events**

The correct answer is c. Connection management information is carried with Local Management Interface (LMI) packets. **debug lmi** is not a valid Cisco IOS command. Therefore, answer a is incorrect. Frame relay events log transmission and reception events, which will not be occurring because the line protocol is down. Therefore, answer b is incorrect. **show frame-relay events** is not a valid Cisco IOS command. Therefore, answer d is incorrect.

Question 10

Which command do you use to reset the counters displayed by the **show frame-relay pvc** command for interface serial 1?

❍ a. **clear counters**

❍ b. **clear counters serial 1**

❍ c. **clear all**

❍ d. **clear interface serial 1**

The correct answer is b. Clearing the serial interface counters also clears all **show** commands that describe traffic statistics on the interface. The **clear counters** command will reset all counters instead of just the serial 1 counters. Therefore, answer a is incorrect. The **clear all** command is not a valid Cisco IOS command. Therefore, answer c is incorrect. **clear interface serial 1** will reset the hardware logic of the serial interface and should not be performed by individuals unless otherwise instructed by Cisco technical support. Therefore, answer d is incorrect.

Need To Know More?

Check out the Internetwork Troubleshooting Guide in the Cisco Connection Online (CCO) documentation. Go to **www.cisco.com/univercd/home/home.htm** and select the Internetwork Troubleshooting Guide link. Within this section are links for troubleshooting WAN connectivity and serial line problems. This information provides several common scenarios as well as the commands to enter to identify and solve the problems.

The Internetwork Troubleshooting Guide in the Cisco Connection Online (CCO) documentation contains helpful information. Go to **www.cisco.com/univercd/home/home.htm** and select the Troubleshooting Internetworking Systems link. Within this section are links for troubleshooting serial line problems and frame relay connections. These sections detail several common configuration problems with the technology internetworking with other systems.

The Frame Relay Forum, located at **www.frforum.com**, was founded to standardize the Frame Relay protocols at an international level. You can find several design specification documents as well as a list of upcoming events such as technical seminars, press releases, and tutorials.

ISDN Basic Rate Interface Issues

Terms you'll need to understand:

- √ Integrated Services Digital Network (ISDN)
- √ Basic Rate Interface (BRI)
- √ Dialer Interface
- √ Point-to-Point Protocol (PPP)
- √ Multilink Point-to-Point Protocol (MLP)
- √ Challenge Handshake Authentication Protocol (CHAP)
- √ Dial-on-Demand Routing (DDR)

Techniques you'll need to master:

- √ Identifying ISDN devices and reference points
- √ Using Cisco IOS commands to isolate problems
- √ Diagnosing ISDN failures
- √ Troubleshooting DDR configurations
- √ Increasing ISDN WAN performance

Integrated Services Digital Network (ISDN) is a relatively inexpensive solution for providing WAN access for small remote offices. ISDN configurations can range from being relatively simple to quite complex, each with its own idiosyncrasies that can be encountered during internetwork troubleshooting. This chapter describes the technology behind ISDN and the Cisco IOS commands that are available to isolate network failures. Several common ISDN issues and how to diagnose them are also covered.

ISDN Background Information

ISDN allows voice and data to be transmitted digitally over the public switched telephone network (PSTN), which was originally designed for analog voice transmission. ISDN is governed by standards set forth by the International Telecommunications Union (ITU), which allows interoperability among a variety of vendor devices. These standards incorporate an official reference configuration, designating responsibilities to devices located at a certain point within the network. Also included are Physical, Data Link, and Network layer protocols to establish and maintain ISDN calls. The following sections cover in detail the standards that have been implemented.

This Cisco IOS is based on international standards and its implementation of ISDN is one of many proofs of this. Spend plenty of time studying standardized concepts and international specifications.

Reference Configuration

The ISDN reference configuration illustrates each of the functional layers and the tasks they must perform. Figure 9.1 shows the different devices and is labeled with the appropriate reference points.

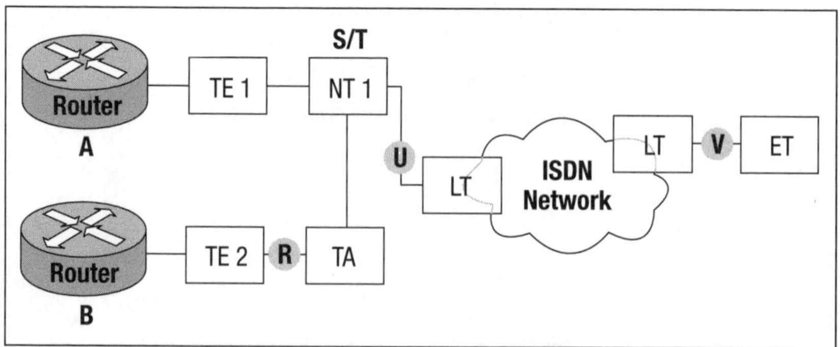

Figure 9.1 A diagram of the ISDN reference configuration.

Devices

ISDN user functions are performed by Terminal Equipment (TE). Terminal Equipment is located at the customer's premises. Multiple TEs can be connected to a single interface. TEs that are not ISDN terminals require a Terminal Adapter (TA). ISDN devices use an S/T connection for communication. Consequently, another device is needed in between—a Network Termination 1 (NT1). Most data communications equipment is available with an NT1 built in. Functions at the carrier's side of an interface are terminated by the Line Termination (LT) and performed by the Exchange Termination (ET). Table 9.1 lists and defines each of the devices described in this section.

Reference Points

The reference configuration defined for ISDN delimits the various functional groupings by reference points. With an ISDN terminal (TE1), there are three reference points between a user and the transmission media. The interfaces are designated as S (which operates at Layers 1, 2, and 3), T (which operates only at Layer 1), and U (between the NT1 and the transmission media). The NT2 and NT1 devices may be merged to form the S/T reference point. Non-ISDN compatible equipment requiring a Terminal Adapter are denoted at reference point R. The reference points, depicted in Figure 9.1, are defined again by the following:

- **R** A conceptual interface between non-ISDN terminals, TE2 terminals, and TAs. Different types of TAs are required for interworking with different TE2s.

Table 9.1 A description of each device in an ISDN network.

Device	Description
TE1	The Terminal Equipment 1 (TE1) is an ISDN terminal.
TE2	The Terminal Equipment 2 (TE2) is a non-ISDN terminal that requires a Terminal Adapter.
TA	The Terminal Adapter (TA) provides analog-to-ISDN protocol conversion.
NT1	The Network Termination 1 (NT1) performs transmission functions similar to a modem.
LT	The Line Termination (LT) is a physical connection to the ISDN switch.
ET	The Exchange Termination (ET) is the logical connection to the service provider's network.

- **S/T** A conceptual reference point between an ISDN terminal, a TE1, and an NT1 or NT2.
- **U** The conceptual interface between an NT1 and an LT.
- **V** The termination point within the local loop and switching functions.

General Functionality

The ISDN BRI line consists of the same twisted pair of wires traditionally used for analog telephone lines; several ISDN devices can connect to this single line. ISDN communication is governed by international standards, which include specifications for all layers of communication.

International Specifications

The ITU has set forth several international standards governing the use of ISDN: I.430 defines the Physical layer, Q.921 defines the Data Link layer, and Q.931 defines the Network layer. Table 9.2 describes each specification in detail.

ISDN Connector

The ISDN RJ-45 connector is wired as specified by the ISO 8877 standard. Pins 3, 4, 5, and 6 provide transmit and receive functionality; the other pins provide power. Pins 1 and 8 can be grounded if the provided power source is not floating. Table 9.3 describes each pin and its associated functionality. As a general rule, most PC cards, routers, and other data communications equipment *do not* require power from the S/T interface. However, ISDN telephones usually *do* require power from the S/T interface.

Generally, power to the S/T interface can be supplied by pins 1 and 2, while NT1 power is supplied by pins 7 and 8. The transmit and receive wire pairs provide two separate channels, pins 3/6 and pins 4/5.

ISDN Interfaces

An ISDN BRI subscriber line consists of two 64Kbps B channels (or *bearer* channels) and one 16Kbps D channel, as shown in Figure 9.2. This type of

Table 9.2 The ITU standards for defining ISDN.

Standard	Function
I.430	The S/T interface is designed according to this standard.
Q.921	Data Link layer protocol over the D channel. Also referred to as Link Access Protocol—D channel (LAPD).
Q.931	Network layer protocol. Provides call setup and teardown, channel allocation, and optional services over the D channel.

Table 9.3 The ISDN RJ-45 connector specifications.

Pin	Color	TE Function
1	Green	Power source [+3 volts]
2	Green/white	Power source [-3 volts]
3	Orange/white	Transmit [+]
4	Blue/white	Receive [+]
5	Blue	Receive [-]
6	Orange	Transmit [-]
7	Brown	Power sink [-2 volts]
8	Brown/white	Power sink [+2 volts]

configuration is commonly called *2B+D*. The B channels are used to carry voice or data, and the D channel is used for protocol negotiation between the user and the ISDN switch, as well as for call setup and teardown. ISDN BRI is delivered over one pair of copper wires to what is known as a U connection.

Service Profile Identifiers

Service Profile Identifiers (SPIDs) identify to the service provider which types of services and features are supported for a given ISDN device. The format of the SPID is usually the 10-digit phone number of the ISDN line, plus a prefix and a suffix that are sometimes used to identify features on the line. There are three primary switch signalling types that the Cisco IOS supports: AT&T 5ESS, Northern Telecom DMS100, and National ISDN-1 (NI1). If an ISDN service provider is using an AT&T 5ESS switch signal with a software revision lower than 5E8, SPIDs are not required. If an ISDN line requires a SPID but one is not supplied correctly, Layer 2 initialization will take place, but Layer 3 will not, and the device will not be able to place or accept calls.

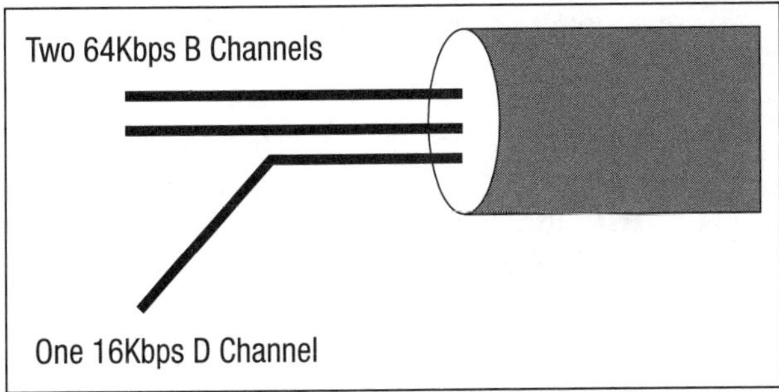

Figure 9.2 ISDN uses a three-channel communication method called 2B+D.

Signaling

Instead of the phone company sending a ring voltage signal to ring the bell in your phone ("In-Band signal"), it sends a digital packet on a separate channel ("Out-of-Band signal"). The Out-of-Band signal does not disturb established connections, and call setup time is very fast. For example, a V.34 modem typically takes 30-60 seconds to establish a connection; an ISDN call usually takes less than 2 seconds. The signaling also indicates who is calling, what type of call it is (data/voice), and what number was dialed. Available ISDN phone equipment is then capable of making intelligent decisions on how to direct the call.

Powering An ISDN Device

Currently the analog phone system provides it's own power—if the power goes out, your phone still works. However, ISDN requires more power than a standard telephone; therefore, each of your ISDN devices must get it's power some other way. Under normal circumstances, your NT1 will be plugged in to your house's power and all of the ISDN devices in your home will get power from the NT1. This is one of the reasons that ISDN uses a four wire system for the network—it allows separate lines for receiving and transmitting and at the same time allows for transmission of power.

Also, those other four unused wires in the 8-pin ISDN jack are specified in the standard to be used for alternate power supplies. Whether these will actually be used remains to be seen, but it is possible that a UPS (uninterruptible power supply) could be added to your NT1, and it could use these auxiliary lines to provide guaranteed power.

Cisco IOS Commands

Several Cisco IOS commands are available to aid you in correctly configuring and troubleshooting ISDN. This section covers, in detail, several of the **show**, **debug**, and **clear** commands that can be used to pinpoint the problems encountered on the local end, the remote end, and, potentially, the ISDN service provider's network.

The show Commands

The Cisco IOS implements several **show** commands that can be used to view the current ISDN configuration of the router. You can potentially use these commands to verify local and remote ISDN connectivity, as well as to isolate network failures. Table 9.4 describes the most commonly used **show** commands. Each command is covered in more detail in the following sections.

Table 9.4 Frequently used show commands for troubleshooting an ISDN BRI internetwork.

Command	Description
show controller bri	Displays the variable contained within the internal BRI controller
show dialer interfaces bri	Displays information about a specific dialer interface and its configured DDR settings
show dialer map	Displays statically and dynamically configured dialer map statements
show interfaces bri	Displays information about the BRI interface and relevant statistics
show isdn status	Displays the status of the three ISDN layers and the locally configured switch type
show ppp multilink	Displays multilink PPP configuration information

show controller bri

The **show controller bri** command displays information about Physical layer connectivity and several other internal controller variables. Also, this command displays information about received datagram errors, as shown in Listing 9.1.

Listing 9.1 The **show controller bri** command displays the Physical layer statistics of the BRI interface.

```
Router>show controller bri 0
BRI unit 0 with Integrated NT1:
Layer 1 is ACTIVATED
D Chan Info:
idb 0x32089C, ds 0x3267D8, reset_mask 0x2
buffer size 1524
[output omitted from listing]
0 missed datagrams, 0 overruns, 0 bad frame addresses
0 bad datagram encapsulations, 0 memory errors
0 transmitter underruns
B1 Chan Info:
Layer 1 is ACTIVATED
idb 0x3224E8, ds 0x3268C8, reset_mask 0x0
buffer size 1524
[output omitted from listing]
0 missed datagrams, 0 overruns, 0 bad frame addresses
0 bad datagram encapsulations, 0 memory errors
0 transmitter underruns
B2 Chan Info:
Layer 1 is ACTIVATED
```

```
idb 0x324520, ds 0x3269B8, reset_mask 0x2
buffer size 1524
[output omitted from listing]
0 missed datagrams, 0 overruns, 0 bad frame addresses
0 bad datagram encapsulations, 0 memory errors
0 transmitter underruns
```

Increasing error counters may indicate a failing BRI interface or a poor line state between the TE and NT1. In the case shown in Listing 9.1, the NT1 is integrated into the BRI unit, so in this case, any line errors may be due to the service provider's network functioning incorrectly. If Layer 1 connectivity is not displayed as *activated*, the connection to the BRI interface may be damaged.

show dialer interfaces bri

Dial on Demand Routing (DDR) provides the triggering mechanism for ISDN call sessions. Dialer lists, groups, and maps are created so that the Cisco router will automatically create and tear down sessions on demand. The **show dialer interfaces bri** command provides information about this process and the router's current dialer configuration. Listing 9.2 displays the output from the command.

Listing 9.2 The **show dialer interfaces bri** command displays DDR and dialer configuration information.

```
Router>show dialer interfaces bri
BRI0 - dialer type = ISDN
Dial String      Successes   Failures    Last called   Last status
5555551212       1           0           00:00:00      successful
5555551212       1           0           00:06:33      successful
0 incoming call(s) have been screened.
BRI0: B-Channel 1
Idle timer (120 secs), Fast idle timer (20 secs)
Wait for carrier (30 secs), Re-enable (15 secs)
Dialer state is data link layer up
Dial reason: ip (s=10.1.1.8, d=10.1.1.1)
Interface bound to profile Dialer1
Time until disconnect 72 secs
Current call connected 00:00:48
Connected to 5555551212 (remote)
BRI0: B-Channel 2
Idle timer (120 secs), Fast idle timer (20 secs)
Wait for carrier (30 secs), Re-enable (15 secs)
Dialer state is idle
```

You can use this tool to confirm the validity of dial strings associated with an interface. It can also be used to verify the reason for DDR initiation, such as the first B channel was activated when the source address 10.1.1.8 sent data to 10.1.1.1. Depending on the router configuration, the second B channel may be activated after a set bandwidth threshold. This command can be used to check for the second B channel's activity.

show dialer map

The **show dialer map** command displays statically and dynamically created dialer statements. These statements can either be configured individually or on a dialer interface. Listing 9.3 displays the output from this command. For example, any traffic destined for IP address 10.1.1.1 will connect to the remote_1 dialer group on the dialer1 interface.

Listing 9.3 The **show dialer map** command displays static and dynamic dialer map statements.

```
Router>show dialer map
Static dialer map ip 10.1.1.1 name remote_1 on Dialer1
Static dialer map ip 10.1.1.2 name remote_2 on Dialer1
Dynamic dialer map ip 10.1.1.3 name remote_3 on Dialer1
```

Dynamic dialer map statements are created when a peer is called, and the statements can only be viewed with the **show dialer map** command. This command is useful for troubleshooting DDR configurations.

show interfaces bri

Both D channel and B channel Data Link and Network layer information can be displayed using variations of the **show interfaces bri** command. As shown in Listing 9.4, the first variation details D channel information, indicating that the line protocol is spoofing. *Spoofing* is a method of lying to DDR so that the routing entry will not be flushed from the routing table. The routing entry allows DDR to initiate a call to the remote ISDN host. The second variation displays information about the B channels. BRI lines listed in the down state may be due to an inactive interface, faulty cabling, or a problem within the service provider's network.

Listing 9.4 The **show interfaces bri** command displays the interface's current status and statistics.

```
Router>show interfaces bri 0
BRI0 is up, line protocol is up (spoofing)
  Hardware is BRI
  MTU 1500 bytes, BW 64 Kbit, DLY 20000 usec,
     rely 255/255, load 1/255
  Encapsulation PPP, loopback not set, keepalive not set
  [output omitted from listing]
```

```
Router>show interfaces bri 0:1
BRI0:1 is down, line protocol is down
  Hardware is BRI
  MTU 1500 bytes, BW 64 Kbit, DLY 20000 usec,
     rely 255/255, load 1/255
  Encapsulation PPP, loopback not set, keepalive not set
  [output omitted from listing]
```

show isdn status

The **show isdn status** command displays information about the three ISDN layers as well as the configured switch type. You can use this information to check whether the ISDN BRI interface is properly communicating with the directly connected hardware and the service provider's ISDN switch. Listing 9.5 displays the output from this command.

Listing 9.5 The **show isdn status** command displays information about each of the three ISDN layers.

```
Router>show isdn status
The current ISDN Switchtype = ntt
ISDN BRI0 interface
    Layer 1 Status:
        ACTIVE
    Layer 2 Status:
        TEI = 64, State = MULTIPLE_FRAME_ESTABLISHED
    Layer 3 Status:
        1 Active Layer 3 Call(s)
    Activated dsl 0 CCBs = 1
        CCB:callid=8003, callref=0, sapi=0, ces=1, B-chan=1
    Number of active calls = 1
    Number of available B-channels = 1
    Total Allocated ISDN CCBs = 1
```

While you're troubleshooting an internetwork, the information provided by the **show isdn status** command can be used to quickly verify the status of ISDN and whether the switch type has been configured correctly. The switch type must match the name of the directly connected device within the local service provider's network.

Switch signaling misconfigurations are very common and can cause very strange results. You will need to contact your local service provider for the switch type used in its ISDN cloud.

show ppp multilink

Both Multilink Point-to-Point Protocol (MLP) and Multilink Multichassis PPP (MMP) configuration information is displayed within the output of the **show ppp multilink** command. In Listing 9.6, a bundle called *remote* has three lines associated with it that can be aggregated across any virtual PPP session.

Listing 9.6 The **show ppp multilink** command displays information about multilink bundle configurations.

```
Router>show ppp multilink
Bundle remote, 3 members, first link is BRI0: B-channel 1
0 lost fragments, 8 reordered, 0 unassigned,
     sequence 0x1E/0x1E rcvd/sent
```

This command can be used to verify that multilink bundles have been activated correctly. Advanced troubleshooting of BRI links utilizing Multilink PPP will require additional verification of the access server's configuration, which is a topic that's beyond the scope of this book.

The debug Commands

As always, **debug** commands should be used sparingly in a production network, but they can and should be used during times of internetwork troubleshooting. ISDN **debug** commands can be used to isolate connection setup and teardown as well as DDR and PPP negotiation and authentication failures. Table 9.5 lists and describes the most commonly used **debug** commands.

Table 9.5 Frequently used debug commands for troubleshooting an ISDN BRI internetwork.

Command	Description
debug bri	Displays information about the Physical layer activation of ISDN B channels
debug dialer events	Displays Dial on Demand Routing (DDR) information
debug isdn events	Displays information about Q.931 call establishment events
debug isdn q921	Displays information about Q.921 Data Link layer access procedures
debug isdn q931	Displays information about Q.931 Network layer call setup and teardown

(continued)

Table 9.5 Frequently used debug commands for troubleshooting an ISDN BRI internetwork (continued).

Command	Description
debug ppp authentication	Displays information about the exchange of Challenge Handshake Authentication Protocol (CHAP) and Password Authentication Protocol (PAP) packets
debug ppp negotiation	Displays Link Control Protocol (LCP) and PPP negotiation packets
debug ppp packet	Displays all PPP packets

debug bri

The **debug bri** command displays the internal Physical layer code used to initialize outgoing calls. Each call requires the B channels to initialize using ISDN code, as shown in Listing 9.7.

Listing 9.7 The **debug bri** command displays Physical layer ISDN codes.

```
Router#debug bri
Basic Rate network interface debugging is on

BRI: write_sid: wrote 1B for subunit 0, slot 2.
BRI: write_sid: wrote 20 for subunit 0, slot 2.
BRI: Starting Power Up timer for unit = 0.
BRI: write_sid: wrote 3 for subunit 0, slot 2.
BRI: Starting T3 timer after expiry of PUP timeout for unit = 0,
     current state is F4.
BRI: write_sid: wrote FF for subunit 0, slot 2.
BRI: Activation for unit = 0, current state is F7.
BRI: enable channel B1
BRI: write_sid: wrote 14 for subunit 0, slot 2.
BRI: disable channel B1
BRI: write_sid: wrote 15 for subunit 0, slot 2.
```

Troubleshooting BRI interfaces normally will be performed with the guidance of a TAC support engineer. Although this command displays Physical layer instruction sets, a few of the generated events can be used to verify that the controller is active. The **write_sid** commands indicate that internal commands are being executed on the BRI interface controller. T3 timers state the time to wait for the interface to activate and normally occur after the expiration of a power-up (PUP) timeout. The selected code shows that the B-Channel1 link transitioned, which could indicate line failures.

debug dialer events

Dialing events occur when an interesting packet has triggered a dialer interface to become active. *Interesting packets* are packets that have been defined by a protocol-specific access list and then bound to a dialer interface. The packets that initiate this event and any errors that may occur can be displayed with the **debug dialer events** command, as shown in Listing 9.8.

Listing 9.8 The **debug dialer events** command displays events used to activate dialer interfaces.

```
Router#debug dialer events
Dial on demand events debugging is on

BRI0: Dialing cause: Serial0: ip (s=10.6.1.1 d=10.6.2.2)
BRI0: No dialer string defined.  Dialing cannot occur.
```

This command can prove useful when you're troubleshooting failures in ISDN line initiation due to traffic that's supposed to trigger the link being defined as *uninteresting*. The **debug dialer events** command can also be useful for tracing snapshot routing processes. If errors are seen, you should check all the dialer configuration statements such as dialer map, dialer string, and dialer group.

debug isdn events

Q.931 call setup and teardown events for the router's ISDN network connection can be viewed using the **debug isdn events** command. The **debug isdn q931** command (which is described a little later in this chapter) provides similar information, but in a different format. The **debug isdn events** command results are shown in Listing 9.9.

Listing 9.9 The **debug isdn events** command displays Q.931 events.

```
Router#debug isdn events
ISDN events debugging is on

received HOST_INCOMING_CALL
 Bearer Capability i = 0x080010
 --------
 Channel ID i = 0x0101
 Calling Party Number i = 0x0000, '555555121202'
 IE out of order or end of 'private' IEs --
 Bearer Capability i = 0x8890
 Channel ID i = 0x89
 Calling Party Number i = 0x0083, '555555121202'
ISDN Event: Received a call from 555555121202 on B1 at 64 Kb/s
ISDN Event: Accepting the call
```

```
received HOST_CONNECT
 Channel ID i = 0x0101
ISDN Event: Connected to 555555121202 on B1 at 64 Kb/s
```

The information displayed from this command can be used to quickly identify misconfigured SPIDs or to verify that the remote host did not accept the connection. Using this command in combination with the **debug isdn q931** or **show isdn status** command might help you isolate problems more quickly.

debug isdn q921

The Q.921 standard defines the connection processes for the logical connection between the router and the service provider's ISDN switch. The **debug isdn q921** command displays the communication process for the ISDN Link Access Protocol—D channel (LAPD) signaling protocol on the D channel. The information displayed by this command will vary in conjunction with the router's role—it's either the calling party or the called party. If the router is the calling party, information about the outgoing call will be shown, as displayed in Listing 9.10. If the router is the called party, commands regarding the incoming call and keepalive messages will be displayed.

Listing 9.10 The **debug isdn q921** command displays Q.921 events.

```
Router#debug isdn q921
ISDN Q921 packets debugging is on

ISDN BR0: TX ->  INFOc sapi = 0  tei = 64  ns = 5  nr = 2
          i = 0x08010705040288901801837006803631383835
ISDN BR0: RX <-  RRr sapi = 0  tei = 64  nr = 6
ISDN BR0: RX <-  INFOc sapi = 0  tei = 64  ns = 2  nr = 6
          i = 0x08018702180189
ISDN BR0: TX ->  RRr sapi = 0  tei = 64  nr = 3
ISDN BR0: RX <-  INFOc sapi = 0  tei = 64  ns = 3  nr = 6
          i = 0x08018707
```

This command will generate a lot of information, and it's very difficult to use for pinpointing service failures. Two common reasons why errors occur while troubleshooting Layer 2 ISDN connectivity are poor D channel line quality and mismatched switch types. The Layer 2 connection establishment process should always proceed as follows:

1. The Terminal Endpoint (TE) and the network initially exchange Receive Ready (RR) frames, listening for someone to initiate a connection.

2. The TE sends an Unnumbered Information (UI) frame with a Service Access Point Identifier (SAPI) of 63 (management procedure, query network) and a Terminal Endpoint Identifier (TEI) of 127 (broadcast).
3. The network assigns an available TEI (in the range 64 to 126).
4. The TE sends a Set Asynchronous Balanced Mode (SABME) frame with a SAPI of 0 (call control, used to initiate a SETUP) and a TEI of the value assigned by the network.
5. The network responds with an Unnumbered Acknowledgement (UA): SAPI = 0, TEI = assigned.
6. At this point, the connection is ready for a Layer 3 setup.

Errors generated by the **debug** command can also point to misconfigured SPIDs if the router sends IDREQs to the CO switch, but a response is not returned.

debug isdn q931

The Q.931 standard defines the Network layer protocols used for user-to-user, circuit-switched connections for D channel communications. This includes setup, connection, release, and disconnection of calls between the Terminal Equipment (TE) and the service provider's ISDN switch. The **debug isdn q931** command displays the call establishment information transmitted between these two devices, as shown in Listing 9.11.

Listing 9.11 The **debug isdn q931** command displays Q.931 events.

```
Router#debug isdn q931
ISDN Q931 packets debugging is on

TX -> SETUP pd = 8 callref = 0x04
 Bearer Capability i = 0x8890
 Channel ID i = 0x83
 Called Party Number i = 0x80, '555555121202'
RX <- CALL_PROC pd = 8 callref = 0x84
 Channel ID i = 0x89
<CodRX <- CONNECT pd = 8 callref = 0x84
TX -> CONNECT_ACK pd = 8 callref = 0x04....
```

You might find it beneficial to also enable the **debug isdn q921** command—this will provide the complete call establishment across the Network and Data Link layers. The most common problems to watch out for while setting up a new ISDN connection involves configuring the correct switch type that the router will be connecting to within the service provider's network (as mentioned earlier) and incorrect SPIDs. Vendors began implementation of the Q.931 protocol specification prior to it becoming a standard. This led to variations of the Q.931 protocol; therefore, the switch type must be defined within the router. The following steps should always occur when an ISDN call is established:

1. Caller sends a SETUP to the switch.
2. If the SETUP is OK, the switch sends a CALL PROC (proceeding) to the calling party and then a SETUP to the called party.
3. The called party gets the SETUP. If it's OK, it rings the phone and sends an ALERTING message to the switch.
4. The switch forwards the ALERTING message to the calling party.
5. When the called party answers the call, it sends a CONNECT message to the switch.
6. The switch forwards the CONNECT message to the calling party.
7. The calling party sends a CONNECT ACK (acknowledge) message to the switch.
8. The switch forwards the CONNECT ACK message to the called party.
9. The connection should now be established.

debug isdn q921 and **debug isdn q931** are very important ISDN troubleshooting commands because they can be used to quickly pinpoint connectivity problems into the service provider's network.

debug ppp authentication

A portion of the Layer 2 connection setup requires caller authentication. This can be in the form of PAP or the more secure CHAP. CHAP uses a three-way handshake for authentication, similar to TCP session establishment; however, in the case of CHAP, a key is exchanged rather than acknowledgements and sequencing numbers. Listing 9.12 displays the output of the **debug ppp authentication** command on a router configured to use CHAP but not configured with the correct username.

Listing 9.12 The **debug ppp authentication** command displays caller authentication messages.

```
Router#debug ppp authentication
PPP authentication debugging is on
```

```
PPP BRI0:1 O CHAP CHALLENGE(1) id 27 len 26
PPP BRI0:1: Send CHAP challenge id=27 to remote
PPP BRI0:1(i): pkt type 0xC223, datagramsize 30
PPP BRI0:1: I CHAP CHALLENGE(1) id 18 len 26
PPP BRI0:1: CHAP challenge from Remote-1
PPP BRI0:1: USERNAME Remote-1 not found.
PPP BRI0:1: Unable to authenticate for peer.
```

The command processed three events describing a PPP CHAP authentication failure for the router/username of Remote-1. In this case, the local router that the **debug** command is processing on has a misconfigured dialer interface. Routers configured with incorrect usernames and passwords are very common mistakes that can lead to hours of misdirected troubleshooting.

debug ppp negotiation

PPP packets transmitted during the initialization of PPP sessions are displayed using the **debug ppp negotiation** command. These negotiations occur normally so that both sides agree on all the Link Control Protocol (LCP) variables. In Listing 9.13, the routers are agreeing on a PPP magic number that will be used for the session (in this case, 2D56AAC).

Listing 9.13 The **debug ppp negotiation** command displays PPP negotiation messages.

```
Router#debug ppp negotiation
PPP protocol negotiation debugging is on

PPP: sending CONFREQ, type = 4 (CI_QUALITYTYPE), value = C025/3E8
PPP: sending CONFREQ, type = 5 (CI_MAGICNUMBER), value = 2D56AAC
PPP: received config for type = 4 (QUALITYTYPE) acked
PPP: received config for type = 5
     (MAGICNUMBER) value = 2D517F1 acked (ok)
PPP Serial0: state = ACKSENT fsm_rconfack(C021): rcvd id 5
PPP: config ACK received, type = 4 (CI_QUALITYTYPE),
     value = C025
PPP: config ACK received, type = 5 (CI_MAGICNUMBER),
     value = 2D56AAC
PPP: ipcp_reqci: returning CONFACK. (ok)
PPP Serial0: state = ACKSENT fsm_rconfack(8021): rcvd id 4
```

CONFACK messages indicate configuration acknowledgements, which are acceptable responses. Indications of configuration failures are flagged by CONFNAK messages. If any of these messages are identified within the output from the command, you should look for PPP configuration mismatches between the neighboring devices.

debug ppp packet

The **debug ppp packet** command displays low-level information about all PPP packets that transit the device. This command may be useful for verifying PPP packet reception, but the information displayed generally can be replaced with some of the more specific PPP debugging commands. The output from the **debug ppp packet** command is displayed in Listing 9.14.

Listing 9.14 The **debug ppp packet** command displays all inbound and outbound PPP packets.

```
Router#debug ppp packet
PPP packet display debugging is on

PPP Serial0: O LCP ECHOREP(A) id 3 (C) magic D21B1
PPP Serial0(o): lcp_slqr() state = OPEN magic = D21B1, len = 48
PPP Serial0(i): pkt type 0xC025, datagramsize 52
PPP Serial0(i): lcp_rlqr() state = OPEN magic = D3254, len = 48
PPP Serial0(i): pkt type 0xC021, datagramsize 16
PPP Serial0: I LCP ECHOREQ(9) id 4 (C) magic D3254
PPP Serial0: input(C021) state = OPEN code = ECHOREQ(9)
    id = 4 len = 12
```

The **clear** Commands

ISDN counters can be used to check for connectivity failures, performance trends, and problem isolation. These counters may need to be reset to provide an appropriate frame of reference while you're troubleshooting ISDN connections. Table 9.6 lists the **clear** commands available to perform this function as well as the command needed to reset the hardware logic of a BRI interface after router configuration changes have occurred.

Common ISDN BRI Issues

Generally, once an ISDN connection has been installed and configured by the service provider, the configuration within the Cisco IOS is simple. However,

Table 9.6 Frequently used clear commands for troubleshooting an ISDN BRI internetwork.

Command	Description
clear counters interface bri	Resets all counters associated with the BRI interface
clear dialer	Resets all dialer statistics
clear interface bri	Resets the hardware logic of the BRI interface

sometimes when the ISDN connection does not operate correctly, it can be a difficult task to troubleshoot and isolate the problem. The next two sections provide sample scenarios that involve setting up a new DDR ISDN connection to a router and troubleshooting performance problems.

Scenario 1: Router Connectivity

The network engineering team has decided that an ISDN connection will serve remote offices that need access to corporate headquarters' email system. DDR will be configured on the ISDN connection because the connection will not be required at all times. The two routers will be connected as shown in Figure 9.3.

Initial Configuration

The new configuration using CHAP, but without using DDR, has been set up on each router, but end-to-end ISDN connectivity has not been established. The following steps should be performed to isolate the problem:

1. Check for initial connectivity with the **show isdn status** command. The three layers should state that they are active or have established a connection. If Layer 1 is not active, the physical hardware or the cabling may have failed. Make sure that pins 4 and 5 are properly terminated within the ISDN cable—they are the pins that receive data from the ISDN networks. Otherwise, if Layer 1 is active, proceed to Step 2.
2. Perform the **show isdn status** command again. If Layer 2 does not show that a connection has been established, use the **debug isdn q921** command to verify that the router is communicating with the switch. Shutting down the interface and reinitializing it can do this, or you can

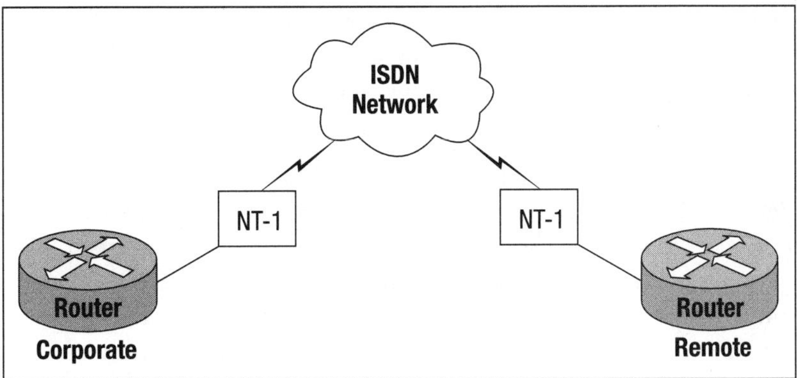

Figure 9.3 The ISDN connection between corporate headquarters and a remote office.

also use the **clear interface bri** command. Also, check that the correct ISDN switch type is configured on the router. Otherwise, if Layer 2 is active, proceed to Step 3.

3. If Layer 3 is not displayed as active by the **show isdn status** command, issue the command **debug isdn q931**. Check for information regarding whether the remote line is busy or the switch type configuration is incorrect. The connection is successfully established once the *calling* party has connected to the *called* party. You can issue the **show dialer** command to view the line connection information. If this occurs but the connection is still dropped, continue to Step 4.

4. Check that PPP negotiation and authentication is performed successfully using the **debug ppp negotiation** and **debug ppp authentication** commands. PPP authentication may need to be configured on one of the devices if errors occur during the PPP negotiation phase. If CHAP authentication fails, verify that the username and passwords are correct on each router and that the dialer map has the correct hostname configured. The ISDN connection between the two routers should now be established.

Dial-On-Demand Routing

Now that the connection between the two offices has been manually established, you've configured the routers to use DDR; however, several attempts at establishing the connection have failed. The following is a partial listing of the key points to check while establishing a DDR connection:

1. Check that the traffic that's supposed to initiate the DDR call is defined as *interesting* within the router's configuration and/or use the **show dialer map** command. If the defined interesting traffic only covers a small range of criteria, change the configuration so that a broad range of traffic generates a DDR call (for example, by permitting all IP traffic). Check the connection with the **show dialer interface** command. If it still fails, continue to Step 2.

2. Verify that the interface recognizes the traffic as interesting using the **debug dialer events** command. This should validate whether the connection is establishing and what's misconfigured. Missing dialer lists or improperly configured access lists may be preventing the traffic from initiating the connection. Use this information to return to the router's configuration and properly configure the dialer interface.

Scenario 2: Performance

The connection between remote locations has been established, but users are complaining that the network's performance is very slow. The first item to check for is line errors or queue drops on the ISDN interface using the **show interfaces bri** command. If a high number appears within the results, issue the **clear counters interface bri** command to set a proper frame of reference for the counter and then reissue the **show interfaces bri** command. Next, if the output or input queues are seeing a high number of drops, configure larger queue sizes on the interface. If the values for the physical errors are incrementing, it's most likely due to the service provider's line quality. You should contact your provider to see whether something can be done to improve it.

Packet drops do not necessarily indicate a problem; this is part of the normal flow control process of connection-oriented protocols such as TCP. The packets dropped will force the sender of the packet stream to decrease its transmit speed, but this may not indicate a problem. Drops are most often caused by "bursty" traffic or because a 10Mbps Ethernet interface is sending a high amount of traffic over a 64Kbps ISDN connection. In this case, you may want to disable fast switching by using the **no ip route-cache** command.

Practice Questions

Question 1

Which **debug** command displays information about Layer 3 call establishments? [Choose the two best answers]

- ❑ a. **debug isdn q921**
- ❑ b. **debug isdn events**
- ❑ c. **debug isdn q931**
- ❑ d. **debug isdn calls**

The correct answers are b and c. These two commands produce similar results but in different formats, which can help in providing more user-friendly debugging information. The **debug isdn q921** command displays Layer 2 information. Therefore, answer a is incorrect. **debug isdn calls** is not a valid Cisco IOS command. Therefore, answer d is incorrect.

Question 2

Which **debug** command should be used to check for invalid PPP usernames and/or passwords?

____

The correct answer is **debug ppp authentication**. This command displays debugging information about both PAP and CHAP authentication.

Question 3

A standard ISDN RJ-45 connector has eight pins. Which ones are used for transmission, as defined by the ISO 8877 standard?

- ❍ a. Pins 4 and 5
- ❍ b. Pins 3 and 6
- ❍ c. Pins 1 and 2
- ❍ d. Pins 7 and 8

The correct answer is b. Pins 3 and 6 provide the positive and negative transmission signals, respectively. Pins 4 and 5 receive positive and negative signals. Therefore, answer a is incorrect. Pins 1 and 2 provide the positive and negative power source. Therefore, answer c is incorrect. Pins 7 and 8 provide the positive and negative power sink. Therefore, answer d is incorrect.

Question 4

What's the name of the Layer 2 standard that the International Telecommunications Union (ITU) has defined for ISDN?

- ❍ a. I.430
- ❍ b. Q.931
- ❍ c. Q.921
- ❍ d. Q.132

The correct answer is c. The Data Link layer protocol over the D channel is defined in the Q.921 standard. The I.430 ITU standard defines the S/T interface. Therefore, answer a is incorrect. The Q.931 standard defines the Network layer protocol that provides call establishment, teardown, and management. Therefore, answer b is incorrect. Q.132 is not a defined ISDN standard. Therefore, answer d is incorrect.

Question 5

What does the ISDN reference model require non-ISDN devices to connect directly into?

- ❍ a. NT1
- ❍ b. TA
- ❍ c. TE2
- ❍ d. LT

The correct answer is b. Terminal Adapters (TAs) provide the analog-to-digital conversion to allow the device to connect to the ISDN network. Only ISDN devices or TAs can connect directly into a Network Termination 1 (NT1) device. Therefore, answer a is incorrect. Non-ISDN devices are actually defined as Terminal Equipment 2 (TE2) devices. Therefore, answer c is incorrect. The Line Termination (LT) is the physical connection to the ISDN switch located within the service provider's network. Therefore, answer d is incorrect.

Question 6

You've just connected your ISDN router to your service provider's network but have not yet configured any SPIDs. The ISDN connection should correctly initialize up to which layer?

❍ a. Layer 1 (Physical).

❍ b. Layer 2 (Data Link).

❍ c. Layer 3 (Network).

❍ d. The connection will not initialize at all.

The correct answer is b. If an ISDN connection requiring a SPID does not have one defined, it will initialize up to Layer 2 and then the Layer 3 call establishment will fail. Therefore, answers c and d are incorrect. Answer a is also incorrect because the Physical layer connection is already established but is not the final initialization point.

Question 7

Performing the **show interfaces bri 0** command on a router describes the line protocol as *spoofing*. What does this mean?

❍ a. Dial on Demand Routing (DDR) has been enabled on the BRI 0 interface, but the connection to the remote location has never been established.

❍ b. The BRI interface has been configured with the **enable spoofing** command so that the ISDN connection never terminates.

❍ c. The router is using Dial on Demand Routing (DDR) to initiate calls. Spoofing is used to stop the routing entry to the remote location from being flushed from the routing table.

The correct answer is c. Spoofing is used to stop routing table entries from being flushed while an ISDN DDR connection is terminated. This allows interesting packets to bring up the remote link automatically. It's not necessarily the case that a remote connection has never been established. Therefore, answer a is incorrect. **enable spoofing** is not a valid Cisco IOS command. Therefore, answer b is incorrect.

Question 8

Which Cisco IOS command will display the status of all three ITU-defined ISDN layers?

- ❍ a. **show isdn status**
- ❍ b. **show controller bri**
- ❍ c. **show interfaces bri**
- ❍ d. **show isdn q931**

The correct answer is a. This command displays information about all three layers (Physical, Data Link, and Network) as well as the ISDN switch type that has been configured. The **show controller bri** command displays only the Physical layer characteristics. Therefore, answer b is incorrect. The **show interfaces bri** command only displays the status of the Physical and Data Link layers. Therefore, answer c is incorrect. **show isdn q931** is not a valid Cisco IOS command. Therefore, answer d is also incorrect.

Question 9

The DDR connection is not being established. Which **debug** command will help the most with identifying why the connection is not becoming active?

- ❍ a. **debug isdn events**
- ❍ b. **show dialer map**
- ❍ c. **debug dialer events**
- ❍ d. **show ppp multilink**

The correct answer is c. The **debug dialer events** command displays events that occur when interesting packets trigger a dialer interface to become active or when these events fail. **debug isdn events** debugs the ISDN connection after the dialer has instantiated a connection. Therefore, answer a is incorrect. The **show dialer map** command displays the DDR entries in the configuration, but this is not a **debug** command. Therefore, answer b is incorrect. The **show ppp multilink** command displays Multilink PPP information and is also not a **debug** command. Therefore, answer d is incorrect.

Question 10

How do you reset the counters displayed by the **show interfaces bri 1** command?

❍ a. **clear bri**

❍ b. **clear arp**

❍ c. **clear interface bri**

❍ d. **clear counters interface bri 1**

The correct answer is d. The **clear counters** command requires the interface name and can then be used to reset individual interface statistics. The **clear bri** command is not a valid Cisco IOS command. Therefore, answer a is incorrect. The **clear arp** command deletes entries from the router's ARP cache. Therefore, answer b is incorrect. The **clear interface bri** command resets the hardware logic of the BRI interface, not the statistical counters. Therefore, answer c is incorrect.

Need To Know More?

Stallings, William. *Advances in ISDN and Broadband ISDN.* IEEE Computer Society Press. Los Alamitos, CA, 1992. ISBN 0818627956. This book covers, in great detail, the low-level processes and features of ISDN—from customer premises to service provider equipment.

Visit the Troubleshooting ISDN Connection page on Cisco Connection Online (CCO) at **www.cisco.com/univercd/home/home.htm**. From there, select Internetworking Troubleshooting Guide and then Troubleshooting ISDN Connections. There you'll find more information about ISDN troubleshooting techniques.

Check out the Integrated Services Digital Network and Point-to-Point Protocol pages at Cisco Connection Online (**www.cisco.com/univercd/home/home.htm**). From the CCO Documentation home page, select Internetworking Technology Overview, and then Integrated Services Digital Network or Point-to-Point Protocol. These two sections provide general background information about each of the technologies. If you had any difficulties reading through this chapter, it's highly recommended that you review each of these sections.

IP Diagnostics

Terms you'll need to understand:

- √ Outgoing and inbound access lists
- √ IP helper addresses
- √ Routing Information Protocol (RIP), Interior Gateway Routing Protocol (IGRP), Open Shortest Path First (OSPF), and Enhanced Interior Gateway Routing Protocol (EIGRP) routing
- √ Multicast routing
- √ Windows Internet Naming Service (WINS)

Techniques you'll need to master:

- √ Understanding the output generated by **show** commands
- √ Debugging TCP/IP protocols
- √ Using **clear** commands
- √ Diagnosing common TCP/IP problems
- √ Routing protocol redistribution
- √ Troubleshooting Microsoft Windows

Troubleshooting a TCP/IP internetwork can involve a variety of tasks, from fixing a failed network interface card to resetting improperly configured routing protocols. No matter what the reasons are for unavailable network services, the final result must be to provide end user connectivity. This chapter describes the most prominent Cisco IOS commands and how they can be used to troubleshoot a network. Also, this chapter lists several common TCP/IP issues as well as the standard procedures for resolving these issues.

Cisco IOS Commands

The **show**, **debug**, and **clear** commands described in this chapter can help you isolate TCP/IP problems related to routing, node connectivity, media performance, and applications.

Memorize all of the **show**, **debug**, and **clear** Cisco IOS commands and their functionality, as listed in this chapter—especially the commands that appear to produce the most informative results.

The show Commands

The **show** commands listed in Table 10.1 should provide enough details, if used properly, for you to diagnose approximately 85 percent of network failures. The remaining types of failures are serious enough that they should be presented to the Technical Assistance Center (TAC) for resolution.

Take the time to study these ten commands. Know what information each one lists and how the commands can be used in a troubleshooting scenario.

show ip access-lists

IP standard and extended access lists are shown via the **show ip access-lists** command (see Listing 10.1). This command can be used after you've retrieved a list bound to an interface or a protocol using the **show ip interface** or **show ip protocols** commands.

Listing 10.1 The output generated by issuing the **show ip access-lists** command.

```
Router>show ip access-lists
Standard IP access list 1
    deny   10.0.0.0, wildcard bits 0.255.255.255
    permit any
Extended IP access list 101
```

Table 10.1 Frequently used IP show commands for troubleshooting an internetwork.

Command	Description
show ip access-lists	Displays the contents of all current IP access lists
show ip arp	Displays the internal Address Resolution Protocol (ARP) cache
show ip eigrp interfaces	Displays EIGRP related information
show ip interface	Displays the current status of IP-configured interfaces
show ip interface brief	Displays a short table of the information shown using **show ip interface**
show ip mroute	Displays the IP multicast routing table
show ip ospf interface	Displays OSPF routing protocol-related information
show ip protocols	Displays enabled routing protocols and their associated information
show ip route	Displays IP routing table entries
show ip traffic	Displays IP traffic statistics for several transport and routing protocols

```
  deny   udp host 10.1.243.50 any log-input
  permit any
```

Access lists always have an implicit **deny any** located at the bottom of the list—keep this in mind during the exam. Also, access lists can literally bring down a network, because all the data at the Transport layer and below can be filtered against.

show ip arp

Use the **show ip arp** command, shown in Listing 10.2, to display the contents of the router's internal ARP cache.

Listing 10.2 The output generated by the **show ip arp** command.

```
Router>show ip arp
Protocol  Address        Age (min)  Hardware Addr   Type  Interface
Internet  10.5.186.100     115      00c0.4f8c.840d  ARPA  Ethernet3/1
Internet  10.5.180.35      181      0060.8367.6720  SNAP  Fddi2/0
Internet  10.5.186.43       -       aa00.0400.6cb7  ARPA  Ethernet3/1
Internet  10.5.180.43       -       0060.3e6f.3d40  SNAP  Fddi2/0
Internet  10.5.186.35       0       0000.0000.0000  ARPA  Ethernet3/1
```

This can be useful in troubleshooting errors with ARP or Reverse ARP (RARP) and in verifying host connectivity. Also, often while you're debugging a problem, the only information that's acquired is the Media Access Control (MAC) address. The ARP table generated by this command allows a lookup of the associated software address, and then a DNS lookup can be performed to retrieve the workstation's host and domain names. The highlighted line demonstrates that each entry displayed by the command contains the IP address (10.5.186.100), the time since the last update (115), the MAC address (00c0.4f8c.840d), the frame level encapsulation type (ARPA), and the router interface that the host is attached to (Ethernet3/1). Table 10.2 describes the column headings in more detail.

An entry in the ARP table that has all zeros for the MAC address means that you've sent an ARP request to the host but haven't received a response back. If you don't receive a response, the all-zeros entry should time out very quickly.

show ip eigrp interfaces

To display interfaces configured with the Enhanced Internet Gateway Routing Protocol (EIGRP) as well as information about those interfaces that relate to EIGRP, issue the command **show ip eigrp interfaces**. If an interface is specified, only that interface will be displayed. Otherwise, all interfaces on which EIGRP is running are displayed. Listing 10.3 displays the output of this command.

Table 10.2 The headings for the show ip arp table.

Column	Description
Address	The network address that corresponds to Hardware Addr
Age (min)	The age, in minutes, of the last update of the cache entry
Hardware Addr	The LAN hardware (or MAC) address that corresponds to the network address
Type	Encapsulation type: ARPA = Ethernet, SNAP = RFC 1042, and ISO1 = IEEE 802.3
Interface	The directly connected interface to which the ARP requests/replies were sent

Listing 10.3 The output of the **show ip eigrp interfaces** command.

```
Router>show ip eigrp interfaces
IP-EIGRP interfaces for process 221

                    Xmit Queue   Mean  Pacing Time  Multicast   Pending
Interface  Peers  Un/Reliable  SRTT  Un/Reliable  Flow Timer  Routes
Fa1/0        0         0/0           0     11/434          50          0
Fa1/1        1         0/0         130      0/10           50          0
Fa2/1        1         0/0          37      0/10          103          0
Fa2/2        1         0/0          19      0/10            0          0
```

Routing processes, at times, may incur strange events, such as route flapping or incorrect route updates and aging. This may be due to the routing protocol's instability or because of misconfigured or even failing devices within the internetwork. Table 10.3 describes the results of issuing the **show ip eigrp interfaces** command.

show ip interface

The **show ip interface** command lists the status of every IP-enabled interface and provides IP-specific information, such as helper addresses, access lists, the status of proxy ARP and split horizon, error codes that may or may not be sent by Internet Control Message Protocol (ICMP), and whether Internet Router

Table 10.3 The columns output from the show ip eigrp interfaces command.

Column	Description
Interface	The interface on which EIGRP is enabled.
Peers	The number of directly connected EIGRP neighbors.
Xmit Queue Un/Reliable	The number of packets remaining in the unreliable and reliable transmit queues.
Mean SRTT	The mean Smooth Round-Trip Time (SRTT), in milliseconds. This is the average of the time it takes for an EIGRP packet to be sent to a neighbor and then for an acknowledgment to be received.
Pacing Time Un/Reliable	Used to determine when EIGRP packets should be sent out on the interface.
Multicast Flow Timer	Maximum number of seconds before the router will send out multicast EIGRP packets.
Pending Routes	Number of routes in the transmit queue waiting to be sent.

Discovery Protocol (IRDP) is enabled. These commands can be very useful in providing information for initial internetwork discovery. The output from the **show ip interface** command is shown in Listing 10.4.

Listing 10.4 Output generated by the **show ip interface** command.

```
Router>show ip interface
Ethernet4/1 is up, line protocol is up
  Internet address is 10.100.1.1 255.255.255.248
  Broadcast address is 10.100.1.7
  Address determined by non-volatile memory
  MTU is 1500 bytes
  Helper address is not set
  Directed broadcast forwarding is disabled
  Multicast reserved groups joined: 224.0.0.1 224.0.0.5 224.0.0.6
  Outgoing access list is not set
  Inbound access list is not set
  Proxy ARP is enabled
  Security level is default
  Split horizon is enabled
  ICMP redirects are always sent
  ICMP unreachables are always sent
  ICMP mask replies are never sent
  IP fast switching is enabled
  IP fast switching on the same interface is disabled
  IP Optimum switching is disabled
  IP Flow switching is disabled
  IP LES Feature Fast switching turbo vector
  IP Null turbo vector
  IP multicast fast switching is disabled
  IP multicast distributed fast switching is disabled
  Router Discovery is disabled
  IP output packet accounting is disabled
  IP access violation accounting is disabled
  TCP/IP header compression is disabled
  Probe proxy name replies are disabled
  Gateway Discovery is disabled
  Policy routing is disabled
  Web Cache Redirect is disabled
  BGP Policy Mapping is disabled
```

Beyond internetwork discovery, this command can also be used to isolate trouble spots, such as misconfigured helper addresses and access lists, or even the fast switching type. The highlighted commands provide valuable information for troubleshooting internetwork problems. The usefulness of each command is described in Table 10.4.

Table 10.4 The relevance of the variables highlighted in the show ip interface command output.

Variable	Description
Helper address	Used to specify the host or broadcast address to retransmit broadcasts from the local network
Directed broadcasts	States whether directed broadcasts are allowed on the interface
Outgoing access-list	Specifies the access list number to be applied to outgoing (from the router) packets
Inbound access-list	Specifies the access list number to be applied to incoming (from the cable) packets
Split horizon	States whether split horizon is enabled on the interface
ICMP redirects	States whether the interface sends ICMP redirect messages
ICMP unreachables	States whether the interface sends ICMP unreachable messages
IP fast switching	States whether fast switching is enabled on the interface
IP Optimum switching	States whether optimum switching is enabled on the interface
IP Flow switching	States whether flow switching is enabled on the interface
Router Discovery	States whether IRDP hosts will be supported on the interface

The switching process enabled on an interface will directly affect the output generated by **debug** commands. This is due to the concept of *process switching*—having every packet go to the CPU. Fast switching, on the other hand, is based on independent traffic flows reaching the CPU only one time.

show ip interface brief

The **show ip interface** command generates statistics for many settings at once. But what if the only information required was the IP address associated with the interfaces and whether the interface was up or down? An excellent command that displays a short table of this information is **show ip interface brief**, as shown in Listing 10.5.

Listing 10.5 The output from the **show ip interface brief** command.

```
Router>show ip interface brief
Interface         IP-Address      OK?  Method    Status   Protocol
Ethernet1/1       10.13.10.1      YES  NVRAM     up       up
Ethernet1/2       unassigned      YES  unset     down     down
Ethernet1/3       10.14.10.1      YES  NVRAM     up       up
```

show ip mroute

This command displays information about the IP multicast routing table, which has results very similar to the standard IP routing table. The **show ip mroute** command, shown in Listing 10.6, lists each multicast entry with the destination group address, uptime, rendezvous point, and incoming/outgoing interfaces.

Listing 10.6 The **show ip mroute** command displays the current multicast routes.

```
Router>show ip mroute
IP Multicast Routing Table
Flags: D - Dense, S - Sparse, C - Connected, L - Local, P - Pruned
       R - RP-bit set, F - Register flag, T - SPT-bit set,
       J - Join SPT
Timers: Uptime/Expires
Interface state: Interface, Next-Hop, State/Mode

(*, 224.0.1.35), 2d14h/00:02:25, RP 10.2.2.1, flags: SJC
  Incoming interface: FastEthernet1/1, RPF nbr 10.2.2.1
  Outgoing interface list:
     Ethernet1, Forward/Sparse, 2d14h/00:02:25
```

You can use this command to verify end-to-end multicast group reservations and session connectivity. Table 10.5 describes the values shown in more detail.

The **show ip mroute active** command limits the display to sources sending at a data rate of greater than or equal to 4Kbps.

show ip ospf interface

The **show ip ospf interface** command can be used to identify explicit routing variables on all interfaces that have IP addresses within the network ranges specified by the Open Shortest Path First (OSPF) routing protocol within the

Table 10.5 Descriptions of the output generated by the show ip mroute command.

Variable	Description
Flags	Provides information about the entry.
(*, 224.0.1.35)	An entry in the IP multicast routing table. The entry consists of the IP address of the source router followed by the IP address of the multicast group. An asterisk (*) in place of the source router indicates all sources.
2d14h/00:02:25	The amount of time, in hours, minutes, and seconds, that the entry has been in the IP multicast routing table.
RP 10.2.2.1	The address of the rendezvous point (RP) router.
Flags: SJC	Information about the entry.
Incoming Interface	The expected interface for a multicast packet sent from the source. If the packet is not received on this interface, the packet is discarded.

running configuration. The command **show ip ospf interface** ***interface name*** can also be issued to show information about a specific interface—for example, **show ip ospf interface ethernet 0**. Listing 10.7 displays the output of this command.

Listing 10.7 Information generated by the command **show ip ospf interface**.

```
Router>show ip ospf interface
Ethernet4/1 is up, line protocol is up
  Internet Address 10.13.10.1/25, Area 0
  Process ID 683, Router ID 192.168.10.1,
     Network Type BROADCAST, Cost: 10
  Transmit Delay is 1 sec, State DR, Priority 1
  Designated Router (ID) 192.168.10.1, Interface address 10.1.10.1
  Backup Designated router (ID) 192.168.10.2,
     Interface address 10.13.10.2
Timer intervals configured,
     Hello 10, Dead 40, Wait 40, Retransmit 5
    Hello due in 00:00:10
  Neighbor Count is 1, Adjacent neighbor count is 1
    Adjacent with neighbor 10.100.1.1
```

OSPF troubleshooting generally requires a great deal of effort in identifying the designated and backup routers, the media type connecting devices, and the routing propagation intervals. This command simplifies the retrieval of this data. The output generated in Listing 10.7 is described in detail in Table 10.6.

Table 10.6 Descriptions of some of the output generated by the show ip ospf interface command.

Variable	Description
Router ID	The ID used by OSPF when propagating routing updates.
Network Type	Available types that can be defined are **BROADCAST**, **POINT-TO-POINT**, and **POINT-TO-MULTIPOINT**. This configuration relies on the media connecting devices, such as frame relay.
Designated Router	Designated router ID and respective interface IP address or hostname.
Backup Designated router	Backup designated router ID and respective interface IP address or hostname.
Timer intervals	Configuration of timer intervals.
Hello	Number of seconds until the next hello packet is sent out of this interface.
Dead	The amount of time hello packets must be received before the neighbor will be considered down.
Wait	The amount of time to wait before flushing a down neighbor out of the neighbor database.
Retransmit	The amount of time before link-state advertisements (LSAs) retransmit.
Adjacent Neighbor	The addresses of neighbors that OSPF adjacencies have been formed with.

Router IDs are reserved by the highest IP address assigned to an interface or, if a loopback interface is defined, its address will be used. If the interface with the highest IP address goes down for any reason, adjacent OSPF routers will assume that the router is down, and routing tables will be completely recalculated and redistributed. The preferred method is for a loopback interface to be defined within the router's configuration. Loopback interfaces are always up as long as the router has power.

show ip protocols

The **show ip protocols** command, shown in Listing 10.8, lists all enabled routing protocols and the associated values of several variables. Use this command to determine whether distribution lists are applied to routing protocols, whether the routing timers are the same across an administrative domain, which interfaces are enabled with the routing protocol, and which other routers the routing tables are being exchanged with.

Listing 10.8 The **show ip protocols** command generates a lot of information about every routing protocol enabled on the router.

```
Router>show ip protocols
Routing Protocol is "eigrp 221"
  Outgoing update filter list for all interfaces is 10
  Incoming update filter list for all interfaces is 20
  Default networks flagged in outgoing updates
  Default networks accepted from incoming updates
  EIGRP metric weight K1=1, K2=0, K3=1, K4=0, K5=0
  EIGRP maximum hopcount 100
  EIGRP maximum metric variance 1
  Redistributing: eigrp 221, ospf 221
  Automatic network summarization is not in effect
  Routing for Networks:
    10.0.0.0
  Passive Interface(s):
    Ethernet1
  Routing Information Sources:
    Gateway         Distance    Last Update
    10.1.1.1          90          1w4d
  Distance: internal 90 external 170

Routing Protocol is "ospf 221"
  Sending updates every 0 seconds
  Invalid after 0 seconds, hold down 0, flushed after 0
  Outgoing update filter list for all interfaces is 10
  Incoming update filter list for all interfaces is 20
Redistributing: static, ospf 683, igrp 75
  Routing for Networks:
    10.0.0.0/8
  Passive Interface(s):
    Ethernet1
  Routing Information Sources:
    Gateway          Distance      Last Update
    10.5.195.1            110      4d14h
    10.137.252.1          110      4d14h
    10.3.8.1              110      05:41:23
  Distance: (default is 110)

Routing Protocol is "igrp 75"
  Sending updates every 90 seconds, next due in 64 seconds
  Invalid after 270 seconds, hold down 280, flushed after 630
  Outgoing update filter list for all interfaces is 10
  Incoming update filter list for all interfaces is 20
  Default networks flagged in outgoing updates
```

```
  Default networks accepted from incoming updates
  IGRP metric weight K1=1, K2=0, K3=1, K4=0, K5=0
  IGRP maximum hopcount 100
  IGRP maximum metric variance 1
  Default redistribution metric is 1544 2000 255 128 1500
  Redistributing: connected, ospf 683 (internal, external 2)
  Redistributing: igrp 75
  Routing for Networks:
    10.103.13.0
  Passive Interface(s):
    Ethernet1
  Routing Information Sources:
    Gateway          Distance       Last Update
    10.103.13.2        100           00:00:31
  Distance: (default is 100)

Routing Protocol is "rip"
  Sending updates every 30 seconds, next due in 1 seconds
  Invalid after 180 seconds, hold down 180, flushed after 240
  Outgoing update filter list for all interfaces is not set
    Ethernet1/0 filtered by 57
  Incoming update filter list for all interfaces is not set
  Default redistribution metric is 1
  Redistributing: rip
  Default version control: send version 1, receive any version
    Interface         Send  Recv   Key-chain
    Loopback0         1     1 2
  Routing for Networks:
    10.202.100.0
  Passive Interface(s):
    Ethernet1
  Routing Information Sources:
    Gateway          Distance       Last Update
    10.202.100.2         255       00:00:06
  Distance: (default is 255)
```

The information contained within the output can be very valuable in troubleshooting routing protocol problems such as route flapping and routing protocol redistribution. Table 10.7 describes the variables displayed in Listing 10.8 in more detail.

show ip route

The **show ip route** command can be used to view the internal routing table entries of all IP routing protocols. The command provides very detailed information regarding the type of routing protocol announcing the route, the route's

Table 10.7 Variables Included in the show ip protocols command.

Variable	Description
Routing Protocol	Specifies the routing protocol in use as well as the process number, if valid.
Sending Updates	Specifies the time interval, in seconds, between the update messages. This only applies to distance-vector routing protocols.
Invalid	Specifies the value of the invalid parameter. This only applies to distance-vector routing protocols.
Hold down	Indicates the current value of the hold-down variable. This only applies to distance-vector routing protocols.
Flushed	Specifies the time until single route entries will be removed from the routing table.
Outgoing Update Filter	Specifies the filter, if any, applied by the **distribute-list out** command.
Incoming Update Filter	Specifies the filter, if any, applied by the **distribute-list in** command.
Redistributing	Identifies the protocols that are being redistributed by the **redistribute** command.
Default Version Control	Identifies the versions of RIP that are being sent and which versions will be accepted.
Default Redistribution Metric	Distance-vector protocols are required to specify this variable.
Routing for Networks	Specifies the networks that are being advertised by the local routing process.
Passive Interface(s)	Specifies the interfaces that are not propagating routing information.
Routing Information Sources	A list of all routing sources that are being used to build the internal routing table.
Distance	The preference level of routes maintained by a routing protocol in comparison to routes administered by another routing protocol. This variable identifies which route is administratively preferred, regardless of internal metrics.

associated administrative and dynamically calculated weights, the default gateway, the time since the last update, and the interface the update was received on. This is all shown in Listing 10.9.

Listing 10.9 Sample output from the **show ip route** command.

```
Router>show ip route
Codes: C - connected, S - static, I - IGRP, R - RIP, M - mobile,
       B - BGP, D - EIGRP, EX - EIGRP external, O - OSPF,
       IA - OSPF inter area, E1 - OSPF external type 1,
       E2 - OSPF external type 2, E - EGP, i - IS-IS,
       L1 - IS-IS level-1, L2 - IS-IS level-2,
       * - candidate default

Gateway of last resort is 10.1.1.1 to network 0.0.0.0
O E1 10.2.1.0/24 [110/151] via 10.200.1.1, 00:13:37, Ethernet0
C    10.100.1.0/29 is directly connected, Ethernet4/1
R    10.1.1.0/24 [120/1] via 10.200.10.1, 00:00:16, Ethernet4/3
I    10.210.0.0/16 [100/9450] via 10.10.3.1, 00:00:34, Serial2/0
B    204.17.221.0/24 [20/10] via 193.3.11.5, 1d17h
B    192.35.226.0/24 [20/10] via 193.3.11.9, 4d03h
```

The **show ip route** command's fields and their descriptions are described using information from the first entry. The OSPF external type 1 entry (O E1) for the 10.2.1.0/24 network, learned 13 minutes and 37 seconds ago, has an administrative distance of 110 and a metric of 151 ([110/151]). The next hop router's IP address is 10.200.1.1, and it is directly connected to the Ethernet0 interface. The other entries located within the table were learned by other routing protocols, but can be identified in a similar manner.

The **show ip route** command can also be further divided by restricting the information returned to one route only (for example, **show ip route 10.1.0.0**). You can also restrict on the type of routing protocols—for instance, **show ip route ospf** would only show routes learned by the OSPF routing protocol.

show ip traffic

The **show ip traffic** command provides generic statistics for several IP protocols, such as ICMP, User Datagram Protocol (UDP), Transmission Control Protocol (TCP), Protocol Independent Multicast (PIM), Internet Group Message Protocol (IGMP), ARP, and routing protocols. Due to the redundancy of several of the fields for each IP protocol, only the IP, ICMP, UDP, and ARP statistics sections returned from this command are shown in Listing 10.10.

Listing 10.10 A partial listing of information generated by the **show ip traffic** command.

```
Router>show ip traffic
IP statistics:
  Rcvd:  2724438798 total, 13264779 local destination
```

```
        5 format errors, 2 checksum errors, 2792697 bad hop count
        0 unknown protocol, 0 not a gateway
        0 security failures, 0 bad options, 791114 with options
  Frags: 5141 reassembled, 0 timeouts, 0 couldn't reassemble
        1587470 fragmented, 6 couldn't fragment
  Bcast: 4014989 received, 1743991 sent
  Mcast: 5700658 received, 111306087 sent
  Sent:  10644501 generated, 2614924472 forwarded
        2691902 encapsulation failed, 372634 no route
ICMP statistics:
  Rcvd: 0 format errors, 0 checksum errors, 39 redirects,
       1446542 unreachable, 229854 echo, 1320 echo reply,
       6 mask requests, 0 mask replies, 162 quench
       0 parameter, 0 timestamp, 0 info request, 0 other
       1232 irdp solicitations, 0 irdp advertisements
  Sent: 59495 redirects, 526 unreachable, 125 echo,
       229854 echo reply, 0 mask requests, 0 mask replies,
       0 quench, 0 timestamp, 0 info reply,
       1626476 time exceeded, 0 parameter problem,
       0 irdp solicitations, 0 irdp advertisements
UDP statistics:
  Rcvd: 4373503 total, 67 checksum errors, 2640712 no port
  Sent: 2480527 total, 633572 forwarded broadcasts
ARP statistics:
  Rcvd: 2018773 requests, 36183 replies, 44098 reverse, 0 other
  Sent: 1917355 requests, 683486 replies (52700 proxy), 0 reverse
```

The IP traffic statistics can be used to verify correct packet propagation, isolate the locations of errors, and generate network baselines. Table 10.8 describes the IP statistics fields.

Several statistics are also provided for ICMP, UDP, and ARP, as described in Table 10.9.

Table 10.8 Some of the IP statistics variables shown in Listing 10.10 and their descriptions.

Type	Variable	Description
Rcvd	Total	The total number of IP datagrams received by the router
	Local Destination	The total number of IP datagrams that were destined for a directly connected network
	Format Errors	Indicates an error in the packet format

(continued)

Table 10.8 Some of the IP statistics variables shown in Listing 10.10 and their descriptions (continued).

Type	Variable	Description
	Bad Hop Count	Occurs when a packet is discarded because its Time To Live (TTL) field was decremented to zero.
	With Options	The number of datagrams processed using options such as record route, source route, and timestamp.
Frags	Reassembled	The number of fragments reassembled by the router.
	Fragmented	The number of fragmentations that have occurred because the sending interface was configured with smaller MTU sizes than the interface the packet was received on.
Sent	Generated	The number of IP datagrams generated by the router.
	Forwarded	The number of IP datagrams forwarded by the router.
	Encapsulation Failed	Usually indicates that the router had no ARP request entry and therefore did not send a datagram.
	No Route	Counted when the Cisco IOS software discards a datagram it did not know how to route.

Table 10.9 Some of the ICMP, UDP, and ARP variables shown in Listing 10.10 and their descriptions.

Protocol	Variable	Description
ICMP	Redirects	The number of ICMP redirect messages sent by the router to the hosts.
	Unreachable	The number of ICMP unreachable messages sent by the router to the hosts.
	Quench	The number of ICMP source quench messages sent by the router to the hosts.
ICMP	Time Exceeded	The number of ICMP packets that have exceeded their TTL values.
	IRDP	The number of hosts requesting their default gateway addresses using ICMP Router Discovery Protocol (IRDP).

(continued)

Table 10.9 Some of the ICMP, UDP, and ARP variables shown in Listing 10.10 and their descriptions (continued).

Protocol	Variable	Description
UDP	No Port	The number of UDP packets received with a destination port.
	Forwarded Broadcasts	The number of UDP broadcasts forwarded by the router. This is set by the helper addresses.
ARP	Reverse	The number of RARP requests answered by the router.
	Proxy	The number of proxy ARP requests that have been received.

The debug Commands

In general, debugging IP protocols can be very difficult because so much data is produced, and it's hard to verify what's actually being sought.

Within the Cisco IOS, several IP debugging commands exist. Table 10.10 lists a few of the most commonly used commands and descriptions of what they display. Each command will be thoroughly described in the following sections and sample output will be shown.

Table 10.10 Frequently used IP debug commands used for troubleshooting an internetwork.

Command	Description
debug arp	Displays information about ARP transactions
debug ip eigrp	Displays information on Enhanced IGRP protocol packets
debug ip icmp	Displays information on ICMP transactions
debug ip igrp events	Displays summary information for IGRP routing messages
debug ip ospf events	Displays information on OSPF-related events
debug ip packet	Displays general IP packet information along with IP security option transactions
debug ip rip	Displays information on RIP routing transactions, including complete routing tables
debug ip routing	Displays information on RIP routing table updates and route cache updates

debug arp

The command **debug arp** provides details of the IP-to-MAC address resolution process, which is the process provided by ARP. If some hosts on the network are not responding but others are, this command will show whether the router is sending and receiving ARP messages. An ARP message contains information indicating whether the message was sent or received, the source and destination MAC addresses and IP addresses, and the interface on which the packet was sent or received. Listing 10.11 shows several ARP replies and transmissions on an internetwork.

Listing 10.11 The **debug arp** command generates useful information for debugging hardware address resolution issues.

```
Router#debug arp
ARP packet debugging is on

IP ARP: sent req src 10.18.22.7 0000.0c01.e117,
     dst 10.18.22.34 0000.0000.0000 FastEthernet1/1
IP ARP throttled out the ARP Request for 10.18.22.7
IP ARP: rcvd rep src 10.18.22.96 0800.2010.b908,
     dst 10.18.22.7 FastEthernet1/1
IP ARP: rep filtered src 10.201.13.7 a0b2.393a.c7d6,
     dst 255.255.255.255 ffff.ffff.ffff FastEthernet1/1
IP ARP: rep filtered src 10.200.10.27 0000.0c00.ac31,
     dst 10.107.29.7 0800.2ac3.5a21
```

If the MAC address is listed as all zeros, it is an ARP request. The receiver of this message will reply to the sender after filling in its own MAC address. Reply filtering occurs when a host on the network attempts to inform the router of an IP address that's not a properly configured address on the locally attached network. If the router were to add this address to its ARP table, the machine would be denied further service on any attached interface. *ARP throttling* means that an ARP request was already issued for the IP address and that the router does not need to send another while it's waiting for the reply.

debug ip eigrp

debug ip eigrp analyzes the EIGRP packets that are sent and received by the router. Use this command to diagnose issues related to routing updates, metric changes, and advertisement requirements. Events processed by this command are shown in Listing 10.12.

Listing 10.12 The information displayed by the **debug ip eigrp** command.

```
Router#debug ip eigrp
IP-EIGRP: Processing incoming UPDATE packet

IP-EIGRP: Ext 142.16.3.0 255.255.255.0 M 386560 - 256000 130560
          SM 360960 - 256000 104960
IP-EIGRP: Ext 142.16.5.0 255.255.255.0 M 386560 - 256000 130560
          SM 360960 - 256000 104960
IP-EIGRP: Ext 142.16.7.0 255.255.255.0 M 386560 - 256000 130560
          SM 360960 - 256000 104960
IP-EIGRP: Processing incoming UPDATE packet
IP-EIGRP: Int 10.68.7.0 255.255.255.0 M 386560 - 256000 130560
          SM 360960 - 256000 104960
IP-EIGRP: Int 10.68.3.0 255.255.255.0 M 386560 - 256000 130560
          SM 360960 - 256000 104960
```

The events processed in Listing 10.12 describe the following information:

- **Lines 1 through 4** These are external (EXT) routing updates with three routes, the computed metrics (M) of composite, inverse bandwidth and delay, and the metric reported by the neighboring router (SM).
- **Lines 5 through 7** These are internal (INT) routing updates with the same information as the external updates.

Because the **debug ip eigrp** command generates large amounts of output, you should use it with extreme caution.

debug ip icmp

This debugging command displays sending and receiving information on the ICMP transactions performed by the router. Debugging ICMP messages can help you troubleshoot end-to-end connectivity problems. For example, the messages generated may indicate that packets are being prohibited administratively, the protocol is unreachable, or IRDP is not working correctly. Sample output from the **debug ip icmp** command is displayed in Listing 10.13.

Listing 10.13 Output from the **debug ip icmp** command.

```
Router#debug ip icmp
ICMP packet debugging is on
```

```
ICMP: echo reply rcvd, src 10.7.210.125, dst 10.7.210.125
ICMP: echo reply sent, src 10.7.66.17, dst 10.7.96.10
ICMP: time exceeded (time to live) sent to 10.14.208.26
     (dest was 10.7.1.9)
ICMP: dst (10.7.1.121) port unreachable rcv from 10.7.1.99
ICMP: dst (255.255.255.255) protocol unreachable rcv from 10.1.1.3
ICMP: source quench rcvd 10.200.1.10
```

ICMP debugging can also be used for detecting network scans and as a rudimentary intrusion detection device.

debug ip igrp events

Use the **debug ip igrp events** command to display summary information about IGRP routing messages that indicate the source and destination of each update as well as the number of routes included in each update. Sample output for the command is displayed in Listing 10.14.

Listing 10.14 Debugging IGRP using the **debug ip igrp events** command.

```
Router#debug ip igrp events
IGRP event debugging is on

IGRP: received update from 10.7.1.2 on Ethernet0
IGRP: Update contains 3 interior, 2 system, and 0 exterior routes.
IGRP: Total routes in update: 5
IGRP: sending update to 255.255.255.255 via Ethernet0 (10.7.10.1)
IGRP: Update contains 1 interior, 2 system, and 0 exterior routes.
IGRP: Total routes in update: 2
```

This output shows that the router has received one update from host 10.7.1.2 and has also sent one update to the broadcast address 255.255.255.255. Here's a description of the three lines of output for both of these updates:

- **Lines 1 and 4** These indicate whether the router sent or received the update packet, the source or destination address, and the interface through which the update was sent or received. If the update was sent, the IP address assigned to this interface is shown.
- **Lines 2 and 5** These lines state the number and types of routes sent.
- **Lines 3 and 6** These indicate the total number of routes sent.

debug ip ospf events

This command displays information on OSPF-related events, such as adjacencies, flooding, designated router selection, and Shortest Path First (SPF) calculations. Listing 10.15 displays the output from the command.

Listing 10.15 Output generated by the **debug ip ospf events** command.

```
Router#debug ip ospf events
OSPF events debugging is on

OSPF: Rcv hello from 10.5.9.253 area 221
      from FastEthernet1/1 10.9.150.2
OSPF: End of hello processing
OSPF: hello with invalid timers on interface Ethernet0
      hello interval received 10 configured 10
      net mask received 255.255.255.0 configured 255.255.255.0
      dead interval received 40 configured 30
```

OSPF events contain hello updates and can detect invalid OSPF configurations. The events processed in Listing 10.15 describe the following information:

- **Lines 1 and 2** These two lines indicate that a hello was received from host 10.5.9.253, located in area 221, on FastEthernet1/1.
- **Line 3** This line detected an invalid dead interval timer but also processed subnet mask information and the hello interval timer.

debug ip packet

IP packet debugging can be useful in analyzing traffic from local hosts connected to remote hosts. Packet details are captured on all packets received, both generated and forwarded. The information acquired includes source and destination addresses, the length of the packet, and whether the packet was forwarded or received by the router (see Listing 10.16).

Listing 10.16 Output from the **debug ip packet** command.

```
Router#debug ip packet
IP packet debugging is on

IP: s=10.2.18.2 (FDDI2/0), d=10.3.8.7, len 100, forward
IP: s=10.2.18.2 (Ethernet), d=255.255.255.255, len 52, rcvd 2
IP: s=10.2.18.3 (ATM2/1), d=224.0.0.5, len 208, rcvd 0
IP: s=10.2.18.6 (local), d=10.2.28.7 (FDDI2/0), len 208, sending
```

Debugging all IP packets can quickly overload the router—the data acquired is overwhelming. To fix this, you can apply either a standard or extended access list to this command. This requires the datagram to be permitted by the access list before the related debugging output is shown. This will restrict the view to only valuable information and reduce router processing overhead.

debug ip rip

Use this command to display information about Routing Interior Protocol (RIP) routing transactions. RIP broadcasts its complete routing table every 60 seconds; the **debug ip rip** command provides information included in these routing updates, along with some error reporting. Listing 10.17 shows a few events logged by the **debug ip rip** command.

Listing 10.17 Output displayed by the command **debug ip rip**.

```
Router#debug ip rip
RIP protocol debugging is on

RIP: received update from 10.3.1.2 on Ethernet4
     10.3.4.0 in 1 hops
     10.3.6.0 in 3 hops
     10.9.13.0 in 16 hops (inaccessible)
     0.0.0.0 in 7 hops
RIP: sending update to 255.255.255.255 via Ethernet4
     subnet 10.3.2.0, metric 1
     subnet 10.3.3.0, metric 3
     10.9.13.0 in 16 hops (inaccessible)
RIP: sending v2 update to 224.0.0.9 via Ethernet3
     0.0.0.0/0 -> 0.0.0.0, metric 16, tag 0
     10.4.0.0/16 -> 0.0.0.0, metric 1, tag 0
RIP: broadcasting general request Ethernet4
RIP: bad version 128 from 10.3.7.1
```

The output shows that the router being debugged has received updates from one router at source address 10.3.1.2 on Ethernet4. This router sent information about three destinations in the routing table update. Notice that the third destination address in the update, 10.9.13.0, is inaccessible because it's more than 15 hops away from the router sending the update. The router being debugged also sent updates to the broadcast address 255.255.255.255 for the RIP version 1 format and a multicast to 224.0.0.9 for the RIP version 2 format. The fourth RIP event is due to an interface being transitioned or a routing table being manually cleared. Finally, the sender of a malformed packet most likely caused the fifth RIP event.

debug ip routing

The **debug ip routing** command displays events pertaining to routing protocol and route-cache update messages. Listing 10.18 shows the output from the command.

Listing 10.18 Use the **debug ip routing** command to view routing protocol update messages.

```
Router#debug ip routing
IP routing debugging is on

RT: add 10.13.7.0/25 via 0.0.0.0, connected metric [0/0]
RT: add 10.13.19.0/25 via 0.0.0.0, connected metric [0/0]
RT: add 10.13.20.0/25 via 0.0.0.0, connected metric [0/0]
RT: add 10.13.24.0/23 via 0.0.0.0, connected metric [0/0]
RT: add 10.20.12.0/26 via 0.0.0.0, connected metric [0/0]
RT: network 10.13.0.0 is now variably masked
RT: closer admin distance for 10.13.20.0, flushing 1 routes
RT: add 10.13.20.0/25 via 10.13.72.2, static metric [1/0]
RT: add 0.0.0.0/0 via 10.20.128.1, ospf metric [110/1]
RT: default path is now 0.0.0.0 via 10.20.12.1
RT: new default network 0.0.0.0
```

The information shown by the command displays the OSPF routing protocol exchanging routing update messages between routers. The command will also display information about other IP routing protocols, such as IGRP, RIP, and EIGRP. Each entry can contain valuable information about network routes, metrics, route flushes, and default network paths. The routing events displayed by this command generally do not occur in a stable network, so a high number of them could be a cause for concern. Increased activity may be due to route flapping, which can be caused by a number of problems, such as hardware failures, routing protocol misconfigurations, or poor connections. You can use this command with the **show ip protocols** command to help isolate inconsistent route-cache and routing update timers.

The clear Commands

While troubleshooting a network, you may need to remove routes from the routing tables or entries from the ARP cache. This and other functions can be performed by using **clear** commands. Only the most relevant IP **clear** commands are described in Table 10.11.

clear arp-cache

The **clear arp-cache** command removes all dynamic entries from the ARP cache, and also clears the fast-switching cache. Clearing the ARP cache can

Table 10.11 Frequently used IP clear commands for troubleshooting an internetwork.

Command	Description
clear arp-cache	Deletes all ARP entries from within the ARP table
clear ip access-list counters	Clears all statistics from access list statements within an access list number
clear ip mroute	Deletes the active routes located in the multicast routing table
clear ip route	Deletes the active routing table

be valuable if a host's network card is replaced and the ARP entry has not expired yet.

Enabling DECnet on an interface regenerates a new MAC address for that interface; this is outlined by the DECnet protocols. This would lead to an invalid entry in other hosts' and routers' ARP caches and there would be no traffic to the interface. The **clear arp-cache** command resolves this issue.

clear ip access-list counters

Access list counters display the number of times each line of the access list configuration has either permitted or denied an IP packet. This logging feature is defined with the **log-input** attribute. Access list counters may need to be cleared when you're troubleshooting application failures as well as when you're attempting to isolate potential network scans by external hackers.

clear ip mroute

The **clear ip mroute** command performs the same function as **clear ip route**, except it uses multicast routes. The routes can be removed by either specifying the host address receiving the multicast session or the multicast group address itself, as shown in Listing 10.19.

Listing 10.19 The **clear ip mroute** command can delete host or group multicast routes or the entire routing table.

```
Router#clear ip mroute ?
  *                    Delete all multicast routes
  Hostname or A.B.C.D  IP name or group address
```

clear ip route

The **clear ip route** command can be used to force routing table recalculations within a routing protocol administrative domain. This can be useful after you've enabled a new interface. Routes can be cleared one at a time or the entire routing table can be deleted, as shown in Listing 10.20.

Listing 10.20 The **clear ip route** command can delete individual routes or the entire routing table.

```
Router#clear ip route ?
  *        Delete all routes
  A.B.C.D  Destination network route to delete
```

The command **clear ip route** * should be used with extreme caution. This deletes all routing entries within a router and disables routing while the table is being rebuilt through the routing protocols. This requires a varying amount of time because the convergence time of each type of routing protocol varies.

Common TCP/IP Issues

Within a TCP/IP environment, you'll find several recurring issues concerning host connectivity, unavailable applications, and routing. These common problems can normally be resolved using standard procedures or circumvented by initially configuring internetwork routers properly. The following sections show some common scenarios involving TCP/IP.

Scenario 1: Host Connectivity

The network is down. This is a typical problem reported by users, but it may have one of several solutions. First, the scope of the problem should be narrowed at the client's workstation. This will define whether the problem is with a single host, multiple hosts, the local network, or a remote network. The following steps detail the sequence of events that should be performed while you're determining the scope of an internetwork failure:

1. Ping the workstation's loopback address (127.0.0.1). This will verify that the TCP/IP stack has been loaded properly. If this is unsuccessful, the TCP/IP stack may be corrupt and a reinstallation may be necessary. If this action is successful, continue to Step 2.

2. Ping the workstation's local IP address. This will check whether the network card and driver are functioning correctly. If this is unsuccessful,

you should verify that the network card is configured correctly and that the local IP address and subnet mask information is correct. If this action is successful, continue to Step 3.

3. Ping a workstation connected on the local network. This will verify that the local workstation can see other directly connected hosts. If this is unsuccessful, you should ensure that all cables are connected correctly and that the remote host is configured correctly. The local workstation ARP table should also be verified for correct address resolution. If this action is successful, continue to Step 4.

4. Ping the workstation's default gateway IP address. This will check whether the workstation can successfully communicate with the locally connected router on the network. If this is unsuccessful, you should verify that the default gateway IP address is correct and that the router's interface is up using the **show ip interface** command. Also check the router's ARP table for correct IP-to-MAC address resolution using the **show ip arp** command. If there isn't an entry listed for the workstation's IP address, verify that the router is responding to ARP requests using **debug arp**. If this action is successful, continue to Step 5.

5. Ping several remote hosts' IP addresses on different networks. If this is unsuccessful, you should find the point of failure using the **traceroute** command. This will identify all routers between the local and remote hosts. Log into the router where the **traceroute** command ends and check for routes to the destination and source addresses using the **show ip route** command. If a route does not exist, check the routing protocols for proper configuration using **show ip protocols**. If this action is successful, continue to Step 6.

The **ping** and **traceroute** commands will not work if an access list has been applied to an interface anywhere between the host and destination IP address restricting the ICMP protocol. This can be verified by using the **debug ip icmp** command.

6. Ping the local workstation using its DNS name. If this is unsuccessful, check the local configuration to verify that the hostname and domain name are correctly defined. Next, check that the IP addresses of the DNS servers are specified correctly and try pinging their IP addresses to verify remote connectivity. If this is still unsuccessful, return to Step 1. If this action is successful, continue to Step 7.

7. Ping another workstation on the local network using its DNS name. If this is unsuccessful, repeat Step 3 to verify local IP connectivity. If Step 3 is successful, use the **nslookup** command to check for name resolution. If this action is successful, continue to Step 8.

8. Ping a remote host using its DNS name. If this is unsuccessful, return to Step 5. If this action is successful, remote connectivity at the IP level using DNS has been verified. If the problem still exists, you now know that the issue lies in either the Transport or Application layer of the OSI model. Common items to check for are host application errors, router-configured access lists, and NetBIOS name resolution using helper addresses.

During the troubleshooting process, stick to a strict methodology. Continue using the same IP addresses and DNS names to try to resolve issues—randomness will greatly reduce the possibility of isolating the problem.

Scenario 2: Unavailable Applications

A user reports that he or she is unable to browse Web sites located on the Internet. Most likely, this issue or any other application-specific failure resides with improperly configured access lists. In this case, the problem may be with an access list prohibiting access on port 80 for a single host, a range of IP addresses, or all hosts.

Use the **traceroute** command to determine the routers between the workstation and the remote Internet site. Log into each of these routers and check for misconfigured access lists using the **show ip access-lists** command. If access lists are found and it's not prohibited to completely remove them from an interface, do so and then check whether connectivity has been restored. If this is strictly prohibited, compare all access lists bound to interfaces between the source and destination address, looking for a reason why access has been restricted for a certain protocol type. Common issues concerning access lists include the ordering of the commands within the list and the implicit **deny all** located at the end of every list.

If IP extended access lists are used, system logging can be enabled independent of each **permit** and **deny** statement within the list. This can aid you in troubleshooting application errors because all blocked IP packets will be sent to the system logs.

Scenario 3: IP Routing

Routing packets across an internetwork can be very straightforward, or it can be an engineer's nightmare. Several routing protocols exist, each with its own idiosyncrasies and special ways to implement unique routing scenarios. Some of the common mistakes made when configuring IP routing include misconfigured network statements, inappropriate use of classful addresses, improperly configured distribute-in and distribute-out access lists, protocol redistribution, and disparate routing protocol timers.

RIP And IGRP

RIP and IGRP are both classful routing protocols, which is where most of the troubleshooting issues with these protocols reside. Every interface within a major network must have the same subnet mask configured, because masking information is not propagated within the routing tables of RIP and IGRP. Figure 10.1 shows a classic misconfiguration of dividing a network with different subnet masks while using a classful routing protocol.

In Figure 10.1, Host 1 attempts to retrieve a file from Host 2. The packet is addressed to 10.4.50.25 and sent to the default gateway (Router C). Router C

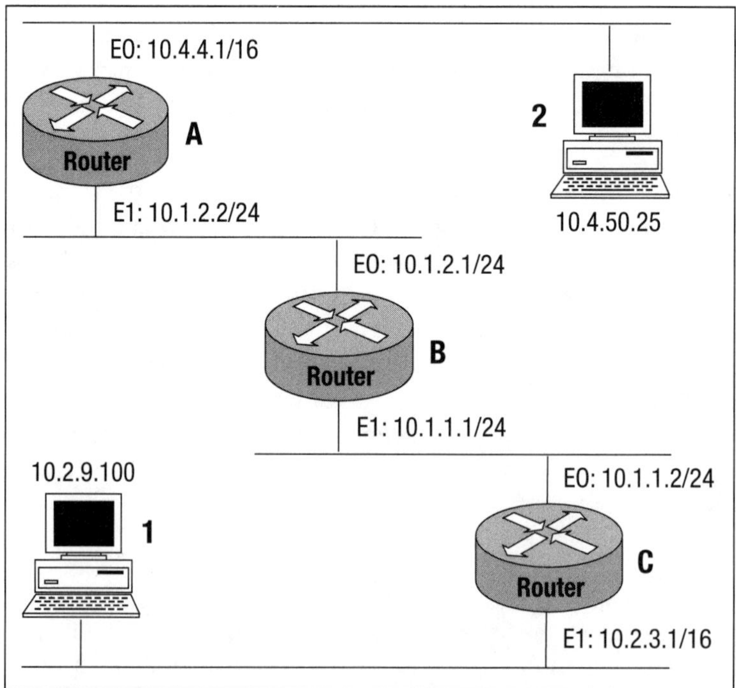

Figure 10.1 An IGRP environment using variable-length subnet masks (VLSMs).

performs a routing table lookup for the destination network using the local subnet mask; the best route to take is to network 10.4.0.0/16 via 10.1.1.1 (Router B). The packet is sent to Router B and another routing table lookup is performed for the destination, again using the local subnet mask. The best route to take to network 10.4.50.0/24 is missing; only the routes to networks 10.1.2.0/24 and 10.4.4.0/24 exist. Therefore, the packet will be dropped by Router B and the connection will never take place.

Beware of any classful routing protocols not adhering to address classes (using VLSMs). This is one of the first things to check for when troubleshooting a RIP- or IGRP-enabled network.

Missing Routes

Redistributing RIP and IGRP routes into OSPF or EIGRP, shown in Figure 10.2, requires the command **redistribute ospf subnets** to be included within the routing protocol configuration. RIP and IGRP are classless routing protocols, so it's expected during redistribution that everything will adhere to standard Class A, B, and C addressing schemas. Including this command redistributes subnet mask information into an exterior routing protocol. Listing 10.21 shows a sample configuration for this situation.

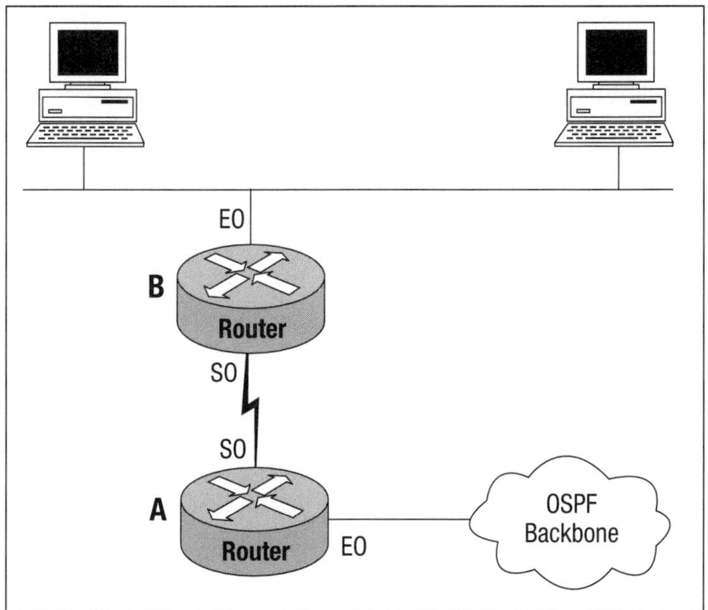

Figure 10.2 Two routers redistributing between OSPF and RIP routing protocols.

Listing 10.21 The running configurations of Routers A and B shown in Figure 10.2.

```
Router A                                 Router B
interface serial 0                       interface serial 0
ip add 10.1.62.2 255.255.0.0             ip add 10.1.6.1 255.255.0.0
!                                        !
interface ethernet 0                     interface ethernet 0
ip add 10.2.72.1 255.255.0.0             ip add 10.10.8.1 255.255.0.0
!                                        !
router rip                               router rip
default-metric 10                        default-metric 10
network 10.1.0.0                         network 10.1.0.0
network 10.2.0.0                         network 10.10.0.0
passive-interface ethernet 0             passive-interface ethernet 0
redistribute ospf 10 subnets
!
router ospf 10
passive-interface serial 0
network 10.1.0.0 0.0.255.255 area 0
network 10.2.0.0 0.0.255.255 area 0
redistribute rip subnets
```

A few more issues can be brought up while viewing the router configurations shown in Listing 10.20, such as the following:

- All data transported between OSPF areas must transit through the backbone area 0.
- The **passive-interface** command disables all routing updates from propagating out of that interface.
- Default metrics for distance-vector protocols are used when redistributing into other protocols.

Scenario 4: Microsoft Windows NetBIOS

Workstations running current Microsoft Windows operating systems require NetBIOS names to operate within a Windows domain. This leads to one of two scenarios: NetBIOS traffic is encapsulated within a TCP/IP packet and a Windows Internet Naming Service (WINS) server is used to resolve NetBIOS names to IP addresses, or native NetBIOS traffic flows across the internetwork using bridging. The latter scenario causes substantially higher amounts of traffic across the entire network because NetBIOS is a nonroutable protocol; therefore, the network has to incorporate bridging or the interfaces must be configured with **ip helper-addresses**. Helper addresses forward network broadcasts and any other traffic specified by the **ip forward-protocol** command set.

A sample network is shown in Figure 10.3 with the router code shown in Listing 10.22.

Listing 10.22 A partial display of the router's configuration, with both bridging and a helper address configured.

```
ip forward-protocol UDP
!
interface Ethernet 0
description "Server Farm"
ip address 10.3.100.1 255.255.255.0
bridge-group 1
!
interface Ethernet 1
description "Marketing Dept"
ip address 10.3.101.1 255.255.255.0
ip helper-address 10.3.100.7
bridge-group 1
!
bridge 1 protocol ieee
```

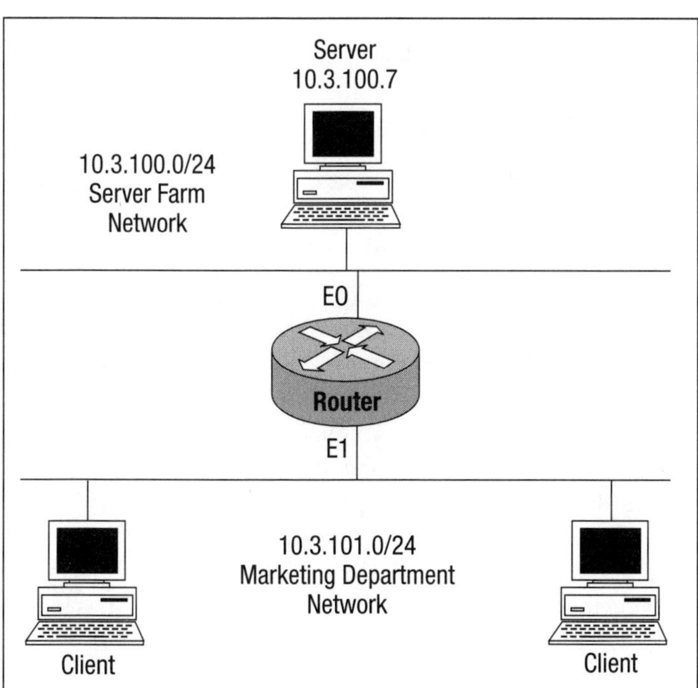

Figure 10.3 A sample client/server environment.

Practice Questions

Question 1

A user located at IP address 10.200.10.27 is reporting that the network is unavailable. Attempts to ping the default gateway are unsuccessful, but the network card is installed properly and pings of the loopback address and locally assigned IP address are successful. Other users on the local network are not experiencing difficulties, so this is an isolated incident. Performing the **debug arp** command produces the following results. What's the best solution to the problem?

```
IP ARP: sent req src 10.18.22.7 0000.0c01.e117,
     dst 10.18.22.34 0000.0000.0000 Ethernet1/1
IP ARP: rep filtered src 10.200.10.27
     0800.2ac3.5a21,
     dst 10.200.10.1 0000.0c00.ac31
```

❍ a. Check the router's interface to see whether the line protocols are up.

❍ b. Nothing, it will eventually start working.

❍ c. Replace the network card and try again.

❍ d. Perform a **clear arp-cache** command on the locally attached router and then attempt to ping the default gateway again.

The correct answer is d. The second event within the **debug arp** output shows that another host might possibly already have an ARP entry into the router for IP address 10.200.10.27. Clearing the ARP cache may solve the problem, or the remote host may be misconfigured and require reconfiguration before the user's workstation will operate correctly. Other users on the local segment are not experiencing any difficulties, so the line protocols on the router's interface are functioning properly. Therefore, answer a is incorrect. Doing nothing may actually work, but this is not necessarily the best solution. Therefore, answer b is incorrect. Replacing the network card could fix the problem, but this is highly unlikely because pings against the loopback address were successful. Therefore, answer c is incorrect.

Question 2

Users are complaining about sporadic availability of services outside their local network. After asking the users for more details and inspecting the local topology, you identify two routers appearing between the users and the services that are only available at certain times. Performing the **show ip route** command on router one shows that the route to the remote network is currently available. Approximately two minutes pass and you issue the command again—this time the route is labelled as possibly down. Five minutes later the command is issued again, and the routing table has removed the route completely. Another five minutes pass by and the command is issued a final time; now the routes are back in the routing table. What is this a common symptom of and how would you point out the problem?

❍ a. Misconfigured distribution lists are denying the propagation of routes. This can be shown by issuing **show ip protocols** and then **show ip access-lists**.

❍ b. Improper routing updates are being issued between the two routers. Turning on debugging using the **debug ip rip** command can verify this.

❍ c. Inconsistent routing protocol timers are causing route flapping. Comparing the results of the **show ip protocols** command on Routers 1 and 2 can identify this.

❍ d. Access lists are configured on the interfaces that deny routing updates. This can be verified by performing **show ip interface** and **show ip access-lists**.

The correct answer is c. Inconsistent routing update timers may produce very strange results, but routes appearing and disappearing directly map to timing issues. Issuing the **show ip protocols** command displays all timers configured for every enabled routing protocol. Distribution lists would never allow the route to show up in a routing table, unlike the sporadic events occurring. Therefore, answer a is incorrect. Improper routing updates may be occurring between the two routers; if the routers were running RIP, this would be the command to issue, but the question does not specify the routing protocol in use. Therefore, answer b is incorrect. Access lists would prevent the routes from ever appearing in the routing table. Therefore, answer d is incorrect.

Question 3

Microsoft Windows workstations configured with NetBIOS are unable to browse servers located within the domain using Network Neighborhood. All the servers are located within the 10.30.27.0/24 network. What could be done so that the workstations can see the servers within their Network Neighborhood? [Choose the two best answers]

- ❑ a. Add an IP helper address of 10.30.27.255 and enable UDP forwarding on the locally attached router
- ❑ b. Add the workstations' local router interface to a bridge group
- ❑ c. Add an access list disabling UDP ports 137, 138, and 139 on a router between the workstations and the servers
- ❑ d. Configure the workstations to use a WINS server rather than broadcasting NetBIOS packets

The correct answers are a and d. Adding a helper address directed to the broadcast address of the network will propagate all UDP packets to all servers located on the 10.30.27.0/24 network. This may not be the most bandwidth-friendly solution, but it will work. NetBIOS packet propagation should not occur on an internetwork at all. Microsoft has developed a server (the WINS server), similar to DNS, that provides mappings between NetBIOS names and IP addresses. Implementing a WINS server would be the most favorable solution. A bridge group might solve the problem, but adding just one interface to a bridge group will not. At least two interfaces need to be in a bridge group for anything to happen. Therefore, answer b is incorrect. NetBIOS traffic occurs on UDP ports 137, 138, and 139. This would not provide connectivity. Therefore, answer c is also incorrect.

Question 4

Several users on a network are reporting that they cannot send email messages, but they can receive new ones. These users are reporting no other problems. What would be the first thing to check?

- ❍ a. Is the locally attached router's interface set as administratively down?
- ❍ b. Are access lists enabled on interfaces located between the clients and their email server denying SMTP traffic (port 25) or are they being denied by the implicit **deny any**?
- ❍ c. Are access lists enabled on interfaces located between the clients and their email server denying POP3 traffic (port 110) or are they being denied by the implicit **deny any**?
- ❍ d. Is the email server currently connected to the network?

The correct answer is b. When individual applications are experiencing connectivity problems, check for access lists enabled on intermediate routers and verify which ports the application requires. This is by far the number one problem experienced by users and network engineers. There are no other users reporting problems, so the router interface cannot be down. Therefore, answer a is incorrect. POP3 is used to retrieve email from a server, and users can receive email, so this is not a POP3 issue. Therefore, answer c is incorrect. Also, the email server is known to be active and connected to the network because users can retrieve their email. Therefore, answer d is also incorrect.

Question 5

A company is moving to using DHCP to propagate workstation network configuration information. The new DHCP clients on network 10.30.1.0/24 are not being assigned IP addresses by the DHCP server with IP address 10.30.2.23. What's the most likely cause of this? [Choose the two best answers]

- ❑ a. The DHCP clients have been configured with an invalid subnet mask.
- ❑ b. The DHCP server is not properly connected to the network.
- ❑ c. The locally attached router is not configured with a helper address pointing to the DHCP server address.
- ❑ d. The hosts are not being assigned IP addresses within the correct address space.

The correct answers are a and c. DHCP clients, by nature, are automatically assigned IP address information, so the subnet mask should not be configured on the workstations. However, if one is still configured during the conversion process, all IP configurations on hosts supersede any values assigned via DHCP. DHCP clients issue broadcasts while attempting to locate a DHCP server; these broadcasts must be forwarded to the appropriate network if the server is not locally connected. Because this is a newly installed DHCP server, it is most likely connected to the network. Therefore, answer b is incorrect. A host not being assigned a valid IP address is a problem of the DHCP server software, and this is most likely not the cause either. Therefore, answer d is incorrect.

Question 6

An organization has standardized running OSPF for its core backbone and RIP for the edge networks, but a few networks are not receiving IP packets. After logging into a router, which command should you issue to find out which interfaces are running OSPF?

❍ a. **show ip protocols**

❍ b. **show ip ospf interface**

❍ c. **show ip interface**

❍ d. **show ip arp**

The correct answer is b. The **show ip ospf interface** command lists routing protocol information about all interfaces with networks enabled by the OSPF routing protocol. The **show ip protocols** command does provide routing information, but only shows the networks that are active in the routing process. Therefore answer a is incorrect. The **show ip interface** command does not contain routing protocol information. Therefore, answer c is incorrect. The **show ip arp** command generates a list of IP-to-MAC address resolutions. Therefore, answer d is also incorrect.

Question 7

Two routers are connected to each other via their 10.20.30.0/24 Ethernet0 interfaces. Each router has been configured to run the RIP routing protocol, as shown in the following output. Why does each router's routing table not list the others router's routes?

```
Router A     Router B
router rip   router rip
passive-interface   passive-interface
       Ethernet0       Ethernet0
network 10.20.15.0  network 10.20.16.0
network 10.20.30.0  network 10.20.30.0
distribute-list 10 out      distribute-list 10 out
! !
access-list 10 permit       access-list 10 permit
       10.20.15.0     10.20.16.0
```

❍ a. The network statements do not contain subnet mask information.

❍ b. The **router rip** statement does not contain a process identifier.

❍ c. The configured access lists stop the propagation of the routes.

❍ d. Both Router A and B have set up Ethernet0 as a passive interface.

The correct answer is d. Passive interfaces stop the propagation of all routing updates to the connected network. Subnet mask information and process identifiers are not required for the RIP routing protocol. Therefore, answers a and b are incorrect. The access lists configured on the routers would permit the locally connected network to propagate. Therefore, answer c is incorrect.

Question 8

If users can access some hosts on the local network but not others, what is most likely the problem?

- ❍ a. An invalid default gateway address.
- ❍ b. An invalid subnet mask is configured on the host workstation.
- ❍ c. The helper address is set up incorrectly on the locally connected router.
- ❍ d. There is an invalid routing table entry in the locally connected router.

The correct answer is b. Invalid subnet masks may make the workstation send packets to the default gateway when actually the destination address is locally connected. Answers a, c, and d are incorrect because they would not prohibit local network connectivity.

Question 9

Issuing the **show ip route** command generates the following output. If a packet enters through interface Ethernet3 that's destined for 10.30.21.154, which interface would it exit out of?

```
Gateway of last resort is 10.1.1.1 to network
     0.0.0.0
O E1 10.30.0.0/16 [110/151] via 10.200.1.1,
     00:13:37, Ethernet1
R    10.2.1.0/24 [120/1] via 10.20.1.1, 00:13:37,
     Ethernet0
C    10.100.1.0/29 is directly connected, Ethernet4/
     1
R    10.30.21.0/24 [120/1] via 10.200.10.1,
     00:00:16, Serial0
```

- ❍ a. Ethernet3
- ❍ b. Serial0
- ❍ c. Ethernet1
- ❍ d. Ethernet4/1

The correct answer is c. The route obtained via the Ethernet1 interface will be preferred over the Serial0 interface because of the administrative distance associated with learning routes via OSPF and RIP. Therefore, answer b is incorrect. The traffic originated from Ethernet3 and there is no routing entry to this interface. Therefore, answer a is incorrect. The Ethernet4/1 interface will be utilized for traffic destined for network 10.2.1.0/24. Therefore, answer d is also incorrect.

Question 10

Users on a single subnet are experiencing limited access to servers on an intranet. After checking the routing tables of the directly connected router, you find that the routes do not appear. Issuing the **show ip protocols** command shows the following results. What would be the best command to enter next to try to narrow the scope of the problem?

```
Routing Protocol is "rip"
  Sending updates every 30 seconds, next due in 1
     seconds
  Invalid after 180 seconds, hold down 180, flushed
     after 240
  Outgoing update filter list for all interfaces is
     not set
  Incoming update filter list for all interfaces is
     not set
    Ethernet1/0 filtered by 57
  Default redistribution metric is 1
  Redistributing: rip
```

❍ a. **show ip arp**

❍ b. **show ip access-list 57**

❍ c. **debug ip rip**

❍ d. **debug arp**

The correct answer is b. The output shows an incoming update filter of 57 assigned to Ethernet 1/0; this could be filtering out routes that are required by downstream hosts. Showing or debugging the ARP cache will not help in narrowing the scope in regards to missing routes. Therefore, answers a and d are incorrect. **debug ip rip** will only display routes and their associated metrics propagated by a neighbor router. Therefore, answer c is also incorrect.

Question 11

When using routing protocols that do not support variable-length subnet masks (VLSMs), such as IGRP and RIP, which problem will most likely occur?

❍ a. Invalid timers

❍ b. Route flapping

❍ c. Convergence time

❍ d. Missing routes

The correct answer is d. Any variance in the subnet mask configured throughout a network running IGRP or RIP will generally not work correctly and cause routes to be missing within the routing tables. Invalid timers will not be affected by VLSMs. Therefore, answer a is incorrect. Route flapping occurs when routes appear and disappear; this is generally caused by invalid timers or when split horizon has been disabled on an interface. Therefore, answer b is incorrect. Convergence time in RIP and IGRP networks is generally large, but it's not affected by VLSMs. Therefore, answer c is incorrect.

Question 12

A workstation's network card is found to be faulty and is replaced. Afterward, the host still cannot connect to the network. After some time, a veteran network engineer realizes the problem, enters a few commands into the router, and everything works. Inspect the results of the local interface's configuration within the following running configuration and select which router command was entered.

```
interface FastEthernet1/1
 description "Marketing LAN"
 ip address 10.13.2.1 255.255.255.128
 ip broadcast-address 10.13.2.127
 no ip directed-broadcast
 arp timeout 0
 bridge-group 1
```

❍ a. **permit ip directed-broadcasts**

❍ b. **clear ip route ***

❍ c. **clear arp-cache**

❍ d. **debug all**

The correct answer is c. An ARP timeout of 0 allows all ARP entries to age an unlimited amount of time. Therefore, the ARP cache still has the old network interface MAC address, and Data Link layer connectivity could not be established. Answers a, b, and d are incorrect because they would have no effect on local network connectivity.

Need To Know More?

Comer, Douglas E. *Internetworking with TCP/IP, volume I.* Prentice Hall. Englewood Cliffs, NJ, 1991. ISBN 0-13468-505-9. This book is a great technical reference for the TCP/IP protocol suite.

Doyle, Jeff. *CCIE Professional Development: Routing TCP/IP, volume I.* MacMillan Technical Publishing. Indianapolis, IN, 1998. ISBN 1-57870-041-8. You may want to read through this book if you feel a bit uneasy about the configuration and troubleshooting of routing protocols.

Microsoft Press. *Internetworking with Microsoft TCP/IP on Windows NT 4.0.* Microsoft Press. Redmond, WA, 1998. ISBN 1-57231-623-3. This Microsoft exam study guide is an excellent resource for more information about Microsoft TCP/IP networking.

For more general IP protocol information, go to the Cisco Documentation home page (**www.cisco.com/univercd/home/home.htm**) and select Internetworking Technology Overview|Internet Protocols.

For more IP troubleshooting scenarios, visit the Cisco Documentation home page (**www.cisco.com/univercd/home/home.htm**). From there, select Internetworking Troubleshooting Guide|Troubleshooting TCP/IP.

From the Cisco Documentation home page (**www.cisco.com/univercd/home/home.htm**) select Troubleshooting Internetworking Systems|Troubleshooting TCP/IP Connectivity. This section has more IP troubleshooting scenarios that can be used to identify common IP issues.

IPX Diagnostics

Terms you'll need to understand:

- √ Service Advertisement Protocol (SAP)
- √ Get Nearest Server (GNS) messages
- √ Routing Information Protocol (RIP)
- √ NetWare Link Services Protocol (NLSP)
- √ Enhanced Internet Gateway Routing Protocol (EIGRP)
- √ IPX NetBIOS Protocol
- √ IPXWAN
- √ Access lists and filters

Techniques you'll need to master:

- √ Verifying IPX network configurations using **show** commands
- √ Using the IPX **debug** command set to isolate and identify problems
- √ Troubleshooting IPX networks using a detailed process

Interconnecting large Novell IPX networks can be a very intense process, requiring a lot of planning and a great deal of discipline. Troubleshooting IPX networks requires an even greater amount of internetwork expertise and an exhaustive analysis of all the types of potential misconfigurations. The following sections cover several of the most commonly used Cisco IOS commands and how they can help isolate IPX problems without you having to disassemble the entire network and start from scratch.

Cisco IOS Commands

When Novell created the concept of an IPX network, no one thought that several individual networks would be interconnected through routers. However, Cisco has kept up with this demand and has provided a valuable command set within the Cisco IOS that can be leveraged while you're trying to isolate a problem with Get Nearest Server (GNS) requests or the IPX routing process. The next few sections will detail the available **show**, **debug**, and **clear** commands.

The **show** Commands

The IPX **show** commands can be used to identify the current network configuration and isolate potential problems while troubleshooting. The most common **show** commands used in diagnosing an IPX network are shown in Table 11.1 and explained further in the upcoming sections.

show ipx access-lists

Access lists can be configured to prohibit IPX traffic at a very granular level. Individual or multiple IPX network numbers, the SAP service type, and GNS response filters can be implemented on individual IPX interfaces. The **show ipx access-lists** command displays every IPX access list configured within the Cisco IOS, as shown in Listing 11.1.

Listing 11.1 The **show ipx access-lists** command displays all IPX access lists that have been configured.

```
Router>show ipx access-lists
IPX access list 800
    permit A4000
IPX sap access list 1000
    deny -1 47
    permit -1
```

When troubleshooting IPX networks, you need to remember that there's always an implicit **deny all** at the end of every access list. Therefore, in the case of

Table 11.1 Frequently used IPX show commands for troubleshooting an internetwork.

Command	Description
show ipx access-lists	Displays all the IPX- and SAP-configured access lists
show ipx eigrp interfaces	Displays all router interfaces configured within the EIGRP routing process
show ipx eigrp neighbors	Displays all directly connected routers running within the same IPX EIGRP process
show ipx interface	Displays all IPX-enabled router interfaces
show ipx interface brief	Displays a short list of information about all IPX-enabled router interfaces
show ipx nlsp database	Displays the contents of the local router's NLSP database
show ipx nlsp neighbors	Displays all directly connected routers running within the same IPX NLSP process
show ipx route	Displays the contents of the IPX routing table
show ipx servers	Displays a list of all servers announced by SAP
show ipx traffic	Displays detailed statistics for all IPX packets that transit the router

access list 800, the only IPX network that will transit through the access list is A4000—all others will be denied. The second access list, 1000, denies only print servers and permits all other SAPs in the last line. This command will help to identify whether access lists are denying network applications and is very useful when used in conjunction with the **show ipx interface** command, which identifies the access list associated with the interface.

show ipx eigrp interfaces

The **show ipx eigrp interfaces** command displays all interfaces configured within the EIGRP routing process. You can specify the routing process or an interface identifier with this command to restrict the output. Listing 11.2 displays the output from the **show ipx eigrp interfaces** command.

Listing 11.2 The **show ipx eigrp interfaces** command displays information on interfaces configured within an EIGRP routing process.

```
Router>show ipx eigrp interfaces
IPX EIGRP Interfaces for process 221
```

```
               Xmit Queue   Mean   Pacing Time   Multicast    Pending
Itf    Peers  Un/Reliable  SRTT   Un/Reliable   Flow Timer   Routes
Et0       1       0/0        4       0/10           50           0
Et1       0       0/0        0       0/10            0           0
```

The output displays that both Ethernet0 and Ethernet1 have IPX addresses that fall into the range specified by the network statements defined within EIGRP routing process number 221. Also, Ethernet0 has one adjacent neighbor, verified by the **Peers** variable, with an average round-trip time of four seconds (displayed by the **Mean SRTT** variable). The **Pending Routes** variable indicates the number of routes that are still waiting to be transmitted. This information can be very useful for verifying that EIGRP has been enabled correctly and that routing updates are being sent appropriately.

show ipx eigrp neighbors

You can use the **show ipx eigrp neighbors** command to display all the directly connected EIGRP neighbors that have been discovered by routing announcements. Listing 11.3 displays the output from this command.

Listing 11.3 The **show ipx eigrp neighbors** command displays information about all directly connected EIGRP neighbors.

```
Router>show ipx eigrp neighbors
IPX EIGRP Neighbors for process 221
H  Address             Interface  Hold    Uptime  Q    Seq  SRTT  RTO
                                  (secs)  (h:m:s) Cnt  Num  (ms)  (ms)
1  11.aa00.01a0.714d  Ethernet1  12      0:12:07 0    601  15    30
0  22.0000.0c71.1a9c  Ethernet0  12      0:12:08 0    602  12    24
```

The first neighbor identified in Listing 11.3 was first learned via the Ethernet1 interface just over 12 minutes ago, and since that time 601 updates have been received, as verified by the sequence number (Seq Num). The Smooth Round-Trip Time (SRTT) and Retransmission TimeOut (RTO) are 15 and 30 seconds, respectively. You can use this information to pinpoint areas that may be encountering increased route flapping due to a dramatic increase in sequencing numbers, or you can use this command to identify the directly connected neighbors that are running the same EIGRP process.

show ipx interface

The **show ipx interface** command displays information about access lists, filters, and routing processes that are configured on each IPX-enabled interface. This command produces a lot of information, as shown in Listing 11.4, but it can prove quite useful while you're troubleshooting an internetwork.

Listing 11.4 The **show ipx interface** command displays several configurable parameters for each IPX-enabled interface.

```
Router>show ipx interface ethernet 0
Ethernet0 is up, line protocol is up
IPX address is 221.0090.2b70.d400, NOVELL-ETHER [up]
Delay of this IPX network,
in ticks is 1 throughput 0 link delay 0
IPXWAN processing not enabled on this interface.
IPX SAP update interval is 60 seconds
IPX type 20 propagation packet forwarding is disabled
  Incoming access list is not set
  Outgoing access list is not set
  IPX helper access list is not set
  SAP GNS processing enabled, delay 0 ms,
output filter list is not set
  SAP Input filter list is not set
  SAP Output filter list is not set
  SAP Router filter list is not set
  Input filter list is not set
  Output filter list is not set
  Router filter list is not set
  Netbios Input host access list is not set
  Netbios Input bytes access list is not set
  Netbios Output host access list is not set
  Netbios Output bytes access list is not set
Updates each 60 seconds aging multiples RIP: 3 SAP: 3
SAP interpacket delay is 55 ms, maximum size is 480 bytes
RIP interpacket delay is 55 ms, maximum size is 432 bytes
RIP response delay is not set
Do not pad odd-length process-switched packets on output
  IPX accounting is disabled
  IPX fast switching is configured (enabled)
  RIP packets received 0, RIP packets sent 0
SAP packets received 1371, SAP packets sent 1781
IPX NLSP is running on primary network 221
    RIP compatibility mode is OFF
    SAP compatibility mode is AUTO (OFF)
    Level 1 Hello interval 20 sec
Level 1 Designated Router Hello interval 10 sec
    Level 1 CSNP interval 30 sec
    Level 1 LSP retransmit interval 5 sec,
LSP (pacing) interval 55 mSec
    Level 1 adjacency count is 1
    Level 1 circuit ID is router.03
    Level 1 Designated Router is router
```

The first section of highlighted code displays the complete IPX network address and the encapsulation being used on the interface. If hosts are having difficulties connecting outside of their LAN, this can be very useful to verify the correct interface network address and encapsulation type. The next highlighted block describes the IPX SAP update interval, whether IPX type 20 packet propagation is enabled, and several filter statements that can be used to identify what access list numbers are associated with the interface. The SAP update interval of all connected interfaces must be the same for an IPX internetwork to function properly. IPX type 20 propagation is required for NetBIOS packet proliferation in networks implementing the IPX NetBIOS protocol. The access lists filter IPX nodes, SAP services and router entries, Get Nearest Server (GNS) requests, and routing table update filters. Access lists are one of the first things you should look for while troubleshooting application failures on any internetwork.

The third highlighted line describes the RIP routing update interval. This time period must be consistent across all directly connected neighbors; otherwise, routing entries may time out prior to receiving an update, which leads to route flapping. The final highlighted output block describes whether fast switching is enabled, the number of RIP and SAP packets received and transmitted, as well as routing protocol information. The **debug ipx packet** command requires IPX fast-switching to be disabled. This will allow all IPX packets to be displayed, rather than just the first packet of a network flow. NetWare Link Services Protocol (NLSP) information, in this case, displays whether RIP and SAP compatibility is enabled and the retransmit intervals for routing updates.

Here are a few of the more important commands to set for some of the values described by the **show ipx interface** command:

- **ipx type-20-propagation** This command enables IPX NetBIOS packets to transmit to other IPX-enabled interfaces.
- **ipx input-sap-filter** This command applies an access list (SAP Input Filter list) to an interface to limit SAP advertisement receipts.
- **ipx output-sap-filter** This command applies an access list (SAP Output Filter list) to an interface to limit SAP advertisement transmissions.
- **ipx output-gns-filter** This command applies an access list (SAP GNS Output Filter list) to an interface so that GNS requests/replies can be relatively controlled.
- **no ipx route-cache** This command disables fast-switching on an IPX interface.

show ipx interface brief

The IPX packet encapsulation type, interface, current status, and network number can be displayed and verified using the **show ipx interface brief** command, as shown in Listing 11.5. This can provide quick interface configuration information for troubleshooting IPX.

Listing 11.5 The **show ipx interface brief** command displays only the critical IPX configuration information.

```
Router>show ipx interface brief
Interface        IPX Network   Encapsulation    Status    IPX State
Ethernet0        unassigned    not config'd     up        n/a
Ethernet1        22166         ARPA             up        [up]
Ethernet2        12900         ARPA             up        [up]
Serial0          1331          SAP              up        [up]
Serial1          1332          NOVELL-ETHER     up        [up]
```

show ipx nlsp database

Routers that interconnect using the NLSP routing protocol maintain route information in adjacencies, link-state, and area address databases. These databases operate together as a single NLSP process to discover and maintain routing information among neighbors. The **show ipx nlsp database** command displays the entries maintained within the link-state packet (LSP) database, as shown in Listing 11.6.

Listing 11.6 The **show ipx nlsp database** command displays entries within the LSP database.

```
Router>show ipx nlsp database
NLSP Level-1 Link State Database: Tag Identifier = notag
LSPID                LSP Seq Num LSP Checksum  LSP Holdtime ATT/P/OL
5000-rsm.00-00 *     0x00000226  0x2C78        5237             0/0/0
5000-rsm.03-00 *     0x000001E2  0xAE1D        6389             0/0/0
Router.00-00         0x0000023B  0x2E07        844              0/0/0
Router.02-00         0x00000237  0x605E        4312             0/0/0
5500-rsm.00-00       0x00000211  0x391A        4657             0/0/0
5500-rsm.03-00       0x000001E4  0xCD8A        1951             0/0/0
```

This command describes each entry in the database using a system identifier, the **LSPID**. Each entry also contains the update sequence number (**LSP Seq Num**) to verify that old information is never received, as well as an **LSP Checksum** to prevent corrupted packets from entering into the NLSP database. The LSP Holdtime is the time, in seconds, until the entry is flushed from the database. The **ATT/P/OL** field describes internal database information that is generally only used by the Cisco Technical Assistance Center (TAC). You can use this command to verify that all routers within a NLSP process area, directly or indirectly connected, have an entry within the database.

show ipx nlsp neighbors

The **show ipx nlsp neighbors** command displays status information about directly connected NLSP neighbors. The command's output, shown in Listing 11.7, reflects three active, adjacent neighbors connected on Ethernet0 subinterfaces. The Holdtime describes the amount of time before the neighbors entry will become inactive, which will be reinitialized each time a keepalive is heard from that router. Similar to OSPF, the Priority field describes the designated router election priority value, which influences which router contains the active information for a given subnetwork.

Listing 11.7 The **show ipx nlsp neighbors** command generates a list of directly connected NLSP-enabled routers.

```
Router>show ipx nlsp neighbors
System Id Interface State Holdtime Priority Cir  Adj  Circuit Id
dtp-21    Et0.2     Up    19       64       mc   mc   dtp-21.03
dtp-12    Et0.1     Up    38       34       bc   mc   dtp-12.02
dtp-12    Et0.1     Up    17       64       bc   bc   dtp-12.02
```

You can use this command to check that NLSP information is being propagated correctly throughout the directly connected NLSP peers and to verify which router is maintaining the database for a given subnetwork. For instance, if a network becomes available, you can determine if it is because the adjacency has been lost or because the remote router's interface has become inactive.

Interfaces that do not display directly connected neighbors might not have NLSP enabled on them. You may want to check the running configuration for the interface-specific **ipx nlsp enable** command.

show ipx route

The contents of the IPX routing table can be displayed using the **show ipx route** command. The routing table contains information about directly connected networks and networks learned via RIP, EIGRP, and NLSP. Listing 11.8 displays the command when used on an internetwork using the EIGRP routing protocol.

Listing 11.8 The **show ipx route** command lists a table of IPX network entries, the cost of using the link, and the interface packets should exit out of.

```
Router>show ipx route
Codes: C - Connected primary network,
c - Connected secondary network, S - Static,
F - Floating static, L - Local (internal), W - IPXWAN
R - RIP, E - EIGRP, N - NLSP, X - External, A - Aggregate
s - seconds, u - uses, U - Per-user static
6 Total IPX routes. Up to 2 parallel paths and 16 hops allowed.
No default route known.
L    221C is the internal network
C    221 (NOVELL-ETHER),  Ethernet1
C    221B (NOVELL-ETHER),  Ethernet0
E    19 [33280/0] via  221.0060.3e86.e220, age 1w6d, 7u, Ethernet1
E    13 [27072/2] via  221.0060.3e86.e220, age 1w6d, 1u, Ethernet1
E    13 [26931/3] via  221B.0060.3e86.e221, age 2d, 31u, Ethernet0
```

This command displays a list of codes that can be used to identify whether each entry was learned because of a local announcement or propagated via a routing protocol. The first highlighted line shows that six total IPX routes are contained in the table and that only two parallel paths will be maintained in the routing table for a given destination network. The next highlighted block contains two routing entries, each to the same destination network (13) but via different interfaces (Ethernet1 and Ethernet0). In this case, the routing process will select the Ethernet0 interface because the listed delay value is less (26931), although the actual hop count is less via Ethernet1 (2). You can also see that the Ethernet0 route is preferred because the path has been selected 31 times by the routing process, as indicated by "31u".

The locally connected router's IPX routing table is one of the first places you should look when users are complaining of problems accessing services on a remote network. The command can also be used with variables (for example, **show ipx route** ***network number***). This can be very useful for quickly identifying incorrect or even missing routing table entries.

The number of parallel paths to maintain within an IPX routing table can be increased to up to six entries using the general **ipx maximum-paths** number of paths command. The default value for this is 1, which provides no redundant network paths.

show ipx servers

The **show ipx servers** command displays a list of IPX servers discovered by SAP advertisements generated by IPX hosts, which are either directly connected routers or servers. Their names, service types, or network numbers can be used to sort the entries displayed in the table. Listing 11.9 displays the output of the command sorted by the server name.

Listing 11.9 The **show ipx servers** command lists IPX servers that have been learned by SAP announcements.

```
Router>show ipx servers name
Codes: S - Static, P - Periodic, E - EIGRP, N - NLSP,
       H - Holddown, + = detail, U - Per-user static
4 Total IPX Servers

Table ordering is based on routing and server info
Type  Name          Net    Address              Port      Route    Hops Itf
N    4 SERVER1      A2204.0000.0000.0001:0451           722560/03   3   E1
N    4 SERVER2      A2204.0000.0000.0001:0451           722560/03   3   E1
N    4 SERVER3      A2204.0000.0000.0001:0451           722560/03   3   E1
N+   4 SERVER4      E2203.0000.0000.0001:0451           722560/03   3   E1
```

Each entry describes how it was learned, the SAP type, the IPX server name, the node address, the route to the server (ticks/hops) via the routing table, the number of hops via the SAP announcement, and the interface used to reach the server. If entries are not showing up within the server table that you believe should be available, check for SAP filters that may be enabled on interfaces between the remote and local router. You may also want to verify that general network connectivity is available between the local and remote hosts.

The **+** code indicates that multiple paths are available to access the server. To view this information, use the **show ipx servers detailed** command.

show ipx traffic

Router traffic statistics can help you isolate problems within an IPX network. The **show ipx traffic** command displays information about the number and types of IPX packets received and transmitted by the router. Listing 11.10 shows the output generated by this command.

Listing 11.10 The **show ipx traffic** command displays system counters for several IPX statistics.

```
Router>show ipx traffic
System Traffic for 221C.0000.0000.0001 System-Name: Router
Rcvd:   865052 total, 0 format errors, 0 checksum errors,
        0 bad hop count, 4 packets pitched,
        865046 local destination, 0 multicast
Bcast:  864910 received, 1409086 sent
Sent:   1409266 generated, 2 forwarded
        0 encapsulation failed, 0 no route
SAP:    0 SAP requests, 0 SAP replies, 43 servers
        0 SAP Nearest Name requests, 0 replies
        0 SAP General Name requests, 0 replies
        0 SAP advertisements received, 24 sent
        12 SAP flash updates sent, 0 SAP format errors
RIP:    0 RIP requests, 0 RIP replies, 25 routes
        0 RIP advertisements received, 0 sent
        0 RIP flash updates sent, 0 RIP format errors
Echo:   Rcvd 0 requests, 0 replies
        Sent 0 requests, 0 replies
        0 unknown: 0 no socket, 0 filtered, 0 no helper
        0 SAPs throttled, freed NDB len 0
Watchdog:
        0 packets received, 0 replies spoofed
Queue lengths:
        IPX input: 0, SAP 0, RIP 0, GNS 0
        SAP throttling length: 0/(no limit),
        0 nets pending lost route reply
        Delayed process creation: 0
EIGRP:  Total received 504284, sent 1008526
        Updates received 73, sent 79
        Queries received 50, sent 4
        Replies received 4, sent 50
        SAPs received 0, sent 0
NLSP:   Level-1 Hellos (sent/rcvd): 399884/266490
        PTP Hellos     (sent/rcvd): 0/0
        Level-1 LSPs sourced (new/refresh): 127/740
        Level-1 LSPs flooded (sent/rcvd): 812/5151
        LSP Retransmissions: 0
        Level-1 CSNPs (sent/rcvd): 0/89121
        Level-1 PSNPs (sent/rcvd): 5/0
        Level-1 DR Elections: 12
        Level-1 SPF Calculations: 348
        Level-1 Partial Route Calculations: 1343
        LSP checksum errors received: 0
        Trace:  Rcvd 0 requests, 0 replies
        Sent 0 requests, 0 replies
```

As shown in the first highlighted block, SAP request and advertisement packet totals can be checked for increasing values. This may be used to identify incorrect SAP or GNS filters that have been implemented on the network. All implemented routing process statistics are also shown by the command. You can use these values to verify that updates are being sent between devices, whether NLSP is enabled, and the number of Designated Router (DR) elections, SPF calculations, and LSP checksum errors. More detailed NLSP information can then be checked using the **show ipx nlsp neighbors**, previously described in this chapter.

The **debug** Commands

Debugging IPX networks can be very difficult because Network layer addresses are usually not software defined; therefore, it becomes laborious to locate misconfigured or failing internetwork hardware. However, if you combine the Network layer addressing with SAP activity or, potentially, routing update messages, troubleshooting the network may become a bit simpler. Table 11.2 outlines the most valuable **debug** commands included in the Cisco IOS arsenal.

debug ipx ipxwan

The **debug ipx ipxwan** command displays information about every interface configured to use IPXWAN. Events are typically only displayed while the IPXWAN protocol is negotiating the link because the command only displays events about state changes and the startup negotiation process. The IPXWAN protocol enables SAP advertisements to be exchanged once, and then only state changes are announced thereafter. This is an excellent traffic reduction as well as cost savings solution for frame relay links. Listing 11.11 displays the output generated by the **debug ipx ipxwan** command during normal operation.

Table 11.2 Frequently used IPX debug commands for troubleshooting an internetwork.

Command	Description
debug ipx ipxwan	Displays information about IPXWAN events
debug ipx packet	Displays all IPX packets that transit the router
debug ipx routing	Displays all IPX routing protocol activities and events
debug ipx sap	Displays the contents of all SAP update packets

Listing 11.11 The **debug ipx ipxwan** command displays messages exchanged when an IPXWAN-enabled link is initialized.

```
Router#debug ipx ipxwan
IPX IPXWAN events debugging is on

IPXWAN: state (Disconnect -> Sending Timer Requests)
        [Serial0/6666:200 (IPX line state brought up)]
IPXWAN: Send TIMER_REQ [seq 0] out Serial0/6666:200
IPXWAN: Send TIMER_REQ [seq 1] out Serial0/6666:200
IPXWAN: Send TIMER_REQ [seq 2] out Serial0/6666:200
IPXWAN: Send TIMER_REQ [seq 0] out Serial0/6666:200
IPXWAN: Rcv TIMER_REQ on Serial0/6666:200, NodeID 6214, Seq 1
IPXWAN: Send TIMER_REQ [seq 1] out Serial0/6666:200
IPXWAN: Rcv TIMER_RSP on Serial0/6666:200, NodeID 6214,
        Seq 1, Del 6
IPXWAN: state (Sending Timer Requests -> Master: Sent RIP/SAP)
        [Serial0/6666:200 (Received Timer Response as master)]
IPXWAN: Send RIPSAP_INFO_REQ [seq 0] out Serial0/6666:200
IPXWAN: Rcv RIPSAP_INFO_RSP from Serial0/6666:200,
        NodeID 6214, Seq 0
IPXWAN: state (Master: Sent RIP/SAP -> Master: Connect)
        [Serial0/6666:200 (Received Router Info Rsp as Master)]
```

The selected output indicates that the router has become the master on the link and is now sending and receiving SAP information. IPXWAN events do not occur frequently, because full SAP tables are only exchanged once, so this command helps to isolate problems during the initial transaction process.

The interface-specific **ipx ipxwan** command will only send SAP announcements once and then sends SAP state change messages thereafter. This is very useful in reducing SAP traffic on limited-bandwidth WAN links.

debug ipx packet

This command generates detailed information about all packets that transit the router. By definition, this command can quickly overload the router with information. Therefore, you should use this command with extreme caution. Also, it should normally be used during times of limited traffic. Each notification displays the source interface and address, the destination address, the packet length, whether the packet is to be forwarded, and the next hop gateway address (gw), as shown in Listing 11.12.

Listing 11.12 The **debug ipx packet** command displays all IPX packets that transit the router.

```
Router#debug ipx packet
IPX packet debugging is on

IPX: Fa1/0.194:A22104.0000.0000.0001->
     11400.00a0.2435.3b17 ln= 32 tc=01,
     gw=AT3/0/0:C000.0010.0d3f.f800
IPX: Fa1/0.194:A22104.0000.0000.0001->
     90004.0020.afd8.3160 ln= 32 tc=01,
     gw=AT3/0/0:C000.0060.5c35.1e80
IPX: Fa1/0.194:A22104.0000.0000.0001->
     20001.0020.af27.3903 ln= 32 tc=00, rcvd, tc:00->01
```

Although this command's use should be limited, it can be useful in debugging new links and verifying the route of packets transiting the router.

IPX packet fast-switching is enabled by default on all interfaces. You must use the **no ipx route-cache** command to disable fast-switching so that you can view all packets that transit the router, rather than just the packets that have yet to be fast-switched.

debug ipx routing

Although the type of routing process may vary—RIP, EIGRP, or NLSP, for example—the **debug ipx routing** command displays information about the update messages sent and received by the router. In Listing 11.13, debugging information is displayed about IPX RIP messages being sent and received.

Listing 11.13 The **debug ipx routing** command generates information about all enabled routing protocols.

```
Router#debug ipx routing
IPX routing events debugging is on

IPXRIP: received update from 13.0800.0744.c093
         221 in 1 hops, delay 2
IPXRIP: sending update to 13:ffff.ffff.ffff via Ethernet 0
         network 10, metric 2, delay 3
         network 11, metric 3, delay 4
```

By default, RIP sends updates every 60 seconds, with each update packet containing up to 50 entries. Therefore, large internetworks would need to send out multiple packets to handle more entries. For example, if 220 entries existed, 4 packets containing 50 entries and 1 containing 20 entries would be sent to every other device running RIP every 60 seconds. Each update contains the announcer's (or sent to) address, the network(s) being announced, and the routing metrics. You can use this command to troubleshoot the IPX routing process and identify why routing tables' entries are missing by checking that routing announcements are being forwarded properly.

debug ipx sap

SAP updates are sent every 60 seconds and can contain up to 7 entries. If many servers are located within an internetwork, the router will send out several updates each minute. The **debug ipx sap** command, as shown in Listing 11.14, displays detailed information about the contents of SAP advertisement packets.

Listing 11.14 The **debug ipx sap** command.

```
Router#debug ipx sap
IPX service debugging is on

IPXSAP: Update type 0x2 len 480 src:B000.aa00.0400.2bbf
        dest:B000.00a0.c911.d995 (4008)
        type 0x4, "MRTG", 302.0000.c0a3.4fbe(4008), 3 hops
        type 0x4, "ACCT", 106.0020.af39.e0ce(6000), 3 hops
        type 0x4, "ENGR", 40.0060.082d.b29a(6000), 4 hops
        type 0x4, "COMM", 36.0060.976e.ee0d(6000), 3 hops
        type 0x4, "HR", 10.00a0.c960.4c6a(6001), 3 hops
        type 0x4, "RECV", 6.0060.0893.9468(6000), 3 hops
        type 0x4, "LEGAL", 6.0060.0893.94bd(6001), 3 hops
```

Each update contains the SAP response type, packet length, and source and destination addresses, as well as each SAP announcement. The SAP announcement contains the service type, name, network address, and socket number, as well as the number of hops to the service. Table 11.3 describes the variations that can be found within each SAP packet announcement.

Table 11.3 The SAP response and service type codes will vary with different SAP messages.

Variable	Description
SAP Response Type	The type of SAP packet sent: 1 (general query), 2 (general response), 3 (GNS request), and 4 (GNS reply).

(continued)

Variable	Description
Table 11.3 The SAP response and service type codes will vary with different SAP messages (continued).	
Service Type	The type code identifies the service type that the server is advertising. There are many possible values for this variable, but here are a few of the most common: 0×4 (file server), 0×6 (gateway), 0×7 (print server), 0×2D (time synchronization), 0×47 (advertising print server), 0×98 (NetWare access server), and 0xFFFF (wildcard [any SAP service]).
Socket Number	The socket number of the sending process: 451 (NetWare Core Protocol), 452 (Service Advertising Protocol), 453 (Routing Information Protocol), 455 (NetBIOS), 456 (Diagnostics), and 4000 through 6000 (sockets used for file and network communications).

You can use this command to help isolate problem areas if users are complaining that IPX services are unavailable in some areas but functioning in others. This could be due to SAP filters or too many SAP advertisements being generated on a WAN link.

The clear Commands

Sometimes values stored within the router do not age properly. Also, when troubleshooting the internetwork, entries may need to be manually removed. Table 11.4 lists four of the most frequently used **clear** commands for IPX networks.

clear ipx cache

The **clear ipx cache** command removes all entries from the IPX fast-switching cache. These entries are used for fast and autonomous switching of IPX packets between router interfaces. You may need to clear the fast-switching cache if IPX cache flows are not aging properly.

clear ipx eigrp neighbors

The EIGRP routing protocol maintains an adjacency database of all neighboring routers. The **clear ipx eigrp neighbors** command can be used to force the router to clear its neighbor table and then attempt to reacquire its neighbor information. You may have to issue this command if the EIGRP router displays announcements that it is "stuck in active mode."

Table 11.4 Frequently used IPX clear commands for troubleshooting an internetwork.

Command	Description
clear ipx cache	Removes entries from the IPX fast-switching cache
clear ipx eigrp neighbors	Removes entries from the EIGRP neighbor table
clear ipx nlsp neighbors	Removes entries from the NLSP neighbor table
clear ipx route	Removes entries from the IPX routing table

clear ipx nlsp neighbors

The NLSP routing protocol, similar to EIGRP, maintains an adjacency database of all neighboring routers. Issuing the **clear ipx nlsp neighbors** command removes all entries from this database and forces a new Shortest Path First (SPF) calculation. Forcing SPF calculations may be useful while you're adding and removing networks to the NLSP routing process.

clear ipx route

The **clear ipx route** command can delete all IPX routes or a subset of routes. For example, if you want to remove only IPX network 100 from the routing table, you would issue the command **clear ipx route 100**. A subnet mask can also be specified with the network number, which allows a range of networks to be removed. If you want to clear all the routes, you would issue the command **clear ipx route** *.

Common IPX Issues

Internetworks vary over time, and configurations that worked correctly yesterday may not provide the same connectivity after equipment has been installed or even after a device has been reloaded. Novell IPX networks are prone to failures just like every other type of network. The next three sections describe scenarios where the network has become unstable or even unusable and the analysis procedure was used to isolate these problems.

Scenario 1: Host Connectivity

A company has placed a new router, Router B, between two networks to provide for future expansion, as shown in Figure 11.1. After the installation is complete, a few users are complaining that certain resources on the Novell network are inaccessible. After questioning the users for more information, you find that individuals located on IPX network 13 cannot access file and print services located on Server_2, and users located on all the IPX networks cannot access services located on Server_1.

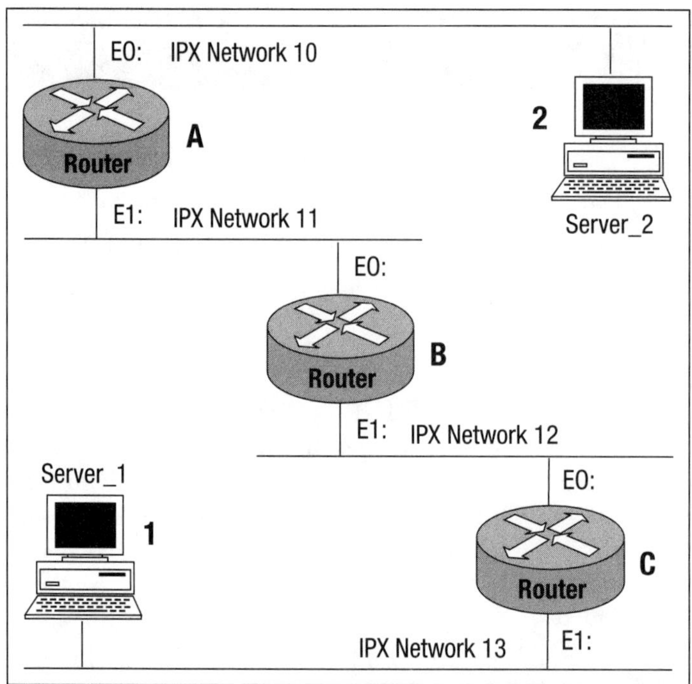

Figure 11.1 The configuration of the company's failing IPX network.

Misconfigured filters can be the cause of severe problems, but they can be temporarily disabled for testing using the **no ipx access-group**, **no ipx input-sap-filter**, and **no ipx output-sap-filter** interface commands.

The first step in a problem of this type is to try to isolate the issue using the standard troubleshooting methodology. The following steps should be performed to reduce the scope of the problem:

1. Verify that the servers and routers are available via the IPX **ping** command on the locally connected LAN. In this case, try pinging Server_1 from a router or workstation located on IPX network 13 (in some cases, this may require an operating system patch). This checks whether Network layer connectivity can be established. If this command fails, verify that the correct network number and encapsulation type have been configured on all the servers and workstations.

   If the router fails to respond to pings, verify that the interface is active and configured with the correct network number and encapsulation type using the **show ipx interface** command. Keep in mind that each router and Novell file server will have at least two addresses assigned to it—the LAN IPX network address and an internal IPX network address—and all addresses must be unique. If IPX pings are successful, continue to Step 2.

All NetWare servers, routers, and clients cabled to a single segment using a common frame type must use the same network address. The reverse is also true: All devices on a common network address must use the same frame type.

2. Check whether services, such as file and print sharing, are accessible by the local router using the **show ipx servers** command. If the server is not listed, try to access any services on Server_1 from a workstation located on IPX network 13. You may also want to compare the output from this command with the Novell server command **display servers**. Also, in some instances, the network address listed is the internal IPX network address rather than the LAN network address.

   If services are not available, make sure that the server is generating SAPs correctly and that the server has properly loaded any NetWare Loadable Modules (NLMs). Also, verify that there are sufficient client licenses available using the Monitor utility screen. You may want to issue the **debug ipx sap** command to view whether the router receives the server's SAPs. If services are available, continue to Step 3.

3. Now that you've verified local connectivity up through the Application layer, you need to check whether remote hosts can ping the server. If these pings fail, verify that all routers are receiving and sending IPX packets using the **show ipx traffic** command. If any of the statistics look suspicious, perform Step 1 on the router. If the Bad Hop Count field is incrementing, there may be a backdoor bridge in the network, which will require a protocol analyzer to identify packet loops. If the pings are successful, continue to Step 4.

4. Verify that routing entries are being correctly propagated throughout the internetwork by checking each router in the local-to-remote data path with the **show ipx route** command. If any routes are missing, you should make sure that IPX routing has been enabled on all routers and that interfaces are included within the IPX routing process in the running configuration (use the **show running-config** command). Also, you should issue the **show ipx interface** command to check for routing update filters and common routing update intervals. If access lists are configured, issue the **show ipx access-lists** command to check their

contents for correctness. The **debug ipx routing** command can also help to identify filters and incorrect routing updates. If routing entries are correct, continue to Step 5.

5. Try accessing the remote services. If this is unsuccessful, issue the **show ipx servers** command to find the remote server's SAP entry. If no entry exists, issue the **show ipx interface** command on each router in the local-to-remote data path to check for SAP filters. You could also use, with extreme caution, the **debug ipx packet** command to check for NetBIOS applications using Novell type 20 packets. IPX NetBIOS packets require the **ipx type-20-propagation** command to be enabled on every interface in the path from the client to the server. If this does not satisfy the problem, an IPX helper address, using the **ipx helper-address** ***network address*** command, may need to be configured on the interface to retransmit broadcasts to another IPX network.

The default IPX ping type sent by the Cisco IOS software uses Cisco's proprietary format. To change this, use the command **ipx ping-default** *type* with the *type* value set to either **novell** or **cisco**.

After several hours of troubleshooting, you identify the following problems within the company's network:

- Server_1 was a new server installed during network changes and was not configured with the correct network number or frame type.
- Router B had a SAP filter enabled that allowed all NetWare SAP services except for types 4 and 7 (file and print services) to be announced out of its Ethernet0 interface.
- Router B was not configured with the correct frame type on its Ethernet1 interface, thus prohibiting traffic from transiting between Routers B and C, which also stops all IPX networks behind Router C from propagating to Router B's or A's routing tables.

While configuring an IPX network, you may need to specify an encapsulation type different from the default. The default encapsulations for Ethernet, token ring, and FDDI are novell-ether, Token Ring-SNAP, and FDDI-SNAP, respectively. Table 11.5 shows the Novell IPX encapsulation names, referenced against the Cisco IOS names.

Table 11.5 Novell IPX encapsulation names versus Cisco IOS names.

Novell	Cisco
Ethernet II	arpa
Ethernet 802.2	sap
Ethernet SNAP	snap
Ethernet 802.3	novell-ether
Token ring	token
Token ring-SNAP	snap

Scenario 2: Increased Remote Network Latency

Users are complaining that over the past six months, remote connectivity to the corporate file servers has become almost unusable due to long download times. After asking the users and IT staff for more information, you learn that the remote connection is a 56Kbps ISDN line between Routers A and B, which then connects into the corporate IPX network, as shown in Figure 11.2. The

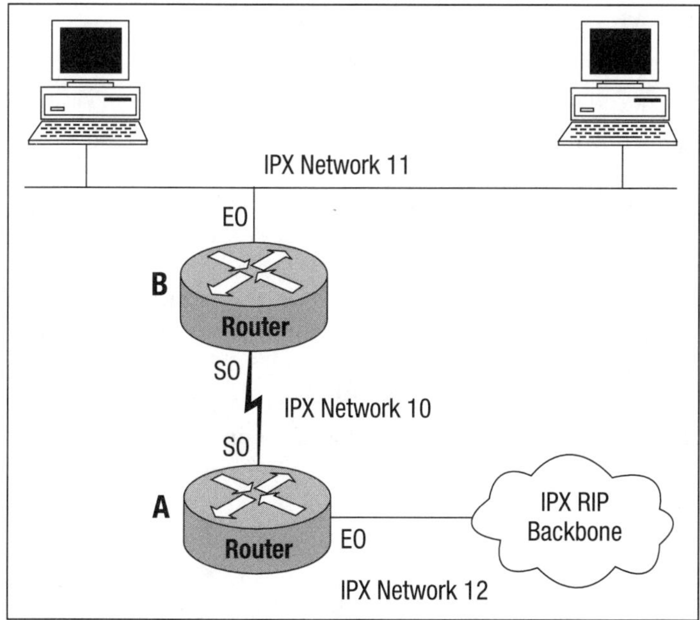

Figure 11.2 The remote office connects into the corporate headquarters through a 56Kbps line attached to the serial 0 interfaces of Routers A and B.

connection currently has full SAP and RIP updates propagating across it. The SAP table contains 1,223 entries, which will therefore require 174 full SAP update packets (each SAP update contains seven entries—1223/7). Each update is 480 bytes, which brings the total bandwidth consumed by SAP updates to 668,160 bits per minute. This means that just under 20 percent of the total bandwidth is consumed by SAP traffic alone. What's more, once you add RIP routing updates as well, the link becomes quite saturated. You can verify the amount of SAP and routing update traffic using the **show ipx traffic** command.

Several solutions exist for this type of scenario that can greatly increase the usable bandwidth of the ISDN link. SAP filters could be applied to each Ethernet0 interface to stop the SAP traffic from propagating through the serial links as well as through the router itself. Devices such as printers and unused remote file services can be easily filtered, as shown in Listing 11.15. You may also want to increase the SAP update interval, which would increase the default update time of one minute to whatever may be feasible. (Keep in mind that this value must be the same on each side of the link.) Simply put, this command used with a value of 10 minutes will decrease the SAP traffic by 90 percent.

Listing 11.15 SAP filters can be placed on interfaces to restrict SAP update message propagation.

```
hostname Router_A                    hostname Router_B
!                                    !
interface Ethernet 0                 interface Ethernet 0
  ipx network 110                      ipx network 120
  ipx input-sap-filter 1000            ipx input-sap-filter 1000
!                                    !
access-list 1000 permit -1 4         access-list 1000 deny -1 47
                                     access-list 1000 permit -1
```

The best solution is to enable IPXWAN on each serial interface, as shown in Listing 11.16. IPXWAN only sends negotiation information during the link's initialization; afterwards, SAP *updates* will be the only packets that transit the link. You could also migrate from RIP to NLSP or EIGRP, which would stop full routing table updates and restrict the updates to only link-state change notifications.

Listing 11.16 IPXWAN can be configured on the serial interfaces to reduce SAP traffic.

```
hostname Router_A                    hostname Router_B
!                                    !
interface serial 0                   interface serial 0
  no ipx network                       no ipx network
  encapsulation ppp                    encapsulation ppp
  ipx ipxwan 1000 Router_A             ipx ipxwan 100 Router_B
```

Scenario 3: NLSP Routing

It has been reported that no Novell file servers can be logged into, even though SLIST, a SAP analysis tool, is producing a full listing of all of the servers. After further analysis, it was noted that all unavailable servers existed on networks where the routers were enabled only with the NLSP routing protocol. Performing a **show ipx nlsp neighbors** command on the routers showed no NLSP neighbors. Further analysis of each router's configuration identified that internal network numbers had not been configured causing NLSP adjacencies to never be completed.

Scenario 4: Cisco IOS Upgrade

After a Cisco IOS upgrade has been performed on a router functioning as an access point for departmental users to an external server farm, users are complaining that they cannot log into the Novell network.

The Cisco IOS default value for GNS response delay was changed from 500 ms to 0 in software release 9.1(13). In this case, the users were running slow machines that missed the quick response from the router. This value can be manually increased using the **ipx gns-response-delay** ***value*** command.

Cisco IOS release 9.21 and later can be configured with the **ipx gns-round-robin** command. This allows the IOS to rotate the server returned to the requesting host in a round-robin fashion. If this is not configured, the router will return the server listed first in the SAP table, which can be shown with the **show ipx servers** command.

Practice Questions

Question 1

Users on IPX network abcd cannot access any Novell services located on IPX network 100. Using the **show ipx interface** command, shown below, you've identified that access list 850 is applied to the router's incoming interface located on IPX network 100. Why is the access list denying services to users on IPX network abcd?

```
Router>show ipx access-list 850
IPX access list 850
    deny 100
```

❍ a. The access list is configured correctly and is not denying access to users on network abcd but only to the users on network 100.

❍ b. Access lists created in the 800 to 899 range declare only the destination IPX address; therefore, no traffic to IPX network 100 will transit through the router interface.

❍ c. All access lists have an implicit **deny all** located at the end of the list. Because the individual IPX network abcd was not explicitly permitted or a **permit any** statement was not included, access from all IPX networks to the 100 network is denied.

The correct answer is c. Access list 850 will not allow any traffic through. Therefore, IPX network 100 users cannot access remote services, and remote users cannot access the 100 network. The access list may be correctly configured, but it's denying access to all users, not just the 100 network users. Therefore, answer a is incorrect. IPX access lists in the range of 800 to 899 can declare either just the source address or the source and destination addresses, but not just the destination. If this access list was supposed to keep traffic from going to network 100, it would read **deny -1 100** (**-1** means *all networks*). Therefore, answer b is incorrect.

Question 2

Which Cisco IOS command will produce detailed IPX routing process information?

____

The correct answer is **debug ipx routing**. This command displays all IPX routing activities and events that can help in troubleshooting an IPX internetwork.

Question 3

After a router's Cisco IOS upgrade, a few of the clients located on a host-only network are having difficulties logging into the Novell environment. It's discovered that the clients having problems are using old 286 machines and network cards. What's the best solution to resolve this problem?

❍ a. Upgrade all client workstations to Pentium III processor-based computers.

❍ b. Install a new Novell server on the local network.

❍ c. Increase the **ipx-gns-response-delay** time on the router.

❍ d. Reduce the number of hosts on the LAN.

The correct answer is c. Cisco IOS 9.1(13) changed the default GNS response delay from 500 ms to 0 ms, which may cause older workstations to miss the GNS response by the local router. Manually increasing this time will solve the problem. Upgrading all the client workstations to the much faster machines or adding a new Novell server to the local LAN would solve the problem, but they're not the best solution because of the high cost factors. Therefore, answers a and b are incorrect. Although reducing the number of hosts on the LAN may decrease the overall latency, it most likely will not have an effect on the workstation correctly receiving the GNS response. Therefore, answer d is incorrect.

Question 4

You've recently replaced an old router with a new Cisco Systems 4000 series router. After you've installed and configured the interfaces with the correct IPX network numbers, the users cannot access remote services. Also, performing the **show ipx servers** command does not list any services. What's the best reason why this is happening?

❍ a. Misconfigured access lists are preventing SAP announcements from propagating through the new router.

❍ b. The frame encapsulation type on the new router is not set to that of the other directly connected devices.

❍ c. IPX routing has not been enabled on the new router.

❍ d. NLSP routing has been configured within the router configuration.

The correct answer is b. The default encapsulation type for Cisco routers is novell-ether. If an internetwork is running a different encapsulation type, it must be specified within the router's configuration. The encapsulation type can be seen using the **show ipx interface** command. Misconfigured access lists may prevent users from accessing services, but this is not the best answer to the problem because it does not explain why IPX servers are not listed in the router. Therefore, answer a is incorrect. Enabling IPX routing will not prohibit SAP packet reception, and services would appear in the SAP table. Therefore, answer c is incorrect. NLSP routing reduces SAP traffic so that only changes are propagated throughout the network, but services would still appear in the SAP table. Therefore, answer d is also incorrect.

Question 5

Remote users are complaining that file services located at corporate headquarters are sporadically available. Checking the remote network router using the **show ipx route** command does not display a route to the corporate network. What's the best reason why this is happening?

❍ a. The routing process on the remote router is missing a network statement.

❍ b. The keepalive timers on the directly connected router interfaces are not set to the same value.

❍ c. Access lists are preventing the network from showing up in the routing table.

❍ d. The interface is disabled.

The correct answer is b. Inconsistent keepalive timers will cause routes to appear and disappear within the IPX routing table. Missing network statements, access list filters, and a disabled interface would prevent any connectivity to the remote network. Therefore, answers a, c, and d are incorrect.

Question 6

You're attempting to use the **debug ipx packet** command to isolate an IPX problem. Which command must you issue first so that you'll be able to truly view all IPX packets that transit the router?

❍ a. **no ipx route-cache**

❍ b. **clear ipx route-cache**

❍ c. **ipx route-cache**

❍ d. **no ipx route cache**

The correct answer is a. The IPX fast-switching cache must be disabled to prevent packet flows. **clear ipx route-cache** would only flush the current entries and then the first packet through for each flow would be seen by the **debug** command. Therefore, answer b is incorrect. **ipx route-cache** would prevent all packets from being seen with the **debug** command. Therefore, answer c is incorrect. Answer d is incorrect because it is not a valid Cisco IOS command.

Question 7

Which command will increase the total number of parallel paths maintained within the IPX RIP routing table to five? As shown in the following **show ipx route 100** command, the routing table currently only maintains one parallel path.

```
Router> show ipx route 100
Codes: C - Connected primary network,
       c - Connected secondary network
       S - Static, F - Floating static, L - Local
       (internal), W - IPXWAN, R - RIP, E - EIGRP,
       N - NLSP, X - External, A - Aggregate,
       s - seconds, u - uses

108 Total IPX routes. Up to 1 parallel paths and 16
     hops allowed.

No default route known.
R 100 [03/02] via 10.0060.5c35.1e80, 48s, Ethernet 0
```

❍ a. **ipx rip maximum-paths 5**

❍ b. **ipx maximum-paths 5**

❍ c. This cannot be done because the maximum number of parallel paths that IPX RIP will support is four.

❍ d. **rip maximum-paths 5**

The correct answer is b. The **ipx maximum-paths** command can be used to increase the number of parallel routers in the router to a maximum of six paths. Therefore, answer c is incorrect. Answers a and d are incorrect because they are not valid Cisco IOS commands.

Question 8

Which commands are defined within the Cisco IOS? [Choose the three best answers]

- ❑ a. **show ipx interface**
- ❑ b. **show ipx eigrp interfaces**
- ❑ c. **show ipx route**
- ❑ d. **clear ipx-route**
- ❑ e. **debug ipx interfaces**
- ❑ f. **show ipx sap traffic**
- ❑ g. **debug sap**

The correct answers are a, b, and c. These three **show** commands will display the IPX-enabled interfaces, the IPX-enabled interfaces defined within the EIGRP routing process, and all the IPX routes, respectively. Answers d, e, f, and g are incorrect because they are not valid Cisco IOS commands.

Question 9

Users are complaining that they're not able to connect to a remote network with IPX NetBIOS applications. Which interface command is required to bridge these packets?

- ❍ a. **ipx bridge**
- ❍ b. **ipx nlsp enable**
- ❍ c. **ipx type-20-propagation**

The correct answer is c. NetBIOS defaults to IPX type-20 packets, and the packets can be transmitted to all interfaces that are enabled with this command. Answer a is incorrect because it's not a valid Cisco IOS command. The **ipx nlsp enable** command enables the NLSP routing process on an interface. Therefore, answer c is also incorrect.

Question 10

Issuing the command **show ipx servers** displays 980 service entries. How many SAP update packets will be sent across the backbone every minute on a network running the NLSP routing protocol?

❍ a. 0

❍ b. 191

❍ c. 15

❍ d. 140

The correct answer is a. The NLSP routing protocol only sends incremental updates, so zero update packets will be sent. Answers b and c are incorrect because these values do not pertain to this question. 140 update packets would be transmitted on a RIP network, but not on a NLSP network. Therefore, answer d is also incorrect.

Need To Know More?

Chappell, Laura A. *Novell's Guide to LAN/WAN Analysis: IPX/SPX*. IDG Books Worldwide, Foster City, CA, 1998. ISBN 0-76454-508-6. This is a great book for brushing up on general Novell network protocols and analysis.

Cisco Systems, Inc. *Cisco IOS Solutions for Network Protocols, Volume II: IPX, AppleTalk, and More*. Macmillan Technical Publishing, Indianapolis, IN, 1998. ISBN 1-57870-050-7. Pages 271 to 599 describe several of the available Cisco IOS commands for IPX networks.

From the Cisco Connection Online (CCO) Documentation home page at **www.cisco.com/univercd/home/home.htm**, select Internetworking Technology Overview|NetWare Protocols. Check out this section for more information on the NetWare protocol suite and IPX internetworking.

From the CCO Documentation home page at **www.cisco.com/univercd/home/home.htm**, select Internetworking Troubleshooting Guide|Troubleshooting Novell IPX. Visit this section to review several more troubleshooting scenarios.

From the CCO Documentation home page at **www.cisco.com/univercd/home/home.htm**, select Troubleshooting Internetworking Systems|Troubleshooting Novell IPX Connectivity. These Web pages have more troubleshooting scenarios for large internetworks.

AppleTalk Diagnostics

Terms you'll need to understand:

- √ AppleTalk Address Resolution Protocol (AARP)
- √ AppleTalk Echo Protocol (AEP)
- √ Zone Information Protocol (ZIP)
- √ Name Binding Protocol (NBP)
- √ Routing Table Maintenance Protocol (RTMP)
- √ Enhanced Internet Gateway Routing Protocol (EIGRP)
- √ ZIP storms

Techniques you'll need to master:

- √ Using Cisco IOS commands to analyze an AppleTalk network
- √ Troubleshooting AppleTalk internetworks
- √ Isolating AppleTalk network failures
- √ Configuring AppleTalk autodiscovery

Although AppleTalk internetworks are easy for users to interconnect into—requiring little or no workstation configuration—they are very difficult to administer. The AppleTalk protocol stack generates a large amount of traffic, creating an administrative nightmare in regards to internetwork configurations. Effective administration requires a great deal of planning in defining adequate networks, zones, routing protocols, and access lists. The following sections outline several of the available Cisco IOS commands and step through some of the more common AppleTalk issues.

Cisco IOS Commands

The more tools that are at a network engineer's disposal, the better the chance he or she has to quickly resolve any AppleTalk network issues. The Cisco IOS contains several **show**, **debug**, and **clear** commands that can be used to identify and troubleshoot an existing AppleTalk network topology.

The show Commands

Once a network is in place and operational, no problems are encountered under normal conditions. However, at the times when the network is not operating efficiently or possibly not at all, the Cisco IOS **show** commands can be used to identify the current state of an AppleTalk network. Table 12.1 describes the most commonly used **show** commands. The next several sections cover these commands in more detail.

show appletalk access-lists

Similar to IP and IPX, misconfigured AppleTalk access lists can be the cause of very unusual internetwork problems, such as only certain applications failing, intermittent or missing network routes, and network access restrictions of a subset of users. The **show appletalk access-lists** command displays a list of only the configured AppleTalk access lists, as shown in Listing 12.1. You should use this list with the **show appletalk interface** command to view the access lists that are bound to a given interface.

Listing 12.1 The **show appletalk access-lists** command generates a list of the configured AppleTalk access lists.

```
Router>show appletalk access-lists
AppleTalk access list 660:
          permit zone Marketing
          permit cable-range 900-950
          deny other-access
```

Table 12.1 Frequently used AppleTalk show commands for troubleshooting an internetwork.

Command	Description
show appletalk access-lists	Displays the configured AppleTalk access lists
show appletalk adjacent-route	Displays only directly connected and neighboring routers' AppleTalk routes
show appletalk arp	Displays the local AppleTalk ARP table
show appletalk eigrp neighbors	Displays a list of directly connected neighbors learned by EIGRP
show appletalk globals	Displays a report of several general AppleTalk settings
show appletalk interface	Displays interfaces configured with the AppleTalk protocol
show appletalk interface brief	Displays a brief table of AppleTalk-enabled interfaces
show appletalk nbp	Displays the NBP lookup table
show appletalk neighbors	Displays a list of the directly connected neighbors learned by all AppleTalk routing protocols
show appletalk route	Displays routes learned by an AppleTalk routing protocol
show appletalk traffic	Displays statistics of AppleTalk traffic by protocol type
show appletalk zone	Displays a list of all internetwork-configured AppleTalk zones

show appletalk adjacent-route

The **show appletalk adjacent-route** command lists the routes to directly connected networks, as well as all routes located on adjacent AppleTalk routers. This information can be used to quickly diagnose problems among a subset of AppleTalk devices. Listing 12.2 shows the output from this command.

Listing 12.2 The **show appletalk adjacent-route** command displays only the directly connected and adjacent networks.

```
Router>show appletalk adjacent-route
Codes: R - RTMP derived, E - EIGRP derived, C - connected,
       A - AURP, S - static, P - proxy
4 routes in internet
```

```
The first zone listed for each entry is its default (primary) zone

C Net 2-3 directly connected, Ethernet0, zone LocalTalk
          Additional zones: 'Marketing','AppleTalk'
R Net 4 [1/G] via 2.203, 8 sec, Ethernet0, zone LocalTalk
C Net 9-12 directly connected, Ethernet1, zone EtherTalk
          Additional zones: 'Accounting','Legal'
R Net 21-21 [1/G] via 500.4, 2 sec, Ethernet2, zone Engineering
```

As shown in the highlighted line of code, this command displays which routing protocol discovered the network (R), the cable-range (4), the hop count/state of the network (1/G), how the route was learned (via 2.203), the time in seconds since the last routing update (8 sec), and the zones for each route. The state of each route can be Good (G), Suspect (S), or Bad (B), which correlates directly to the time since a routing update was last received. The first zone listed is considered the *primary zone*, and all other zones are labeled as *secondary*. All routers on each individual AppleTalk network must agree on the primary zone.

show appletalk arp

Dynamic AppleTalk ARP (AARP) entries are created in the local ARP cache for addresses that the router is unaware of. Hardware entries are addresses of locally defined interfaces; table entries are then used to resolve AARP requests to MAC addresses. The AppleTalk ARP entries contained within the local cache can be displayed with the **show appletalk arp** command, as shown in Listing 12.3.

Listing 12.3 The **show appletalk arp** command lists the contents of the local ARP cache.

```
Router>show appletalk arp
Address  Age(min) Type     Hardware Addr       Encap  Interface
2.133        4    Dynamic  0800.096c.13b2.0000 SNAP   Ethernet4/1
2.161        -    Hardware aa00.0400.2bbf.0000 SNAP   Ethernet4/1
2.203       10    Dynamic  0800.89a2.4349.0000 SNAP   Ethernet4/1
3.104        9    Dynamic  0800.074e.1ef5.0000 SNAP   Ethernet4/2
3.161        0    Dynamic  0005.02cd.3056.0000 SNAP   Ethernet4/3
9.23         5    Dynamic  0000.9474.8e21.0000 SNAP   Ethernet4/5
```

As shown in the highlighted line of code, individual entries display the AppleTalk address (2.203), the age of the entry in minutes (10), how the entry was learned (Dynamic), the MAC address of the device (0800.89a2.4349.0000), the protocol encapsulation type (SNAP), and the interface the AARP reply packet was received on (Ethernet4/1). ARP entries are removed from the table after 240 minutes. The types of entries can either be Dynamic, Hardware, or

Pending. Dynamic entries are learned by AARP, Hardware entries are learned from an internal interface, and Pending entries are waiting for a response from the host. ARP entries can be used to verify device connectivity up to the locally connected router, thus providing problem isolation while troubleshooting an internetwork.

show appletalk eigrp neighbors

EIGRP provides similar functionality for AppleTalk as it does for the IP and IPX protocol stacks. You can use the **show appletalk eigrp neighbors** command to list all directly connected devices running the AppleTalk EIGRP routing protocol, as shown in Listing 12.4.

Listing 12.4 The **show appletalk eigrp neighbors** command displays directly connected devices running AppleTalk EIGRP.

```
Router>show appletalk eigrp neighbors
AT/EIGRP Neighbors for process 100, router id 90
Address     Interface    Holdtime  Uptime     Q      Seq   SRTT   RTO
                         (secs)    (h:m:s)    Count  Num   (ms)   (ms)
4.101       Ethernet2    29        0:05:31    0      82     3     20
3.129       Ethernet2    28        1:29:35    0      331    5     21
```

This command displays the EIGRP routing process identifiers and the AppleTalk addresses of all directly connected devices, as well as other valuable information that can be used to isolate a problem. The minutes or hours that are indicated by the Uptime field may indicate that a router has reloaded, or drastically incrementing sequence numbers (Seq Num) may indicate an improper routing configuration.

show appletalk globals

AppleTalk internetworks may contain a variety of environment-dependent configurations. The **show appletalk globals** command displays details on general AppleTalk settings, such as ZIP, RTMP, and AARP maintenance update intervals. Listing 12.5 displays the output from this command.

Listing 12.5 The **show appletalk globals** command is a valuable resource for isolating AppleTalk internetwork trouble spots.

```
Router>show appletalk globals
AppleTalk global information:
  Internet is incompatible with older, AT Phase1, routers.
  There are 139 routes in the internet.
  There are 76 zones defined.
```

```
Logging of significant AppleTalk events is disabled.
ZIP resends queries every 10 seconds.
RTMP updates are sent every 10 seconds.
RTMP entries are considered BAD after 20 seconds.
RTMP entries are discarded after 60 seconds.
AARP probe retransmit count: 10, interval: 200 msec.
AARP request retransmit count: 5, interval: 1000 msec.
DDP datagrams will be checksummed.
RTMP datagrams will be strictly checked.
RTMP routes may not be propagated without zones.
Routes will not be distributed between routing protocols.
Routing between local devices on an interface
   will not be performed.
IPTalk uses the udp base port of 768 (Default).
AppleTalk EIGRP is not enabled.
Alternate node address format will not be displayed.
Access control of any networks of a zone hides the zone.
```

The first highlighted section states that the configured AppleTalk network is not compatible with Phase I networks. Phase I compliance requires cable ranges to cover no more than one network number (for example, 13-13), and multiple zones cannot be assigned to these cable ranges. The second section describes the configured ZIP, RTMP, and AARP update intervals—in this case, the values listed are the default settings. The RTMP values must be consistent across an AppleTalk internetwork; otherwise, routes may disappear and reappear dynamically. The other values do not need to be consistent, but a stable network is not guaranteed.

The **show appletalk globals** command generates a large amount of general AppleTalk configuration details and is a very useful troubleshooting tool. Make sure that you fully understand how this command can be used to identify problems in an AppleTalk internetwork.

show appletalk interface

The **show appletalk interface** command lists the configured AppleTalk information for all router interfaces (see Listing 12.6).

Listing 12.6 The **show appletalk interface** command displays configured AppleTalk interface information.

```
Router>show appletalk interface
Ethernet0 is up, line protocol is up
  AppleTalk protocol processing disabled
Ethernet1 is up, line protocol is up
```

```
  AppleTalk protocol processing disabled
Ethernet2 is up, line protocol is up
  AppleTalk cable range is 2-3
  AppleTalk address is 2.161, Valid
  AppleTalk primary zone is "LocalTalk"
  AppleTalk additional zones: "AppleTalk", "Marketing"
  AppleTalk port configuration verified by 2.203
  AppleTalk discarded 16 packets due to input errors
  AppleTalk address gleaning is disabled
  AppleTalk route cache is enabled
```

As shown in Listing 12.6, Ethernet0 and Ethernet1 are not configured with the AppleTalk protocol, whereas the Ethernet2 interface is. Also displayed is the AppleTalk network cable range, the local address and whether it's valid, primary and additional zones, port verification status, and whether route caching has been enabled on the interface.

As with IP and IPX, *route caching* (also known as *fast-switching*) must be disabled for you to view all AppleTalk packets transiting the router. An AppleTalk address may be listed as having a Port configuration mismatch, which indicates that the Cisco router detected another AppleTalk router on that network (with address x.y). One of the primary rules for AppleTalk is that all routers that share a network must use the same configuration for that network. This includes the cable-range or network numbers used, the default, or primary, zone and the names of each of the other zones. You can use this information to verify that a newly configured interface is functioning correctly and that zones are properly set up (for example, the Standard primary zone for all directly connected routers).

show appletalk interface brief

Sometimes you may only require a brief synopsis of the current status of the AppleTalk interfaces. The **show appletalk interface brief** command, shown in Listing 12.7, can be used to quickly provide the AppleTalk address and line/protocol status of every router interface.

Listing 12.7 The **show appletalk interface brief** command can be used to quickly identify AppleTalk interfaces and their addresses.

```
Router>show appletalk interface brief
Itf    Address     Config         Status/Line Proto  Atalk Proto
Eth 0  unassigned  not config'd   up                 n/a
Eth 1  66.49       Extended       up                 up
Ser 0  666.123     Extended       up                 up
Ser 1  12900.78    Extended       up                 up
```

show appletalk nbp

The Name Binding Protocol (NBP) maps node names to AppleTalk addresses—similar to IP's Domain Name Service (DNS). The **show appletalk nbp** command displays each entry registered by the router, as shown in Listing 12.8.

Listing 12.8 The **show appletalk nbp** command displays the contents of the router's NBP table.

```
Router>show appletalk nbp
  Net Adr Skt Name                     Type           Zone
   42  84 254 router.FastEthernet1/1   ciscoRouter    Accounting
   42  84   8 router                   SNMP Agent     Accounting
   66 153 254 router.FastEthernet1/2   ciscoRouter    Legal
   66 153   8 router                   SNMP Agent     Legal
    2 161 254 router.Ethernet4/3       ciscoRouter    LocalTalk
    2 161   8 router                   SNMP Agent     LocalTalk
```

Each router interface registers a unique name within the table, such as router.FastEthernet1/1, which is then mapped to its address of 42.84. This device is of the type ciscoRouter and is located in the Accounting zone. An SNMP agent identified this device's name as *router*. You can use this information to verify that devices are registering their information with the locally connected router and becoming active on the network.

show appletalk neighbors

The **show appletalk neighbors** command, shown in Listing 12.9, displays EIGRP, RTMP, and AppleTalk Update-Based Routing Protocol (AURP) routing information about all directly connected routers.

Listing 12.9 The **show appletalk neighbors** command lists the routing protocol for each directly connected router.

```
Router>show appletalk neighbors
AppleTalk neighbors:
  20.5          Ethernet1/1, uptime 1w3d, 6 secs
        Neighbor has restarted 232 times in 12w4d.
        Neighbor is reachable as a RTMP peer
  210.109       Ethernet1/2, uptime 1w3d, 2 secs
        Neighbor has restarted 8 times in 12w4d.
        Neighbor is reachable as a RTMP peer
```

As shown in the highlighted line of code, each entry lists the neighbor's AppleTalk address (20.5), the local interface it's connected to (Ethernet 1/1), the length of its uptime (1 week, 3 days, and 6 seconds), the number of restarts

(232 times in 12 weeks and 4 days), and how the neighbor's entry was learned (RTMP).

You can specify an AppleTalk address with this command for much more granular information about an individual router entry, such as the number of routing updates and ZIP packets received. This command can be used to verify neighbor connectivity and whether packet updates are being received during times that routes may be unavailable or zones are not transferring correctly.

show appletalk route

The **show appletalk route** command displays either all route entries or only specified entries located within the routing table. For example, the command **show appletalk route 6** would only list the entry for AppleTalk network 6. Listing 12.10 displays the output of the **show appletalk route** command when used on a Phase II AppleTalk internetwork.

Listing 12.10 The **show appletalk route** command displays the entire AppleTalk routing table.

```
Router>show appletalk route
Codes: R - RTMP derived, E - EIGRP derived, C - connected,
       A - AURP, S - static  P - proxy
5 routes in internet

The first zone listed for each entry is its default (primary) zone

C Net 2-3 directly connected, Ethernet0, zone LocalTalk
          Additional zones: 'ECT 221','AppleTalk'
R Net 4 [1/G] via 12.203, 7 sec, Ethernet0, zone LocalTalk
R Net 6-6 [1/G] via 2.173, 2 sec, FastEthernet8/1, zone Public
          Additional zones: 'LocalTalk','Marketing'
R Net 7-7 [1/G] via 2.173, 2 sec, FastEthernet8/0, zone Accounting
C Net 9-12 directly connected, Ethernet1, zone EtherTalk
          Additional zones: 'Legal','Engineering'
```

This command generates the same output as that described for the **show appletalk adjacent-route** command, except that the routes contained here are of a much broader scope. The entries are AppleTalk internetwork-wide rather than just the adjacencies. Troubleshooting poor or even nonexistent connectivity is very difficult. You can use this command in conjunction with the AppleTalk version of **traceroute** and **ping** to understand the path an AppleTalk packet takes through the internetwork. Then you can pinpoint the problem areas.

show appletalk traffic

The AppleTalk protocol, by nature, generates a lot of traffic—ZIP packets, NBP packets, RTMP packets, AARP packets, and standard Datagram Delivery Protocol (DDP) packets. These detailed AppleTalk traffic statistics can all be displayed with the **show appletalk traffic** command. Listing 12.11 displays the output from this command.

Listing 12.11 The **show appletalk traffic** command displays detailed statistics about AppleTalk packets.

```
Router>show appletalk traffic
AppleTalk statistics:
  Rcvd:  328628805 total, 0 checksum errors, 2097 bad hop count
         19834383 local destination, 0 access denied
         0 for MacIP, 0 bad MacIP, 0 no client
         0 port disabled, 0 no listener
         0 ignored, 0 martians
  Bcast: 867254 received, 14019321 sent
  Sent:  25604913 generated, 12063048 forwarded,
         289629873 fast forwarded, 7091269 loopback
         0 forwarded from MacIP, 0 MacIP failures
         5040 encapsulation failed, 2277 no route, 0 no source
  DDP:   46090560 long, 0 short, 0 macip, 31 bad size
  NBP:   21990357 received, 43 invalid, 0 proxies
         12 replies sent, 23848805 forwards, 12520459 lookups,
         17776 failures
  RTMP:  6884386 received, 96 requests, 0 invalid, 0 ignored
         4951201 sent, 0 replies
  ATP:   0 received
  ZIP:   22499 received, 27687 sent, 16085 netinfo
  Echo:  3 received, 0 discarded, 0 illegal
         0 generated, 3 replies sent
  Responder:  0 received, 0 illegal, 0 unknown
         0 replies sent, 0 failures
  AARP:  4443210 requests, 6192 replies, 45720 probes
         3178 martians, 2 bad encapsulation, 0 unknown
AppleTalk statistics:
         176659 sent, 1 failures, 5953 delays, 5038 drops
  Lost: 0 no buffers
  Unknown: 0 packets
  Discarded: 0 wrong encapsulation, 0 bad SNAP discriminator
  AURP: 0 Open Requests, 0 Router Downs
        0 Routing Information sent, 0 Routing Information received
        0 Zone Information sent, 0 Zone Information received
        0 Get Zone Nets sent, 0 Get Zone Nets received
        0 Get Domain Zone List sent,
        0 Get Domain Zone List received, 0 bad sequence
```

As long as the command displays that AppleTalk traffic is being sent and received with very few checksum or encapsulation errors, you know that the interface is configured correctly at Layer 2. Encapsulation failures may indicate that there are Phase I and Phase II router incompatibility problems. The highlighted sections provide information about Layer 3 and higher protocols that can be used to troubleshoot a link that's working, but incorrectly. Rising long, short, or macip DDP statistics verify that DDP is functioning correctly. An increase in the bad size variable indicates that the packets being received are not the same size as the original packets sent.

NBP data can be used to verify that hosts are correctly receiving name lookups and replies from the router or are forwarding them appropriately to a remote router. Reception and replies of internetwork routing events by RTMP and AURP packets can be verified through the number of received and sent packets or zone variables. If these values are not incrementing, there may be access lists preventing routing traffic, or the routing protocol may be incorrectly configured for one or more AppleTalk networks. The statistics located in the ZIP section can be used to verify that zone messages are being sent and received. If these counters are incrementing rapidly, a ZIP storm may be occurring. A *ZIP storm* occurs when invalid routes are being injected into the internetwork.

AppleTalk Echo Protocol (AEP) packets are sent and replied to each time a ping is initiated. A host can verify its network connectivity by checking here to see whether the ping packets are being received. Each AppleTalk-to-MAC address resolution (or vice versa) requires AARP reply and request packets. The AARP section not only shows counters for the requests and replies but also for martians. *Martians* are AARP packets that the router did not understand. Large values for the martian counters may indicate that a bridge has been improperly inserted into the network.

show appletalk zone

Zone Information Table entries map zone names to network cable ranges. A single zone name can be correlated with a single cable range or with multiple cable ranges, as shown in Listing 12.12. For example, the Legal zone is associated with three cable ranges and one network number. You can also specify a zone name with this command to restrict the result set to cable ranges, locally configured interfaces, and associated access lists.

Listing 12.12 The **show appletalk zone** command displays the zone name to network cable range correlations.

```
Router>show appletalk zone
Name                           Network(s)
Marketing                      30-30
```

```
Accounting                          229
Engineering                         2-2 2010-2010
Research                            3620-3620
Executive                           441-441
EtherTalk                           9-12
Legal                               222 2220-2220
                                    2221-2221 2222-2222
Total of 7 zones

Router>show appletalk zone marketing
AppleTalk Zone Information for Marketing:
  Valid for nets: 30-30
  Interface (1 use): Ethernet0
  Not associated with any access list.
```

This is an excellent command to use in mapping an internetwork's logical topology while you're troubleshooting (if a logical network diagram doesn't already exist).

The debug Commands

Tracing AppleTalk internetwork problems back to the true source can be a very tedious task. There are numerous **debug** commands included within the Cisco IOS that can help you isolate misconfigurations and performance issues. These commands, listed in Table 12.2 and described in the following sections in more detail, must be used with extreme caution because they may generate a large amount of data.

Table 12.2 Frequently used AppleTalk debug commands for troubleshooting an internetwork.

Command	Description
debug apple arp	Displays packet information about local AARP replies and requests
debug apple events	Displays local AppleTalk internetwork events
debug apple nbp	Displays NBP packet contents
debug apple packets	Displays information about packets received by the router
debug apple routing	Displays packets containing AppleTalk routing information
debug apple zip	Displays ZIP packet contents

debug apple arp

The **debug apple arp** command displays information about packets containing local AARP replies and requests. Listing 12.13 displays the output from this command.

Listing 12.13 The **debug apple arp** command enables debugging of the AARP.

```
Router#debug apple arp
AppleTalk ARP debugging is on

at_arp: valid'g src: 20.124, 0800.07af.e189;
        target: 20.100, 0000.0000.0000
AARP: Request from src 20.124(0800.07af.e189) for trgt 20.100
```

The highlighted line displays the AARP request, including validation of the source AppleTalk and MAC addresses and the target address with the MAC address of 0000.0000.0000. The next line acknowledges that the packet contains a valid AARP request. The receipt of valid AARP packets verifies that the network problem is not at the Physical layer, although Data Link layer errors may still be present.

debug apple events

Several types of unique events occur with AppleTalk internetworks, such as routing table and neighbor updates, interfaces going up and down, and discovery mode information. The **debug apple events** command, shown in Listing 12.14, displays this information. This can be very useful when you're trying to discover why an internetwork is unstable.

Listing 12.14 The **debug apple events** command lists the local AppleTalk events.

```
Router#debug apple events
AppleTalk Events debugging is on

Ether1: AT: Resetting interface address filters
%AT-5-INTRESTART: Ether1: AppleTalk port restarting;
     protocol restarted
Ether1: AppleTalk state changed; unknown -> restarting
Ether1: AppleTalk state changed; restarting -> probing
%AT-6-ADDRUSED: Ether1: AppleTalk node up; using address 20.101
Ether1: AppleTalk state changed; probing -> acquiring
%AT-6-ACQUIREMODE: Ether1: AT port initializing; acquiring net
     configuration
Ether1: AppleTalk state changed; acquiring -> requesting zones
```

```
Ether1: AppleTalk state changed; requesting zones -> verifying
Ether1: AppleTalk state changed; verifying -> checking zones
Ether1: AppleTalk state changed; checking zones -> operational
```

This **debug** code describes an interface resetting on the network and then stepping through the AppleTalk initialization process. Due to the nature of the AppleTalk protocol stack, it's possible that the interface will process this command set several times because of assigned addresses that are already in use on the network. This will occur much more frequently in larger AppleTalk networks because of limited address assignment space. A high volume of generated messages may indicate an unstable network. This command will not display any events in a stable network.

debug apple nbp

The Name Binding Protocol (NBP) retrieves a remote host's AppleTalk software address by sending a query to the remote host's directly connected router and performing an NBP table lookup. The **debug apple nbp** command displays the NBP lookup and reply packets, as shown in Listing 12.15.

Listing 12.15 The **debug apple nbp** command generates events for NBP lookup and reply packets.

```
Router#debug apple nbp
AppleTalk NBP packets debugging is on

AT: NBP ctrl = LkUp, ntuples = 1, id = 236
AT: 6.40, skt 254, enum 0, name: =:Server@Accounting
AT: NBP, LkUp handler, ntups=1

AT: NBP ctrl = LkUp, ntuples = 1, id = 118
AT: 20.97, skt 253, enum 0, name: =:Server@Marketing
AT: NBP, LkUp handler, ntups=1

AT: NBP ctrl = LkUp, ntuples = 1, id = 227
AT: 20.158, skt 254, enum 0, name: DL234 Color LaserWriter:
    TANDEM LaserWriter@Marketing
```

The debugging information displays the type of NBP packet (ctrl = LkUp), which can be either a lookup or reply packet. Each event also displays the AppleTalk address and the resolved name and zone (Server@Marketing).

If there are problems in the network that may be due to NBP lookups, you should enable NBP debugging on all routers in between the host and remote machines. This will allow you to isolate the problem spot within the internetwork. Large internetworks may produce a great deal of traffic, so this command should be used with extreme caution.

debug apple packets

The **debug apple packets** command, shown in Listing 12.16, generates events on a per-packet basis for both received and transmitted data. This command can be used in combination with other AppleTalk **debug** commands, such as **debug apple routing** and **debug apple zip**, to further increase the granularity of acquired information.

Listing 12.16 The **debug apple packets** command displays packets received and transmitted from the router or an individual interface.

```
Router#debug apple packets interface ethernet 0
AppleTalk packets debugging is on for interface Ethernet0

Ethernet0: input AT packet: enctype SNAP, size 73
           04002BBF080089A243490051AAAA03080007809B|004900000006
           000200CB020202418800033 8FE000F46696C6557617665205365 7
           27665721346696C6557617665205265706F7369746F
Ethernet0: encap'ed output packet AT packet: enctype SNAP,
           size 618 0000000000000000000000000000000000000000|090
           007FFFFFFAA0004002BBF025CAAAA03080007809B$0254E14B000
           00002FFA1010101000208A10002800003820006810006820007 81
AT: src=Ethernet0:2.161, dst=2-3, size=583, 103 rtes,
    RTMP pkt sent
```

You can see that an RTMP packet was sent out of the Ethernet0 port to the address 2.161, which contains 103 routes. This same packet is also the one defined in the second event labeled Ethernet0, so that you can verify that the correct transmission size was sent and the correct encapsulation type was used.

This command can generate large amounts of output, so it's a good idea to restrict the debugging to only individual interfaces. This will also provide better management of the data being presented. In general, this command won't be used much, but it's good to have within your troubleshooting arsenal.

debug apple routing

RTMP and/or EIGRP packets must provide the mechanism to construct and maintain routing tables throughout an internetwork. Every router must periodically broadcast—and therefore receive from other routers—RTMP packets through each of its ports. The **debug apple routing** command displays each routing packet as it's transmitted and received, along with information about the routes contained in the packet update. Listing 12.17 shows the output from this command.

Listing 12.17 The **debug apple routing** command displays local routing events.

```
Router#debug apple routing
AppleTalk RTMP routing debugging is on
AppleTalk EIGRP routing debugging is on

AT: RTMP from 50.8 (new 0, old 69, bad 0, ign 5, dwn 0)
AT: RTMP from 6.49 (new 0, old 100, bad 0, ign 2, dwn 0)
AT: RTMP from 6.49 (new 0, old 29, bad 0, ign 0, dwn 0)
AT: src=Ethernet0:2.161, dst=2-3, size=583, 103 rtes,
    RTMP pkt sent
```

As you can see in the highlighted code, RTMP packet events contain the source AppleTalk address (50.8) and information about the announced routes (new 0, old 69, bad 0, ign 5, and dwn 0), representing the number of new, old, bad, ignored, and poison reversed routes. This command can be used to monitor and troubleshoot routing protocol update message contents for invalid route announcements and for appropriate route aging. Events are also generated if network addresses are misconfigured or are conflicting within the AppleTalk internetwork.

debug apple zip

Zone Information Protocol (ZIP) packets maintain the entries stored in the Zone Information Table. The **debug apple zip** command, shown in Listing 12.18, displays the zone discovery and list query packets.

Listing 12.18 The **debug apple zip** command displays ZIP packets received by the router or an individual interface.

```
Router#debug apple zip interface ethernet 1/1
AppleTalk ZIP Packets debugging is on for interface Ethernet1/1

AT: Recvd ZIP cmd 5 from 20.136-6
AT: Answering ZIP GetNetInfo rcvd from 20.136 via Ethernet1/1
AT: Sent GetNetInfo reply to 20.136 via Ethernet1/1
AT: Answering ZIP GetNetInfo rcvd from 20.154 via Ethernet1/1
AT: Sent GetNetInfo reply to 20.154 via Ethernet1/1
AT: net 100, zonelen 9, name Marketing
```

ZIP discovery and query packets may contain information about a neighbor requesting the default zone or the local router sending responses to zone queries. For instance, the last AT event is responding to a zone name lookup (Marketing) for network 100. This command can also be used to detect the presence of a ZIP storm. For example, if no routers on a specific cable range contain the zone name that corresponds to a network number being announced within routing tables, a ZIP storm is occurring.

The clear Commands

AppleTalk counters, ARP table entries, and routing neighbor entries sometimes need to be cleared or reset while you're troubleshooting an internetwork. Table 12.3 lists and defines the most commonly used Cisco IOS **clear** commands.

Testing AppleTalk Protocols

AppleTalk protocols such as AARP, EIGRP, and NBP can be tested using the special Cisco IOS **test appletalk** command. This is a very useful tool you can utilize while troubleshooting host resolution and connectivity without involving the actual host machine or application. Listing 12.19 displays the different AppleTalk protocols that can be tested and a more detailed look at the format for testing NBP.

Listing 12.19 The special Cisco IOS command **test appletalk** can send customized AARP, EIGRP, and NBP packets.

```
Router#test appletalk
Router(atalk test)#?
  arp     APPLETALK ARP test commands
  eigrp   APPLETALK EIGRP test commands
  end     Exit AppleTalk test mode
  nbp     AppleTalk NBP test commands
```

Table 12.3 Frequently used AppleTalk clear commands for troubleshooting an internetwork.

Command	Description
clear appletalk arp	Deletes all entries or a specific entry from the local AppleTalk ARP table
clear appletalk eigrp neighbors	Deletes all AppleTalk EIGRP neighbors from the neighbor table
clear appletalk interface	Resets the software logic of a specific AppleTalk interface
clear appletalk nbp	Deletes all entries or a specific entry from the NBP table
clear appletalk neighbor	Deletes all entries or a specific entry from the AppleTalk neighbor's table
clear appletalk route	Deletes a specific network entry from the AppleTalk routing table
clear appletalk route-cache	Deletes all AppleTalk entries from the fast-switching cache
clear appletalk traffic	Resets the AppleTalk traffic counters

```
Router(atalk test)#nbp ?
  confirm      Confirm NBP
  lookup       Send NBP Lookup
  parameters   Set NBP timeouts
  poll         Poll all devices in internet

Router(atalk test)#nbp lookup =:macintosh:c5@Marketing
(15n,20a,253s)[1]: 'userA:Macintosh IIcx@Marketing'
(15n,56a,251s)[1]: 'userB:Macintosh II@Marketing'
```

Four types of NBP tests can be performed:

- **nbp confirm** Sends out an NBP confirm packet to the specified AppleTalk device
- **nbp lookup** Searches for NBP devices in a specific zone
- **nbp parameters** Sets the parameters used in NBP lookup and pool tests
- **nbp poll** Searches for all devices in all zones

The NBP commands are useful for checking service availability when zones are listed within the Apple Chooser but services are not. An example of the NBP **lookup** command is included in the listing. In this case, a lookup was performed for all services containing the word *macintosh* within the Marketing zone. The result set lists two devices with their network identifications—for example, socket number 253 at network address 15.20.

AppleTalk Discovery

Dynamic address configuration can take place on a network that already has at least one operational AppleTalk router through the AppleTalk discovery mode (this is called a soft seed router). If an interface is placed in discovery mode when no other operational router is located on the network, the interface will not become active. A router interface can be placed into discovery mode by issuing the interface-specific command **appletalk address 0.0** for Phase I networks or **appletalk cable-range 0-0** for Phase II networks. Discovery mode can be very useful when you're making network changes or adding a router to an existing network.

Make sure to disable AppleTalk discovery mode using the **no appletalk discover** command. If this is left enabled on an internetwork and all devices on a network are shut down (for example, if there's a power failure), all the discovery mode-enabled interfaces will not become active.

Common AppleTalk Issues

AppleTalk internetworks generate a large amount of management traffic, all of which must be functioning properly. Troubleshooting AppleTalk networks can be a very painstaking process. Locating incorrectly configured zone names, cable ranges, and access lists by checking ZIP, NBP, AARP, and routing protocol packets is very difficult. The following few sections describe some of the more common AppleTalk internetwork troubleshooting scenarios.

Scenario 1: Host Connectivity

AppleTalk users are complaining that the network is down at corporate headquarters. Several changes, such as zone- and cable-range restructuring and access list implementation, occurred over the weekend to the running and startup configurations of Routers A, B, and C. Also, several new workstations were installed on AppleTalk network cable range 16-16, all of which are having difficulties attaching to the network. Figure 12.1 illustrates the configuration of the AppleTalk internetwork.

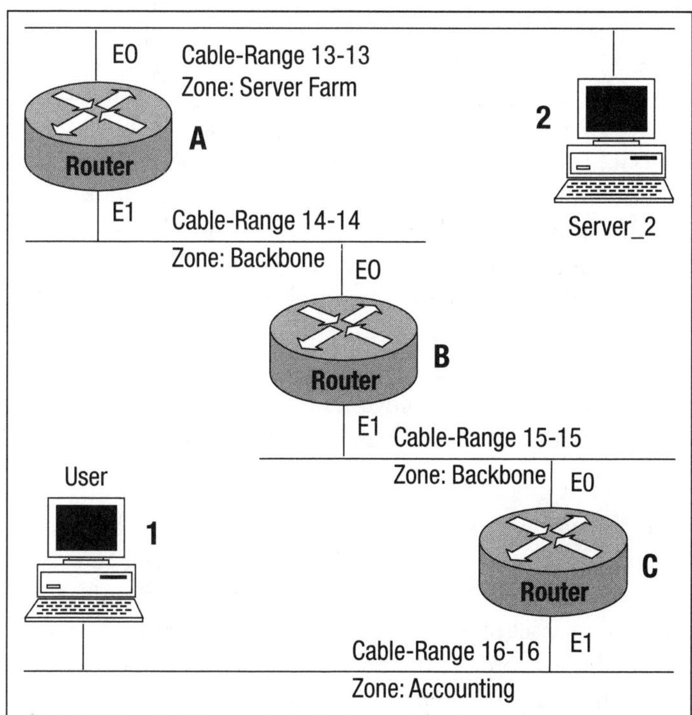

Figure 12.1 A snapshot of corporate's AppleTalk internetwork.

The first step in isolating a problem of this type is to try and define what has changed between when the network worked properly and now. In this case, there is no network change documentation and no TFTP server is set up to store the router configurations; therefore, restoring the initial configuration is not an option. The following steps should be performed to reduce the scope of the problem:

1. Check whether the user workstations are accessible via the AppleTalk version of the **ping** command from the locally connected router. In this case, attempt to ping the user workstation from another locally connected workstation. This checks whether Network layer connectivity can be established. If the ping fails, check whether the AppleTalk network protocol is selected within the Network control panel (this depends on the type of network connection). If the correct AppleTalk network protocol is not chosen, select it and attempt to ping the workstation again. You may also want to check whether the local network cable is plugged into the back of the computer and the appropriate wall jack or even try rebooting the machine if it's an isolated problem. If the workstation-to-workstation pings are successful, continue to Step 2.

2. Try to ping the workstation from the locally connected router—in this case, Router C. If the **ping** command is unsuccessful, check that the locally connected router interfaces are operational using the **show appletalk interface** command. If the interface is down, there may be an address conflict, a broken cable, or the interface may not be administratively enabled. If conflicting network addresses are shown in the **show appletalk interface** command, check for the correct cable range. You may also want to use the **debug apple arp** command to view ARP conflicts and potentially obtain the MAC address of the misconfigured device. Disabling the interface and then performing a **show appletalk route** command can check for duplicate network numbers. If the route still exists, you know that another router is announcing this address space. If AppleTalk pings are successful, continue to Step 3.

3. Check whether the user workstation can see a list of zones within the Apple Chooser menu. If a list of zones appears, Network layer and higher connectivity is established, and ZIP is functioning properly. Otherwise, if only a subset of lists or no lists at all appear, there may be a problem with the locally connected router. Issue the **debug apple zip** and **debug apple events** commands to try to isolate the problem. If the interface looks to be operational, continue to Step 4.

4. Issue the **show appletalk traffic** command to check whether a ZIP storm is in progress by looking for a rapidly incrementing ZIP received

counter. If a ZIP storm is in progress, use the **show appletalk traffic** and **show appletalk route** commands to locate the misconfigured router and remove the invalid routes. If a network is displayed in the table, a node on that network is probably not responding to ZIP requests; the result is the ZIP storm. Determine why the node is not responding to ZIP requests. ZIP storms can result from a defect in the software running on the node. Contact the vendor to determine whether there is a known problem. You could also use the **debug apple zip** command to verify that the user workstations' requests are propagating to the local router and beyond. If zones are appearing within the Chooser, continue to Step 5.

5. There may be access lists configured on an interface that are stopping certain application packets, such as ZIP, NBP, routing updates, and so on, thus causing missing zones and inaccessible AppleTalk devices. This can be verified using the **show appletalk interface** and **show appletalk access-lists** commands. If an access list is configured, unbind the access list from the interface and check whether connectivity is restored. Misconfigured access lists can cause several strange events, such as sporadic or missing routes, individual host or application loss of connectivity, and missing ZIP and NBP information. If access lists are known not to be the problem, continue to Step 6.

6. Check for Phase I/II violations and inconsistent maintenance intervals for AARP, RTMP, or ZIP using the **show appletalk globals** command. The update intervals must be consistent across an internetwork; otherwise, unknown results may occur. Phase compatibility requires Phase I networks to not span cable ranges, and multiple zones cannot be assigned to a single cable range. In the example, the network is Phase I compliant. If the global variables look consistent across the internetwork, continue to Step 7.

7. Verify that the configured routing protocols are sending update messages to directly connected neighbors with the **show appletalk neighbors** command. If a neighbor is missing, there may be an access list misconfigured or the interface may not be configured within the routing process. If multiple routing processes are enabled on the router, verify that route redistribution is taking place correctly using the **show appletalk route** command.

While making changes to a router's configuration within an AppleTalk internetwork, turn on AppleTalk event processing with the **debug apple events** command. If a syslog server is available, you may also want to enable AppleTalk event logging using the **appletalk event-logging** command.

Troubleshooting the corporate internetwork led to the discovery of several misconfigured access lists that prohibited routing updates and ZIP traffic to propagate through the intermediate router, Router B. Access lists are commonly misconfigured, and the best solution to isolate this type of problem is to disable all access lists and verify whether connectivity is restored. There may be political and/or administrative security issues involved with this that limit the possibility of completely removing an access list.

Scenario 2: AppleTalk Zone Changes

A new CEO has been named at a large company and several departmental moves are taking place throughout the campus. One of the moves involves the marketing department migrating from building 110 to building 130. Each building is located behind different Cisco 7500 series routers and will require the AppleTalk zones to be removed from the old router and placed into the new location.

Internetwork moves, changes, and upgrades occur frequently, and so can changes in the location of AppleTalk zones. This can be tricky, though, because zone names are not immediately flushed from the Zone Information Table—they normally require approximately 10 minutes to age out of the table. Zone changes require a four-step process:

1. Disable the AppleTalk protocol for all interfaces attached to the network(s) that contain the zone for about 10 minutes.
2. Configure the new zone list on all directly connected routers.
3. Enable the AppleTalk protocol on all interfaces.
4. Issue the **show appletalk zones** command to verify that the removed zone is no longer listed.

AppleTalk interfaces, by default, will not initialize if the local router's zone list conflicts with a neighbor's list. Some instances may require the interface to become enabled even though the zone list is conflicting with other routers. This can be done with the **appletalk ignore-verify-errors** command. Statically defining AppleTalk addresses and ignoring errors are elements of a hard seed router. After you use this command and the network has once again restabilized, make sure you disable it.

Practice Questions

Question 1

Which Cisco IOS command displays information about ZIP and RTMP update intervals?

❍ a. **show appletalk neighbors**

❍ b. **show appletalk globals**

❍ c. **show appletalk zip**

❍ d. **show appletalk updates**

The correct answer is b. The **show appletalk globals** command displays a report of several of the general AppleTalk settings, such as the total number of routes and zones, protocol update intervals, and routing protocol specifics. The **show appletalk neighbors** command displays a list of directly connected AppleTalk neighbors learned via a routing protocol. Therefore, answer a is incorrect. The **show appletalk zip** command lists the entries in the Zone Information Table. Therefore, answer c is incorrect. Answer d is incorrect because it is not a valid Cisco IOS command.

Question 2

Which special Cisco IOS commands can be used to check individual NBP lookups and confirms? [Choose the two best answers]

❑ a. **test nbp**

❑ b. **test appletalk**

❑ c. **nbp lookup** and **nbp confirm**

❑ d. **show appletalk traffic**

The correct answers are b and c. The **test appletalk** command reveals the command set, such as **nbp lookup** and **nbp confirm**, that can verify service availability for AARP, EIGRP, and NBP packets. **test nbp** is not a valid Cisco IOS command. Therefore, answer a is incorrect. The **show appletalk traffic** command will display information about the sending and receiving of NBP packets, but it does not check individual command success and failure. Therefore, answer d is also incorrect.

Question 3

Enter the command to display debug information regarding EIGRP, RTMP, or AURP routing protocols.

____

The correct answer is **debug apple routing**. This command displays information about every enabled AppleTalk routing protocol.

Question 4

A workstation cannot resolve AppleTalk names to their addresses, but it can ping the local router interface's AppleTalk address. Which Cisco IOS command can be used to display the AppleTalk name-to-address mapping table?

____

The correct answer is **show appletalk nbp**. This command displays the Name Binding Protocol (NBP) table, which contains individual AppleTalk names-to-address entries, similar to the Domain Name Service (DNS).

Question 5

The same workstation in Question 4 is still not able to resolve AppleTalk names. Which **debug** command issued on the local router might display information that would help identify the problem?

❍ a. **debug apple arp**

❍ b. **debug apple nbp**

❍ c. **debug apple zip**

❍ d. **show debug nbp**

The correct answer is b. The **debug apple nbp** command displays the contents of NBP packets, which can be useful for verifying that the workstation is sending NBP requests to the local router. The **debug apple arp** command displays MAC-to-AppleTalk address resolutions, which are already confirmed to be working because the pings are successful. Therefore, answer a is incorrect. ZIP packets contain zone information and may need to be checked if zones are not showing up in the workstation's Apple Chooser menu, but this is not the case. Therefore, answer c is also incorrect. Answer d is incorrect because it is not a valid Cisco IOS command.

Question 6

The marketing department is moving from one office building to another; they will also be transitioning their AppleTalk zone from behind one router to another. You have just disabled the AppleTalk protocol from the old network interface. Approximately what is the shortest amount of time you should wait before configuring the zone list on the new interface?

❍ a. 10 minutes

❍ b. 15 minutes

❍ c. 1 hour

❍ d. 30 minutes

The correct answer is a. It takes about 10 minutes for Zone Information Table entries to age out of all AppleTalk internetwork routers. The other answers would provide enough time to age out the entries, but they are not the shortest amount of time. Therefore answers b, c, and d are incorrect.

Question 7

You would like to remove all the routes from the AppleTalk routing table. Which Cisco IOS command will perform this function?

❍ a. **clear appletalk route ***

❍ b. **clear appletalk route**

❍ c. **delete appletalk routes**

❍ d. None of the above

The correct answer is d. The **clear appletalk route** command can only be used to remove individual AppleTalk routes, unlike the IP and IPX versions, which can delete the entire routing table. Therefore, answers a, b, and c are incorrect.

Question 8

The AppleTalk internetwork suffered severe problems over the weekend, causing all the core routers to crash. Afterward, the network engineering team analyzed the logs stored on the syslog server but found absolutely no events pertaining to the AppleTalk protocol. What's the most likely cause of this?

❍ a. No AppleTalk events occurred and therefore none were logged.

❍ b. The routers did not have **appletalk event-logging** enabled.

❍ c. The syslog server was down.

The correct answer is b. AppleTalk events are not logged by default—they must be turned on with the **appletalk event-logging** global configuration Cisco IOS command. Although it's possible that no events were logged, it's not the most likely cause. Generally, if a network suffers severe degradation, there will be at least minimal system logging available that can be used to isolate the problem. Therefore, answer a is incorrect. If the syslog server was down, the engineers would not have been able to analyze any logs at all. Therefore, answer c is incorrect.

Question 9

Users are complaining that the network has become very slow and that zones are sporadically appearing within the Chooser. You issue the **show appletalk traffic** command on a router because you think that there may be a ZIP storm in progress. Which statistical counter would back up your theory?

❍ a. RTMP requests

❍ b. ZIP sent

❍ c. ZIP received

❍ d. NBP failures

The correct answer is c. A rapidly incrementing ZIP received counter usually indicates that a ZIP storm is in progress. The RTMP requests counter tracks the number of times neighboring routers have solicited for a routing update. Therefore, answer a is incorrect. Cisco routers will not propagate ZIP packets received if the associated network cable-range is unknown. Therefore, answer c is incorrect. NBP failures would cause name resolution problems but would not result in missing zones. Therefore, answer d is incorrect.

Question 10

Which network interface would traffic destined for address 21.100 exit the router from, as shown by the **show appletalk route** command performed below?

```
Router>show appletalk route
Codes: R - RTMP derived, E - EIGRP derived, C -
     connected,
       A - AURP, S - static  P - proxy
2 routes in internet

The first zone listed for each entry is its default
     (primary) zone

R Net 4 [1/G] via 12.203,
     7 sec, Ethernet1, zone LocalTalk
R Net 7-7 [1/G] via 2.173,
     2 sec, FastEthernet8/0, zone Accounting
R Net 21-21 [1/G] via 10.173, 2 sec, FastEthernet8/
     1, zone Public
     Additional zones: 'LocalTalk','Marketing'
```

❍ a. Ethernet1

❍ b. FastEthernet8/0

❍ c. FastEthernet8/1

❍ d. Net 21-21

The correct answer is c. The routing table entry learned by RTMP (R) passes all data destined for network cable range 21-21 (Net 21-21) to the next hop host of 10.173 (via 10.173) out of interface FastEthernet8/1. Answers a and b are incorrect because only data destined for Networks 4 and 7 will transit the interfaces. Answer d is also incorrect because the question asked for the interface's name, not the network's numbers.

Need To Know More?

Cisco Systems, Inc. *Cisco IOS Solutions for Network Protocols, Volume II: IPX, AppleTalk, and More.* Macmillan Technical Publishing. Indianapolis, IN, 1998. ISBN 1578700507. Pages 5 to 270 describe several of the available Cisco IOS commands for AppleTalk networks.

Sidhu, Gursharan S., Richard F. Andrews, and Alan B. Oppenheimer. *Inside AppleTalk, 2nd Edition.* Addison-Wesley. Reading, MA, 1990. ISBN 0-201-55021-0. A firm understanding of the inner workings of AppleTalk is required for troubleshooting. This book discusses and explains the AppleTalk protocols at great length.

From the CCO Documentation home page at **www.cisco.com/univercd/home/home.htm**, select Internetworking Technology Overview|AppleTalk. These Web pages can help you find more information about AppleTalk internetworks in a Cisco environment.

From the CCO Documentation home page at **www.cisco.com/univercd/home/home.htm**, select Internetworking Troubleshooting Guide|Troubleshooting AppleTalk. This section contains several more AppleTalk troubleshooting scenarios.

From the CCO Documentation home page at **www.cisco.com/univercd/home/home.htm**, select Troubleshooting Internetworking Systems|Troubleshooting AppleTalk Connectivity. Check out these pages for even more common AppleTalk troubleshooting scenarios.

Catalyst 5000 Series

Terms you'll need to understand:

- ✓ Supervisor engine
- ✓ Route Switch Module (RSM)
- ✓ Spanning Tree Protocol (STP)
- ✓ Virtual LANs (VLANs)
- ✓ Inter-Switch Link (ISL)
- ✓ Switch Port Analyzer (SPAN)
- ✓ Cisco Catalyst IOS

Techniques you'll need to master:

- ✓ Resolving errors with host connectivity
- ✓ Determining the bridge root port
- ✓ Analyzing VLANs with SPAN
- ✓ Troubleshooting RSM VLAN configurations
- ✓ Troubleshooting ISL encapsulated interfaces

The Catalyst 5000 family of switches consists of the 5000 and 5500 series product lines and is well designed for deployment within small- to mid-size enterprise backbones. The Catalyst series supports frame and cell switching, Fast EtherChannel, Gigabit EtherChannel, Fiber Distributed Data Interface (FDDI), token ring, Asynchronous Transfer Mode (ATM), virtual LANs, and IP multicast. This chapter covers in detail the Catalyst 5000 family architecture, line modules, switching methods, and troubleshooting tools as well as the Catalyst software command set.

Architecture

Five variations of the Catalyst switch exist: 5000, 5002, 5500, 5505, and 5509. Each design shares the same set of interface modules and software features but varies in total line module density and support, as shown in Table 13.1.

Each platform distinguishes itself from the others by the number and type of line modules supported. For example, the Catalyst 5500 supports LightStream 1010 line modules using the Catalyst's 5Gbps cell-forwarding matrix. Although support may vary with the series, the entire Catalyst family of switches is built on the same modular design and general internal architecture.

Table 13.1 The Cisco Catalyst 5000 family of switches.

Platform	Slots	Supports
Catalyst 5000	5	Supports all supervisor engines, 1.2Gbps backplane, and up to four additional line modules, including the Route Switch Module.
Catalyst 5002	2	Supports supervisor engines I and II, 1.2Gbps backplane, and one additional line module.
Catalyst 5500	13	Redundant support for supervisor engines II and III, 3.6Gbps backplane, and up to 12 additional line modules, including the Route Switch Module, the Switch Route processor, and the LightStream 1010 switch processor and embedded cell-relay fabric with a 5Gbps backplane.
Catalyst 5505	5	Redundant support for supervisor engines II and III, 3.6Gbps backplane, and up to four additional line modules, including the Route Switch Module.
Catalyst 5509	9	Redundant support for supervisor engines II and III, 3.6Gbps backplane, and up to eight additional line modules, including the Route Switch Module.

Modular Design

The modular design provides scalability for design enhancements and support for increasing the total port density for additional users. Available modules include, but are not limited to, the supervisor engines; Ethernet/Fast Ethernet, Gigabit, and ATM line cards; and route switch processors.

The Supervisor Engines

The supervisor engines I, II, and III can be swapped among the Catalyst family members. The supervisor engines provide switching and network management, and use various media types as uplink ports. Each successive supervisor engine builds upon its predecessors, with the supervisor III engine containing the most recent feature sets. The supervisor III engine may contain fixed uplink ports or can be purchased in a modular fashion, thus allowing a variation of uplink ports to be configured. It can also be used in conjunction with the NetFlow Feature Cards (NFFCs) I and II, providing quality of service (QoS), Layer 3 gigabit switching, protocol filtering, and advanced data exporting support. The supervisor engine module also has a list of up to 1,024 MAC addresses that it uses for multiple purposes, such as assigning unique identifiers for each VLAN spanning tree bridge.

Line Cards

The Catalyst architecture built upon line modules provides flexibility in transmission media and data link selection due to the wide array of port availability. Line cards are available in several variations for 10/100 Ethernet, Gigabit Ethernet, FDDI, token ring, and ATM. The bottom five slots of the Catalyst 5500 can even be populated with Cisco LightStream 1010 for providing Layer 2 ATM switching.

Catalyst 5000 series switches allow the removal and replacement of line modules without powering off the switch (this is known as *hot swapping*). The system reports console messages about module removals and insertions, as shown in Listing 13.1. During the removal or insertion process, the system performs the following tasks:

1. Scans the backplane for configuration changes.
2. All newly inserted switching modules are initialized. The software notes any removed modules and configures them as administratively shut down.
3. All previously configured interfaces on the switching module are placed back to the state they were in when they were removed. Newly inserted interfaces are left unconfigured and placed in the administratively shut down state.

4. All new interfaces have diagnostic tests performed on them. If they pass these tests, the system is operating normally. If, on the other hand, they fail these tests, the system resumes normal operation but places the newly inserted modules into faulty states.

Listing 13.1 Line modules can be removed and inserted without power cycling.

```
Catalyst_5500>
Mon November 2 1998, 16:24:52 Module 2 has been removed
Catalyst_5500>
Mon November 2 1998, 16:24:55 Module 2 has been inserted
Catalyst_5500>
Mon November 2 1998, 16:25:12 Module 2 is online
Catalyst_5500>
```

To avoid erroneous failure messages, allow at least 15 seconds for the system to reinitialize. Note the current configuration of all interfaces before you remove or insert another switching module.

Route Switch Module

The Route Switch Module (RSM) is a router module that runs Cisco IOS software and plugs directly into the Catalyst 5000 series switch backplane, thus providing multiprotocol routing. The Catalyst 5000 series switches view the RSM as a module with a single trunked port and one MAC address. The RSM provides high-performance, multilayer switching and routing services between switched virtual LANs (VLANs).

Internal Processing

The Catalyst switch comprises several custom application-specific integrated circuits (ASICs), which greatly increase the overall performance of the switch. The ASICs provide software logic written to a chip that may encapsulate frames at the switch port or service management processes. Figure 13.1 shows the primary components of a Catalyst 5000 family switch. The different parts of the switch are discussed in the following sections.

SAINT/SAGE

SAINT (Synergy Advanced Interface and Network Termination) is a high-performance 10/100 Ethernet ASIC. It performs the Ethernet frame encapsulation within the port interface before the frames cross the internal

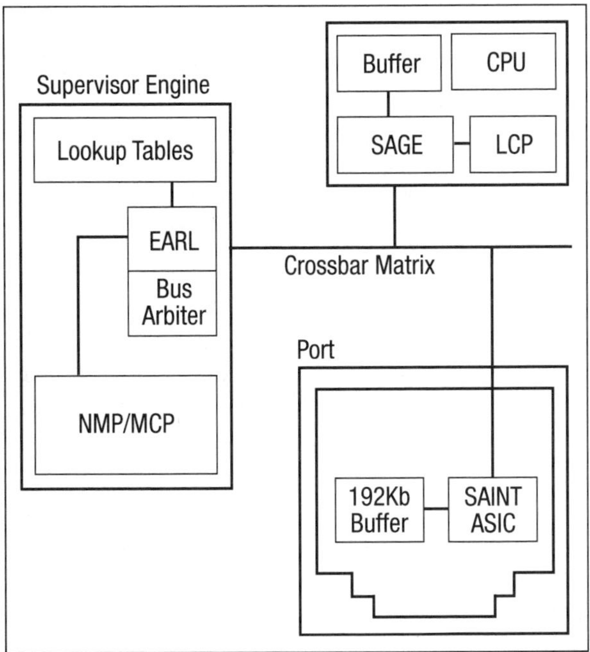

Figure 13.1 The internal architecture of the Cisco Catalyst 5000 switch.

backbone. The packet buffer attached to the SAINT ASIC provides a total of 192K of storage—168K for frames exiting the port and 24K for frames entering. SAGE (Synergy Advanced Gate-Array Engine) ASIC provides similar functionality as SAINT, but it's used with non-Ethernet applications, such as FDDI, token ring, and ATM. SAINT and SAGE both also perform ISL encapsulation and de-encapsulation on frames configured on trunking ports.

Enhanced Address Recognition Logic

The Enhanced Address Recognition Logic (EARL) chip is a switch component similar to a learning bridge that stores MAC addresses within its content-addressable memory (CAM). The EARL chip learns the source MAC addresses dynamically and stores them within the CAM, along with VLAN and other port information. The port information learned from the entries is then used to forward packets to their destination.

The supervisor engine module has separate hardware that supports switching and network management. This separation allows the EARL chip to forward packets across the switching bus even if the network management processor fails.

Management Processors

The network management processor (NMP) provides system control, configuration, diagnostics, and general network management functions. NMP provides SNMP-based network monitoring and executes separate instances of the Spanning Tree Protocol for each VLAN installed. The master control processor (MCP) communicates information between the line control processors (LCPs) and the NMP on a serial bus at a line rate of 761Kbps.

Line Control Processor

Individual line modules contain LCPs that process information sent by the MCP. The LCP runs the boot code residing on the local Read-Only Memory (ROM) and performs diagnostic tests on all local hardware. After completing all tests, the LCP notifies the MCP of the current status of the line module.

Phoenix

The Phoenix ASIC connects the switching busses available in the Catalyst 5500 architecture and provides a 3.6Gbps backplane by interconnecting three 1.2Gbps switching busses. The ASIC acts simply as a Gigabit bridge, providing full-duplex connectivity between the switching busses at a line rate of 1Gbps.

Switching Methods

The switching method determines how quickly a switch can forward a packet. Three switching modes are supported: fast-forward, fragment-free, and store-and-forward:

- **Fast-forward switching** Uses the *cut-through technique* to forward packets. This technique begins forwarding the packets immediately after receiving the destination addresses.
- **Fragment-free switching** Also uses the cut-through method but checks for collision fragments and does not forward this information.
- **Store-and-forward technique** Stores the entire packet and checks for consistency before transmitting the packet to its destination.

Figure 13.2 displays a frame that is received by the switching mode prior to being switched to the destination port.

If a network is experiencing frame or alignment errors, the store-and-forward method can be used to ensure that these errors are not propagated to the rest of the network. Store-and-forward is the method used to transport packets between 10Mbps and 100Mbps ports.

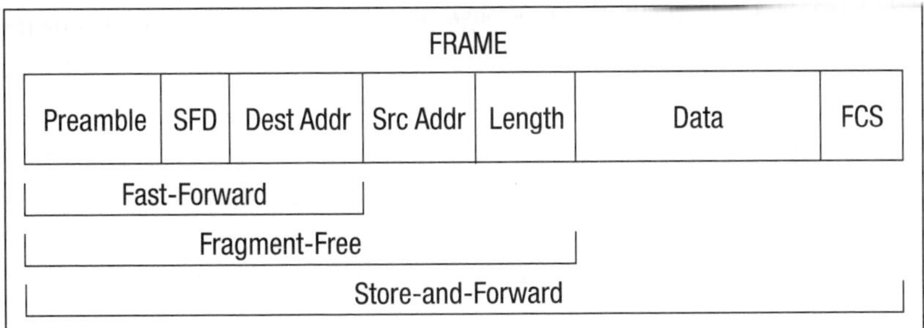

Figure 13.2 The Catalyst 5000 family supports three different switching methods.

Spanning Tree Algorithm

When you're creating fault-tolerant internetworks, a loop-free path must exist between all nodes in a network. A spanning tree algorithm is used to calculate the best loop-free path throughout a Catalyst 5000 series switched network. Placing a port in blocking mode restricts the bridge from transferring any data through that port. When you're determining the network topology, this needs to be taken into account, because it may have an extremely adverse effect on overall network performance. When Spanning Tree Protocol (STP) topology becomes stable based on default parameters, the path between the source and destination stations in a switched network might not be the most ideal. For instance, connecting higher-speed links to a port that has a higher number than the current root port can cause a spanning tree recalculation and a root port change. The goal is to make the fastest link the root port.

Virtual LANs

A VLAN on a Catalyst 5000 is essentially a broadcast domain. Only end stations within the VLAN receive packets that are unicast, broadcast, and multicast (flooded) from within the VLAN. VLANs can easily provide security barriers between multiple end stations that are connected into the same switch or even the same line module. Every port can be in its own VLAN, thus preventing others from seeing even broadcast traffic.

VLANs are considered broadcast domains and contain only one network identity (for example, 10.0.0.0/8). The greatest benefit of incorporating VLANs is the ease in management of departmental moves and political security issues.

VLAN trunks are created between individual devices (switches and routers) across single physical connections to carry traffic originating from multiple

VLANs. Up to 1,000 VLANs can be multiplexed on a single interface using Inter-Switch Link (ISL) on Fast Ethernet, the 802.10 specification for FDDI, or LAN emulation on ATM.

The Virtual Trunking Protocol (VTP) manages the VLAN trunks within a management domain. Each switch within the domain can serve in one of three modes within the domain—server, client, or transparent. Table 13.2 describes the various modes that a switch can be configured as.

The Dynamic Trunking Protocol (DTP) manages trunk negotiation in Catalyst 5000 series software release 4.2 and later. DTP supports autonegotiation of both ISL and IEEE 802.1Q trunks. In prior releases, trunk negotiation was managed by the Dynamic Inter-Switch Link (DISL) protocol. DISL supports autonegotiation of ISL trunks only.

If trunking is performed across two or more links between switches, you should set up load balancing across the links using **set spantree portvlanpri** to distinguish which VLANs have priority on which links.

Table 13.2 A switch can be configured as a VTP server or client or as transparent.

VTP Mode	Description
Server	Switches configured in this mode can create, modify, and delete VLANs and specify other configuration parameters (such as the VTP version) for the entire VTP domain. The VLAN configurations are saved in nonvolatile memory. VTP server is the default mode.
Client	In this mode, VTP clients behave like VTP servers, but they cannot create, change, or delete VLANs within the management domain. The VLAN configurations are not saved in nonvolatile memory.
Transparent	In this mode, VTP transparent switches do not participate within a VTP domain. Transparent switches forward VTP advertisements that are received from other switches, but they're not active within the management domain. You can create, modify, and delete VLANs in this mode. VLAN configurations are saved in nonvolatile memory, but they're not advertised to other switches.

Inter-Switch Link

Inter-Switch Link (ISL) encapsulates Ethernet packets with an ISL header and a checksum, as shown in Figure 13.3. The header is 30 bytes in length; therefore, the maximum length for an ISL packet is the standard frame length (1,518 bytes for Ethernet) plus the 30 bytes, which equals 1,548 total bytes for Ethernet.

The ISL header contains several fields that describe the embedded frame, but only a few may prove useful while you're debugging. The source address is the MAC address of the switch port sending the frame, whereas the destination address is a multicast address set to the hexadecimal value 01-00-0C-00-00. The type field indicates the encapsulated frame type, and the VLAN field is a 15-bit value used to distinguish the frames from different VLANs.

Intel manufactures an ISL-aware network interface card that allows a computer to assign address space within any VLAN that's trunked on the switch port.

IEEE 802.1Q

The standards track VLAN protocol, 802.1Q, was developed within the IEEE and ratified in 1998. The standard is very similar to ISL. It uses the same idea of source and destination addresses, along with the VLAN identifier, but it's 12 bits in size.

IEEE 802.1Q trunks are not supported prior to Cisco Catalyst IOS software release 4.1. In 4.1 they can be defined using the **encapsulation dotq** command.

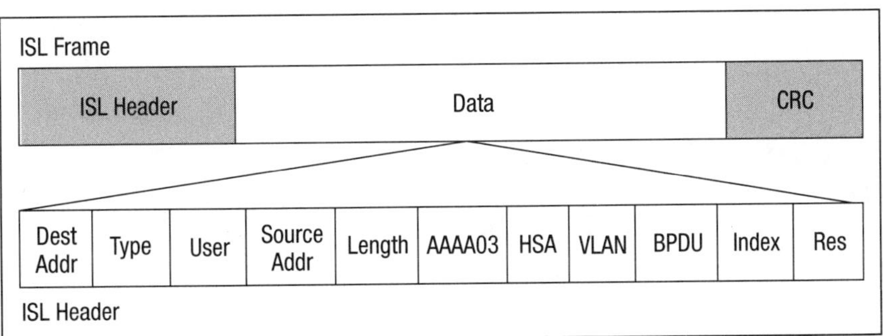

Figure 13.3 ISL encapsulates a standard Ethernet frame with a header and a checksum.

Troubleshooting Tools

Catalyst switches provide their own set of troubleshooting tools in addition to the ones mentioned in Chapter 4. Self-diagnostics of internal ROM and line modules detect hardware failures, whereas embedded RMON agents and the Switch Port Analyzer (SPAN) provide traffic-analysis tools.

Power-On Self-Tests

The Catalyst switch performs self-diagnostic tests on the internal architecture of the system, including Nonvolatile Random Access Memory (NVRAM), Dynamic Random Access Memory (DRAM), Level 2 cache, and the EARL chip. The information displayed during a system startup is shown in Listing 13.2. If any of these diagnostic tests report negative results, a hardware failure has occurred, and the Technical Assistance Center (TAC) should be contacted immediately.

Listing 13.2 During the system boot process, several diagnostic tests are performed.

```
System Power On Diagnostics
NVRAM Size .. .................512KB
ID Prom Test ..................Passed
DPRAM Size ....................16KB
DPRAM Data 0x55 Test ..........Passed
DPRAM Data 0xaa Test ..........Passed
DPRAM Address Test ............Passed
Clearing DPRAM ................Done
System DRAM Memory Size .......32MB
DRAM Data 0x55 Test ...........Passed
DRAM Data 0xaa Test ...........Passed
DRAM Address Test  ............Passed
Clearing DRAM .................Done
EARL++ ........................Present
EARL RAM Test .................Passed
EARL Serial Prom Test .........Passed
Level2 Cache ..................Present
Level2 Cache test..............Passed
```

Module LEDs

The LEDs on the front panel of the line modules indicate the status of the system. Each line module has different indicators to represent the initialization process and the current operational status. The LEDs will flash during startup and then should turn green when a successful initialization process is completed.

Supervisor Module

The supervisor engine line module has system status, fan, power supply, active, and switch load indicators to describe the current operational status of the module itself, along with the entire chassis. The left section of the line card is shown in Figure 13.4.

The state of the LED displays the current condition of the module. Table 13.3 shows the various operational states that the LEDs can indicate.

Line Module

Every line module installed into a Catalyst switch has a global module indicator as well as individual port indicators. These LEDs will vary by the technology being supported. Figure 13.5 shows a section of an Ethernet 10/100 24-port line module.

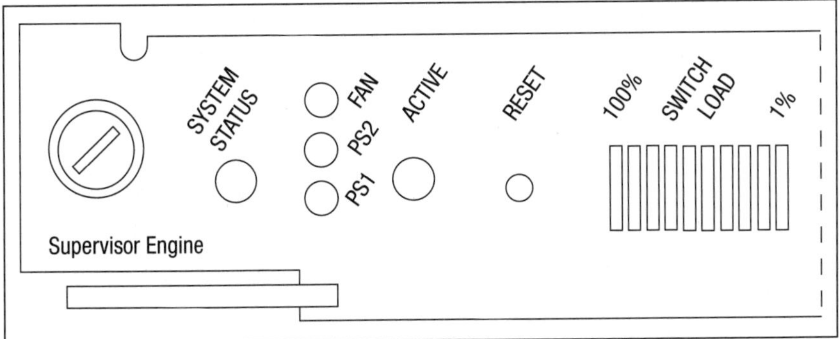

Figure 13.4 The supervisor module has five LEDS and a variable switch load panel to monitor hardware activity.

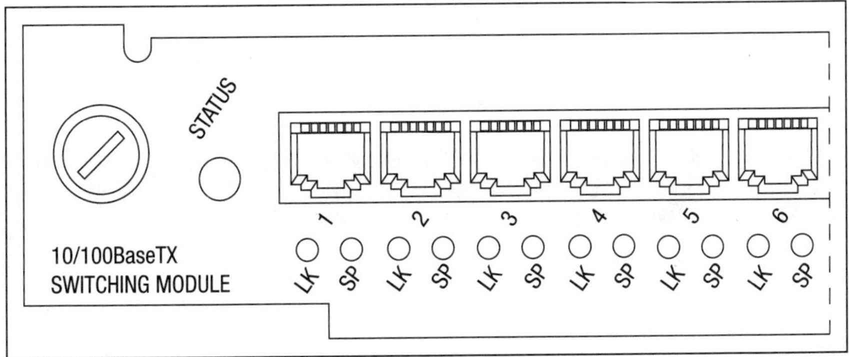

Figure 13.5 Line modules have a status indicator, and each port has a link LED and possibly a 10/100MB indicator.

The module displayed in Figure 13.5 shows several LEDs that are standard on most types of line modules. Each indicator and what the various representations mean are described in Table 13.4.

Table 13.3 The supervisor module LEDs may indicate correct operation or a hardware failure.

Indicator	LED	Description
System Status	Green	All diagnostic tests passed.
	Red	The diagnostic test failed or the module is disabled.
	Orange	The redundant power supply is installed but not turned on or not receiving input, or the fan module failed.
Fan	Green	The fan is operational.
	Red	The fan has failed.
PS1	Green	The left bay power supply is operational.
	Red	The left bay is not operational, is switched off, or is not receiving input.
	Off	The left bay is turned off or is not installed.
PS2	Green	The right bay power supply is operational.
	Red	The right bay is not operational, is switched off, or is not receiving input.
	Off	The right bay is turned off or is not installed.
Active	Green	The supervisor engine is operational and active.
	Orange	The supervisor engine is in standby mode.
Switch Load	Varies	The approximate percentage of traffic, in multiples of 10 percent, crossing over backplane.

Table 13.4 The line modules' LEDs indicate diagnostic failures and the operational status and speed of the ports.

Indicator	LED	Description
Status	Green	All diagnostic tests passed.
	Red	A test other than an individual port test failed.
	Orange	Self-test diagnostics are currently running or the module is disabled.

(continued)

Table 13.4 The line modules' LEDs indicate diagnostic failures and the operational status and speed of the ports (continued).

Indicator	LED	Description
LK	Green	A signal has been detected and the port is operational.
	Orange	The link has been disabled by software. Flashing orange indicates that the link is bad and has been disabled due to a hardware failure.
	Off	No signal has been detected.
SP	Green	The port is operating at 100Mbps.
	Off	The port is operating at 10Mbps.

Route Switch Module

Like all line modules, the Route Switch Module (RSM) provides its own status LEDs to indicate hardware and software failures. RSMs have three indicators to relay the current state of the module: status, CPU halt, and enabled. Each LED is shown in Figure 13.6 and described in Table 13.5.

Embedded RMON

The embedded mini-RMON Management Information Base (MIB) provides the statistics, history, alarms, and events groups with an agent monitoring every Ethernet, Fast Ethernet, and token ring port in the Catalyst 5000. The

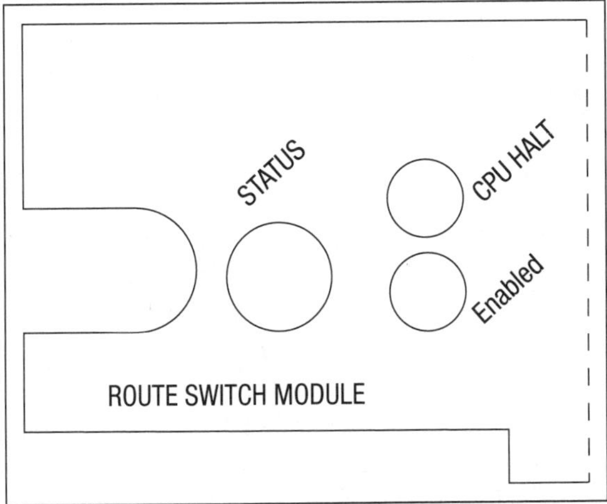

Figure 13.6 The Route Switch Module has indicators for the status of the module and the CPU and whether the module is active.

Table 13.5 The RSM's indicators provide operational status information.

Indicator	LED	Description
Status	Green	All diagnostic tests passed.
	Orange	Self-test diagnostics are running, the system boot is in progress, or the module is currently disabled.
	Red	A module reset is in progress or it failed diagnostics.
CPU Halt	Green	The RSM is operating normally.
	Off	The RSM has had a processor hardware failure.
Enabled	Green	The IP microcode is loaded, and the RSM is operational.
	Off	The RSM is disabled.

alarms and events groups can be used to create robust management solutions by automatically alerting network administrators when thresholds are exceeded.

Switch Port Analyzer

Errors, misconfigurations, and host application failures still occur on VLANs, just as they do on the average network configuration. However, due to the general concept of a switch, only traffic designated for a MAC address located on the end of a switch port will enter the switch port, unless it's a VLAN broadcast. This makes it difficult to troubleshoot host application issues when the traffic generated by the host cannot be seen. The Switch Port Analyzer (SPAN) allows an administrator to duplicate traffic received on a single port or multiple ports to a remote connection, as long as they are all configured in the same VLAN. This information can then be used by an external network analyzer or RMON probe for in-depth traffic analysis.

System Logging

By default, similar to a Cisco router, system logging messages are sent to the console and Telnet sessions. You can enable and disable the logging state for the console session by entering the **set logging console** command. You can then issue the command **show logging** to verify the current logging parameters. You can also enable or disable the logging status for the current Telnet session by entering the command **set logging session**. The logging severity level for each logging facility can be set using the **set logging level** command, similar to the Cisco IOS command levels detailed in Chapter 4, under System Categories.

Cisco Catalyst 5000 IOS Commands

Cisco Catalysts run their own version of software that's different from the software run on Cisco routers. Configuration and troubleshooting commands come in three types: **set**, **show**, and **clear**. **set** commands are used to make configuration changes. **show** and **clear** commands, similar to the Cisco router IOS, display the results of the currently running configuration and clear stored information, respectively.

The **set** Commands

Although the **set** commands will not be discussed in detail, a few of these commands will be referenced in this chapter. Table 13.6 displays these commands and gives a brief description of what they do.

Configuring the sc0 interface with an IP address and subnet mask allows you to access the switch CLI via Telnet from a remote host. The sc0 interface should be assigned to an active VLAN configured on the switch (the default is VLAN 1). Make sure the IP address you assign is in the same subnet as other stations in that VLAN. After you configure the interface, a default route will have to be installed using the **set ip route 0.0.0.0 default gateway address** command.

Table 13.6 Frequently used Catalyst set commands for troubleshooting an internetwork.

Command	Description
set interface	Sets the network interface configuration
set ip route	Adds entries to the IP routing table
set logging	Enables/disables message logging to the console and sets the message severity
set port	Sets port variables such as duplex mode, speed, Fast EtherChannel, and name
set span	Enables/disables the switch port analyzer and sets the source and destination ports
set spantree	Sets spanning tree information
set trunk	Configures port trunking
set vlan	Creates and configures options for VLANs
set vtp	Sets VLAN trunking protocol information

The **show** Commands

Several **show** commands are available to help you troubleshoot Catalyst performance degradation and response and hardware failures. These commands are listed in Table 13.7 and covered in more detail in the following sections.

show cam dynamic

The **show cam dynamic** command displays the Catalyst switch's transparent bridging table (or CAM table). When a frame enters the switch, the destination address is looked up in the CAM table. If the address exists in the table, the frame is switched according to the information retrieved from the table; otherwise, the frame is flooded to all ports contained in the same VLAN. CAM entries can either be entered statically or acquired dynamically as frames enter and leave the switch. The output of the **show cam dynamic** command is shown in Listing 13.3.

Table 13.7 Frequently used Catalyst show commands for troubleshooting an internetwork.

Command	Description
show cam dynamic	Displays the content addressable memory
show cdp neighbors	Displays CDP information
show config	Displays the current system configuration
show interface	Displays information about the network interfaces
show log	Displays the error log for the system or a specific module
show modules	Displays currently installed module information
show port	Displays port information by individual port, module, or entire system
show spantree	Displays spanning tree information for a VLAN or port
show system	Displays system information such as power supply status, internal temperature, uptime, and contact information
show test	Displays the results of the diagnostic test
show trunk	Displays trunking information by individual port, module, or entire system
show version	Displays software and hardware version
show vtp domain	Displays VTP domain information

Listing 13.3 The **show cam dynamic** command displays the contents of the dynamically learned information in the CAM table.

```
Catalyst_5500> show cam dynamic
* = Static Entry. + = Permanent Entry. # = System Entry.
R = Router Entry. X = Port Security Entry

VLAN  Dest MAC/Route Des   Destination Ports or VCs/[Protocol Type]
----  -----------------   ---------------------------------------
190   00-00-0c-07-ac-00   1/1 [ALL]
1     00-90-2b-70-d4-00   1/1 [ALL]
190   00-00-0c-8e-e1-08   2/10 [ALL]
1003  00:10:0b:93:23:fe   1/1
Total Matching CAM Entries Displayed = 4
```

show cdp neighbors

Cisco's proprietary data link protocol exists within the Catalyst IOS as well as the Cisco router IOS. CDP provides Network layer addresses, the IOS version deployed on the Cisco product, and the active ports on each end of the connection. Listing 13.4 displays the output of the **show cdp neighbors** command on the Catalyst switch.

Listing 13.4 The router and switch versions of the **show cdp neighbors** command return identical results.

```
Catalyst_5500> show cdp neighbors detail
Device-ID: Router.company.com
Device Addresses:
  IP Address: 10.17.86.1
  Novell address: abababab.0
Holdtime: 176 sec
Capabilities: ROUTER
Version:
  Cisco Internetwork Operating System Software
  IOS (tm) RSP Software (RSP-JSV-M), Version 12.0(2)XE1,
     EARLY DEPLOYMENT RELEASE SOFTWARE (fc1)
  TAC:Home:SW:IOS:Specials for info
  Copyright (c) 1986-1999 by cisco Systems, Inc.
Platform: cisco RSP1
Port-ID (Port on Device): FastEthernet1/0/0
Port (Our Port): 2/1
```

For CDP to work correctly, ports must be configured to announce information via CDP with the command **set cdp enable**.

show config

The **show config** command lists the current configuration of the Catalyst switch. It can be considered a combination of the Cisco IOS **running-config** and **startup-config** commands. Commands entered into the switch are stored in NVRAM immediately, so there's no need for two separate files. The output from the **show config** command is broken into sections, such as system settings, protocol settings, and module settings. This command can be very useful if several configured parameters need to be viewed at one time.

show interface

Remote access to the Catalyst switch is available via tools such as Telnet, if the logical sc0 interface is configured. The sl0 interface is a SLIP interface that a modem can be attached to for remote access. By default, both interfaces reside in VLAN 1, but they can reside in any VLAN available on the switch. To view the current configuration of the sc0 and sl0 interfaces, perform the **show interface** command (see Listing 13.5).

Listing 13.5 To check the configuration of the logical interfaces within the Catalyst switch, issue the **show interface** command.

```
Catalyst_5500> show interface
sl0: flags=51<UP,POINTOPOINT,RUNNING>
     slip 0.0.0.0 dest 0.0.0.0
sc0: flags=63<UP,BROADCAST,RUNNING>
     vlan 1 inet 10.7.6.2 netmask 255.255.255.0
              broadcast 10.7.6.255
```

This command displays the current state of the logical interfaces, the IP address, and the netmask and broadcast addresses for the sc0 interface. If remote access isn't available, this should be the first place to go to verify that the configuration is correct.

show log

Event logs provide after-the-fact information and are available through the **show log** command. Listing 13.6 shows the information provided by this command, such as individual module resets, reloads, checksum failures, and power supply failures.

Listing 13.6 Issue the **show log** command to check for system failures, reboots, and module resets.

```
Catalyst_5500> show log
Network Management Processor (ACTIVE NMP) Log:
  Reset count:   2
  Re-boot History: Mar 30 1999 09:27:52 0, Mar 30 1999 17:19:25 0

  Bootrom Checksum Failures:   0   UART Failures:               0
  Flash Checksum Failures:     0   Flash Program Failures:      0
  Power Supply 1 Failures:     3   Power Supply 2 Failures:     2
  Swapped to CLKA:             0   Swapped to CLKB:             0
  Swapped to Processor 1:      0   Swapped to Processor 2:      0
  DRAM Failures:               0
  Exceptions:                  0

NVRAM log:

Module 2 Log:
  Reset Count:   1
  Reset History: Tue Feb 23 1999, 12:23:32
```

In addition to the logs available through this command, the Catalyst switch can be configured to use the syslog server, which is identical to the one used by the Cisco IOS. This can provide the informational detail required for advanced troubleshooting within a central file store.

show modules

The **show modules** command can be used to retrieve a listing of the current line modules installed in the switch. The data displayed contains information about the hardware, firmware, and software version on the ROM chips of each line module, as well as the range of potential MAC addresses and serial numbers for each module. Listing 13.7 provides the output of the **show modules** command.

Listing 13.7 The **show modules** command provides a summary of the modules and associated installed software.

```
Catalyst_5500> show modules
Mod Module-Name Ports Module-Type      Model    Serial-Num Status
------------    ----  ---------------- -------- ---------- ------
1               2     100BaseFX MMF Sup WS-X5530  010905488 ok
2               24    10/100BaseTX Ethe WS-X5224  007458695 ok
3               1     Route Switch      WS-X5302  011474046 ok

Mod MAC-Address(es)                        Hw   Fw      Sw
-- -------------------------------------- --- ------ --------
1   00-50-53-73-70-00 to 00-50-53-73-73-ff 2.0 3.1.2   4.3(1a)
```

```
2   00-e0-1e-ec-da-b8 to 00-e0-1e-ec-da-cf 1.3 3.1(1) 4.3(1a)
3   00-e0-1e-92-44-e8 to 00-e0-1e-92-44-e9 7.0 20.11  12.0(1a)

Mod Sub-Type Sub-Model Sub-Serial Sub-Hw
--  -------- --------  ---------- ------
1   NFFC     WS-F5521  0010918162 1.1
1   uplink   WS-U5533  0011452029 1.0
```

The information obtained by this command can aid you in tracking Catalyst IOS software versions for the supervisor module and each individual line card. This can be useful if a known bug exists for a particular version of the IOS and you need to find out if an upgrade is required.

show port

The **show port** command provides general port information as well as port errors and collisions. The command can be extended to display information about port capabilities, filters, security, status, trunking, and several other switches. Listing 13.8 displays the output of the **show port** command.

Listing 13.8 One of the many options for the **show port** command is displayed here.

```
Catalyst_5500> show port 4/4
Port Name      Status    Vlan Level  Duplex Speed Type
---- --------  --------  ---- ------ ------ ----- ------------
 4/4 Marketing connected 100  normal   full    10 10/100BaseTX

Security Secure-Src-Addr Last-Src-Addr Shutdown Trap
-------- --------------- ------------  -------- ------
disabled                               No       enabled


                                 Channel Channel Neighbor Neighbor
Broadcast-Limit Broadcast-Drop mode    status  device   port
--------------- -------------- ------  ------  -------- --------
              -              0 auto    up

Align-Err  FCS-Err    Xmit-Err   Rcv-Err    UnderSize
---------- ---------- ---------- ---------- ---------
         1          0          0          0         0

Single-Col Multi-Coll Late-Coll Excess-Col Carri-Sen Runts Giants
---------- ---------- --------- ---------- --------- ----- ------
   4785392    4171071         0          4         0     1      0

Last-Time-Cleared
----------------------
Fri May 21 1999, 15:14:59
```

The information obtained by this command can be used to verify connectivity, increases in line errors or collisions, correct VLAN settings, and port security settings. If a host is having difficulty connecting to the network, this is a good location for verifying that the correct settings are configured in the Catalyst for the user's switch port.

The **show port status** command lists all ports on the Catalyst switch and displays vital information for troubleshooting, such as port status, VLAN, duplex, speed, and media type.

show spantree

A separate spanning tree is defined for each VLAN created on a Catalyst switch. Spanning tree information can be viewed via the **show spantree** command, as shown in Listing 13.9.

Listing 13.9 Spanning tree information can be viewed by issuing the **show spantree** command.

```
Catalyst_5500> show spantree
VLAN 100
Spanning tree enabled
Spanning tree type          ieee

Designated Root             00-10-0b-93-20-00
Designated Root Priority    32768
Designated Root Cost        12
Designated Root Port        1/1-2
Root Max Age   20 sec    Hello Time 2  sec   Forward Delay 15 sec

Bridge ID MAC ADDR          00-50-53-73-70-00
Bridge ID Priority          32768
Bridge Max Age 20 sec    Hello Time 2  sec   Forward Delay 15 sec

Port   Vlan  Port-State    Cost  Priority Fast-Start Group-Method
----   ----  ----------    ----  -------- ---------- ------------
 1/1-2 100   forwarding      12        32   disabled       channel
 2/1   100   forwarding     100        32    enabled
MAC    Rcv-Frms Xmit-Frms Rcv-Multi Xmit-Multi Rcv-Broad Xmit-Broad
----   -------- --------- --------- ---------- --------- ----------
 1/1   51364795 186215879  47839920   23307734  13492421   13400450
 1/2   63863782  88959979  50357093   11730806  10859656   11577597
 2/1   36502371  50956488   4779385   24521146    563578     998337
```

This command can be used to list the type of STP used, the current MAC address and priority of the root bridge, and the MAC address of the bridge for the designated VLAN. This information can be very useful in finding performance bottlenecks due to root bridge selection or incorrectly configured bridging protocols, such as using the DEC encapsulation instead of IEEE.

show system

The **show system** command provides information regarding the system contact, environment status, uptime, and levels of utilization. Listing 13.10 shows the output of this command.

Listing 13.10 The **show system** command displays system and environment information.

```
Catalyst_5500> show system
PS1-Status PS2-Status Fan-Status Temp-Alarm Sys-Status
---------- ---------- ---------- ---------- ----------
ok         none       ok         off        ok

Uptime d,h:m:s Logout     PS1-Type   PS2-Type   Modem   Baud
-------------- ------     --------   --------   ----    ----
18,01:42:41    none       WS-C5008A  none       disable 9600

Traffic Peak Peak-Time                   System Name
------- ---- --------------    -------- -------------
0%      0%   Tue May 25 1999, 12:22:55 Catalyst_5505

System Location          System Contact
--------------------     --------------
Building 30 - Wing C     MIS Department
```

If hundreds of routers are within a management domain, the contact information may become very useful during times of failure. This information is also available through SNMP; therefore, any network management system can poll for this information and store it within its database.

show test

The **show test** command displays the results of the supervisor module diagnostic tests. If the Catalyst has a redundant supervisor engine, you can issue the **show test** command with any switch to see results of both tests, or you can enter the module number with the command to limit the results, as shown in Listing 13.11.

Listing 13.11 The **show test** command displays the results of all diagnostic tests performed on the supervisor engine.

```
Catalyst_5500> show test 2
Network Management Processor (NMP) Status: (. = Pass, F = Fail,
    U = Unknown)
   ROM: .     RAM: .  DUART: .  FLASH-EEPROM: .  Sre-EEPROM: .
   NVRAM: .  Temperature: .  PS (3.3V): .  PS (12V): .  PS(24V): .

 8051 Diag Status for Module 2(. = Pass, F = Fail, N = N/A)
   CPU           : .  Ext Ram 0 : .   Ext Ram 1: .  Ext Ram 2: N
   DPRAM         : .  LTL Ram 0 : .   LTL Ram 1: N  LTL Ram 2: N
   BootChecksum: .  CBL Ram 0 : .   CBL Ram 1: N  CBL Ram 2: N
   Saints        : .  Pkt Bufs  : .   Repeaters: N  Sprom     : .
   SAINT Status :
    Ports 1  2  3
    -------------
          .  .  .
 Packet Buffer Status :
    Ports 1  2  3
    -------------
          .  .  .
 System Diagnostic Status : (. = Pass, F = Fail, N = N/A)
  Module 2: MCP Status:
                        NewLearnTest:        .
                        IndexLearnTest:      .
                        DontForwardTest:     .
                        MonitorTest:         .
                        DontLearn:           .
                        FlushPacket:         .
                        ConditionLearn:      .
                        EarlLearnDiscard:    .
 PMD Loopback Status :
  Ports 1  2  3
  -------------
        .  .  .
```

The **show test** command performed on a supervisor engine III will display results about all onboard ASICs used, such as the Phoenix, to connect the two switching buses.

show trunk

Entering the **show trunk** command displays the actively trunking ports and the VLANs allowed on each port within the VTP management domain (see

Listing 13.12). To display the trunking configuration for a port that's not actively trunking, specify the module and port number of the port you want to display. The RSM port displays as a port that's always trunking, with allowed and active VLANs for each VLAN configured on the RSM.

Listing 13.12 The **show trunk** command displays the status of all trunked ports and the VLANs allowed on each one.

```
Catalyst_5500> show trunk
Port      Mode         Status
----      ----         ------
 3/1      on           trunking

Port      Vlans allowed on trunk
----      ----------------------
 3/1      1-1005

Port      Vlans allowed and active in management domain
----      ---------------------------------------------
 3/1      1,46,66,96,114,127,172,203,205,210,212,214,223-224

Port      Vlans in spanning tree forwarding state and not pruned
----      -------------------------------------------------------
 3/1      1,46,66,96,114,127,172,203,205,210,212,214,223-224
```

The **show trunk** command can be used if VLANs are not appearing on a trunked port. The VLANs may have been pruned from the port or are not currently active within the management domain.

show vtp domain

A VTP domain (also called a *VLAN management domain*) is made up of one or more interconnected switches that share the same VTP domain name. A switch can be configured to be in one (and only one) VTP domain. Each domain can have multiple switches configured as VTP servers or clients or as transparent mode. The **show vtp domain** command displays the configured VTP domain name, the current version of the VTP database, the locally configured VTP mode, and the total number of VLANs within the domain. This information and more is shown in Listing 13.13.

Listing 13.13 VTP domain information is made available by issuing the **show vtp domain** command.

```
Catalyst_5500> show vtp domain
Domain Name          Domain Index VTP Version Local Mode  Password
-----------          ------------ ----------- ----------  --------
Company.Bldg         1            2           server      -
```

```
Vlan-count Max-vlan-storage Config Revision Notifications
---------- ---------------- --------------- ------------
10         1023             9               enabled

Last Updater    V2 Mode  Pruning  PruneEligible on Vlans
------------    -------  -------  ----------------------
0.0.0.0         enabled  enabled  2-1000
```

The **clear** Commands

Various internal tables may require individual entry removals or complete flushing of the entire cache while you're attempting to troubleshoot Catalyst issues. The commands shown in Table 13.8 are the most widely used **clear** commands for solving switching problems.

Cisco IOS Commands

Routing, whether it's done by an RSM or an external router, requires Cisco IOS software. A few commands, including **show** and **debug**, exist within the IOS that pertain only to the VLAN architecture, and they return valuable information. These commands will be covered in detail because they can help you during the troubleshooting process.

The **show** Commands

A couple of **show** commands are available to display VLAN information within the Cisco router IOS. Table 13.9 describes these commands, and the following two sections cover them in more detail.

Table 13.8 Frequently used Catalyst clear commands for troubleshooting an internetwork.

Command	Description
clear arp	Deletes all entries in the ARP cache
clear cam	Deletes all entries in the CAM table
clear counters	Clears all MAC and port counters
clear ip route	Clears all IP routing table entries
clear port	Clears all MAC or protocol filters on a port
clear trunk	Resets all trunk ports and clears all information from the trunk table
clear vlan	Deletes a VLAN from the VTP management domain

Table 13.9 The show commands available for viewing VLAN information on a router.

Command	Description
show interfaces vlan	Displays configured parameters and statistical information about a VLAN interface
show vlans	Displays the configured VLANs, the encapsulation type used, and the configured Network layer protocols

show interfaces vlan

The same information is returned from the **show interfaces vlan** ***vlan number*** command as the standard **show interfaces** command described in Chapter 7.

show vlans

The **show vlans** command is used to display VLANs that are routed by an external router (also dubbed a *router on a stick*). This information, as shown in Listing 13.14, describes the type of VLAN encapsulation (ISL or 802.1Q), the interface the VLAN is trunked on, and the Network layer addresses assigned to the VLAN.

Listing 13.14 VLAN information is displayed by the **show vlans** command.

```
Router>show vlans
Virtual LAN ID:  1 (Inter Switch Link Encapsulation)
   vLAN Trunk Interface:  FastEthernet1/0.1
   Protocols Configured:  Address:       Received:      Transmitted:
           IP              10.170.1.1         9347            494762

Virtual LAN ID:  194 (Inter Switch Link Encapsulation)
   vLAN Trunk Interface:  FastEthernet1/0.194
   Protocols Configured:  Address:        Received:     Transmitted:
           IP             10.10.19.1        3180406         81726139
           IPX       ababa.00e0.3400.4820   820844         40144287
        Bridging            Bridge Group 1      730228          9445847
```

The **show vlans** command can be used to quickly determine all VLANs configured on an external router and their associated network addresses. This can be very useful when you're troubleshooting encapsulation issues and need to determine whether each Network layer protocol is transmitting and receiving traffic.

The debug Commands

Again, only a few **debug** commands exist for troubleshooting bridging and VLAN issues, but they can provide crucial information as to decreasing performance and misconfigurations. Table 13.10 lists the two primary **debug** commands within the Cisco IOS.

debug vlan packets

The **debug vlan packets** command displays only packets with a VLAN identifier that the router is not configured to support. This command allows you to identify other VLAN traffic on the network. The output shown in Listing 13.15 indicates that an unknown encapsulation was used to generate the VLAN packet with a VLAN ID of 8. It was also received on subinterface FastEthernet1/0.8, and this interface was not configured to route or switch this type of VLAN packet.

Listing 13.15 The router can view misconfigured VLAN information through the **debug vlan packets** command.

```
Router#debug vlan packets
Virtual LAN packet information debugging is on
vLAN: Received ISL encapsulated UNKNOWN packet bearing colour ID 8
      on interface FastEthernet1/0.8 which is not configured to
      route or bridge this packet type.
```

This command can be used to troubleshoot misconfigurations for VLANs that are currently unreachable.

debug spanning events

The **debug spanning events** command can be used to observe changes in bridged interfaces through the various spanning tree port states. In the spanning tree debugging information shown in Listing 13.16, notice how a new root has been elected on interface Ethernet 4/2 and that the new topology change is sent.

Table 13.10 **Debug commands can help track down bridge errors and misconfigured VLAN encapsulations.**

Command	Description
debug vlan packets	Displays VLAN information on packets received that the interface is not configured to support
debug spanning events	Displays information on spanning tree topology changes

Listing 13.16 Spanning tree topology events can be viewed with the **debug spanning events** command.

```
Router#debug spanning events
Spanning Tree event debugging is on
ST: Heard root 500-0000.0c49.7cda on Ethernet 4/2
    Supersedes 899-0000.0c87.ab91
ST: new root is 500, 0000.0c49.7cda on port Ethernet 4/2, cost 101
ST: sent Topology Change Notice on Ethernet4/2
ST: Topology Change rcvd on Ethernet4/3
```

Because the spanning tree algorithm operates at Layer 2 and all addresses are at this level, it's very difficult to trace bridge misconfigurations. This command can help to determine why performance on a switched LAN is poor, such as when spanning tree root elections occur every five seconds.

Common Catalyst 5000 Issues

Although the Catalyst 5000 family can be primarily plug-and-play switches, the more complex networks will always run into troubleshooting issues within any type of environment. Some of these common problems are host and application failures, spanning tree calculations, VLAN misconfigurations, and lost passwords.

Scenario 1: Host Connectivity

A new host requires a connection to a production Catalyst switch already in use by several other individuals. If the connection is to be to another switch, the following issues should be thought about in advance:

- Latency and host CPU utilization increases with the number of switches in a network.
- Broadcast traffic increases in large networks.
- More instabilities may arise in a large network due to changes in the bridge spanning tree algorithm.

After a host is connected to port 2/6 on the switch, the user reports that he or she is not able to use the network and that pinging the default gateway times out (but **ping** does respond to the local host address). The default gateway is a router connected to the switch's uplink port on the supervisor engine. The switch is also only servicing one VLAN (with the default of 1). In this case, the following steps should be performed to troubleshoot the problem:

1. First, check the link light located on line module 2 to verify that the physical connection is up. If this light is not lit, the network cable may need to be replaced. Otherwise, continue to Step 2.

2. Check the Catalyst switch port to verify that it's enabled, set at the proper speed, duplexed, and in the correct VLAN for the host's IP address by using the **show port 2/6** command. If the port is not enabled, issue the command **set port enable 2/6**. If the port is not in the proper VLAN, it can be set using the **set vlan** ***VLAN number*** **2/6** command. If the port is not set at the correct speed, use the **set port speed 2/6** ***speed*** command. If the duplex mode is incorrect, change it using the **set port duplex 2/6** ***mode*** command. Perform the **show port 2/6** command again; the port should now be in the connected state. Proceed to Step 3.

3. Verify that the correct port address entries are shown in the switch's CAM table by issuing the **show cam dynamic** command for port 2/6 and the uplink supervisor module port(s). If the entries appear to be invalid, issue the **clear cam** command. Otherwise, proceed to Step 4.

4. If the user is correctly connected to the switch, the next item to check is whether the router, acting as the user's default gateway, is configured correctly. Use the technique shown in Step 2 to verify that the port is set to the correct VLAN, speed, and duplex. If this is correct, proceed to Step 5.

5. Check that the switch's ARP table contains the correct information by issuing the **show arp** command. On the switch, this should only show the uplink router interface MAC address. If this address is incorrect, perform the **clear arp** command. If the problem still persists, make certain that the physical infrastructure and hardware are correctly inserted and intact.

Every time a port is attached or removed and the spanning tree is turned on, the ports appear to be locked up during the spanning tree calculation (learning mode for 15 seconds). If you have a loop-free environment in the switch environment (such as connecting a user workstation), you can turn off spanning tree on this port. There's a **set portfast enable** command that addresses this spanning tree learning time (forwarding delay). It should also be noted that IPX workstations require this to be enabled or else Get Nearest Server (GNS) requests will not be processed in time and it will appear as if the workstation is unable to login to the network.

Scenario 2: Packet Looping

Network management system alarms have been triggered due to a dramatic increase in input and output packets on the bridged ports. Bridged ports can sometimes result in looping if a backdoor bridge has been accidentally installed or if the incorrect encapsulation type is instantiated on a bridged interface.

If an unknown bridge has been inserted into the network, use a protocol analyzer to examine the source MAC address of all remote nodes. If a frame from a remote node includes a MAC address not from the locally connected router, it's known that this packet arrived through the backdoor bridge. Next, identify the manufacturer of the bridging device through the universally assigned MAC assignments (for example, all MAC addresses beginning with 0000-0c are assigned to Cisco Systems).

Two different bridging spanning tree algorithms may exist on an internetwork—IEEE and DEC. Use the **show span** command to determine whether multiple root bridges exist in the network and whether multiple spanning algorithms are in use. If both bridging types are in use, reconfigure all bridges with a standard algorithm. The most commonly utilized spanning tree algorithm is IEEE.

Scenario 3: STP Port Blocking

The Spanning Tree Protocol (STP) calculates loop-free Layer 2 data paths while still providing path redundancy. Each switch participating in a LAN generates Bridge Protocol Data Unit (BPDU) messages that can result in the election of a new root bridge. The root bridge serves as the logical center to a spanning tree network.

A network management system is reporting several election processes of a new spanning tree root within the Catalyst environment. If the common core, distribution, and access layered model distinguishes the network, then it would make sense for the highest layer to become the spanning tree root for all bridge groups. This can be accomplished via one of two methods: The port cost can be set by the command **set spantree portcost** ***port cost*** or the port priority can be set using the command **set spantree portpri** ***port priority***.

The spanning tree protocol will decide which port to disable based on three criteria: the port cost, the port priority, and the MAC address. Spanning tree will determine which port to disable using the following steps:

1. Spanning tree will first determine what the individual port cost is on each port connected to the bridge loop; it will then disable the port with the highest cost.
2. If the port costs are equal on all ports, spanning tree then checks for the lowest bridge priority. The bridge with the highest priority will have a port placed in blocking mode, and all other bridges will continue to function.

3. If the port cost and priority are all equal, spanning tree will check the MAC address and disable the port with a highest MAC address.

Scenario 4: Application Failures

A Microsoft Windows host reboots its computer, and the computer reports a duplicate NetBIOS name located on the network in the event log. The host computer is located in a VLAN 120, along with 150 other Microsoft Windows and Novell NetWare computers. As shown in Listing 13.17, the **set span** command can be used to mirror the traffic from VLAN 120 to a port that's connected to a protocol analyzer. This will allow all NetBIOS announcement frames to be captured by the analyzer, and the IPX or IP address of the misconfigured host can be identified.

If the switch has not learned of the MAC address and it's not stored in its CAM table, the frame is broadcast out of the entire group of switch ports within the designated VLAN.

Listing 13.17 The **set span** command can mirror traffic by VLAN number. The **show span** command displays the current SPAN configuration.

```
Catalyst_5500> (enable) set span 120 4/9 both enable
Enabled monitoring of VLAN 120 transmit/receive traffic by port 4/9

Catalyst_5500> (enable) show span
Status       : enabled
Admin Source: VLAN 120
Oper Source : Port 4/4
Destination : Port 4/9
Direction    : transmit/receive
```

Scenario 5: Misconfigured Virtual LANs

Your office building's network infrastructure was upgraded over the weekend using Catalyst 5500 switches and a 7513 router. Individual floors of users located within your building are not able to access remote network services—the first and second floors are operational while the third and fourth floors are not. Approximately half of the users on the fifth floor are not able to connect to remote networks. Further investigation of the problem reveals that the network problems are grouped by subnetworks, which could mean incorrect network configurations.

You can configure routing for virtual LANs using the Catalyst 5000 in two different ways: using an RSM and attaching a router to a VLAN trunking port using ISL encapsulation. Each method has its own benefits and downfalls, but, in essence, they provide the same functionality.

Route Switch Module

The RSM provides simple inter-VLAN routing using the existing backplane of the Catalyst switch. VLANs are configured on the switch with a unique VLAN identifier. This identifier must match the VLAN interface name used by the RSM, as shown in Listing 13.18.

To toggle between the router and switch sessions, enter the command **session** *RSM module number*. To perform a complete reset of the RSM hardware and software, issue the command **reset** *RSM module number*.

Listing 13.18 Using VLAN information from the Catalyst switch, the RSM can be configured to route for the VLANs.

```
Catalyst VLAN Information
VLAN Name                               Status    Mod/Ports, Vlans
---- ------------                       ------    ----------------
1    default                            active    1/1,2/1-12
2    Marketing LAN                      active    4/1-12

RSM Configuration
description Default Management VLAN
interface VLAN1
ip address 10.1.1.1 255.255.255.0
ipx network 1
appletalk cable-range 1-1
appletalk zone Default_Mgmt
!
interface VLAN2
description Marketing LAN
ip address 10.2.2.2 255.255.255.0
ipx network 1
appletalk cable-range 2-2
appletalk zone Marketing_LAN
```

If the VLAN number is incorrect within the Catalyst's configuration you can use the **set vlan** ***vlan number port numbers*** command to correct it. The router configuration will require a new interface to be created with the appropriate

VLAN number if it's found to be incorrect. Entering terminal configuration mode and then entering the command **interface VLAN *number*** can do this. IP, IPX, and AppleTalk configurations are performed identically to any other router, because the RSM runs standard Cisco IOS.

External Router

An external router can provide inter-VLAN routing using ISL or dot1q encapsulation between the switch and the routers; this is also known as a *router on a stick*. Subinterfaces are then configured on the router port identifying each ISL-encapsulated VLAN. Listing 13.19 displays the current configuration of the Catalyst switch and the external router.

Listing 13.19 Using VLAN information from the Catalyst switch, an external router can use ISL encapsulation to route for the VLANs.

```
Catalyst VLAN Information
VLAN Name                               Status    Mod/Ports, Vlans
---- ------------                       ------    ----------------
10   Novell Netware Servers             active    2/1-6,3/1-6
100  Windows NT Servers                 active    2/6-12,3/6-12
101  Client Workstations                active    4/1-24,5/1-24

Router Configuration
interface FastEthernet 2/1
no ip address
!
interface FastEthernet 2/1.10
description Novell NetWare Servers
ipx network 10
encapsulation isl 10
!
interface FastEthernet 2/1.100
description Windows NT Servers
ip address 10.100.100.1 255.255.255.0
encapsulation isl 100
bridge-group 50
!
interface FastEthernet 3/1.101
description Client Workstations
ip address 10.100.101.1 255.255.255.0
ipx network 101
encapsulation isl 101
bridge-group 50
!
bridge 50 protocol ieee
!
```

Mistakes, such as using an incorrect encapsulation VLAN identifier or not setting the catalyst switch port as trunked, are commonly found while browsing through the switch and router configurations. The router interface must also be configured utilizing subinterfaces, but the selected subinterface name is at the engineer's discretion. If VLAN routing is still not performing correctly, use the **debug vlan packet** command that's available on the router—this could provide valuable information in the troubleshooting process. It's also possible that the router's interface may be the bridged port that's in a blocking state. If this is the case, the VLAN interface may not become active. Logging into the switch and performing a **show port** command on the switch port the router is connected to will display the current bridging state. If the port is in blocking mode, initiating the **debug span tree** command should identify the root bridge, and the **set spantree** command on the switch will change the priority level of the catalyst port.

Although the naming conventions used for the subinterfaces are up to the engineer, it's widely recommended that the names reflect the associated IP network number, because IP is the predominant networking protocol. Therefore, interface Ethernet 1/1.200 would be configured with a 200-network address, such as 10.1.200.0/24.

Scenario 6: Password Recovery

Someone who is now on vacation has configured the password for a Catalyst 5500 switch, and users are complaining of high latency while performing intradepartmental file transfers. You must be able to perform privileged-level commands to set the VLAN to be monitored by SPAN, and the password is currently unavailable. To recover a lost password on a Catalyst 5000 family switch, the following steps must be performed:

1. You must be on the console. Reboot the device.
2. Press Enter at the password prompt (there's a null password for the first 30 seconds).
3. Type in the word "enable".
4. Press Enter again at the password prompt (again, there's a null password for the first 30 seconds).
5. Change the password using the **set password** and **set enablepass** commands.

Scenario 7: Auto-Negotiation

Auto-negotiation is an optional function of the Fast Ethernet standard that enables devices to automatically exchange information over a link about speed and duplex capabilities. Auto-negotiation should not be used to support network infrastructure devices such as routers and switches but should instead be used to support end workstations. Port duplex mode is not detectable at the 10 Megabit interface speed. One of the most common causes of performance loss is when one 10 Megabit port of a link is operating at half duplex while the other port is operating at full duplex. You can use the **show port** command to verify the current operating state of each end of the link. It should be noted that a duplex mismatch may or may not result in an error message; therefore, another indication of a duplex mismatch is rapidly increasing Frame Check Sequence (FCS) and alignment errors on the half duplex side, and runts on the full duplex port.

Practice Questions

Question 1

The protocol identified in the IEEE 802.10 specification is the VLAN transport mechanism used by which type of trunking media?

❍ a. FDDI

❍ b. ATM

❍ c. Fast Ethernet

The correct answer is a. IEEE 802.10 encapsulates FDDI. Fast Ethernet is encapsulated with Cisco's proprietary ISL protocol or the new IEEE 802.1Q standard, and ATM uses LAN emulation. Therefore, answers b and c are incorrect.

Question 2

What are the functions of the SAINT and SAGE ASICs? [Choose the two best answers]

❑ a. Performing frame encapsulation

❑ b. Processing information from the MCP

❑ c. Storing the CAM table

❑ d. Performing ISL encapsulation

The correct answers are a and d. SAINT provides ISL and Ethernet frame encapsulation, and SAGE performs ISL and all other data link protocol encapsulations. SAINT is an ASIC located at the switch port, and SAGE requires data to transfer across the backplane for encapsulation. The LCP handles information sent by the MCP. Therefore, answer b is incorrect. The CAM table is stored within RAM. Therefore, answer c is incorrect.

Question 3

The router for a Catalyst switched network is currently experiencing a high amount of traffic containing CRC errors. Which switching method should the switches be using to stop propagating this type of traffic?

❍ a. Fragment-free

❍ b. Fast-forward

❍ c. Store-and-forward

❍ d. Error-free

The correct answer is c. Store-and-forward receives the entire frame and validates the checksum before sending the frame to its destination. This would stop all corrupted frames from transiting the network any further. Fast-forward begins sending the frame as soon as the destination MAC address is processed, and fragment-free sends the frame just before receiving the data. Neither one of these switching methods will recognize whether the frame's checksum is valid prior to propagating the frame because it's not received yet. Therefore, answers a and b are incorrect. The error-free switching method does not exist. Therefore, answer d is incorrect.

Question 4

What's the minimum packet size for an ISL-encapsulated Ethernet frame?

❍ a. 128 bytes

❍ b. 94 bytes

❍ c. 1,548 bytes

❍ d. 30 bytes

The correct answer is b. ISL adds a 26-byte header and a 4-byte checksum, and the standard Ethernet frame ranges in size from 64 bytes to 1,518 bytes. Therefore, the minimum frame size using ISL encapsulation would be 64 + 30, which equals 94 bytes. Therefore, answers a, c, and d are incorrect.

Question 5

Performing the **show spantree** command on a Catalyst switch displays that the root bridge is not the Catalyst's port. Which command would have the highest probability of making the Catalyst port the root bridge?

❍ a. **set spantree portcost**

❍ b. **set spantree portpri**

❍ c. **set spantree root**

❍ d. Restarting the Catalyst switch

The correct answer is a. The individual port cost is the first metric compared by the spanning tree algorithm, so setting the cost to the lowest value possible would increase the chances of it becoming the root bridge by the largest percentage. The port priority is evaluated second to the cost, so this does not have the highest probability of promoting the bridge to root. Therefore, answer b is incorrect. **set spantree root** is not a valid Cisco Catalyst IOS command. Therefore, answer c is incorrect. Restarting the Catalyst switch will only force a new spanning tree election. This is forced because the port is just becoming active. Therefore, answer d is also incorrect.

Question 6

A VLAN trunk is set up between a Catalyst switch and a router to provide routing services for the trunked VLANs. After you configure the subinterfaces for the ISL trunked interface, all but VLAN 120 becomes active. What could cause this type of result? [Choose the two best answers]

❑ a. The subinterface on the router is configured with the IEEE 802.1Q encapsulation.

❑ b. The VLANs allowed on the trunking port do not include VLAN 120.

❑ c. The interface is not named VLAN120.

❑ d. The physical wiring has been cut.

The correct answers are a and b. After the ratification of IEEE 802.1Q, two encapsulation methods exist for VLANs: ISL and dotq. If the incorrect encapsulation type is configured on the link, the VLAN will not become active. Also, if the VLAN is disabled on the trunked port, it will not become active either. The naming convention of **interface VLAN** ***number*** is only required for

RSM interfaces. Therefore, answer c is incorrect. If the wiring were cut, the other VLANs would not have become active. Therefore, answer d is incorrect.

Question 7

What could cause the supervisor engine module's system status LED to be orange? [Choose the two best answers]

- ❑ a. A redundant power supply is installed but not turned on.
- ❑ b. The fan module has failed.
- ❑ c. The module systems diagnostic test failed.
- ❑ d. The supervisor module is in standby mode.

The correct answers are a and b. The supervisor module indicator will also be orange if it's no longer receiving any input from the chassis backplane. The status indicator will turn red if the diagnostic tests fail. Therefore, answer c is incorrect. If the supervisor goes into standby mode, the active indicator, not the system status LED, turns orange. Therefore, answer d is incorrect.

Question 8

A user operating a workstation connected to port 6/3 on the Catalyst switch is complaining of poor response time. Which command would need to be issued in the Catalyst switch to monitor traffic, if the protocol analyzer is plugged into port 7/1?

- ❍ a. **set span 6/3 7/1 both**
- ❍ b. **set span 7/1 6/3 both**
- ❍ c. **set span port 6/3 port 7/1 direction both**
- ❍ d. **set span 120 7/1 both**

The correct answer is a. In this case, the **set span** command requires the source port, the destination port, and the direction in which to monitor traffic. Answer b reverses the command and places the destination port first. Therefore, answer b is incorrect. Answers c and d are incorrect because they both do not adhere to Cisco Catalyst IOS guidelines for the **set span** command.

Question 9

Security policy states that all potential MAC addresses on a network must be documented. Which switch command will provide the available MAC addresses for each line module inserted into the chassis?

- ❍ a. **show vlans**
- ❍ b. **show modules**
- ❍ c. **show arp**
- ❍ d. **show cam**

The correct answer is b. The **show modules** command displays all modules that are inserted into the chassis and their associated MAC address ranges. Displaying VLAN information will not provide a list of MAC addresses, it will only show information about each individual VLAN configured. Therefore, answer a is incorrect. The ARP and CAM tables will only show currently active MAC addresses, not potential addresses. Therefore, answers c and d are also incorrect.

Question 10

Which Cisco IOS configuration statements are required for an RSM to become active on VLAN 50? [Choose the two best answers]

- ❑ a. Add an interface on the RSM using the configuration mode command **interface VLAN50**.
- ❑ b. Add the correct encapsulation statement for ISL or 802.1Q.
- ❑ c. **set rsm-vlan active** must be configured on the Catalyst switch.
- ❑ d. Place the interface in a bridge group or add Network layer addresses.

The correct answers are a and d. For the RSM to become active in any sense, the interface name must be configured using the VLAN number, and it also requires data link bridging or a Network layer address. RSMs do not require VLAN encapsulation statements, and external routers do. Therefore, answer b is incorrect. **set rsm-vlan active** is not a valid Cisco Catalyst IOS command. Therefore, answer c is incorrect.

Question 11

Which Cisco IOS **debug** command can resolve ISL encapsulation issues received on a router functioning as a "router on a stick"?

❍ a. **debug spanning events**

❍ b. **debug vlan packets**

❍ c. **debug isl packets**

❍ d. **debug isl router**

The correct answer is b. The **debug vlan packets** command will display all unsupported VLAN encapsulations and IDs. **debug spanning events** only provides information about the spanning tree protocol and its events. Therefore, answer a is incorrect. **debug isl packets** and **debug isl router** are not valid Cisco router IOS commands. Therefore, answers c and d are incorrect.

Question 12

A server was located on a hub connected to the Catalyst switch port 5/1, which is on VLAN 100. It has now been moved to another hub connected to port 6/3 on the same Catalyst switch. Which commands can be issued to delete the MAC address entry pointing server traffic to port 5/1? [Choose the two best answers]

❑ a. **clear cam dynamic 100**

❑ b. **clear arp**

❑ c. **delete cam**

❑ d. **clear cam static 100**

The correct answers are a and d. Because the server was on a hub connected to the switch, either the CAM table has mapped those MAC addresses or static entries have been configured to the connected switch port. This information will need to either age out or be manually cleared out (in this case, all MAC addresses associated with VLAN 100 are removed). The ARP table does not contain addresses learned by ports. Therefore, answer b is incorrect. **delete cam** is not a valid Cisco Catalyst IOS command. Therefore, answer c is incorrect.

Need To Know More?

Hein, Mathias and David Griffiths. *Switching Technology in the Local Network: From LAN to Switched LAN to Virtual LAN*. International Thompson Computer Press. London, UK, 1997. ISBN 1-85032-166-3. This is a great book that details all types of switched internetworks.

Perlman, Radia. *Interconnections: Bridges and Routers*. Addison-Wesley. Reading, MA, 1992. ISBN 0-201-56332-0. This book describes all the low-level fundamentals of bridging and routing—an excellent resource.

Check out the Catalyst 5000 family of products at the Cisco Web site (**www.cisco.com**). From the home page, select Products|LAN Switches|Catalyst Family of LAN Switches. There you'll find product and technical information about the Catalyst 5000 family.

Sample Test

In this chapter, I provide pointers to help you develop a successful test-taking strategy, including how to choose proper answers, how to decode ambiguity, how to work within the Cisco testing framework, how to decide what you need to memorize, and how to prepare for the test. At the end of the chapter, I include 61 questions on subject matter that pertains to Cisco Exam 640-506, "Support 2.0".

Questions, Questions, Questions

There should be no doubt in your mind that you're facing a test full of specific and pointed questions. Exam 640-506 consists of 61 randomly selected questions. You may take up to 75 minutes to complete the exam and need a score of 696 out of 1,000 to pass the exam.

For this exam, questions belong to one of six basic types:

- Multiple-choice with a single answer
- Multiple-choice with multiple answers
- Multipart with a single answer
- Multipart with multiple answers
- Simulations (that is, you must answer a question based on Cisco IOS command output)
- Fill in the blank (you must type out your answers without using the abbreviations that many Cisco administrators are used to using)

Always take the time to read a question at least twice before selecting an answer, and always look for an Exhibit button as you examine each question. Exhibits include graphics information that's related to a question. An exhibit is usually a screen capture of program output or GUI information that you must examine to analyze the question's contents and to formulate an answer. The Exhibit button brings up graphics and charts used to help explain a question, provide additional data, or illustrate program behavior.

Not every question has only one answer; many questions require multiple answers. Therefore, you need to read each question carefully to determine how many answers are necessary or possible and to look for additional hints or instructions when selecting answers. Such instructions often occur in brackets immediately following the question itself (as they do for all multiple-choice, multiple-answer questions). Unfortunately, some questions do not have any right answers and you're forced to find the "most correct" choice.

Picking Proper Answers

Obviously, the only way to pass any exam is to select enough of the right answers to obtain a passing score. However, Cisco's exams are not standardized like the SAT and GRE exams; they're far more diabolical and convoluted. In some cases, questions are strangely worded, and deciphering them can be a real challenge. In those cases, you may need to rely on answer-elimination skills.

Almost always, at least one answer out of the possible choices for a question can be eliminated immediately because it matches one of these conditions:

- ➤ The answer does not apply to the situation.
- ➤ The answer describes a nonexistent issue, an invalid option, or an imaginary state.
- ➤ The answer may be eliminated because of the question itself.

After you eliminate all answers that are obviously wrong, you can apply your retained knowledge to eliminate further answers. Look for items that sound correct but refer to actions, commands, or features that are not present or not available in the situation that the question describes.

If you're still faced with a blind guess among two or more potentially correct answers, reread the question. Try to picture how each of the possible remaining answers would alter the situation. Be especially sensitive to terminology; sometimes the choice of words ("remove" instead of "disable") can make the difference between a right answer and a wrong one.

Only when you've exhausted your ability to eliminate answers, but remain unclear about which of the remaining possibilities is correct, should you guess at an answer. An unanswered question offers you no points, but guessing gives you at least some chance of getting a question right; just don't be too hasty when making a blind guess.

Decoding Ambiguity

Cisco exams have a reputation for including questions that can be difficult to interpret, confusing, or ambiguous. In my experience with numerous exams, I consider this reputation to be completely justified. The Cisco exams are tough, and they're deliberately made that way.

The only way to beat Cisco at its own game is to be prepared. You'll discover that many exam questions test your knowledge of things that are not directly related to the issue that a question raises. This means that the answers you must choose from—even incorrect ones—are just as much a part of the skill assessment as the question itself. If you don't know something about most aspects of CIT, you might not be able to eliminate obviously wrong answers because they relate to a different area of CIT than the area the question at hand is addressing. In other words, the more you know about the Cisco IOS and troubleshooting Cisco internetworks, the easier it will be for you to tell a right answer from a wrong one.

Questions often give away their answers, but you have to be Sherlock Holmes to see the clues. Often, subtle hints appear in the question text in such a way that they seem almost irrelevant to the situation. You must realize that each question is a test unto itself and that you need to inspect and successfully navigate each question to pass the exam. Look for small clues, such as access-list modifications, problem isolation specifics (such as which layers of the OSI model are not functioning correctly), and invalid Cisco IOS commands. Little things like these can point at the right answer if properly understood; if missed, they can leave you facing a blind guess.

Another common difficulty with certification exams is vocabulary. Be sure to brush up on the key terms presented at the beginning of each chapter. You may also want to read through the Glossary at the end of this book the day before you take the test.

Working Within The Framework

The test questions appear in random order, and many elements or issues that receive mention in one question may also crop up in other questions. It's not uncommon to find that an incorrect answer to one question is the correct answer to another question, or vice versa. Take the time to read every answer to each question, even if you recognize the correct answer to a question immediately. That extra reading may spark a memory or remind you about a Cisco router or Catalyst switch Internetwork Operating System (IOS) feature or function that helps you on another question elsewhere in the exam.

Deciding What To Memorize

The amount of memorization you must undertake for an exam depends on how well you remember what you've read and how well you know the Cisco IOS by heart. The tests will stretch your recollection of the router's commands and functions.

At a minimum, you'll want to memorize the following kinds of information:

- The resources and tools available to administer and troubleshoot a Cisco internetwork.
- A standard troubleshooting technique for adequately diagnosing network problems.
- General Switching, IP, IPX, AppleTalk, Frame Relay, and ISDN concepts.
- The basic **show** and **debug** commands for IP, IPX, AppleTalk, frame relay, and ISDN diagnostics.

- The general **show** commands for troubleshooting the Catalyst 5000 series switches using the Cisco Catalyst IOS.

If you work your way through this book while sitting at a Cisco router (actually, you may need a group of routers) and try to manipulate this environment's features and functions as they're discussed throughout the book, you should have little or no difficulty mastering this material. Also, don't forget that The Cram Sheet at the front of the book is designed to capture the material that's most important to memorize; use this to guide your studies as well.

Preparing For The Test

The best way to prepare for the test—after you've studied—is to take at least one practice exam. I've included one here in this chapter for that reason; the test questions are located in the pages that follow (and unlike the preceding chapters in this book, the answers don't follow the questions immediately; you'll have to flip to Chapter 15 to review the answers separately).

Give yourself 105 minutes to take the exam, keep yourself on the honor system, and don't look at earlier text in the book or jump ahead to the answer key. When your time is up or you've finished the questions, you can check your work in Chapter 15. Pay special attention to the explanations for the incorrect answers; these can also help to reinforce your knowledge of the material. Knowing how to recognize correct answers is good, but understanding why incorrect answers are wrong can be equally valuable.

Taking The Test

Relax. Once you're sitting in front of the testing computer, there's nothing more you can do to increase your knowledge or preparation. Take a deep breath, stretch, and start reading that first question.

There's no need to rush; you have plenty of time to complete each question. Both easy and difficult questions are intermixed throughout the test in random order. Don't cheat yourself by spending too much time on a hard question early on in the test, thereby depriving yourself of the time you need to answer the questions at the end of the test. If you feel like you can cross out a couple of incorrect answers immediately for a question, then evaluate the remaining possibilities and guess from there. This will at least increase the chance of selecting the correct answer.

That's it for pointers. Here are some questions for you to practice on.

Sample Test

Question 1

In the ISDN reference model, what are non-ISDN devices defined as?

- ❍ a. NT1
- ❍ b. TA
- ❍ c. TE2
- ❍ d. LT

Question 2

You would like to remove all the routes from the AppleTalk routing table. Which Cisco IOS command will perform this function?

- ❍ a. **clear appletalk route ***
- ❍ b. **clear appletalk route**
- ❍ c. **delete appletalk routes**
- ❍ d. None of the above

Question 3

During a new installation, you've configured the local router for IPX on network ABAB. However, when you configure your Novell file server using 802.2 encapsulation, it's unable to see system resources. What's the most likely cause of the problem?

- ❍ a. The file server's network card is bad.
- ❍ b. SAP is unsupported using 802.2 encapsulation.
- ❍ c. There's a missing IP address statement in the router.
- ❍ d. There's a mismatched frame type.

Question 4

The **debug arp** command produced the following results:

```
IP ARP: sent req src 10.10.1.1 0000.0cab.1a47,
        dst 10.100.1.1 0000.0000.0000
IP ARP: rcvd rep src 10.100.1.1 0800.2010.a12c,
        dst 10.10.1.1
IP ARP: rcvd req src 10.101.1.1 0000.0cac.127a,
        dst 10.101.2.67
```

What's the MAC address of the workstation with the IP address 10.100.1.1?

❍ a. 0000.0cab.1a47

❍ b. 0000.0000.0000

❍ c. 0800.2010.a12c

❍ d. 0000.0cac.127a

Question 5

The router for a Catalyst switched network is currently experiencing a high amount of traffic containing CRC errors. Which switching method should the switches be using to stop propagating this type of traffic?

❍ a. Fragment free

❍ b. Fast forward

❍ c. Store and forward

❍ d. Error free

Question 6

What Cisco IOS command displays information about OSPF-related events?

____

Question 7

Which **debug** command displays information about Layer 3 call establishments? [Choose the two best answers]

- ❑ a. **debug isdn q921**
- ❑ b. **debug isdn events**
- ❑ c. **debug isdn q931**
- ❑ d. **debug isdn calls**

Question 8

Which Cisco product works with HP Openview and Sun Net Manager third-party network management products?

- ❍ a. Netsys Baseliner
- ❍ b. CiscoWorks 2000
- ❍ c. VlanDirector
- ❍ d. Traffic Director

Question 9

You've recently captured a large amount of IPX traffic using a protocol analyzer. What's the easiest way to restrict the packets you view to only the packets destined for the IPX network ABAB?

- ❍ a. Configure a capture filter.
- ❍ b. Configure a display filter.
- ❍ c. Configure a router access list.
- ❍ d. Set the protocol analyzer's interface frame type to Ethernet II.

Question 10

Which Cisco IOS command generates a list of direct mappings between the Network layer protocol address and the frame relay data link control identifier (DLCI)?

____

Question 11

Distance-vector routing protocols are more susceptible to routing loops than link-state routing protocols. Which techniques have been implemented within the distance-vector protocols to limit the chances of routing loops occurring? [Choose the three best answers]

❑ a. Hold-down timers

❑ b. Dijkstra algorithm

❑ c. Split horizon

❑ d. Poison reverse

❑ e. Updates sent with changes only

Question 12

Which of the following is most likely to be caused by using a classless IP address space?

❍ a. Invalid OSPF routes

❍ b. Invalid EIGRP routes

❍ c. Incorrect routing update timers

❍ d. Invalid RIP or IGRP routes

Question 13

You would like to have a more redundant WAN link and have taken on the task of installing a backup ISDN line. Initially the line comes up and begins working, but as soon as you begin configuring CHAP, the connection is broken and cannot be reestablished. What **debug** command displays the output from CHAP three-way handshakes?

____

Question 14

On a frame relay network, a high number of dropped packets in conjunction with rapidly increasing FECN and BECN values could be a warning sign of what?

❍ a. Poor line quality

❍ b. A saturated connection

❍ c. An incorrectly configured serial interface

❍ d. Failing Cisco hardware

Question 15

Based on the output from the following **show ip route** command, what's the administrative distance of OSPF?

```
Router>show ip route
[output omitted from listing]
O E1 10.2.1.0/24 [150/151] via 10.200.1.1,
        00:13:37, Ethernet0
C    10.100.1.0/29 is directly connected, Ethernet4/
     1
R    10.1.1.0/24 [120/1] via 10.200.10.1,
        00:00:16, Ethernet4/3
I    10.210.0.0/16 [100/9450] via 10.10.3.1,
        00:00:34, Serial2/0
B    204.17.221.0/24 [20/10] via 193.3.11.5, 1d17h
B    192.35.226.0/24 [20/10] via 193.3.11.9, 4d03h
```

❍ a. 150

❍ b. 120

❍ c. 151

❍ d. 100

Question 16

ICMP can be used for which of the following tasks? [Choose the two best answers]

- ❑ a. Echo and reply messages for testing node reachability
- ❑ b. As a reliable transport protocol for host applications
- ❑ c. Multicast group inclusion and removal
- ❑ d. Router address automated discovery

Question 17

Performing the **show interfaces** command generates the following output. From this output, what's most likely to be the problem?

```
Router>show interfaces FastEthernet1/0
FastEthernet1/0 is up, line protocol is up
     [output omitted from listing]
     0 input packets with dribble condition detected
     2604306051 packets output, 4065876293 bytes,
     0 underruns
     0 output errors, 1375681 collisions,
     1783 interface resets
     0 babbles, 0 late collision, 0 deferred
     0 lost carrier, 0 no carrier
     1 output buffer failures,
     0 output buffers swapped out
```

- ❍ a. High data throughput has saturated the Fast Ethernet connection.
- ❍ b. A high number of interface resets.
- ❍ c. Excessive collisions.
- ❍ d. There's no way to know because only one **show interfaces** command is listed.

Question 18

By default, how often are IPX SAPs sent out of an individual router interface?

❍ a. Every 60 seconds

❍ b. Every 90 seconds

❍ c. Every 30 seconds

❍ d. Every 120 seconds

Question 19

Which Cisco IOS command lists the IPX servers that have been learned by SAP announcements?

❍ a. **show ipx servers**

❍ b. **display servers**

❍ c. **show servers**

❍ d. **show ipx route**

Question 20

An incorrect network address has been configured on a frame relay subinterface. Which command needs to be issued after the network address is correctly reconfigured?

❍ a. **clear counters serial**

❍ b. **clear ip arp**

❍ c. **delete frame arp**

❍ d. **clear frame-relay-inarp**

Question 21

Which Cisco IOS command displays information about Phase I/II compatibility?

❍ a. **show appletalk neighbors**

❍ b. **show appletalk globals**

❍ c. **show appletalk zip**

❍ d. **show appletalk updates**

Question 22

After you've upgraded the local router from an older IOS version, several Ethernet II frame type IPX clients are unable to connect to the Novell file server. Which response is the best solution to resolve this problem?

❍ a. Enable IPX type-20 propagation.

❍ b. Change the router's frame type to novell-ether.

❍ c. Increase the ipx gns-response-delay timer on the router.

❍ d. Downgrade the router's IOS back to its previous version.

Question 23

A serial interface misses three consecutive keepalives. Which interface status will be displayed by the **show interfaces** command?

❍ a. Serial 0 is up, and the line protocol is down

❍ b. Serial 0 is down, and the line protocol is up

❍ c. Serial 0 is up, and the line protocol is up

❍ d. Serial 0 is down, and the line protocol is down

Question 24

Users on an Ethernet II IPX network are not able to access any network information. Performing the **show interfaces** command generates the following information. What's most likely the problem?

```
Router>show interfaces ethernet 0
Ethernet0 is up, line protocol is up
  Hardware is cxBus Ethernet,
    address is aa00.0400.2bbf (bia 00e0.3400.4883)
  Internet address is 10.7.1.1/24
  MTU 1500 bytes, BW 10000 Kbit, DLY 1000 usec,
     rely 255/255, load 1/255
  Encapsulation NOVELL-ETHER, loopback not set,
     keepalive set (10 sec)
```

❍ a. The MAC address that the interface is responding to is aa00.0400.2bbf instead of the burned-in address, 00e0.3400.4883.

❍ b. The users are attempting to connect at 100Mbps speeds rather than 10Mbps.

❍ c. The encapsulation type needs to be changed to ARPA.

❍ d. The encapsulation type needs to be changed to SAP.

Question 25

Which of the following reasons might initiate a route to be learned through the wrong interface, thus causing a routing loop?

❍ a. A misconfigured network statement.

❍ b. Split horizon is disabled on the interface.

❍ c. A misconfigured autonomous system number.

❍ d. Incorrect route redistribution.

Question 26

Which instrument can verify fiber-optic installations?

❍ a. OTDR

❍ b. Protocol analyzer

❍ c. Cable tester

❍ d. TDR

Question 27

Which section of CCO enables you to purchase and configure Cisco products over the Internet?

❍ a. Documentation

❍ b. Software Center

❍ c. Cisco Purchasing

❍ d. Cisco Marketplace

Question 28

A standard ISDN RJ-45 connector has eight pins. Which ones are used for reception, as defined by the ISO 8877 standard?

❍ a. Pins 4 and 5

❍ b. Pins 3 and 6

❍ c. Pins 1 and 2

❍ d. Pins 7 and 8

Question 29

A user operating a workstation connected to VLAN 120 on the Catalyst switch is complaining of poor response time. Which command would need to be issued in the Catalyst switch to monitor traffic if the protocol analyzer is plugged into port 5/6?

❍ a. **set span 5/1 5/6 both**

❍ b. **set span 5/6 5/1 both**

❍ c. **set span port 5/1 port 5/6 direction both**

❍ d. **set span 120 5/6 both**

Question 30

You would like to have all system log messages go to the router's internal buffer. Which command will perform this?

❍ a. **logging internal**

❍ b. **logging buffered**

❍ c. **logging monitor**

❍ d. **logging console**

Question 31

Which command will display all directly connected Cisco devices and information about the devices' software, data link, and network configurations?

____

Question 32

Which of the following commands displays the contents of the IP routing table?

❍ a. **show ip arp**

❍ b. **show ip route**

❍ c. **show route**

❍ d. **display ip route**

Question 33

The local office installs a Cisco 2500 series router, and the remote office installs a Nortel (formerly Bay Networks) router. Which frame relay encapsulation type should be run between the two routers?

❍ a. IETF

❍ b. CISCO

❍ c. Frame

❍ d. Serial

Question 34

Which of the following are acceptable methods for packet switching? [Choose the three best answers]

❑ a. NetFlow

❑ b. Autonomous

❑ c. Phantom

❑ d. Generic

❑ e. Optimum

Question 35

Which step of the troubleshooting model may require contacting affected users and checking network baselines?

❍ a. Implementing an action plan

❍ b. Defining the problem

❍ c. Gathering facts

❍ d. Documenting the solution

Question 36

Debug and system errors are sent where by default?

❍ a. The syslog server.

❍ b. The console.

❍ c. The internal buffer.

❍ d. Messages are not recorded.

Question 37

What's the function of the Phoenix ASIC in a Catalyst 5500 switch?

❍ a. It performs frame encapsulation.

❍ b. It processes information from the MCP.

❍ c. It connects the switching busses available in the Catalyst 5500 architecture and provides a 3.6Gbps backplane.

❍ d. It stores the CAM table.

Question 38

Users in a remote office are complaining that they're intermittently not able to access the corporate database. Issuing the **show interfaces serial** command on the router reveals that the serial connection between corporate headquarters and the remote office is experiencing numerous carrier transitions. Which command could also be issued on the router to help in diagnosing the problem?

❍ a. **show controllers cbus**

❍ b. **debug atm-sig all**

❍ c. **debug serial interface**

❍ d. **debug all**

Question 39

Which of the following addresses is a valid AppleTalk address?

❍ a. 10.1.10.1

❍ b. 100.13

❍ c. 13

❍ d. ABAB.00c0.43ab.12da

Question 40

You've recently converted from completely process-switching packets to fast-switching, and now you would like to see how many packets are using each method. What command will provide these statistics for you?

____

Question 41

After you've captured several packets on an Ethernet IPX network with your protocol analyzer, the counter reads "2,113 frames received, 113 frames captured." What do these two statistics mean?

❍ a. 2,000 frames contained invalid checksums and were dropped.

❍ b. Excessive collisions are being seen on the network.

❍ c. The protocol analyzer is set for the wrong Ethernet frame type.

❍ d. 2,113 frames were seen by the network interface, but 113 frames met the criteria specified in a traffic filter.

Question 42

What's the standard SAP type for Novell file servers?

❍ a. 1

❍ b. 4

❍ c. 7

❍ d. 24

Question 43

What could cause the supervisor engine module's active status LED to be orange?

❍ a. A redundant power supply is installed but not turned on.

❍ b. The fan has failed.

❍ c. The module systems diagnostic test failed.

❍ d. The supervisor module is in standby mode.

Question 44

How do you tell the difference between an 802.3 (RAW) Ethernet frame and an Ethernet II frame?

❍ a. There is no difference between the two frame formats.

❍ b. Ethernet II includes DSAP and SSAP addresses.

❍ c. 802.3 (RAW) includes the 802.2 LLC header.

❍ d. Ethernet II frames include a type field, whereas 802.3 (RAW) frames include a length field.

Question 45

What ISDN command displays multilink PPP configuration information?

____

Question 46

You've just connected your ISDN router to your service provider's network but have not yet configured any SPIDs. The ISDN connection should correctly initialize up to which layer?

❍ a. Layer 1 (Physical).

❍ b. Layer 2 (Data Link).

❍ c. Layer 3 (Network).

❍ d. The connection will not initialize at all.

Question 47

IP helper addresses are displayed by issuing what Cisco IOS **show** command?

____

Question 48

Issuing the **show ip route** command generates the following output. If a packet enters through interface Ethernet2 that's destined for 11.1.31.154, what is the next hop IP address?

```
Gateway of last resort is 10.1.1.1 to network
     0.0.0.0
O E1 10.30.0.0/16 [110/151] via 10.200.1.1,
       00:13:37, Ethernet1
R    10.2.1.0/24 [120/1] via 10.20.1.1,
       00:13:37, Ethernet0
C    10.100.1.0/29 is directly connected, Ethernet4/
     1
R    10.30.21.0/24 [120/1] via 10.200.10.1,
       00:00:16, Serial0
```

❍ a. 10.200.10.1

❍ b. 10.200.1.1

❍ c. 10.1.1.1

❍ d. 10.20.1.1

Question 49

Which command displays information about overflow, memory, and buffer errors for the Serial 1 interface?

❍ a. **show serial 0**

❍ b. **show ip interface brief**

❍ c. **show interfaces serial 1**

❍ d. **show controllers serial 1**

Question 50

Which tool is most useful for analysis of redesign, reconfiguration, and stress testing within a Cisco network?

❍ a. A cable tester

❍ b. Cisco Netsys Baseliner

❍ c. An oscilloscope

❍ d. Network Management Systems

Question 51

Connectionless protocols, such as UDP, have what advantage over connection-oriented protocols?

❍ a. Increased network traffic

❍ b. Windowing and flow control

❍ c. Reliable data stream

❍ d. Less network traffic

Question 52

Which commands are defined within the Cisco IOS? [Choose the three best answers]

❑ a. **show ip interface**

❑ b. **show ip eigrp interfaces**

❑ c. **show ip route**

❑ d. **clear ip-route***

❑ e. **debug ip interface**

❑ f. **show ip globals**

❑ g. **debug ip all**

Question 53

Performing the **show interfaces** command generates the following results:

```
Ethernet0 is up, line protocol is up
  Hardware is cxBus Ethernet,
     address is aa00.0400.2bbf (bia 00e0.3400.4883)
  Internet address is 10.7.16.1 255.255.255.0
```

Which MAC address will the interface respond to?

❍ a. 255.255.255.0

❍ b. aa00.0400.2bbf

❍ c. 00e0.3400.4883

❍ d. 10.7.16.1

Question 54

A VLAN trunk is set up between a Catalyst switch and a router to provide routing services for the trunked VLANs. After you configure the subinterfaces for the ISL trunked interface, all but VLAN 120 becomes active. What could cause this type of result? [Choose the two best answers]

❑ a. The subinterface on the router is configured with the IEEE 802.1Q encapsulation.

❑ b. The VLANs allowed on the trunking port do not include VLAN 120.

❑ c. The interface is not named VLAN120.

❑ d. The physical wiring has been cut.

Question 55

Which Internet protocol can hosts use to discover all locally attached router addresses?

❍ a. IGMP

❍ b. UDP

❍ c. IRDP

❍ d. ICMP

Question 56

Users are complaining that they're not able to connect to a remote network with IPX NetBIOS applications. Which interface command is required to bridge these packets?

❍ a. **ipx bridge**

❍ b. **ipx nlsp enable**

❍ c. **ipx type-20-propagation**

❍ d. **ipx gns-response-delay**

Question 57

A workstation's network card is found to be faulty and is replaced. Afterward, the host still cannot connect to the network. After some time, a veteran network engineer realizes the problem, enters a few commands into the router, and everything works. Inspect the results of the local interface's configuration within the following running configuration and select which router command was entered.

```
interface FastEthernet1/1
 description "Marketing LAN"
 ip address 10.13.2.1 255.255.255.128
 ip broadcast-address 10.13.2.127
 no ip directed-broadcast
 arp timeout 0
 bridge-group 1
```

❍ a. **permit ip directed-broadcasts**

❍ b. **clear ip route ***

❍ c. **clear arp-cache**

❍ d. **debug all**

Question 58

Several users on a network are reporting that they cannot execute Telnet sessions to offsite locations. These users are reporting no other problems. What would be the first thing to check?

❍ a. Check whether the locally attached router's interface has been set as administratively down.

❍ b. Check whether access lists enabled on interfaces located between the clients and the remote server are denying port 23 or are denied by the implicit **deny any**.

❍ c. Check whether access lists enabled on interfaces located between the clients and the remote server are denying port 21 or are denied by the implicit **deny any**.

❍ d. Check whether the users are currently connected to the network.

Question 59

The DDR connection is not being established. Which **debug** command will help the most with identifying why the connection is not becoming active?

❍ a. **debug isdn events**

❍ b. **show dialer map**

❍ c. **debug dialer events**

❍ d. **show ppp multilink**

Question 60

Performing the **show interfaces ethernet0** command generates the following output. From this output, what number correlates to a possible overextended LAN?

```
Router# show interfaces ethernet0
1.   Ethernet 0 is up, line protocol is up
2.   Hardware is MCI Ethernet, address is
     aa00.0400.0134 (via 0000.0c00.4369)
3.   Internet address is 131.108.1.1, subnet mask is
     255.255.255.0
4.   MTU 1500 bytes, BW 10000 Kbit, DLY 1000 usec,
     rely 255/255, load 1/255
5.   Encapsulation ARPA, loopback not set, keepalive
     set (10 sec)
6.   ARP type: ARPA, PROBE, ARP Timeout 4:00:00
7.   Last input 0:00:00, output 0:00:00, output hang
     never
8.   Output queue 0/40, 0 drops; input queue 0/75, 2
     drops
9.   Five minute input rate 61000 bits/sec, 4 pack-
     ets/sec
10.  Five minute output rate 1000 bits/sec, 2 pack-
     ets/sec
11.  2295197 packets input, 305539992 bytes, 0 no
     buffer
12.  Received 1925500 broadcasts, 0 runts, 0 giants
13.  3 input errors, 3 CRC, 0 frame, 0 overrun, 0
     ignored, 0 abort
14.  0 input packets with dribble condition detected
15.  3594664 packets output, 436549843 bytes, 0
     underruns
16.  8 output errors, 1791285 collisions, 10 inter-
     face resets, 0 restarts
```

Question 61

Give four of the commands that are included in the output of the **show tech-support** Cisco IOS command.

____

Answer Key

1. c
2. d
3. d
4. c
5. c
6. **debug ip ospf events**
7. b, c
8. b
9. b
10. **show frame-relay map**
11. a, c, d
12. d
13. **debug ppp authentication**
14. b
15. a
16. a, d
17. d
18. a
19. a
20. d
21. b
22. c
23. a
24. c
25. b
26. a
27. d
28. a
29. d
30. b
31. **show cdp neighbors detail**
32. b
33. a
34. a, b, e
35. c
36. b
37. c
38. c
39. b
40. **show interfaces stats**
41. d
42. b
43. d
44. d
45. **show ppp multilink**
46. b
47. **show ip interfaces**
48. c
49. d
50. b
51. d
52. a, b, c
53. b
54. a, b
55. c
56. c
57. c
58. b
59. c
60. 16
61. *See page 404.*

Question 1

The correct answer is c. Non-ISDN devices are actually defined as Terminal Equipment 2 (TE2) devices. Only ISDN devices or TAs can connect directly into a Network Termination 1 (NT1) device. Therefore, answer a is incorrect. Terminal Adapters (TAs) provide the analog-to-digital conversion to allow the device to connect to the ISDN network. Therefore, answer b is also incorrect. The Line Termination (LT) is the physical connection to the ISDN switch located within the service provider's network. Therefore, answer d is incorrect.

Question 2

The correct answer is d. The **clear appletalk route** command can only be used to remove individual AppleTalk routes, unlike the IP and IPX versions, which can delete the entire routing table. Therefore, answers a, b, and c are incorrect.

Question 3

The correct answer is d. The default encapsulation type for Cisco routers is novell-ether, or 802.3 (RAW), which is what the Novell file server needs to be configured for. Answer a is not the best choice because this is a new installation and the interfaces are most likely OK. SAPs are supported within all frame encapsulations because they occur at a higher layer in the OSI model. Therefore answer b is incorrect. Answer c is also incorrect because this is on an IPX network, not an IP network.

Question 4

The correct answer is c. Station 10.100.1.1 replied to station 10.10.1.1 with its MAC address of 0800.2010.a12c. Answer a is incorrect because it's the MAC address of station 10.10.1.1. The 0000.0000.0000 contained in the first IP ARP statement identifies that station 10.10.1.1 has issued an ARP request for the MAC address of station 10.100.1.1. Therefore, answer b is incorrect. The second IP ARP statement is station 10.100.1.1, sending an ARP reply back to station 10.10.1.1 with its MAC address of 0800.2010.a12c. Answer d is incorrect because it's the MAC address of station 10.101.1.1.

Question 5

The correct answer is c. The store-and-forward switching method receives the entire frame and validates the checksum before sending the frame to its destination. This would stop all corrupted frames from transiting the network any further. The fast-forward switching method begins sending the frame as soon as the destination MAC address is processed, and the fragment-free switching method sends the frame just before receiving the data. Neither one of these switching methods will recognize whether the frame's checksum is valid prior to propagating the frame because it's not received yet. Therefore, answers a and b are incorrect. The error-free switching method does not exist. Therefore, answer d is incorrect.

Question 6

The correct answer is **debug ip ospf events**. This command displays information about OSPF-related events, such as adjacencies, designated router selection, and SPF calculations.

Question 7

The correct answers are b and c. These two commands produce similar results but in different formats, which can help in providing more user-friendly debugging information. The **debug isdn q921** command displays Layer 2 information. Therefore, answer a is incorrect. **debug isdn calls** is not a valid Cisco IOS command. Therefore, answer d is incorrect.

Question 8

The correct answer is b. CiscoWorks 2000 integrates with HP Openview standalone and Web-version applications. Netsys Baseliner only integrates with CiscoWorks 2000, not third-party products. Therefore, answer a is incorrect. VlanDirector and Traffic Director are also integrated with the CiscoWorks 2000 product line, but they're also individual applications. Therefore, answers c and d are incorrect.

Question 9

The correct answer is b. Display filters are used to restrict the view of previously captured packets. Capture filters limit the packets that are buffered by the protocol analyzer prior to viewing. Therefore, answer a is incorrect. Access lists may limit the actual packets you'll see in an analyzer, but they will also affect all other computers on the network. Therefore, answer c is incorrect. Setting the protocol analyzer's frame type to Ethernet II would restrict all captured packets to the Ethernet II frame type, but you need to restrict what's seen to only IPX network ABAB packets. Therefore, answer d is also incorrect.

Question 10

The correct answer is **show frame-relay map**. DLCI-to-Network layer mappings can be viewed directly using this command.

Question 11

The correct answers are a, c, and d. Distance-vector routing protocols implement split horizon, poison reverse, triggered updates, and hold-down timers to reduce the changes of routing loops. Answer b is incorrect because this is the algorithm employed by the link-state routing protocol OSPF. Answer e is also incorrect because this is a general function of link-state routing protocols.

Question 12

The correct answer is d. RIP and IGRP are both classful routing protocols and therefore cannot handle VLSMs. OSPF and EIGRP routing protocols can handle classless IP addresses and VLSMs. Therefore, answers a and b are incorrect. Routing update timers are handled independently of the address space. Therefore, answer c is incorrect.

Question 13

The correct answer is **debug ppp authentication**. This command can be used to identify CHAP misconfigurations such as incorrect or missing usernames and passwords.

Question 14

The correct answer is b. The frame relay network notifies each end station of congestion encountered within the network via FECNs and BECNs—which could be due to a saturated connection—thus notifying you that additional bandwidth may be required. Line transitions may indicate poor line quality. Therefore, answer a is incorrect. Misconfigured serial interfaces or failing Cisco hardware would not cause FECNs or BECNs to be produced with the service provider's frame relay network. Therefore, answers c and d are incorrect.

Question 15

The correct answer is a. Although the default administrative distance for OSPF is 110, in this case, the network has been configured to use an administrative distance of 150. Answers b, c, and d are incorrect because they identify the RIP administrative distance, OSPF route's metric, and IGRP's administrative distance, respectively.

Question 16

The correct answers are a and d. The ping utility uses ICMP for echo and echo reply messages, whereas IRDP uses ICMP to generate advertisements for router IP addresses for locally connected workstations. TCP is the reliable transport protocol for IP. Therefore, answer b is incorrect. Multicast group changes are handled by IGMP. Therefore, answer c is incorrect.

Question 17

The correct answer is d. This is only one instance of the information generated by the **show interfaces** command; the collisions, resets, and high throughput may have occurred months ago. Therefore, answers a, b, and c are incorrect. In general, for an accurate representation of the data, either several instances of the command should be issued in succession or the **clear counters** command should be performed.

Question 18

The correct answer is a. SAP packets are sent out every 60 seconds, which can saturate an ISDN connection. Although the SAP interval can be changed (using the **ipx sap-interval** command) to 30, 90, or 120 seconds (or any other value), because the question asks for the default value, answers b, c, and d are incorrect.

Question 19

The correct answer is a. The **show ipx servers** command generates a list of server names, service types, network numbers, the number of hops to the server, and the interface the SAP advertisement was received on. Answers b and c are incorrect because they're not valid Cisco IOS commands. The **show ipx route** command displays the IPX routing table. Therefore, answer d is incorrect.

Question 20

The correct answer is d. This command will force new DLCI-to-network address mappings by deleting all the entries in the frame relay Inverse ARP table. **clear counters serial** will only clear the statistical counters available for the various frame relay **show** commands. Therefore, answer a is incorrect. Clearing the IP ARP table will delete all IP-to-MAC address correlations, which is not what's required. Therefore, answer b is incorrect. **delete frame arp** is not a valid Cisco IOS command. Therefore, answer c is incorrect.

Question 21

The correct answer is b. The **show appletalk globals** command displays a report of several of the general AppleTalk settings, such as the total number of routes and zones, protocol update intervals, and routing protocol specifics, as well as phase compatibility. The **show appletalk neighbors** command displays a list of directly connected AppleTalk neighbors learned via a routing protocol. Therefore, answer a is incorrect. The **show appletalk zip** command lists the entries in the Zone Information Table (ZIT). Therefore, answer c is incorrect. Answer d is incorrect because it is not a valid Cisco IOS command.

Question 22

The correct answer is c. The Cisco IOS default value for GNS response delay was changed from 500 ms to 0 in newer software releases, which sometimes leads to older workstations not acknowledging the router's response quickly enough. IPX type 20 packets are IPX NetBIOS packets, which would not be affected by a router upgrade. Therefore, answer a is incorrect. The network was working prior to the router upgrade, so the frame type is already correctly set. Therefore, answer b is incorrect. Downgrading the router to its previous IOS may solve the problem, but it's not the best solution. If the router is running this old of an IOS version, it needs to be upgraded anyway. Therefore, answer d is incorrect.

Question 23

The correct answer is a. After a serial interface misses three consecutive keepalives, the line is brought down and reset, which would cause the Physical layer to still be up but the line protocol to be down. Therefore answers b, c, and d are incorrect.

Question 24

The correct answer is c. The default encapsulation is still set on the Ethernet 0 interface (NOVELL-ETHER), and because this is an Ethernet II network, the encapsulation type should be ARPA. Even though the interface will respond with the MAC address that is not the burned-in address, this should not cause any problems. Therefore, answer a is incorrect. The users could be connecting into a 100Mbps switch that connects to the router at 10Mbps speeds. Therefore, answer b is incorrect. The SAP encapsulation type is used with the Ethernet 802.2 frame types. Therefore, answer d is incorrect.

Question 25

The correct answer is b. Disabling split horizon makes a distance-vector routing protocol susceptible to routing loops because it allows routing announcements to be propagated out of the interface on which they were originally received. Misconfigured network statements and autonomous system numbers wouldn't allow the routes to propagate at all. Therefore, answers a and c are incorrect. Route redistribution would cause routes to be learned through the wrong interface. Therefore, answer d is incorrect.

Question 26

The correct answer is a. Optical time domain reflectors (OTDRs) analyze fiber media using optical pulses. Protocol analyzers provide realtime traffic analysis and dissemination of packets. Therefore, answer b is incorrect. Cable testers check the physical continuity and termination of networking cables. Therefore, answer c is incorrect. TDRs send electrical signals along a metallic cable. Therefore, answer d is incorrect.

Question 27

The correct answer is d. The Marketplace also provides shipment tracking as well as maintenance contract and warranty information. The Documentation section provides Cisco product catalogs and configuration manuals. Therefore, answer a is incorrect. The Software Center provides online IOS and network management software new releases and upgrades. Therefore, answer b is incorrect. Answer c is incorrect because the Cisco Purchasing section does not exist within CCO.

Question 28

The correct answer is a. Pins 4 and 5 provide the receive positive and negative signals. Pins 3 and 6 provide the positive and negative transmission signals, respectively. Therefore, answer b is incorrect. Pins 1 and 2 provide the positive and negative power source. Therefore, answer c is incorrect. Pins 7 and 8 provide the positive and negative power sink. Therefore, answer d is incorrect.

Question 29

The correct answer is d. In this case, the **set span** command requires the source VLAN, the destination port, and the direction in which to monitor traffic. Answers a and b would be used to span port 5/1 to port 5/6 and vice versa, respectively. Answer c is incorrect because it does not adhere to Cisco Catalyst IOS guidelines for the **set span** command.

Question 30

The correct answer is b. The **logging buffered** command sends all logging messages to an internal buffer. Answer a is incorrect because it's not a valid Cisco IOS command. The **logging monitor** command limits the logging to virtual terminal sessions only. Therefore, answer c is incorrect. The **logging console** command limits the logging to the console port only. Therefore, answer d is incorrect.

Question 31

The correct answer is **show cdp neighbors detail**. This command lists the Network layer addresses and other information using Cisco's proprietary Cisco Discovery Protocol (CDP). This command will only work if each end of the connection is configured within each router's configuration with the **cdp enable** command.

Question 32

The correct answer is b. The **show ip route** command displays the router's internal routing table, providing detailed information about each individual route. The **show ip arp** command displays the local ARP table, which contains the IP-address-to-MAC-address resolutions. Therefore, answer a is incorrect. Answers c and d are incorrect because they are not valid Cisco IOS commands.

Question 33

The correct answer is a. The IETF standardized frame relay encapsulation allows routers from disparate vendors to communicate. The CISCO encapsulation method is proprietary—only Cisco devices can communicate via this protocol. Therefore, answer b is incorrect. Answers c and d are incorrect because they are not Data Link layer encapsulations.

Question 34

The correct answers are a, b, and e. The NetFlow, Autonomous, and Optimum switching methods are all acceptable switching methods that can be used to increase the overall performance, statistical collecting resources, and reliability of a network. Answers c and d are incorrect because they are not valid Cisco switching methods.

Question 35

The correct answer is c. While gathering facts about a network problem (Step 2), you should question users and check historical information and network baselines for as much information as possible. Implementing an action plan is the fifth step in the troubleshooting model, where you're executing, step by step, the procedures outlined in Step 4, "Create an action plan." Therefore, answer a is incorrect. Defining the problem (Step 1) involves developing a clear statement of the problem and its scope. Therefore, answer b is incorrect. Documenting the solution is the last step in the troubleshooting model and requires a document to be prepared, summarizing the events that occurred while you were troubleshooting the problem. This document should then be stored within a help desk database. Therefore, answer d is incorrect.

Question 36

The correct answer is b. All system logs are sent to the console by default, which also produces the most system overhead. Therefore answers a, c, and d are incorrect.

Question 37

The correct answer is c. SAINT provides ISL and Ethernet frame encapsulation. SAGE performs ISL and all other data link protocol encapsulations. Therefore, answer a is incorrect. The LCP handles information sent by the MCP. Therefore, answer b is incorrect. The CAM table is stored within RAM. Therefore, answer d is incorrect.

Question 38

The correct answer is c. Debugging the serial interface will provide information on line timing, which is generally the reason carrier transitions occur. This information can then be used to distinguish whether the problem is on the local interface, within the carrier's network, or on the remote interface. The **show controllers cbus** command would show the version of microcode that's installed, but this would not help in resolving an intermittent issue. Therefore, answer a is incorrect. The **debug atm-sig all** command would only debug ATM signaling events, not serial events. Therefore, answer b is incorrect. The **debug all** command would overload the router with all types of debugging material and would not prove useful. Therefore, answer d is also incorrect.

Question 39

The correct answer is b. AppleTalk addresses are composed of a 16-bit network address and an 8-bit node address, which makes all values between 1 and 255 available for the network address and all values between 1 and 253 available for the node address (the node address values 254 and 255 are reserved). Answer a is incorrect because it's a valid IP address. Answer c is incorrect because it does not contain the host portion of the AppleTalk address. Answer d is incorrect because it's a valid IPX address.

Question 40

The correct answer is **show interfaces stats**. This command displays switching information for processor, fast, and distributed switching.

Question 41

The correct answer is d. Traffic filters can be set on protocol analyzers so that only relevant traffic can be captured. A protocol analyzer only counts valid packets in the received frames field; errors may be shown in invalid, collision, or other fields. Therefore, answer a is incorrect. All captured data does not include collisions; this is a separate statistic. Therefore, answer b is incorrect. If the wrong frame type was selected on the network, no traffic would be seen. Therefore, answer c is incorrect.

Question 42

The correct answer is b. The other SAP types characterize the following:

- SAP type 1 defines the user.
- SAP type 7 defines a print server.
- SAP type 24 defines a remote bridge server.

Therefore, answers a, c, and d are incorrect.

Question 43

The correct answer is d. The supervisor module active indicator will only be orange if it's in standby mode. The PS1 and PS2 LEDs monitor the power supplies. Therefore, answer a is incorrect. The Fan LED monitors would indicate a fan failure. Therefore, answer b is incorrect. A system diagnostics failure would be indicated by a red system status LED. Therefore, answer c is incorrect.

Question 44

The correct answer is d. Ethernet II and 802.3 (RAW) frames are very similar, except for swapping the length and type fields with one another. Therefore, answer a is incorrect. Answers b and c are incorrect because the LLC header, which contains DSAP and SSAP addresses, is only contained in Ethernet 802.2 and Ethernet SNAP frames.

Question 45

The correct answer is **show ppp multilink**. This command can then be used to verify that multilink bundles have been activated correctly.

Question 46

The correct answer is b. If an ISDN connection requiring a SPID does not have one defined, it will initialize up to Layer 2 and then the Layer 3 call establishment will fail. The Physical layer connection is already established but is not the final initialization point. Therefore, answer a is incorrect. The ISDN connection does not establish SPID negotiation. Therefore, answer c is incorrect. Call and link establishment will perform correctly. Therefore, answer d is incorrect.

Question 47

The correct answer is **show ip interfaces**. This command displays the current configuration parameters of all IP-configured interfaces, including helper addresses, access lists, and switching method.

Question 48

The correct answer is c. Because there's no route listed for the 11.1.31.154, it will be transmitted to the next hop address, 10.1.1.1, which is the gateway of last resort. Therefore, answers a, b, and d are incorrect.

Question 49

The correct answer is d. The **show controllers serial** command displays low-level information about serial interfaces, such as installed serial line cards, the type of cable installed, line errors, and the internal hardware logic. Answer a is incorrect because it's not a valid Cisco IOS command. The **show ip interface brief** command displays a short table that includes each interface name and associated IP address. Therefore, answer b is incorrect. The **show interfaces serial** command displays IP address, encapsulation type, and protocol errors but not memory-related errors. Therefore, answer c is incorrect.

Question 50

The correct answer is b. Cisco Netsys Baseliner can compile current infrastructure configurations and then analyze their design for performance. The configurations can then be altered prior to implementation on a production network. Remember that when answering questions, you should look for the most specific answer as well as an answer based around Cisco technology. Answers a and c are incorrect because cable testers and oscilloscopes are used to verify infrastructure integrity. Network management systems (NMSs) can be used to analyze a Cisco network, but not to the extent that Cisco Netsys Baseliner can, by using proprietary extensions. Therefore, answer d is incorrect.

Question 51

The correct answer is d. UDP has a smaller header size than the connection-oriented protocol TCP and does not require packet acknowledgements. Therefore, answer a is incorrect. Answers b and c describe methods included within TCP and are also incorrect.

Question 52

The correct answers are a, b, and c. These three **show** commands will display the IP-enabled interfaces, the IP-enabled interfaces defined within the EIGRP routing process, and all the IP routes, respectively. Answers d, e, f, and g are incorrect because they're not valid Cisco IOS commands.

Question 53

The correct answer is b. The two MAC addresses displayed represent the MAC address that the interface will respond to and the MAC address that was physically imprinted by the manufacturer, in that order. aa00.0400.2bbf and 00e0.3400.4883 are the two MAC addresses listed in reverse. Answers a and d are the subnet mask and interface IP address, respectively, not the MAC addresses. Therefore, answers a and d are incorrect. 00e0.3400.4883 is the burned-in address (BIA), not the software-configured address. Therefore, answer c is incorrect.

Question 54

The correct answers are a and b. With the ratification of IEEE 802.1Q, two encapsulation methods exist for VLANs: ISL and dotq. If the incorrect encapsulation type is configured on the link, the VLAN will not become active. Also, if the VLAN is disabled on the trunked port, it will not become active. The naming convention of **interface VLAN***number* is only required for RSM interfaces. Therefore, answer c is incorrect. If the wiring was cut, the other VLANs would not have become active. Therefore, answer d is incorrect.

Question 55

The correct answer is c. ICMP Router Discovery Protocol (IRDP) provides router information to locally attached hosts. The Internet Gateway Management Protocol (IGMP) subscribes hosts to local multicast sessions. Therefore, answer a is incorrect. The User Datagram Protocol (UDP) is the Transport layer connectionless protocol for IP. Therefore, answer b is incorrect. The Internet Control Message Protocol (ICMP) provides end-to-end control messages at the Network layer. Therefore, answer d is incorrect.

Question 56

The correct answer is c. NetBIOS defaults to IPX type 20 packets, and the packets can be transmitted to all interfaces that are enabled with this command. Answer a is incorrect because it's not a valid Cisco IOS command. The **ipx nlsp enable** command enables the NLSP routing process on an interface. Therefore, answer b is incorrect. The GNS response delay command changes the delay when responding to Get Nearest Server (GNS) requests. Therefore, answer d is incorrect.

Question 57

The correct answer is c. An ARP timeout of 0 allows all ARP entries to age an unlimited amount of time. Therefore, the ARP cache still has the old network interface MAC address, and Data Link layer connectivity could not be established. Answers a, b, and d are incorrect because they would have no effect on local network connectivity.

Question 58

The correct answer is b. When individual applications are experiencing connectivity problems, check for access lists enabled on intermediate routers and verify which ports the application requires. This is by far the number one problem experienced by users and network engineers. There are no other users reporting problems, so the router interface cannot be down. Therefore, answer a is incorrect. Port 21 is used by FTP, and this is not an FTP issue. Therefore, answer c is incorrect. Also, the users are connected to the network correctly because they're not experiencing any other problems. Therefore, answer d is incorrect.

Question 59

The correct answer is c. The **debug dialer events** command displays events that occur when interesting packets trigger a dialer interface to become active or when these events fail. **debug isdn events** debugs the ISDN connection after the dialer has instantiated a connection. Therefore, answer a is incorrect. The **show dialer map** command displays the DDR entries in the configuration, but this is not a **debug** command. Therefore, answer b is incorrect. The **show ppp multilink** command displays Multilink PPP information and is also not a **debug** command. Therefore, answer d is incorrect.

Question 60

The correct answer is 16. The number of collisions counts how many messages have been retransmitted due to an Ethernet collision. This is usually the result of an overextended LAN (Ethernet or transceiver cable too long, more than two repeaters between stations, or too many cascaded multiport transceivers).

Question 61

The correct answers are any four of the following **show appletalk traffic, show bootflash:, show bootvar, show buffers, show context, show controllers, show controllers cbu, show diagbus, show interfaces, show ip traffic, show novell traffic, show process cpu, show process memory, show running-config, show stacks**, and **show version.**

Glossary

Address Resolution Protocol (ARP)—Used to dynamically discover the low-level physical network hardware address that corresponds to the high-level IP address for a given host. ARP is limited to physical network systems that support broadcast packets that can be heard by all hosts on the network. It is defined in RFC 826.

AppleTalk—Apple Computer's proprietary networking protocol.

AppleTalk Address Resolution Protocol (AARP)—Used to dynamically discover hardware addresses that correspond to AppleTalk software addresses and vice versa.

AppleTalk Echo Protocol (AEP)—Used to send datagrams to other AppleTalk devices and receive a duplicate of the datagram. Ping is an application that uses this protocol.

AppleTalk Filing Protocol (AFP)—Conducts the dialogue between a user's computer and an AppleShare server.

AppleTalk Session Protocol (ASP)—Establishes a session between programs on the communicating computers and synchronizes the communications.

AppleTalk Transaction Protocol (ATP)—Directs the AppleTalk transaction process by setting up a reliable exchange pathway.

AppleTalk Update-Based Routing Protocol (AURP)—A link-state AppleTalk routing protocol.

Application layer—The top layer of the network protocol stack. The Application layer is concerned with the semantics of work (for example, formatting electronic mail messages). How to represent that data and how to reach the foreign node are issues for lower layers of the network.

Asynchronous Transfer Mode (ATM)—A high-performance, cell-oriented switching and multiplexing technology that utilizes fixed-length packets to carry different types of traffic.

autonomous switching—A packet switching method available in 7500-series routers that is similar to fast switching, but faster.

Basic Rate Interface (BRI)—A digital, WAN-oriented data communications ISDN service consisting of two B channels at 64Kbps and one D channel at 16Kbps (2B+D).

Border Gateway Protocol (BGP)—An exterior gateway protocol defined in RFCs 1267 and 1268.

broadcast—A special type of multicast packet that all nodes on the network are always willing to receive.

cable tester—A device that can be used to identify faulty or improperly terminated wiring.

Challenge Handshake Authentication Protocol (CHAP)—A security mechanism used to periodically verify the identity of a peer using a three-way handshake.

channel service unit/data service unit (CSU/DSU)—A digital modem generally used in conjunction with a T1 digital connection.

Cisco Connection Online (CCO)—Cisco's Web site, which can be used to search for documentation and technical support and to purchase new products.

Cisco Discovery Protocol (CDP)—Cisco's proprietary Layer 2 protocol that can discover device-level information, such as Network layer addresses, hardware type, and IOS version.

connectionless—The data communication method in which communication occurs between hosts with no previous setup. Packets between two hosts may take different routes, as each is independent of the other. UDP is a connectionless protocol.

connection-oriented—The data communication method in which communication proceeds through three well-defined phases: connection establishment, data transfer, and connection release. TCP is a connection-oriented protocol.

CSMA/CD (Carrier Sense Multiple Access with Collision Detection)—The access method used by local area networking technologies such as Ethernet.

cyclic redundancy check (CRC)—A method of error correction using an identification byte sent with the packet to determine transmission problems.

data communications equipment (DCE)—The serial or RS-232 port that a modem or interim-communication device connects to.

data-link connection identifier (DLCI)—A unique number assigned to a PVC endpoint in a frame relay network. It identifies a particular PVC endpoint within a user's access channel in a frame relay network and has local significance only to that channel.

Data Link layer—The OSI layer that is responsible for data transfer across a single physical connection or a series of bridged connections between two network entities.

data terminal equipment (DTE)—The RS-232 interface that a computer, router, or other end-communication device connects to.

Datagram Delivery Protocol (DDP)—Network layer protocol in the AppleTalk protocol suite that communicates with the link access protocols of the Physical and Data Link layers to deliver datagrams.

debug commands—The low-level command set available within the Cisco IOS that can be used to troubleshoot Cisco device, protocol, and network errors.

default route—A routing table entry that is used to direct packets addressed to networks not explicitly listed in the routing table.

Dijkstra's algorithm—An algorithm that is sometimes used to calculate routes given a link and nodal state topology database.

dialer interface—A virtual interface created to ease the configuration of dial-up interfaces.

Distance-Vector Multicast Routing Protocol (DVMRP)—The original IP multicast routing protocol created to run over both multicast- and nonmulticast-capable routers.

Domain Name System (DNS)—A general purpose distributed, replicated data query service. Its principal use is to look up host IP addresses based on hostnames. The style of hostnames now used in the Internet is called *domain name*, because they are the style of names used to look up anything in the DNS.

Dot1q—A standardized format for frame tagging to communicate VLAN membership information across multiple, multivendor devices.

Dynamic Host Configuration Protocol (DHCP)—Enables a DHCP client to dynamically obtain an IP address for a fixed length of time from a DHCP server.

encapsulation—The technique used by layered protocols in which a layer adds header information to the protocol data unit from the layer above.

Enhanced Internet Gateway Routing Protocol (EIGRP)—An enhanced version of IGRP that functions similarly to a link-state routing protocol.

Ethernet—A 10/100/1000 megabit per second baseband Physical and Data Link layer specification, originally designed by Xerox.

Exterior Gateway Protocol (EGP)—A protocol that distributes routing information to the routers that connect autonomous systems. The term *gateway* is historical, as *router* is currently the preferred term. There is also a routing protocol called EGP defined in RFC 904.

fast-forward—A switching method that uses cut-through forwarding to quickly transmit packets within a Catalyst switch.

Fiber Distributed Data Interface (FDDI)—A high-speed (100Mbps) LAN standard. The underlying medium is fiber optics, and the topology is a dual-attached, counter-rotating token ring. See also: *local area network*, *token ring*.

fiber optic—A type of transmission medium that utilizes optical glass pairs to send light signals.

fragment-free—Uses the cut-through forwarding method to check for collision fragments so that corrupted data is not propagated.

Frame Check Sequence (FCS)—Any mathematical formula which derives a numeric value based on the bit pattern of a transmitted block of information and uses that value at the receiving end to determine the existence of any transmission errors.

Frame relay—Provides a packet-switching data communications capability across WANs.

Get Nearest Server (GNS) requests/replies—Packets sent by NetWare-enabled devices to locate services.

ICMP Router Discovery Protocol (IRDP)—Used to automatically discover all directly connected router addresses.

Integrated Services Digital Network (ISDN)—A switched digital transmission service provided by a local telephone company's switching office.

Interior Gateway Protocol (IGP)—A protocol that distributes routing information to the routers within an autonomous system. The term *gateway* is historical, as *router* is currently the preferred term.

Interior Gateway Routing Protocol (IGRP)—A distance-vector routing protocol developed by Cisco that is used in TCP/IP networks. It was originally designed in 1986.

Internet Control Message Protocol (ICMP)—An extension of the Internet Protocol (IP) that allows for the generation of error messages, test packets, and informational messages related to IP. It is defined in RFC 792.

Internet Group Management Protocol (IGMP)—A signaling protocol used to establish, maintain, or remove multicast groups on a subnet.

Internet Protocol—The most fundamental protocol in the Internet. IP is the basic transport method for high layer protocols.

Internetwork Operating System (IOS)—Cisco's general network device operating system.

Internetwork Packet Exchange/Sequenced Packet Exchange (IPX/SPX)—Novell's flagship network protocol. IPX is Novell NetWare's LAN communication protocol. SPX works on top of IPX and is responsible for flow control.

Inter-Switch Link (ISL)—Cisco's proprietary VLAN trunking protocol.

IP address—A number identifying the network address of a machine using the TCP/IP protocol.

IPXWAN—A start-up end-to-end negotiations protocol used to reduce the amount of RIP and SAP management traffic transiting WAN links.

Logical Link Control (LLC)—The upper portion of the Data Link layer, as defined in IEEE 802.2. The LLC sublayer presents a uniform interface to users of the Data Link layer service. Beneath the LLC sublayer is the MAC sublayer.

Media Access Control (MAC) address—The hardware address assigned to the network device at the manufacturing facility.

multicast—Network traffic that is disseminated to selected nodes.

Multilink PPP—Allows multiple data streams to be used as a single transmission pipe.

Name Binding Protocol (NBP)—Used by AppleTalk to look up an entity's address in the name table.

NetBIOS—A Session layer communications service used by client and server applications in IBM token ring and PC LAN networks.

NetFlow switching—A highly intelligent flow cache management system that provides detailed data collection and efficient processing of security access lists.

NetWare Core Protocol (NCP)—A collection of file server functions for remote file access and printing on server.

NetWare Link Services Protocol (NLSP)—Novell's link-state routing protocol designed to overcome IPX RIP limitations.

network baseline—Defines the typical protocol activity of all devices within a network's infrastructure.

network monitor—Software that monitors the network for performance and degradation.

Open Shortest Path First (OSPF)—An IGP, link-state routing protocol intended for use in large networks.

optical time domain reflector (OTDR)—Analyzes fiber media using optical pulses rather than electronic signals.

OSI reference model—A seven-layer structure designed to describe computer network architectures and the way that data passes through them. This model was developed by the ISO in 1978 to clearly define the interfaces in multivendor networks and to provide users with conceptual guidelines regarding the construction of such networks.

packet—The unit of data sent across a network. *Packet* is a generic term used to describe a unit of data at all levels of the protocol stack, but it is most correctly used to describe application data units.

Packet Internet Groper (ping)—A program used to test and debug network connections. It sends out an echo and expects a specified host to reply in a specified time frame.

permanent virtual circuit (PVC)—A virtual circuit that is permanently established, saving the time associated with circuit establishment and tear-down.

Physical layer—The OSI layer that provides the means to activate and use physical connections for bit transmission. The Physical layer provides the procedures for transferring a single bit across a physical medium.

Point-to-Point Protocol (PPP)—Provides a method for transmitting packets over serial point-to-point links. It is defined in RFC 1171.

port—A Transport layer demultiplexing value. Each application has a unique port number associated with it.

Presentation layer—The OSI layer that determines how application information is represented (encoded) while in transit between two end systems.

Primary Rate Interface (PRI)—An ISDN standard for provisioning of 1.544 Mbps, which uses 23 "B" channels of 64Kbps each and one signalling "D" channel of 64 Kbps.

process switching—A switching method that sends every packet to the route processor, which performs a routing table lookup to identify which interface to send the packet to.

protocol—A formal description of message formats and the rules two computers must follow to exchange those messages. Protocols can describe low-level details of machine-to-machine interfaces (such as the order in which bits and bytes are sent across a wire) or high-level exchanges between allocation programs (such as the way two programs transfer a file across the Internet).

protocol analyzer—Shows the contents of data packets, which can be used to help diagnose low-level network protocol problems.

Protocol Independent Multicast (PIM)—A multicast routing protocol that runs over an existing unicast infrastructure.

Remote Monitoring (RMON)—Allows agents, which collect statistics and periodically update a network management system (NMS), to be deployed on network devices.

Reverse Address Resolution Protocol (RARP)—Provides the reverse function of ARP. RARP maps a hardware MAC address to an IP address.

route—The paths that network traffic takes from source to destination.

Routing Information Protocol (RIP)—A routing protocol based on the Bellman-Ford (or distance-vector) algorithm.

Serial Line Internet Protocol (SLIP)—A protocol used to run IP over serial lines, such as telephone circuits or RS-232 cables, interconnecting two systems. SLIP is defined in RFC 1055.

Service Advertising Protocol (SAP)—NetWare network services use this protocol to inform clients of their presence.

Service Profile Identifier (SPID)—Identifies to the phone company what types of services and features are supported for a given device. SPIDs are optional in the ISDN standard but are usually required in North America.

Session layer—OSI layer that provides the means for dialogue control between end systems.

set commands—Cisco Catalyst IOS commands used to change a switch's running configuration.

show commands—Cisco Catalyst and router IOS commands that generally display the current running configuration and its effect on the network.

silicon switching—The packet-switching method employed by the silicon switch processor (SSP).

Simple Network Management Protocol (SNMP)—An Application layer protocol that facilitates the exchange of management information between network devices.

Spanning Tree Protocol (STP)—A link management protocol that provides path redundancy while preventing packet loops.

split horizon—A method of avoiding routing loops that are caused by including routes in updates sent to the gateway from which they were learned.

store and forward—A data communications technique that accepts messages, stores them, and then forwards them as addressed in the message header.

subnet mask—The subnet portion of an IP address. In a subnetted network, the host portion of an IP address is split into a subnet portion and a host portion using an address (subnet) mask.

Switch Port Analyzer (SPAN)—Monitoring software embedded in the Cisco Catalyst IOS that allows traffic to be mirrored to another port.

T1—An AT&T term for a digital carrier facility used to transmit a DS-1 formatted digital signal at 1.544 megabits per second.

time domain reflector (TDR)—A device that transmits a signal down a cable, which can be used to measure the cable's length, resistance, attenuation, and crosstalk, as well as to identify cable faults to within inches.

token ring—A ring topology that uses a supervisory "token" that is passed from station to station around the ring. Computers must have the token in order to transmit and do so using the entire bandwidth of the communication medium.

traceroute—A utility used to identify the path taken by a packet from source to destination.

Transmission Control Protocol (TCP)—A connection-oriented, Transport layer protocol that ensures individual packet delivery.

Transport layer—The fourth layer of the OSI model responsible for the reliable delivery of data.

tunneling—The encapsulation of protocol A within protocol B, such that A treats B as though it were a Data Link layer protocol. Tunneling is used to get data between administrative domains that use a protocol that is not supported by the Internet.

unicast—Direct network traffic between two nodes.

User Datagram Protocol (UDP)—A connectionless, Transport layer protocol that does not guarantee packet delivery.

Virtual Channel Identifier (VCI)—A unique numerical tag as defined by a 16-bit field in the ATM cell header that identifies a virtual channel over which the cell is to travel.

virtual circuit—A service that is implemented on top of a network. It can be either connection-oriented or connectionless.

virtual LAN (VLAN)—A logical grouping of network nodes that act as if they are connected to a single, shared-media network.

Virtual Path Identifier (VPI)—An eight-bit field in the ATM cell header, which indicates the virtual path over which the cell should be routed.

Windows Internet Naming Service (WINS)—A Microsoft-based service for Windows workstations, similar to DNS, used to resolve NetBIOS names to IP addresses.

Zone Information Protocol (ZIP)—Maintains the network-number-to-zone-name mapping of the AppleTalk network.

Index

Bold page numbers indicate sample exam questions.

L

Q

R

S

T

U

V

W

Z